NATIVE AMERICAN
RENAISSANCE

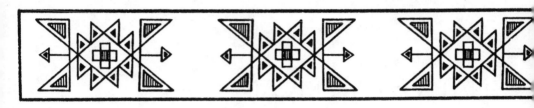

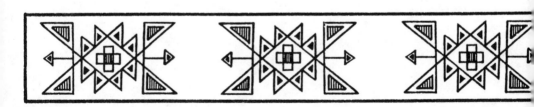

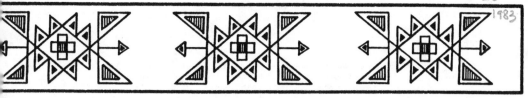

NATIVE AMERICAN RENAISSANCE

KENNETH LINCOLN

UNIVERSITY OF CALIFORNIA PRESS • BERKELEY LOS ANGELES LONDON

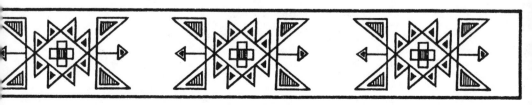

Portions of this study have been published elsewhere. Chapter 1, "—Old like hills, like stars," was delivered as a lecture at the Fourth Annual Symposium of American Indian Issues in Higher Education, UCLA American Indian Studies Center, Los Angeles, May 1980 and published among the proceedings, AMERICAN INDIAN ISSUES IN HIGHER EDUCATION (Los Angeles: UCLA American Indian Studies Center, 1981). The essay was revised and reissued in Houston Baker's THREE AMERICAN LITERATURES (New York: Modern Language Association, 1982) and again revised for Brian Swann's SMOOTHING THE GROUND (Berkeley, Los Angeles, London: University of California Press, 1982). Chapter 2, "Crossings," first appeared as the introduction to a special translation issue of UCLA's AMERICAN INDIAN CULTURE AND RESEARCH JOURNAL 4 (1980); it was revised and reprinted in Baker's THREE AMERICAN LITERATURES and in Swann's SMOOTHING THE GROUND. Chapter 3, "Ancestral Voices in Oral Traditions," originally appeared in THE SOUTHWEST REVIEW 60 (Spring 1975) as "Native American Tribal Poetics"; it was revised and reprinted in UCLA's AMERICAN INDIAN CULTURE AND RESEARCH JOURNAL 4 (1976) as "Tribal Poetics of Native America," the preferred title; it was again revised and reprinted in Baker's THREE AMERICAN LITERATURES and in Swann's SMOOTHING THE GROUND. Chapter 4, "A Contemporary Tribe of Poets," first appeared in a special ethnomusicological issue of UCLA's AMERICAN INDIAN CULTURE AND RESEARCH JOURNAL 6 (1982) as a review essay. Selected portions of chapter 5, "Word Senders: Black Elk and N. Scott Momaday," appeared in Baker's THREE AMERICAN LITERATURES. A condensation from chapter 6, "Trickster's Swampy Cree Bones," appeared in Baker's THREE AMERICAN LITERATURES. Studies of James Welch's first novel, WINTER IN THE BLOOD, and volume of poetry, RIDING THE EARTHBOY 40, printed here in chapter 7, "Blackfeet Winter Blues: James Welch," originally appeared in MELUS (Multi-Ethnic Literature of the United States) 6 (Spring 1979) as "Back-Tracking James Welch"; the sections were revised and reprinted in Baker's THREE AMERICAN LITERATURES. In chapter 7 also, the study of James Welch's second novel, THE DEATH OF JIM LONEY, first appeared as a review in the special translation issue of UCLA's AMERICAN INDIAN CULTURE AND RESEARCH JOURNAL 4 (1980). "The Now Day Indi'n" opening chapter 8, was originally published in a longer version, "The Now Day Indi'n," in FOUR WINDS: THE INTERNATIONAL FORUM FOR NATIVE AMERICAN ART, LITERATURE, AND HISTORY 3 (Summer 1982). Introductions to J. Ivaloo Volborth, Barney Bush, and Paula Gunn Allen first appeared as Forewords to first volumes of poetry published in the "Native American Series," UCLA American Indian Studies Center: J. Ivaloo Volborth, THUNDER-ROOT: TRADITIONAL AND CONTEMPORARY NATIVE AMERICAN VERSE (1978); Barney Bush, MY HORSE AND A JUKEBOX (1979); Paula Gunn Allen, SHADOW COUNTRY (1982). These Forewords were revised and republished in Baker's THREE AMERICAN LITERATURES. Parts of the opening of chapter 9, "Grandmother Storyteller: Leslie Silko," originally appeared in the "Introduction: Native Literatures" of Special Issue Number 2 on American Indian Translation, AMERICAN INDIAN CULTURE AND RESEARCH JOURNAL 4 (1980). My thanks to all of these publications for permission to reprint.

University of California Press
Berkeley and Los Angeles, California

University of California Press, Ltd.
London, England

Copyright © 1983 by The Regents of the University of California

Library of Congress Cataloging in Publication Data

Lincoln, Kenneth.
    Native American Renaissance.

    Bibliography
    1. American literature—Indian authors—History and criticism. 2. American literature—20th century—History and criticism. 3. Indians in literature. I. Title.
PS153.I52L6   1983   810'.9'897   82-17450
ISBN 0-520-04857-1

Printed in the United States of America

1 2 3 4 5 6 7 8 9

TO ALFONSO ORTIZ

"sending a voice"

His name was Cheney, and he was an arrowmaker. Every morning, my father tells me, Cheney would paint his wrinkled face, go out, and pray aloud to the rising sun. In my mind I can see that man as if he were there now. I like to watch him as he makes his prayer. I know where he stands and where his voice goes on the rolling grasses and where the sun comes up on the land. There, at dawn, you can feel the silence. It is cold and clear and deep like water. It takes hold of you and will not let you go.

—N. Scott Momaday, Kiowa
THE WAY TO RAINY MOUNTAIN

⚒ CONTENTS ⚒

ACKNOWLEDGMENTS

Thanks to the UCLA American Indian Studies Center and English Department for research funds, support from colleagues, and the generosity of many friends. I owe special debts to scholars in other disciplines. Alfonso Ortiz, Tewa anthropologist, stood by my literary studies over the years. The historian, Gary B. Nash, tested my sense of style against the truth of things. William Bright, American Indian linguist, shared concerns over the poetry and science of good translation. N. Scott Momaday, Kiowa novelist and poet, extended timely encouragement from the start and support through a decade of changes. Howard Norman, the Cree ethnologist, remained a brother through the contraries, as Paula Gunn Allen, Laguna poet, was there as a sister through all the stories. The Cherokee ethnomusicologist, Charlotte Heth, provided leadership in the diverse field of Native American Studies. Kenneth Morrison at UCLA worked next to me as an American Indian historian. Raymond J. DeMallie offered long-distance anthropological feedback. Al Logan Slagle (Cherokee), professor of law at UC Berkeley, grew from my student into teacher and friend.

My literary colleagues have given me a disciplined home from which to stray, and I am appreciative. S. Page Stegner, novelist and Nabokov critic, drew me out of Nebraska at nineteen. F. Douglass Fiero worked beside me learning, in some measure, how to teach, write, and think. Paul Sheats, my chairman, assured me this study matters. Calvin Bedient inspired critical imagination, Jascha Kessler struck firm lines of argument, Gerald Goldberg held out for courage, and Richard Cross remained a friend to trust. Raymund Paredes bet our work would last. The Americanist, Richard Lillard, tended a house at the end of the lane. William S. Merwin believed in this work, and Brian Swann smoothed the ground. Stan Thompson, nuclear chemist, swore we ought to give it all back to the original caretakers.

My students over ten years in Indian classes have given daily responses to sharpen my thinking. I am particularly indebted to Edelgard Ditmars, Virginia Jackson, Greg Sarris, and Patrick Hubbard, whose insights kept me going. Elaine Childers and Cori Steinberg helped with the notes. Victoria Pasternack encouraged clarity at the cost of metaphor. Jeanette Gilkison, my departmental secretary, stood loyal through this study's longest days.

ACKNOWLEDGMENTS

Recalling her grandmother's words in hard times, Karin Jones promised all along that cream rises to the top.

Uncounted American Indian friends from hundreds of tribal backgrounds, UCLA to Old Oraibi to northwest Nebraska, told me to come back and keep writing. The memories of those no longer living, Jennie and Felix Lone Wolf, Minnie and Bill Monroe, Emma Monroe, Terry Monroe, Lawrence Antoine, John (Fire) Lame Deer, and Dawson No Horse, give reason to continue.

My Lakota brother, Mark Monroe of Alliance, Nebraska, baked bread when I was a boy, adopted me into the Oglala Sioux with the warrior's name, *Mato Yamni*, and taught me more about Native America than all the books. *Hetchétu alóh!*

Rachel, my daughter, grew into a young woman as this book was taking shape. She knows, more than any, the dedications.

First and final thanks to my parents, Eldon and Helen Lincoln, whose grandparents bore families in the northern plains, and who passed on some of America's native life.

Kenneth Lincoln

Beverly Glen Canyon, Los Angeles
Spring 1982

✦ INTRODUCTION ✦
"Sending A Voice"

Tuⁿka'shila	Grandfather,
ho uwa'yiⁿ kte	a voice I am going to send
nama'lion ye	hear me
maka' sito'mniyaⁿ	all over the universe
ho uwa'yiⁿ kte	a voice I am going to send.
nama'lion ye	Hear me,
Tuⁿka'shila	Grandfather,
wani' ktelo'	I will live.
epelo'	I have said.

—Red Bird, Lakota Sun Dance Prayer[1]

"WHAT-MOVES-MOVES"

Among the Lakota on the northern plains where I was raised, "sending a voice" invoked the sensible and mysterious powers that move the world. James R. Walker, one of the first white ethnologists at Pine Ridge, South Dakota, worked with direct descendants and contemporaries of Crazy Horse, Red Cloud, Spotted Tail, Gall, and Black Elk. After talking with "several old Indians, including George Sword," Walker wrote to Clark Wissler, his sponsor in the Bureau of American Ethnology in 1915: "each and all declaring that *Skan* was the sky, and was also a spirit that was everywhere, and that gave life and motion to everything that lives or moves. Every interpreter interpreted *Taku Skanskan* as 'What Moves-moves,' or that which gives motion to everything that moves."[2] This power that moves the moving world, vast as the sky itself, can still be petitioned through *Tate*, or the wind, in a person's own voice. The *Niya*, or "life-breath," is the body's soul in Lakota belief, and through this "life-breath," the world's powers can be called, prayed, sung, chanted, ceremonialized, even reasoned with or admonished, if the petitioner lives rightly, in accord with natural rituals. These daily rites, "sending a voice," align with the passage of sun, moon, stars, planets, animals, winds, seasons, visions, winter counts, peoples, and timeless generations of spirits, passed on, passing on. Such voices make up tribal cultures, past and present; their oral and written literatures are acknowledged in this book.

Ritual appeals to "What Moves-moves" call upon the special language of "sending a voice" among the Lakota. A totemic creation hears and speaks with these voices, as the Indian world is believed to be made up of natural exchanges, alive through a reciprocal language of interdependencies. In ritual kinship, for example, the Lakota emerge from ceremonies singing out "*Mitakuye oyasin*," or "All my relatives." Just so in other tribes, the word "totem" itself derives from the Ojibwa for "my fellow clansman."[3] It is thus central to note that the bonds of the Indian world turn on a tribal sense of relation to all being.

A conception of the human voice invoking power, *waka^n* or "holy-mysterious" in the presence of "What Moves-moves," underlies some five hundred Native American literatures. This regard for a voice of power remains pan-Indian, despite relative differences over time and degrees of acculturation to modern, non-Indian ways. Indian literary history spans older oral traditions (crying for vision or recounting honorable deeds, telling tribal stories or chanting personal songs, making medicine or entreating spirits, retelling the communal past or prophesying the future) over the long cultural odyssey into written contemporary poetry, fiction, essay, drama, and treatise. And so, tracing the connective threads between the cultural past and its expression in the present is the purpose of *Native American Renaissance*.

"DEEP-ROOTED THINGS"

The Modoc scholar, Michael Dorris, writes from the Native American Studies Program of the first "Indian" university in the United States, Dartmouth College: "Native American cultures and their respective literatures are not ornamental and historical artifacts of America's past, but are both ancient and ongoing—and as complicated as those of any other of the world's peoples."[4] Why, then, have there been four hundred years of American silence toward these native literatures? Why the relative ignorance of Indian cultures and voices? Dell Hymes argues that non-Indians have been "telling the texts not to speak."[5]

Our failures to hear partly stem from the tragedies of tribal dislocation and mistranslation, partly from misconceptions about literature, partly from cultural indifference. Hymes returns to opaque ethnological texts with a freshly reconstructive linguistics; his anthropology is premised on hearing the original language before attempting any translation. He would *reproduce* the Native American oral literatures as literature in their own contexts: a case in point, his own retranslations of Pacific Northwest verse-texts, first transcribed by Boas and Sapir. Hymes concludes *"In Vain I Tried to Tell You": Essays in Native American Ethnopoetics* (1981) with a rhetorical challenge, "Do these texts, restored to something like their true form, have power to move us, as part of the first literature of our land?"[6]

The question of a "power to move us" has been raised and left unanswered by Americans for several hundred years. In 1931, Mary Austin romanticized a poetics born out of the rhythms of the land, springing from "deep-rooted aboriginal stock" among American Indians-at-large. Austin championed the "first-born literature of our native land"; two generations ago, she complained that "it is still easier to know more of Beowulf than of the Red Score of the Delaware, more of Homer than of the Creation Myth of the Zuñi, more of Icelandic sagas than of the hero myths of Iroquois and Navajo."[7] And, a decade earlier, poets such as Lawrence, Pound, Williams, and the new-founded Imagists noted Harriet Monroe's 1920 publication of an "aboriginal number" in *Poetry: A Magazine of Verse.* Mary Austin, Alfred Kreymborg, Nelson Crawford, and William H. Simpson offered personal versions of "native" American verse to acquaint readers with their own Indian country, adoptive ancestors, natural life, and regional language. In "The Painted Desert," Emma Hawkridge wrote:

> Over the wasteland a strong wind goes;
> Like captured heat lies the cactus rose.
> The desert sings:
> Sand-precious flowers and quick lizards lie
> In a world like the brazen bowl of the sky—
> Sun-captured things.
> Color and distance come weaving their dances,
> Mystery-full the great silence advances;

> Then, at your hand,
> Marvelling, mortals unfold strange wings.
> Delicate, fabulous land![8]

Though awash with sentiment, this poetry was at home in America, less wracked, less displaced (if less technically arresting) than T. S. Eliot's anomie from a European *Waste Land* two years later.

A radical, postwar change was taking place in Western arts and sciences. In the July 1921 issue of *The Dial*, Pablo Picasso and Wyndham Lewis sculpted tactile abstractions; D. H. Lawrence apologized to the underworld in "Snake"; William Carlos Williams sketched slender riddles in the American idiom; W. B. Yeats wrote from his *Autobiography* of the Irish renaissance; and Marianne Moore struck a native insight in "When I Buy Pictures."

> It comes to this: of whatever sort it is,
> it must acknowledge the forces which have made it;
> it must be 'lit with piercing glances into the life of things';
> then I 'take it in hand as a savage would take a looking-glass.'

The Dial reviews spoke directly to nativist concerns: Edward Sapir, American Indian linguist and student of Franz Boas, commented on Max Müller's *The Mythology of All Races*, and Mary Austin heralded Frank Hamilton Cushing's Zuñi ethnography, "the search for native sources of inspiration in the poetry and drama and design of Amerind art."[9] Yet, Henry James, Ezra Pound, and T. S. Eliot immigrated back to Europe, removed from Austin's "top-soil of human experience laid next to the earth by the earliest Americans." In the September 1921 *Dial*, Eliot wrote a letter home of primitive upheavals in London's art scene: Picasso, Artur Rubinstein, Stravinsky's *Sacre du Printemps*, and Fraser's *The Golden Bough*, in Eliot's words, "a revelation of that vanished mind of which our mind is a continuation."[10] And Eliot went away to shore up the runes of his own anthropoetics.

Eliot, Yeats, Joyce, Pound, Williams, and Austin, in their iconoclastic ways, sought primal artistic origins in "deep-rooted things," as Yeats chanted his "deep heart's core" in Ireland.[11] The search for grounded traditions was an American quest, in particular, given the westering relocation of peoples and cultures. Wanting freedom from the shadows of Europe, Walter Channing in the 1815 *North American Review* had called for an American literary rootedness in "native" ways and words indigenous to this Western land, its seasons and weathers, its vastly varied topography, its many and diverse peoples, its ecological history, first represented in the literatures of American Indian tribes. Channing wrote: "In the oral literature of the Indian, even when rendered in a language enfeebled by excessive cultivation, every one has found genuine originality."[12] What Gary Snyder generations later would call *The Old Ways* was not an imposed sense of "culture" from other lands, but a natural and native "literature" arising from American peoples, integrated within their own local places and communities.[13]

William Carlos Williams, a hundred years after Channing and a model for Snyder, was still trying to hear and shape American literature out of a "language of the tribe." His attentions, primarily in *Paterson*, to the shared American idioms and submerged currents of natural poetic mythology, including Indian legend, led back to "romantic" breakthroughs in the poetry of cultural experience, better termed humanist, or even nativist, literatures. Wordsworth and Coleridge first experimented with "the language of men speaking to men" in the 1798 *Lyrical Ballads*, as Yeats in the twentieth century listened among his own people for "passionate, normal speech" to give flesh to his poetry.[14]

Donald Wesling has explored the organic premises in this shift of consciousness toward "the poem not as an object but as practice," just as folklorists and ethnologists now begin to appreciate literature as process and performance, not written product alone, among Indian cultures and elsewhere (*The Chances of Rhyme: Device and Modernity*, 1980).[15] In *Roots of Lyric* (1978), Andrew Welsh goes so far as to correlate "primitive poetry" and "modern poetics": "Our search is not for primal sources but for basic structures of poetic language, whether they are found in a Bantu riddle or a poem by Donne, in a Cherokee charm or a song by Shakespeare. If the poetics of one leads us in some suggestive way to the poetics of the other, we will have discovered something about the language of poetry without involving ourselves in either genetic or psychological assumptions."[16] So Welsh's study concerns poetry less as form than riddle, emblem, image, ideogram, charm, chant, rhythm, and naming.

Some artists have been at work with these "primitive" assumptions since the Renaissance. Foster-fathering the not-so-noble Caliban, a half-breed savage in the image of the "new" world Tupinamba "cannibals" of Brazil, Prospero speaks a graced version of the white man's burden at the end of *The Tempest*: "this thing of darkness I / acknowledge mine"

5

(5.1.275–276). The line stands as Shakespeare's coda to his art. Rousseau dreamed primitive adoptions in the eighteenth century and Thoreau in the nineteenth. By the 1920s Ezra Pound had resurrected the "ideogrammatic method" of poetry, sparked by cave paintings in southern France, Indian petroglyphs, and Ernest Fenollosa discovering the concrete nature of the Chinese language itself. There could be a literature of tangible, organic forms *in* the world. Pound and others proselytized against calcified art forms, where the artist sees, hears, and minds a poetry of real things by "watching *things* work out their own fate."[17] For Pound, the shapes and sounds of literature should be as convincingly animate as natural objects, or as Fenollosa put it, "the single phrase, charged, and luminous from within."[18]

A generation later, Charles Olson found the American equivalent to Oriental ideograms in Mayan "glyphs" (also evident in the Lenape *Walum Olum* on birch bark and Iroquois beaded wampum belts). These sign-words seemed tactile, intrinsically formed, and "open" to response. They projected a physical sense of literature and language, communal and worldly. Olson termed such radicals of presentation "projective" verse, that is, moving through the world and projecting the "power to move us," summoned by Hymes. Olson argued for a poetic language in the world, people up to their hips in things, attuned with "the secrets objects share."[19] With the Mayas of the Yucatan, Charles Olson rediscovered himself a poet among people. He wrote to Robert Creeley in 1951:

> When I am rocked by the roads among any of them—kids,
> women, men—their flesh is most gentle, is granted, touch is
> in no sense anything but the natural law of flesh, there is none
> of that pull-away which, in the States, causes a man for all the
> years of his life the deepest sort of questioning of the rights of
> himself to the wild reachings of his own organism. The admis-
> sion these people give me and one another is direct, and the in-
> dividual who peers out from that flesh is precisely himself, is a
> curious wandering animal like me.[20]

D. H. Lawrence, following the likes of Bodmer, Maximilian, and Catlin who culture-hopped from Europe to Native America, reinspired modernist forays into the Indian world. Lawrence was Whitman's continental counterpart and Olson's godfather, but he was not so sure what could be brought back intact: "White people always, or nearly always, write sentimentally about Indians. . . . The highbrow invariably lapses into sentimentalism like the smell of bad eggs" (*Mornings in Mexico*, 1927).[21] New Mexico's "Lorenzo," in company with Mabel Dodge, was no exception. Drawn by what he saw as cultural animism and natural ceremony in Native American tribalism, Lawrence broke with European encrustations, "high" poetic formalisms to Victorian propriety. He came West in a twentieth-century replay of America's break from the Old World. Lawrence was hungry for the genuine, the natural, the real; he thought "free" verse the honest literary equivalent of "native" Americans openly moved by a language of the living earth. So Lawrence came to Native America compelled to write from natural passions, "the insurgent naked throb of the instant moment."[22]

No less than Americans, European artists were seeking tribal renewal: a language of the natural self, a sense of aesthetic ground, a participant audience. Back home in Wales, Dylan Thomas played out the "Red Man" myth of native wildness:

> On my haunches, eager and alone, casting an ebony shadow,
> with the Gorsehill jungle swarming, the violent, impossible
> birds and fishes leaping, hidden under four-stemmed flowers
> the height of horses, in the early evening in a dingle near Car-
> marthen, my friend Jack Williams invisibly near me, I felt all
> my young body like an excited animal surrounding me. . . .
> There, playing Indians in the evening, I was aware of me my-
> self in the exact middle of a living story, and my body was my
> adventure and my name.[23]

REEMERGENCE

Most Indian writers today, over one hundred published, were born since World War II. A generation before, Ezra Pound and associates prepared a non-Indian literati for the new nativism with its organic forms and subjects: the eidetic image, the musical cadence, the intrinsic song of spoken language, the visionary passion that charges words with meaning, the nonformalist rediscovery of art *in* things. When Indian writers began to emerge in the 1960s, Momaday, Welch, Silko, and Ortiz at first, they were recognized as outside the great traditions of Western literature. They, in turn, were shaped by what they recognized and relearned from contemporary literature, as non-Indian modernists had been discovering native art forms. Paula Gunn Allen,

7

from Laguna Pueblo, says that she could hear "Indian" premises in Pound's clarity of language, in Williams's search for an American idiom, in Gertrude Stein's firm lines, in Olson's "glyphs," and in Allen Ginsberg's chanted poetry. And the converse is true: Pound's musical arguments for literature, set forth in *The A B C of Reading*, make cross-cultural sense to Indians versed in tribal ceremony, Paula Allen adds.[24] Literature was no longer strictly formal in America, but form in some measure shaped by content.[25] And the progressions from ritual through dance and music to poetic language also made sense, Pound insisted, among the older troubadour poetries of southern France, the Confucian odes of ancient China, the Homeric epics of classical Greece, the courtly literature of Renaissance Italy, or the ballad traditions of England and America. The native ground may well be terra firma for literary tradition in any culture.

Grounded Indian literature is tribal; its fulcrum is a sense of relatedness. To Indians tribe means family, not just bloodlines but extended family, clan, community, ceremonial exchanges with nature, and an animate regard for all creation as sensible and powerful. Tribe means an earth sense of self, housed in an earth body, with regional ties in real things. Tribe means ancestral history, the remembered presence of grandmothers and grandfathers gone before. Tribe means spiritual balance through inherited rituals and an ever present religious history, not "back there" in time, but continuously reenacted, even as it changes form. Tribe means the basics of human community shared, lean to fat, a catalyst to the creation of common bonds against suffering. And given four hundred sad years of Indian dispossession, tribe often means nonwhite inversions of the American mainstream, a contrary ethnicity and dark pride, even to a people's disadvantage.

The Native American renaissance here targeted, less than two decades of published Indian literature, is a written renewal of oral traditions translated into Western literary forms. Contemporary Indian literature is not so much new, then, as regenerate: transitional continuities emerging from the old. The misnomer "Indian," ironically so, now binds many native peoples, several thousand tribes spread all over the Western Hemisphere (perhaps thirty to sixty million aboriginal Americans in the fifteenth century) first glossed wrongly by Columbus as one mythical subgroup. Indian writers today have stepped into the bicultural "forest's edge" that once designated treaty-making between older peoples of the wood and newer settlers of the clearing. Now most Indians speak English as a first language, in some degree integrate into American life, despite reservations, and learn of other Indians and cultures, as well as relearning their own. These days, the center of a country or city powwow may be one Indian drum of "All Nations." Analogous "native" American tribal histories, distinct within America as nations within a nation, serve to bridge old barriers, Hopi against Navajo, for example, or Lakota against Chippewa. Such are the new Indian alliances in a Native American renaissance. So Indian writers more or less share a common ground.

There is no codified discipline to approach these materials in their cultural diversities. A scholar should attend to culture-specific differences among tribes, but also recognize the pan-Indian acculturations that reunify tribal Americans among themselves and across tribes. The old healer Black Elk was Lakota, an Oglala Sioux, rather than "Indian," and he gave John Neihardt a life story that translated into *Black Elk Speaks*. But "Black Elk" is an Anglicized character drawn from the living visionary, *Hehaka Sapa*, blind and preliterate on the South Dakota prairies in 1931, whose Lakota is translated, transcribed, edited, revised, and shaped by the writer John Neihardt. Neihardt's book now influences "Indian" writers from many disparate tribes, who write in English and think of themselves as Indian—Oglala Sioux, or Tsimshian, or Chickasaw—as well as American. In belief of the strengths of those bonds, this study would seek further to tribalize Native American writers and their respective cultures.

Native American Renaissance is neither anthropology nor literary criticism, strictly speaking, but a hybrid. The book moves toward understanding "a multi-cultural event," as Paula Gunn Allen characterizes her Laguna-English-Arabic-Spanish-Lakota-German upbringing on the edges of Pueblos, "a confluence of cultures."[26] The study's methodology is interdisciplinary, collating literature, folklore, history, religion, handcraft, and the expressive arts; it demands of the scholar and the reader a cross-referenced mind, informed with due homework, freshly engaging multiple texts, asking variable questions, feeling for insights, hazarding perceptions. This book engages, to quote my Lakota brother, literature of "the now day Indi'n."

"RE-EXPRESSIONS"

Jarold Ramsey in *College English*, October 1979, discussed the "new" field of teaching American Indian literature and drew attention to "the interaction, for better or worse, of ethnographic scholarship and criticism."

He pointed to "the extraordinary fusion of cultural inheritance and imaginative innovation" in modern Indian writers.[27] These multiple perspectives involve looking backward and forward at once, from ethnic origins to modernist freedoms. The pioneer in this field was Roy Harvey Pearce with *The Savages of America: A Study of the Indian and the Idea of Civilization* (1953), followed twenty years later by Richard Slotkin's *Regeneration Through Violence: The Mythology of the American Frontier, 1600–1860*. Comparativist American Indian history of ideas generated such progeny as Robert F. Berkhofer's *The White Man's Indian: Images of the American Indian from Columbus to the Present* (1978) and Frederick Turner's *Beyond Geography: The Western Spirit Against the Wilderness* (1980).

Literary studies per se have been fewer and farther between. The most pertinent essays of a hundred years are gathered in Abraham Chapman's *Literature of the American Indians* (1975), among them Daniel G. Brinton's early monograph, *Aboriginal American Authors and Their Productions* (1883). Margot Astrov prefaced her anthology of traditional Indian translations, *The Winged Serpent* (1946), with an extended essay on what scholars now call American Indian "ethnopoetics." Arthur Grove Day, student of Yvor Winters, moved farther into the literatures with a discursive anthology of translations, *The Sky Clears: Poetry of the American Indians* (1951).

More recently, Karl Kroeber has collected and republished four classic essays on Indian oral narrative by contemporary revisionist ethnologists, Jarold Ramsey, Dennis Tedlock, Barre Toelken, and Dell Hymes, in *Traditional American Indian Literatures* (1981). Kroeber's anthology is complemented by Brian Swann's *Smoothing the Ground: Essays on Traditional and Contemporary American Indian Literature* (1982), twenty-one essays by leading anthropologists, linguists, ethnologists, and literary critics, reflecting the present state of the art. Paula Allen's *Studies in American Indian Literature* (MLA 1983) presents curriculum essays in teaching Native American literature.

Not until Charles R. Larson's *American Indian Fiction* (1978) was there a book-length study of Indian literatures, old or new, and this analysis of a few novels regrettably thins out against the complexity and depth of the materials. Alan R. Velie looks at Momaday, Welch, Silko, and Vizenor in *Four American Indian Literary Masters* (1982), but he slides away from the texts with questions of biography, theme, and non-Indian artistic influences. Whether the literatures carry "the power to move us," raised by Dell Hymes, still begs critical response. What is "Indian," specifically, about Indian writings? What is ''seeing from a native eye,'' Barre Toelken asks, and to rephrase his Navajo informant, Henry Yellowman, how many kinds of words will it hold?

Helen Addison Howard has published an informative monograph, *American Indian Poetry* (1979), to introduce those early century intermediaries, from Alice Fletcher to Frances Densmore to Lew Sarett, drumming and chanting through poetry readings, who ''re-expressed'' Indian verse in English, as Mary Austin put it. Most recently, the English-born poet and translator, Brian Swann, has reworked the transcriptions of seventeen pioneering ethnologists: ''adaptations from the work of'' Natalie Curtis, Frances Densmore, John R. Swanton, Edward Sapir, Gertrude P. Kurath, Francis La Flesche, James Mooney, Frank G. Speck, Ruth Bunzel, Jeremiah Curtin, and others in *Song of the Sky: Versions of Native American Songs & Poems* (1983).[28] These recreations of older translations are formally improvisational, as with Jerome Rothenberg's *Shaking the Pumpkin* (1972), and poetically inventive, as with William Brandon's *The Magic World* (1971); yet Swann's ''re-expressions'' are judiciously experimental and responsible to the sources. Excising repetitions and vocables, but providing ethnographic and musical notation, Swann shapes the song-poems visually on the acoustic canvas of the page. Round dance songs come round typographically. Spirit songs ascend the page and circle. Hunting songs step with empathic care. Planting songs open the ground walked upon verbally. D. Dematracapoulou heard a northern California Wintu shaman sing in 1929, and Swann's adaptation pictures the dance.[29]

                                    above
                              rise
                        will   swaying
                  of people   like women
          The spirits

                                          while men dance,

                        swaying with dandelion puffs
                  in their hands.

These words ideogrammatically play out the ''song'' of the poem. Prelinguistic vocables register as lyric overtones within the graphic designs, their echoes freed in the silence that cushions words.

"SENDING A VOICE"

Academic quarterlies such as the *American Indian Culture and Research Journal, MELUS* (Multi-Ethnic Literature of the United States), *The American Indian Historian*, and the *American Indian Quarterly* have been publishing Native American scholarship for almost a decade, paralleled by *Sun Tracks, Contact II, Greenfield Review, Blue Cloud Quarterly, Wassaja,* and *Akwesasne Notes* for general readers. The Association for the Study of American Indian Literature has organized scholars and published a newsletter, *SAIL,* since 1977. Such journals as *Parabola, Four Winds, Alcheringa,* and the *American Indian Art Magazine* regularly feature Indian literary materials. Special "Native American" issues of *Shantih* (Summer–Fall 1979), *Denver Quarterly* (Winter 1980), *Beloit Poetry Journal* (Winter 1979–80), *The Georgia Review* (Fall 1981), *Book Forum* (1981), and *The Greenfield Review* (Winter 1981–82) have introduced the major and less well-known Indian writers, among those already noted, Carroll Arnett, Jim Barnes, Peter Blue Cloud, Joseph Bruchac, Diane Burns, Barney Bush, Ward Churchill, Joy Harjo, Lance Henson, Jamake Highwater, Roberta Hill, Linda Hogan, Maurice Kenny, Tony Long Wolf, Duane Niatum, Nila Northsun, William Oandasan, J. Ivaloo Volborth, and Anna Lee Walters. Anthologies such as *The Remembered Earth, Carriers of the Dream Wheel,* and *The Third Woman* have offered nearly a hundred more Indian writers.

The quality of this emerging literature is, without question, uneven, and every Indian who writes is not de facto a "poet." Yet the commitment to a common tribal voice—a "native" American access to the cultural sources of literature in daily song and story—is ancient and ongoing. Art is not on the decorative edges of Indian cultures, but alive at the functional heart: in blankets that warm bodies, potteries that store food, songs that gather power, stories that bond people, ceremonies that heal, disciplines that strengthen spirits. The potential for distinguished literature, and even more importantly, a supportive literary tradition, is high, perhaps higher than in any other enclave of American culture today. Jim Barnes hears Montana by telephone, the "talking wire" so essential to tribal networking across relocated America:

> The distance drums your words into my ears; it's good
> to hear your voice backed by the force of snow.

> I speak of things small enough to ride the wires, the
> Dakota winds. I try to find a certain power of
> words to make the distance thin.

"SENDING A VOICE"

> And growing in my ears are the sounds I think we know:
> the flight of low geese, the awesome scream of
> owls, the sudden fall of skree.[30]

The "certain power of words" among old-time and "now day Indi'ns," as my Lakota brother updates tribal America, shapes the oral and written texts that inspire this book.

Native American Renaissance is a selective study of American Indian literatures, beginning with turn-of-the-century field work. Critical discussion of translations from history, folklore, and ethnography suggests the larger time and terrain, relatively undocumented and seldom considered literary soil, of some five hundred tribal peoples native to North America. These oral traditions lead into adaptations of the past among present Indian writers, hundreds of poets and prose artists, as yet undiscovered.

"I go backward, look forward," a Swampy Cree storyteller says, "as the porcupine does." The body of *Native American Renaissance* focuses on issues in Indian translation, literary history, tribal poetics, and the seminal writings of Pulitzer novelist N. Scott Momaday (Kiowa), Black Elk (Lakota holy man) by way of John Neihardt's retelling, Howard Norman's Cree translations, James Welch's poetry and prose (Blackfeet/Gros Ventre), Simon Ortiz's verse (Acoma Pueblo), Wendy Rose's poetry and drawings (Hopi/Miwok), and Leslie Silko's fiction (Laguna mixed-blood). Indian artists from myriad cultures today share a collective sense of American origins, deep-rooted in the land. Though diverse, they overlap in "native" concerns for kinship and tribal ways of thinking, shaped culturally over thousands of years, still viable. These peoples are witnesses to a common sense of dispossession forced on them as native "Indians." Their mythically storied, prelapsarian origins before the European "invasion" and their mutual sense of historical displacement, the dream and its descent, transcend factional differences in a shared struggle for cultural survival and rebirth.

At best, Native American Studies is a holistic art, since Indian cultures traditionally exist contiguously with their environments, grounded in their rituals and ceremonies, enacting their histories each day. This integration is still ideally retained, even if some tribes, such as the Southwest Pueblos, seem more *in situ* physically than others, the terminated Menominee of Wisconsin or Klamath of Oregon, for example. The scholar's methods, correspondingly, must be syncretic and exploratory, as the "literary" reader opens to new ways of observing and registering the world through Indian concepts of literature and language, not necessarily Western. It is not often easy. There is a critical "other" to be worked through here, before ever conceiving to reach the "not-other other" Victor Turner seeks through symbolic anthropology.[31]

In *Tristes Tropiques* Claude Lévi-Strauss recalls that as a novice he declined philosophy and law as self-referential, skirted geology as too widely defined in nonhuman terms, and bypassed psychology as too individually oriented. He thought by way of the new science of anthropology, open to improvisation, to fuse geological time, psychological humanism, and the epistemological concerns of philosophy with the disciplines of legal reasoning.[32] Lévi-Strauss and structural anthropology offer one of many international approaches to native cultural studies, balanced by the more immediate ethnography of scholars in direct contact with Indian peoples. Most of us fall somewhere between.

Native American Renaissance is necessarily multidisciplinary. Continuing tribal cultures give rise to a scattering of interpretations that intersect history, music, religion, theater, philosophy, heuristics, ethics, politics, sociology, and the arts. Living out particular lives, Indians hold their own in formed views on tribal continuity, from ideological theory to empirical data. Converging in American literature, hundreds of tribal voices now facet a Native American renaissance: one pluralistic body of diverse peoples newly voiced in contemporary history. These peoples are "sending a voice" with the "power to move us."

In the beginnings, the Lenape of "New" England held and historically noted on the bark of birch trees, their *Walum Olum* or "painted record,"

> All had cheerful knowledge,
> all had leisure
> all thought in gladness.[33]

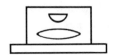

1

"OLD LIKE HILLS, LIKE STARS"

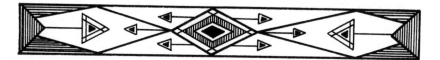

"I do not know how many there are of these songs of mine," Orpingalik told Knud Rasmussen among the Netsilik Eskimo. "Only I know that they are many, and that all in me is song. I sing as I draw breath."[1] Vital as breath itself, the oral literatures of native cultures lie deeply rooted in America. Radically diverse languages, life styles, ecologies, and histories have survived more than forty thousand years "native" to America. Perhaps the people can be imagined even farther back, "older than men can ever be—old like hills, like stars," Black Elk dreams his tribal ancestors.[2] Origin myths speak of ancient emergence from this land.

An introductory review of Indian history, known to some, obscure for many, sets a necessary background for discussing the literature. By official count, three hundred and fifteen "tribes" remain in the United States, where once four to eight million peoples composed five hundred distinct cultures speaking as many languages.[3] The working definition of "Indian," though criteria vary from region to region, is minimally a quarter blood and tribal membership. Roughly seven hundred thousand Native Americans survive as full-bloods or "bloods," to use the reservation idiom, mixed-bloods whose parents derive from different tribes, and half-bloods or "breeds" with one non-Indian parent. Another half million or more blooded Indian people live as whites. Over half of the Indian population now lives off the fifty-three million acres of federal reservation lands.

Whether an Alaskan Tlingit fishing village of forty extended kin, or the Navajo "nation" of one hundred and forty thousand Diné in Arizona, Utah, and New Mexico, each tribe can be traditionally defined through a native language, an inherited place, and a historical set of traditions. Their oral literatures are made up from a daily speech, a teaching folklore, a ritual sense of ceremony and religion, a heritage passed on generation to generation in songs, legends, morality plays, healing rites, event-histories, social protocol, jokes, spiritual rites of passage, and vision journeys to the sacred world. These cultural traditions evolved before the Old World "discovered" the New World. Many have survived changing circumstances and remain strong today. The distinguished Nobel poet, Jorge Luis Borges, for years taught "American Literature" beginning with George Cronyn's anthology, *The Path on the Rainbow* (1918), noting that native literature in translation "surprises by its contemplative perception of the visual world, its delicacy, its magic, and its terseness."[4]

Given their diversities, Native American peoples acknowledge specific and common inheritance of the land. They celebrate ancestral ties. They share goods and responsibilities, observe natural balances in the world, and idealize a biological and spiritual principle of reciprocation.[5] Personal concerns lead into communal matters. Black Elk opens his life story, a remembered history that is carried on not as autobiography but tribal history, as follows: "It is the story of all life that is holy and is good to tell, and of us two-leggeds sharing in it with the four-leggeds and the wings of the air and all green things; for these are children of one mother and their father is one Spirit."[6]

Literatures, in this sense, do not separate from the daily contexts of people's lives; the spoken, sung, and danced language binds the people as the living text of tribal life. "Firmly planted. Not fallen from on high: sprung up from below," Octavio Paz, the Mexican poet, says of native arts. The voiced word, like the handmade object, the right-told tale, the well-shaped poem, speaks of "a mutually shared physical life" (Octavio Paz, *In Praise of Hands*), not as icon, commodity, or art for its own precious sake. Words move among things in usable beauty. "A glass jug, a wicker basket, a coarse muslin huipil, a wooden serving dish: beautiful objects, not despite their usefulness but because of it."[7]

The many native peoples with ancient tenure in America remain as varied as the land itself—forest, prairie, river, valley, seacoast, mountain, tundra, desert, and cliff-dwelling peoples. They have lived as farmers, food gatherers, fishermen, and hunters inseparable from the land. Their cultures and histories differ as widely as terrain and climate, flora and fauna; but all native tribes look back to indigenous time on this "turtle island," as Iroquois origin myths envision the continent, unified in an ancient ancestral heritage. The Hopi village of Old Oraibi, on the third mesa in northern Arizona, has stood for at least eight hundred and fifty years. Canyon de Chelly, on the Navajo reservation near the Four Corners area, has been occupied continuously for two and one half thousand years. In contrast, the landscape east of the Mississippi carries slim living evidence of once powerful tribes who settled the forests. Among many others, the Powhatans saved Jamestown colony with gifts of green corn in the first severe winter of 1607. Until the 1830s the Five Civilized Tribes (Cherokee, Choctaw, Chickasaw, Creek, and Seminole) inhabited the Southeast and adapted successfully to new ways. In Colonial America the Ohio River and Great Lakes tribes lived along a western frontier, and "at the forest's edge" the Iroquois Confederacy treated as equal powers with the Confederation of United States in the eighteenth century.

What Indians gave in the exchanges between immigrants and natives is not so much remembered as what was taken from them, primarily the richest lands—fertile valleys for farming, mountains rifted with minerals, grazing lands for stock, coastal fishing shores, river passages, forests of game. The Indians' intimate knowledge of American ecology rescued many pilgrims and pioneers from hardship, or even death, in a continent the newcomers viewed as "wilderness." Indian cultivations such as beans, maize, squash, hickory, pecan, pumpkin, and sweet potatoes fed the new Americans; Indian skills in gathering native foods saved settlers from their own agricultural failures (the first Thanksgiving of 1621, for example, where Indians and pilgrims ate, among other foods, corn and eel). Indian expertise in hunting secured the bounty of the animal food pack of America—turkey, deer, buffalo, rabbit, salmon, sturgeon, shellfish, among hundreds of other game. Indians contributed over a third of the medicines we now use synthetically, 220 drugs in the National Formulary, according to Virgil Vogel's native pharmacopoeia—astringents, cathartics, childbirth medicines, febrifuges, vermifuges, emetics, poisons, antibiotics, diabetes remedy, and contraceptives, including quinine, cocaine, tobacco, and techniques of birth control.

Native Americans showed uneasy settlers a love and regard for the living land, premised on coexisting in harmony with its demands. Native governments, such as the Iroquois Confederacy, set models for new political experiments in representative democracy and tribal alliances; it was of no small significance to Franklin, Jefferson, and Washington that Iroquois meant "We-the-People." Indians gave names for rivers, mountains, lakes, cities, counties, streets, and over half the states. And they believed in the bonding and animating powers of words—to invoke and actualize the world through a language of experience. Words were not notational labels or signs, visually affixed to a blank page for material transaction: words were beings in themselves, incantatory, with spirits and bodies. Stories, songs, visions, and names lived empirically in the world, and people could seek them for power, identity, beauty, peace, and survival.

The many treaties and speeches spanning three centuries of white contact represent the first recorded Indian literatures. The precision and eloquence of Indian oratory highlight these first American "chronicle plays," Constance Rourke observes.[8] The Indians "spoke as free men to free men," Lawrence Wroth notes, "or often indeed as kings speaking to kings."[9] For over two hundred years ceaseless invasion and even military defeat could not dislodge the Indian spirit of rightful place in America. Fleeing seventeen hundred miles into the bitter winter of 1877, Chief Joseph finally had to surrender the Nez Percé. He grieved with dignity:

> My people, some of them, have run away to the hills and have
> no blankets, no food. No one knows where they are—perhaps
> they are freezing to death. I want to have time to look for my
> children and see how many of them I can find. Maybe I shall
> find them among the dead. Hear me, my chiefs, I am tired.
> My heart is sad and sick. From where the sun now stands I
> will fight no more forever.[10]

The people could be killed or captured or "reserved," but not defeated. In 1883 Sitting Bull told reservation bureaucrats:

> I am here by the will of the Great Spirit, and by His will I am
> a chief. My heart is red and sweet, and I know it is sweet, be-
> cause whatever passes near me puts out its tongue to me; and
> yet you men have come here to talk with us, and you say you
> do not know who I am. I want to tell you that if the Great
> Spirit has chosen anyone to be the chief of this country, it is
> myself. [Senate Report #283][11]

While fighting to preserve their own cultural integrity, Indians survived national policies of removal, starvation, warfare, and genocide. The Indian Bureau was first established under the War Department in 1824. Within its boundaries the United States warred against native peoples and guaranteed political settlements for military alliances, the sale of lands, acquiescence to the reservation system, and the surrender of mineral rights. Vine Deloria discusses the 389 broken treaties in *Of Utmost Good Faith*, the opening words of the Northwest Ordinance of 1787, the first treaty signed by George Washington in the Continental Congress:

> The utmost good faith shall always be observed toward the
> Indians, their lands and property shall never be taken from
> them without their consent; and in their property, rights, and
> liberty, they shall never be invaded or disturbed, unless in just
> and lawful wars authorized by Congress; but laws founded in
> justice and humanity shall from time to time be made, for
> preventing wrongs being done to them, and for preserving
> peace and friendship with them.[12]

"They were chasing us now," Black Elk remembers of the nineteenth century, "because we remembered and they forgot."[13]

Beginning in the 1830s many Indian cultures were "removed" to the "Great American Desert" west of the Mississippi, despite the acculturative success of the Five Civilized Tribes. This forced migration was more a diaspora under presidential decree and military escort. Andrew Jackson promised the Eastern tribes:

> Say to them as friends and brothers to listen to their father,
> and their friend. Where they now are, they and my white
> children are too near to each other to live in harmony and
> peace. . . . Beyond the great River Mississippi . . . their father
> has provided a country large enough for them all, and he advises them to move to it. There their white brothers will not
> trouble them, and they will have no claim to the land, and
> they can live upon it, they and all their children, as long as
> grass grows and waters run.[14]

Already settled in the West, the Plains Indians resisted the intrusion. They militarily protested encroachment from Eastern tribes shoved west and an invasion of land-grabbing, gold-searching, buffalo-slaughtering, treaty-violating white immigrants who brought with them the railroad, guns, plows, fences, plagues, alcohol, and the Bible. The West wasn't wild until the whites came, Indians complained. They lived at home in land earlier considered by whites deserted.

19

The "Indian Wars" lasted from the 1860s to the Wounded Knee Massacre in 1890. From 1881 to 1883 the government employed marksmen to slaughter the remaining two and a half million buffalo, once fifteen million in 1700, the life-support of the plains tribes.[15] The seasonal migrations of mid-American Indians, following the game, were disrupted forever. Soldiers herded the survivors onto reserves of waste land, issued "citizen's dress" of coat and trousers, and ordered the "savages" to "civilize." The secretary of the interior commented in 1872 on killing the buffalo to starve Indians onto reservations: "A few years of cessation from the chase will tend to unfit them for their former mode of life, and they will be the more readily led into new directions, toward industrial pursuits and peaceful habits."[16]

The transition did not take place so easily or soon; over a hundred years later many Indian peoples are still caught between cultures, living the worst conditions of both. Their lands contain half the uranium and one-third the strip mine coal in the United States (the coal alone worth perhaps a trillion dollars), and yet some reservations suffer the worst hardship in America—incomes at half the poverty level, five years average schooling, the highest national alcoholism and suicide rates, substandard housing and social services, infant mortality, tuberculosis, and diabetes in multiples beyond any other minority in the country, resulting in an average lifespan of forty-four years.[17] For all the positive collaborations between Indians and newcomers to America, there runs a deeply bitter history, inherited for better or worse by "native" American writers.

The national myth of civilizing a virgin land, Fitzgerald's "green breast of the new world" in *The Great Gatsby*, has been revised by the historian Francis Jennings in *The Invasion of America*: "The American land was more like a widow than a virgin. Europeans did not find a wilderness here; rather, however involuntarily, they made one. . . . The so-called settlement of America was a *re*settlement, a reoccupation of a land made waste by the diseases and demoralization introduced by the newcomers."[18] It is an old and shameful wound, still open—a story largely fabled in the popular mind and seldom taught honestly in American schools, a history of murder and cultural suppression and displacement from native lands. This last grievance, still active, is most commonly dramatized in the Long March of the Five Civilized Tribes when over a third of the people died on forced relocation to Oklahoma. Asked his age by a census taker in 1910, the old Creek, Itshas Harjo, answered with a memory purely elegiac:

I have passed through many days and traveled a long way,
the shadows have fallen all about me and I
can see but dimly.
But my mind is clear and my memory has not failed me.
I cannot count the years I have lived.
All that I know about my age is that I was old enough
to draw the bow
and kill squirrels at the time of the second emigration of the
Creeks and Cherokees from the old country under
the leadership of Chief Cooweescoowee.
I was born near Eufaula, Alabama, and left there
when about fifteen years of age and the trip
took about a year,
for the peaches were green when we left Alabama and the
wild onions plentiful here when we arrived.[19]

Despite the poetry of such natural observation, Indian traditions were dismissed as barbaric and pagan. The Commissioner of Indian Affairs stated in 1889:

> The Indians must conform to "the white man's ways,"
> peaceably if they will, forcibly if they must. They must adjust
> themselves to their environment, and conform their mode of
> living substantially to our civilization. This civilization may
> not be the best possible, but it is the best the Indian can get.
> They cannot escape it, and must either conform to it or be
> crushed by it.[20]

Children "kidnapped" into government boarding schools, as Indians saw it, were ridiculed for their Indian names, stripped of their tribal dress, denied their customs, and punished for speaking native tongues. Eventually their elders were shamed from belief in the ancestral spirit world, animal totems, and vision powers, a speaking landscape sacredly interdependent with the people. Culture after culture, beginning with Cortez's destruction of Tenochtitlan in 1521, witnessed deicide as conquered tribes were forced to abandon their own beliefs and buckle to Christianity.

A more insidious oppression threatens Indians today under melting-pot policies of assimilation, direct and indirect coercion of tribes to adapt to mainstream American culture. The disastrous "termination" policies of the 1950s are currently being revived in congressional bills to abrogate treaties; and "when someone says 'termination,'" writes an anthropologist of the

Montana Blackfeet, "the Indians hear 'extermination.' ''[21] America's most diverse minorities of Native Americans hold the status, independently, of "domestic dependent nations" (Supreme Court Justice John Marshall's opinion of 1831), that is, nations within a nation whose members are legally entrusted "wards" of the federal government, yet remain "sovereign," and occupy separate land salvaged from the one hundred and forty million acres allotted under the 1887 Dawes Act.[22] Indians are legally cast as children who cannot grow up and answer prodigally to the Great White Father.

Historical irony notwithstanding, traditional native literatures celebrate spiritual and worldly harmonies. Yet there is a danger of misdirected romanticism, fueled by pastoral myths of the noble savage and nostalgic regression to the Garden of Eden. Indians and non-Indians alike tend to gloss contemporary reservation life and visions of the-way-things-used-to-be. America still fails to see the Native American as an individual with a tribal, human identity, directed by a history that informs the present. "To be an Indian in modern American society," Vine Deloria writes in *Custer Died for Your Sins*, "is in a very real sense to be unreal and ahistorical."[23]

The transparent "Indian," a film and fictional stereotype, lingers more as a silhouette—the only minority figure anonymously enshrined on our currency, the "Indian-head" nickel, now an artifact. And the true history of national Indian affairs shapes an oftentimes bitter resistance to "the American way." D. H. Lawrence wrote in *Studies in Classic American Literature* (1923):

> The desire to extirpate the Indian. And the contradictory
> desire to glorify him. Both are rampant still, to-day.
> The bulk of the white people who live in contact with the
> Indian to-day would like to see this Red brother exterminated;
> not only for the sake of grabbing his land, but because of the
> silent, invisible, but deadly hostility between the spirit of the
> two races. The minority of whites intellectualize the Red Man
> and laud him to the skies. But this minority of whites is mostly
> a high-brow minority with a big grouch against its own
> whiteness.[24]

When America catches the shadow of native peoples on its money and names professionally competitive teams the Warriors, the Indians, the Redskins, or the Aztecs (not to mention a Pontiac automobile, the Winnebago recreation vehicle, or "Geronimo!" as a battle cry), the stereotype surely reaches down through a sentimental myth of the noble savage into "the bloody loam" of national history. The Indian warrior, who has been warred against, refracts an image that covers several million lives destroyed or violently "removed" from their native earth.[25] And today, there seem "so few of them left," Frederick Turner observes in his *North American Indian Reader*, "so far away from the centers of population."[26] This, too, is open to dispute, since Native Americans represent the fastest growing minorities in America. Indians have doubled in population between 1950 and 1970, and more than half now live in cities.

If the people are proportionately few in number, they remain many in ancient diversities and stand mythically large in the national consciousness. We would do well to appreciate their literatures as origins of native cultural history in America. Here lies the seedbed for a renaissance in American literature.

2

CROSSINGS

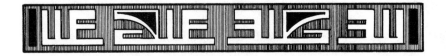

Beseeching the breath of the divine one,
His life-giving breath,
His breath of old age,
His breath of waters,
His breath of seeds,
His breath of riches,
His breath of fecundity,
His breath of power,
His breath of strong spirit,
His breath of all good fortune whatsoever,
Asking for his breath
And into my warm body drawing his breath,
I add to your breath
That happily you may always live.
                    —Zuñi, 47th Annual BAE Report, 1929–1930
                    RUTH BUNZEL, translator

"LISTEN"

Crossings of breath: every "word" translates the world we experience by aural or visual signs. Words embody reality. When language works, in flesh or print, our known world comes alive *in* words, animate and experiential. With more than one epistemological complex in this metamorphic process, any translator must look two ways at once—to carry over, as much as possible, the experiential integrity of the original; to *re*generate the spirit of the source in a recreated text. Two differing tongues and respective art-ists reciprocate in translation, and they speak to dissimilar audiences. Indian translation is at once more complex than translating from written French, for example, into the literary forms of a cognate English. Older North American Indian literatures derive from oral traditions, for the most part, of twelve racial subtypes and five hundred cultures and thousands of years, altogether unrelated to written European languages, cultures, and histories.

Native American literature, in brief, is literature *and* culture in transla-tion. When the tribal ear listens ceremonially at one end of this continuum, and the existential eye scans the printed page at the other, questions of form and function, of how cultures use language, of why artists pursue certain lit-erary designs, of why audiences relate culturally to their literatures, natur-ally come into play.

One language may be assumed magically powerful and alive with spirits, the other aesthetically functioning to transmit ideas. If the tribal poet sings at the center of an integrated ethics, beauty, and use among his people, how can the translator carry over Native American oral traditions into printed words in books for modern readers? The hundreds of indigenous literatures are permeated with religion, mythology, ritual, morality, heuris-tics, national history, social entertainment, economic skills, magic formulas, healing rites, codes of warfare, strategies of hunting, planting, and food-gathering, visions and dreams, love incantations, death chants, lullabies, and prayers. "From what you say," Ikinilik told Knud Rasmussen in the arctic North, "it would seem that folk in that far country of yours *eat* talk marks just as we eat caribou meat" (Utkyhikhalingmiut Eskimo).[1]

Ikinilik's remark points to the split between language as product and language as process. Tribal peoples may be justifiably apprehensive of a writ-ten form of literature that fixes spiritual ideas. Peter Nabokov reminds us that the first Cherokee shamans to adapt Sequoyah's 1821 syllabary of eighty-six characters, the earliest known "talking leaves" north of the Rio Grande, hid their transcriptions in trees and attics, fearful of exploitation.[2] Their fears were not unfounded, given the many anthropological misunder-standings and abuses of sacred tribal materials.

"Good translation of any literature," Jeffrey F. Huntsman posits, "re-quires a native or near-native sensitivity to both languages, and few trans-lators have the foresight to request a bilingual birth."[3] So the working model in this field would be collaborative translation, intertribal and truly reciprocal, as in such collaborative works as *Sun Chief, Son of Old Man Hat,*

The Autobiography of a Papago Woman, Crashing Thunder, My People the Sioux, Black Elk Speaks, Lame Deer Seeker of Visions, and *Fools Crow,* among other "as-told-to" life stories recorded this century. Copyright here is a cross-cultural issue. Rather than making up the world as an isolate poet-maker, the creative native artist participates in the common reality of things, by way of singing, storytelling, or writing. This collaborative artist, honored by what words are entrusted in him, passes on things-as-they-are.

The most basic paradigm of translation before writing is, simply speaking, one person listening to another tell his story. Even with writing, this human exchange occurs before an "as-told-to" text is ever written and published. Here is the radical in American Indian translation, since there is often no set text to check against variations in performance. But further still, consider the variables in *Black Elk Speaks, Being the Life Story of a Holy Man of the Oglala Sioux* (1932), perhaps the most ubiquitous text in Native American Studies, *"as told through* John G. Neihardt (*Flaming Rainbow*)," the credit reads.

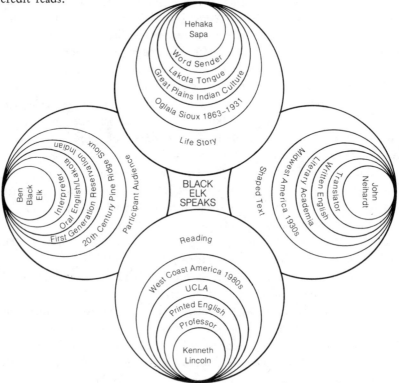

CROSSINGS

My nation, behold it in kindness!
The day of the sun has been my strength.
The path of the moon shall be my robe.
A sacred praise I am making.
A sacred praise I am making.
                    —Black Elk's Heyoka Song[4]

Four people, supported by a larger audience, "translate" this Indian story as history. At any one moment (or "word") here, overlapping sets of at least six variables come into play:

(1) an *individual* in his or her own psychogenetic complex;
(2) a personal *role* in the event;
(3) the *medium* involved;
(4) the *space/time* of the event (synchronic time cutting across a culture);
(5) the *cultural matrix* around the event (diachronic time encompassing cultural history);
(6) and the *performance* itself.

Hehaka Sapa (Black Elk) sat down on the South Dakota prairie for several months with John Neihardt, family, and friends in the spring of 1931, recalling half a century of his life as an Oglala Sioux healer. His son, Ben Black Elk, translated the spoken Lakota into English speech, as Neihardt asked questions in return, translated back into Lakota by Ben Black Elk, and recorded in stenographic notes by Neihardt's daughter, Enid. Black Elk, a purblind "holy man" or *wicasa waka*^{n}, spoke out of a performing textual vortex. It was a tribal telling, as distinct from a set biographical story, and the telling took place among extended family, interspersed with friends' commentaries (Standing Bear, who also did the illustrations, Iron Hawk, and Fire Thunder). Ben Black Elk had to find the extemporaneous oral English for these Lakota tongues. Neihardt later translated these "translations" into a written text, working from his daughter's transcriptions, exercising poetic license with the notes, sometimes even speaking for the holy man. The reader, half a century later, many removes from the Great Plains, opens the book and tries to assimilate the published account.

To move from Black Elk's memories, through his son's spoken English, through Neihardt's transcriptions, to the reader's study spans a century. The translation proceeds from visionary-healer, telling and singing his people's story, through an interpreter-son, hearing much of his father's "Great Vision" for the first time, through poet-translator, who would "write" the story, to literate recipient, who reads the book. Plains Indian mysticism then translates from a life story, through a son's heritage, through field anthropology, to the public at large. Personalities gradate from visionary native informant, through first-generation reservation Indian, through creative writer, to general reader. To note these passages raises questions about how one moves toward, or slides away from, genuine translation. Huntsman cautions: "The inherent differences between languages, combined with symbolism, figurative or metaphoric manipulation of ordinary language, secret or esoteric language, and fossils of earlier, now archaic language, all contribute to a maddening arabesque of many varieties of meaning that only the most perceptive and careful translator should confront."[5]

American Indian translation carries special challenges, from the self-translation of a contemporary Lakota, such as Luther Standing Bear or Lame Deer, to translation-by-interpretation, in the case of Black Elk and John Neihardt or Frank Fools Crow and Thomas Mails. The radicals of oral tradition, tribal secrets, uncommon perceptions and cultural points of view, historical animosities, and differing artistic or "literary" traditions dog a sensitive translator. A step removed from the personal level come translations of tribal myth and history, medicine and religion, philosophy and language. These demand validation across a tribal group of people, and agreements are hard to strike. Even more complex are narrative and song translations that would assume literary, musical, and linguistic distinctions in both languages. The collaborative team must have expertise at either end of the translative paradigm to do any justice to the original performance. Their translation would seek "the power to move" a literary reader in the second language, culture, mind-set, and textual experience.

Charles Olson says all poetry is a projection from one place "over to" another; his concern with poetic translation feeds into this discussion.[6] Translation, if an original oral performance is to survive in a written story or poem, must project "over to" another culture. The word "tradition," from Latin *trans* plus *dare* or "to give over," bears a cognate etymology with "translation," defined through the prefix "trans-" as "to the other side of, over, across." But language does not just relay data as a cognitive system. The translated event, in its new literary form, must reemerge as a poem or shaped prose, a musical pattern with origins in dance and song tapping the underlying rhythms of the language. The poem/translation must present an insight into this given world, an arrangement of sound and sense like no other before it, or strike an ancient revelation of the workings of human nature, specific to a place, time, and culture. And all the while, without distorting the original, Walter Benjamin argues that "a free translation bases the text on its own language. It is the task of the translator to release in his own language that pure language which is under the spell of another, to liberate the language imprisoned in a work in his re-creation of that work."[7] Poems must work, word for word, line by line, *as poetry* when translated.

Transliterated ethnography in itself is not necessarily poetry, any more than are folkloric motifs or anthropological paradigms. Literal translations may flat-footedly betray the original, failing to regenerate music, structural pattern, clarity, or depth of perception. In this regard, folklorists, linguists, and poets such as Dell Hymes, William Bright, and Brian Swann are beginning to show that many traditional Indian texts, mistaken for prose, are highly patterned verse structures. It is an old rediscovery, to go back to Ezra Pound, resurrecting issues of translation in the Confucian odes, Homeric epics, and Scripture.[8]

"A real translation is transparent," Benjamin argues, "it does not cover the original, does not block its light, but allows the pure language, as though reinforced by its own medium, to shine upon the original all the more fully."[9] Within its cultural integrity, *all* poetry, in original text or rendered into another language/culture, is an act of translation from life *into* the medium of language. The original "poem" or song, described by Black Elk as the "sacred language" of "a great Voice . . . silent" of a vision, springs from a preverbal illumination in the seer's imagination, perhaps from the gods themselves.

In *Selected Translations 1968–1978* the American poet, W. S. Merwin, adds: "When I tried to formulate practically what I wanted of a translation, whether by someone else or by me, it was something like this: without deliberately altering the overt meaning of the original poem, I wanted the translation to represent, with as much life as possible, some aspect, some quality of the poem which made the translator think it was worth translating in the first place."[10] And many removes later we ask of the translation: Does the poem honor the source of the original, re-present its inherent cultural values? Does the poem sing with an echo of the original music, recreate rhythm, tone, syntax, or structure? Does the poem freshly penetrate things? Does it succeed accurately in form and style? Does the poem

29

give expression to a genuine and arresting truth, or offer insight and meaning in the world? To question authenticity in translation, to look back to a poem's origins, is to look forward to issues concerning the very nature and uses of poetry itself.

ORIGINAL CARE

Since the early ethnology and folklore of almost a century ago, laying the ground for the sciences of archaeology, anthropology, and linguistics, a new literary interest in Native America has developed. An old American curiosity with Indians was accelerated by alternative cultural explorations in the 1960s. Anthologies of traditional Indian song-poems, dream visions, narrative cycles, speeches, and life stories illustrate the remarkable variety and depth of literatures in hundreds of tribal cultures. Beginning with Natalie (Curtis) Burlin's *The Indians' Book* (1907) and George Cronyn's *The Path of the Rainbow* (1918), other anthologies followed in time: Margot Astrov's *The Winged Serpent* (1946), A. Grove Day's *The Sky Clears* (1951), John Bierhorst's *In the Trail of the Wind* (1971), *Four Masterworks of American Indian Literature* (1974), and *The Red Swan* (1976), Thomas Sanders and Walter Peek's *Literature of the American Indian* (1973), Gloria Levitas and others' *American Indian Prose and Poetry* (1974), Frederick Turner's *North American Indian Reader* (1974), Alan Velie's *American Indian Literature* (1979), and the more experimental (and controversial) *Shaking the Pumpkin* (1972) by Jerome Rothenberg and *The Magic World* (1971) by William Brandon.

Indeed, a number of America's writers, from Thoreau dying with the word "Indians" on his breath, to novelists such as Cooper and Melville, Faulkner and Hemingway, Berger and Kesey, to contemporary poets Hugo, Snyder, Merwin, Rexroth, Olson, Levertov, Bly, Rothenberg, Creeley, Kelly, Berg, Simpson, Wagoner, Swann, Norman, and Tedlock, have found a need to "go native," with varying degrees of authenticity. They have sought a more integral relation to this land, artists' uses among people, a tribal language and audience, and raw material in the myth and history and imagination of America. These poets seek to reinvent, on their own cultural terms, an original relationship to the spoken word, a sensitivity to spirit of place and natural environment, a responsive bond with a tribal audience.

The artistic interest in this land's first poetries signals an involvement in the life and immediacy of America's "language of the tribe," as Williams wrote. "Not for himself surely to be an Indian, though they eagerly sought to adopt him into their tribes, but the reverse: to be *himself* in a new world, Indianlike" (*In the American Grain*).[11] Other peoples cannot assume to be Indians; but they can translate, discover, or rediscover their own cultural family and place in this earth. It is a matter of gathering the tribes, adopting one another anew; and still it won't be easy. As diverse peoples, we must come to accept mutual differences to overcome that "gulf of mutual negation" Lawrence saw yawning between Indian and American cultures imported later in history.[12]

Granted the honest intentions coloring faulty translations, how can we correct "the 'wilderness' poet approach," noted by Jeffrey Huntsman, which finds a "tranquilly recollecting rhymer in every tree"?[13] How unlock the American stereotypes of Hiawatha and Pocahontas, a damned Injun Joe and sainted Tekawitha, and bring things up to date? How see Native Americans for the many and diverse peoples and pasts and regions they comprise? Too many afterimages perpetuate the feathered, naked, promiscuous, warring, lawless, cannibal stereotype of the Brazilian Tupinamba, misrepresented grossly in the first New World woodcuts to surface in Germany about 1505: "They also fight with each other. They also eat each other even those who are slain, and hang the flesh of them in smoke. They live one hundred and fifty years. And have no government" (*The New Golden Land*).[14] This misrepresentation is patently absurd, yet etched in "historical" documents and still dangerously at large in the fantasies of the American populace. More recently, how avert the commercial travesty and cultural exploitation of *Hanta Yo*, a will-to-power rendition of the Teton Sioux under a Lakota title meaning, not as Ruth Beebe Hill supposed, "Clear the path," but more "Get out of the way"?[15] How ward off ethnic slumming among Indians?

After four hundred years, Americans can start again with more accurate translations of Indian America. A translation can miss the truth of place and cultural history, looking sideways in space and time, or mar the delicacies of recreative poetry, mirroring instead its intrusive culture. A well-versed Indian anthropologist wrote that he queries the artifice of Brandon's *The Magic World* and Rothenberg's *Shaking the Pumpkin* because they "decontextualize so much that, very often, one can no longer recognize from where—from what people's singular genius—a given piece came after they have worked it over" (correspondence, 16 September 1979). At the same time, in a recent issue of *Western American Literature*, H. S. McAllister defends the "revolutionary" thrust of Rothenberg's experiments in "total translation," even if all the reworkings do not work all the time. It is a question of authentic license within the scope of "loose" translation. With Trickster's room "for messing around," Rothenberg in the spirit of oral improvisation attempts a poem-for-poem translation "not only of the words but of all sounds connected with the poem, including finally the music itself."[16] His former co-editor of *Alcheringa*, Dennis Tedlock, succeeds more consistently, if not so inventively, in *Finding the Center: Narrative Poetry of the Zuñi Indians*.

Surely these are matters of cultural understanding and poetic taste: Who does the translating and reworking? How skillfully do they recreate the song-poem? How clearly are the objectives and frame stated at the outset, so no reader is misled? There should always be consultation with the tribal originators of the translation.

Then, too, the poems must work in English. Do they have a "power to move us"? Levertov's Aztec adaptations in *Shaking the Pumpkin* ring true, Olson's Mayan myths seem to touch readers with ancient narrative arts, and Merwin's "Crow Versions" graze the spirit-echo of the original songs notated by Lowie:

> I am climbing
> everywhere is
>
> coming up

McAllister defends the intent of *Shaking the Pumpkin's* experimentation, apart from the total success: "These new translations, like the originals, are vital poetry, and the essential alienness of the originals has been translated as well as the words."[17] McAllister goes on to discuss participatory immersion (taking active part in the environmental "field" of a poem) with leads from Edward Hall, Marshall McLuhan, Walter Ong, and Barre Toelken, among others:

> For us, the word is a third-hand, highly abstracted symbol,
> finite in the sense that its quantity is determined by its letters,

discrete in the sense that it occupies visual space on the page. Its "thingness" is the visual structure we call the alphabet. Because of our deeply grounded literacy, which impinges on our total sense of language, the word is for us primarily (though not exclusively) a visual entity. For a non-literate poet or culture, the word is unambiguously oral/aural.

The aural word, though not infinite, is finite in a continuum rather than being clearly bounded like the visual word; the aural word is a portion of the flow which makes up our sound environment. The non-literate is more comfortable than the literate with the sense of language as a flow of sound, because that is how his ear perceives language, and he has not had the perception contradicted by knowledge of the discrete segments of meaning that appear on the page. However, he also perceives words as discrete "things," but this individuation is different from ours, again because of the lack of an abstracted visual mode like our alphabet. With the image of written language to cue us, we have no difficulty imagining what the aural poet means if he says that words are pebbles of meaning, but that very image of written language makes us see as a metaphor what he may mean as a literal statement.[18]

Yes, and perhaps this is why Rothenberg and others seem at times strained or gimmicked. Their reworkings can be self-indulgently Westernized in attempts at free translations from oral cultures. Disregarding the integrity of the original transcriptions too often, Brandon has been charged with abusing the texts in *The Magic World*, even though his spatial arrangements and verse compositions go far in revitalizing the song-poems *as poems*.[19] Form is never free, poets say, any more than insight, regardless of new or old discoveries.

Still, more critically, what is the proper recreation to carry performance into print, dance onto the page, ceremony into the classroom, one language and sense of reality over into new ones? These are not dead acts, or ones that succeed without imagination. In brief, begin with caution against defacing the original; know or work with a bicultural native who knows firsthand the language and culture; listen truly; dig down for the spark in the tinder; proceed with attention to the way *translated* language takes shape, on the page, relayed in the mind and body, *as a poem*.

NATIVE FORMS

"The poem's form," McAllister offers, "is the sound it makes when spoken."[20] Translations must therefore risk the forms of reality in song-poems, since the world of experience does not lie flat on a page, or always justify its margins, or behave only according to conventional rhyme and meter. The page serves as visual canvas, with dimensions, perspectives, and energies around words-as-objects-in-space, moving according to acoustic design among other objects in space. At the same time, this translative risk cannot violate a second audience's expectations, vis-à-vis the boundaries of reality, or the traditional behaviors of poetry. To push too hard on the recreative metaphor is possibly to lose song and shape through overstylization.

A translated poem may hang mobile in space like the leaves on a tree. It may serpentine through a Hopi rain dance in stately choral strophes, arrange itself in a Navajo origin myth as patiently as strata in a canyon wall, or burst freely around Plains drumming and chanting. A translation may lap quietly as lake ripples beaching on a Chippewa shore, or stalk powerfully through darkness over a broken Iroquois terrain. It may soar with the Trickster Raven over the Pacific Northwest, or descend into itself, as kachina gods disappearing into a kiva. The original song, in its human reality, the transplanted poem, in its spatial equivalent, are measured, shaped, imaged, pitched movements in space.

> Good Christ what is
> a poet—if any
>   exists?
>
> a man
> whose words will
>   bite
>   their way
> home—being actual
>
> having the form
>   of motion
>
> At each twigtip
>
> new

upon the tortured
body of thought
        gripping
the ground

a way
        to the last leaftip
—W. C. Williams, "The Wind Increases"[21]

One should first listen to the song-poets on these issues, from all cultures and times, for their life *is* poetry, not theory. Certainly they master poetic form and function beyond the ethnologists, linguists, structural anthropologists, or literary critics, who by and large do not write (perhaps even seriously read, sad to say) poetry in any language.

All the warm nights
sleep in moonlight

keep letting it
go into you

do this
all your life

do this
you will shine outward
in old age

the moon will think
you are
the moon

—Swampy Cree[22]

Who knows more about the performing of words than the "word senders" themselves, who speak for their people without needing interpretation?

It was the pictures I remembered and the words that went
with them; for nothing I have ever seen with my eyes was so
clear and bright as what my vision showed me; and no words
that I have ever heard with my ears were like the words I
heard. I did not have to remember these things; they have remembered themselves all these years.
—Black Elk, Oglala Sioux[23]

CROSSINGS

Everybody sang. We felt as if a beautiful thing was coming.
Because the rain was coming and the dancing and the songs.

> Where on Quijota Mountain a cloud stands
> There my heart stands with it.
> Where the mountain trembles with the thunder
> My heart trembles with it.

That was what they sang. When I sing that song yet it
makes me dance.

—Maria Chona, Papago[24]

A description in the *Iliad* or the *Odyssey*, unlike one in the
Aeneid or in most modern writers, is the swift and natural
observation of a man as he is shaped by life.

—W. B. Yeats[25]

> No tool 'gainst tiger,
> no boat for river.
> That much, no more,
> and they know it;
> but above all to be precise
> at the gulf's edge
> or on thin ice.

—Confucius, *Shih-Ching*[26]

To me it seems more and more as though our customary consciousness lives on the tip of a pyramid whose base within us
(and in a certain way beneath us) widens out so fully that the
farther we find ourselves able to descend into it, the more
generally we appear to be merged into those things that, independent of time and space, are given in our earthly, in the
widest sense worldly, existence.

—Rainer Maria Rilke[27]

. . . if he is contained within his nature as he is participant in
the larger force, he will be able to listen, and his hearing
through himself will give him secrets objects share. And by an
inverse law his shapes will make their own way.

—Charles Olson[28]

> *Ajaja—aja—jaja,*
> The lands around my dwelling
> Are more beautiful

36

CROSSINGS

From the day
When it is given me to see
Faces I have never seen before.
All is more beautiful,
All is more beautiful,
And life is thankfulness.
These guests of mine
Make my house grand,
Ajaja—aja—jaja.

> —Improvised Song of Joy sung to Knud
> Rasmussen by Takomaq, Iglulik Eskimo
> woman, as she prepared tea[29]

The author's conviction on this day of New year is that music begins to atrophy when it departs too far from the dance; that poetry begins to atrophy when it gets too far from music. . . .

> —Ezra Pound[30]

In regard to the songs, Dreamer-of-the-Sun told me that I may pray with my mouth and the prayer will be heard, but if I *sing* the prayer it will be heard *sooner* by *Wakan' Tanka.*

> —Red Weasel, Standing Rock Sioux[31]

I am ashamed before the earth;
I am ashamed before the heavens;
I am ashamed before the dawn;
I am ashamed before the evening twilight;
I am ashamed before the blue sky;
I am ashamed before the sun.
I am ashamed before that standing within me which speaks with me.
Some of these things are always looking at me.
I am never out of sight.
Therefore I must tell the truth.
I hold my word tight to my breast.

> —Old Torlino, Navajo[32]

Whatever culture or history, genuine literature opens up its audience, inside and out: words that move us come alive with the unforgettable intensity of sacred objects, naturally concise and precise. These words break down through the surfaces of the world into our deepest selves, as Rilke suggests, spiritual beings embodying experience, moved tonally and in rhythm with the motions of all things. Words with a "power to move us," from Black Elk to Yeats to Confucius, liven people—heard by the gods, humbled within the universe and their inner being, sacredly close to their common language.

First and finally, the words must *sing*, as Albert Lord says of oral formulaic tradition, not "*for* but *in* performance," a notion no less applicable to translated Native American oral literatures than to Homeric epics.[33] "Text" is only a stop-time facet of the embracing mode and texture of a cultural performance, Toelken and Dundes and others remind us. "But the Indian, you take away everything from him, he still has his mouth to pray, to sing the ancient songs," says Pete Catches, Pine Ridge Sioux medicine man.[34]

CAUTIONS

A translator must take care not to package chants and ceremonial texts (music, religion, medicine, history) into technological and commercial artifacts. Without the care of tribal validation, print can temporarily ossify the spirit of dance, song, narration, healing ritual, prayer, or private witness to a world responsive to interior needs. The spiritual distinctions must be observed, the energies kept alive, even if this means silence and no translation. "Because there is a difference, and there will always be a difference," Lame Deer, the Rosebud Sioux healer believes, "as long as one Indian is left alive. Our beliefs are rooted deep in our earth, no matter what you have done to it and how much of it you have paved over. And if you leave all that concrete unwatched for a year or two, our plants, the native Indian plants, will pierce that concrete and push up through it."[35]

Not everyone wants his or her shadow translated and caught, notwithstanding Edward Curtis's ethnographic genius and photographic skills. Some cultures do not care to "share" tribal ways and values with the non-Indian world (witness the Northern Cheyenne controversy over translated tribal secrets in Hyemeyohsts Storm's *Seven Arrows*). Traditionalists resent sacred implements on display in museums (the Smithsonian or Southwest Museum as antiquarian dumping grounds for native North America). Many

Indians resist the recording of songs, ceremonies, and customs to serve as data in Bureau of Ethnology and American Anthropological reports. Vine Deloria, the Sioux political trickster of *Custer Died for Your Sins*, dubs much anthropology the work of "ideological vultures" scavenging for tenure.[36] In this regard, anthropology bears the bite of a restless westering society that imperializes native societies, knowingly or unknowingly, with an indiscreet appetite for *other* cultures. Western man, to the Indian, unappeasedly hungers for travel and exploration and conquest, for the new, exotic, and untouched, out of a dearth of self-definition within inchoate cultural traditions. The sins of translation, here, result from assuming to escape one's own culture, while imposing a cultural bias on "the other," even unconsciously.

"The Indian has been for a long time generalized in the imagination of the white man," N. Scott Momaday observes. "Denied the acknowledgment of individuality and change, he has been made to become in theory what he could not become in fact, a synthesis of himself."[37] Deloria finds that such generalizations cause Native Americans to live in the "shadows of a mythical super-Indian."[38] The Nez Percé Chief Joseph addressed Congress in 1879:

> [In Washington] I have heard talk and talk, but nothing is
> done. Good words do not last long unless they amount to
> something. Words do not pay for my dead people. They do
> not pay for my country, now overrun by white men. . . .
> Good words will not give my people good health and stop
> them from dying. Good words will not get my people a home
> where they can live in peace and take care of themselves. I am
> tired of talk that comes to nothing. It makes my heart sick
> when I remember all the good words and the broken promises.
> There has been too much talking by men who had no right to
> talk. Too many misrepresentations have been made, too many
> misunderstandings have come up between the white men about
> the Indians.[39]

"The people" themselves want to be heard, not spoken for or paraphrased. To repeat a plea from Indians everywhere, ceremonial texts must not be reduced to market products or cultural oddities. Translations should preserve their traditional contexts, respond to their participant audiences, maintain their sacred and medicinal powers (even if this means protection *from* translation), and keep alive their improvisational and traditional tellers and singers. A translator simply must have cultural experience with the people he translates. The critical issues are ones of basic survival. "The best story teller is one who lets you live if the weather is bad and you are hungry," William Smith Smith told Howard Norman, Swampy Cree translator. "Maybe it won't be easy to hear, inside the story, but it's there. Too easy to find you might think it was too easy to do."[40]

"I go backward, look forward, as the porcupine does," Jacob Nibènegenesábe, tribal historian, said to Norman of Swampy Cree traditions.[41] The past is always "back there," for anybody. A people's inherited cultural burrow may "look forward" to their present lives, rounded on the quills of time; personal and collective history manifests itself in who we are, where we make our home, how we live with one another, why we place ourselves in nature as-we-are. Indians and non-Indians may meet over common bicultural concerns and mutual translations. The stories and songs, the origins of things, are always with us. Rightly translated, sung, and told, the old ways rise up through the new ways.

Translation is a historical crossing, finally, from manifest to manifesting cultures, past-to-present enacted through people. Each cultural bearer, American and Native American, would guard against mistranslation, misrepresentation, and misunderstanding. Controversies over breed and blood, urban and "res," conservation and progress, "going back" and coming forward, your tribe and mine, set up the dynamics of being who we are in the world. In Indian thought, we are native to ourselves, tribal to our given peoples, relative to all life forms, ritual to powers that spirit us. The original "What-Moves-moves" in the world renews all of us continually, constantly, at our best without fear of change, trusting in seasonal continuities. The renaissance or rebirth of all cultures, alive in spoken, sung, and signed literatures, lies here in acts of translation.

3

ANCESTRAL VOICES
IN ORAL TRADITIONS

Here through art I shall live for ever.
Who will take me, who will go with me?
Here I stand, my friends.
A singer, from my heart I strew my songs,
my fragrant songs before the face of others.
I carve a great stone, I paint thick wood
my song is in them.
It will be spoken of when I have gone.
I shall leave my song-image on earth.
  My heart shall live, it will come back,
  my memory will live and my fame.
I cry as I speak and discourse with my heart.
Let me see the root of song,
let me implant it here on earth so it may be realized.
        —Aztec, *Cantares Mexicanos* (Gordon Brotherston,
            Image of the New World, 1979)

The values and perceptions in older oral literatures underlie contemporary Indian writing. Without question a renaissance or "rebirth" springs from roots deep in the compost of cultural history, a recurrent past. Indian novelists look back to storytelling and "winter count" historians telling tribal time by imaging events on animal skins. Poets recall visionary singers and healers who draw the people together in ceremony. Dramatists remember ritual priests and cultural purveyors of daily tribal life. Essayists reach back to political leaders and orators in council. It is a time when words empower ethical ways of living, good medicine, secular entertainment, spiritual vision, utilitarian arts, politics, and the skills of surviving each day.

The literary synthesis in this chapter is gleaned from ethnography, folklore, and linguistics. It speaks collectively for Native American tribal literatures. The chapter presents an overview of the old ways, mythologized by modern Indians, as well as Americans-at-large. These are the cultural myths of Native America, more or less historically verifiable, and certainly real to American Indians as images. Their aesthetics turn on a sense of tribe, that is, an extended family that reciprocates among people, places, history, flora and fauna, spirits and gods.

In similar synthesis, the anthropological paradigms of George and Louise Spindler, to cite a respected example, are less "culture-specific," as anthropologists say, than cross-tribal profiles of Indian life, distinct in mindset from mainstream America. In *Native American Tribalism* D'Arcy McNickle, the Flathead historian, summarizes the Spindlers' inventory in a psychosociological profile of American Indian cultural traits over time and many tribes: restrained, giving, individualist, stoic, courageous, awed of the world, in-joking, presently oriented, and spiritually minded.[1] These pan-Indian coordinates risk generalization, to be sure, and there will always be exceptions. Such cultural adjectives are still useful as basic introductions to Indian ways. The purpose of such an overview is to authenticate and clarify broad cultural truths behind images of Indians in America.

TRIBAL POETICS

With notable exceptions (Mayan, Mixtec, and Aztec hieroglyphics), North American tribal peoples lived without depending particularly on written languages per se. Visualized inscriptions, carvings, paintings, and etchings constituted native "writing" north of Mexico. Pictographs and petroglyphs were inscribed in stone all over the North American landscape. In addition, there were ritual codes embedded in artifacts portraying tribal forms of literature: Algonkin birchbark scrolls, Iroquois shell-beaded wampum belts, Sioux winter count pictography on buffalo skins, Northwest cedar totem poles, Southwest sandpaintings, pottery and weaving designs almost everywhere.[2]

But for the most part, basic to common Indian life, oral cultures lived mouth to mouth, age to age, as the people passed on a daily culture. Their literatures survived as remembered myths and rituals, song-poems and narrative tales, legends and parables. Once these oral works were translated into English and printed in books, America began to recognize, belatedly, the long presence of Native American literatures.[3]

How do members of Indian cultures look upon their languages and literatures? A. Grove Day writes in *The Sky Clears*:

> The Indians made poems for many reasons: to praise their gods and ask their help in life; to speak to the gods through dramatic performances at seasonal celebrations or initiations or other rites; to work magical cures or enlist supernatural aid in hunting, plant-growing, or horsebreeding; to hymn the praises of the gods or pray to them; to chronicle tribal history; to explain the origins of the world; to teach right conduct; to mourn the dead; to arouse warlike feelings; to compel love; to arouse laughter; to ridicule a rival or bewitch an enemy; to praise famous men; to communicate the poet's private experience; to mark the beauties of nature; to boast of one's personal greatness; to record a vision scene; to characterize the actors in a folk tale; to quiet children; to lighten the burdens of work; to brighten up tribal games; and sometimes, to express simply joy and a spirit of fun.[4]

Words are believed to carry the power to make things happen, ritualized in song, sacred story, and prayer. This natural force is at once common as daily speech and people's names. The empowering primacy of language weds people with their native environment: an experience or object or person exists interpenetrant with all other creation, inseparable from its name. And names allow people to see themselves and the things around them, as words image the spirits in the world.

A common tribal language is essential. Oral traditions unify a people, just as they poeticize the common speech. For the most part still today, tribal cultures express themselves through spoken literatures. The people's "literary history" is a function of memory, imagination, daily and seasonal ritual. The arts of language remain communally open; the word is a tribal bond. According to Vine Deloria, Jr., the original names of twenty-seven different tribes meant, in various forms, *the people*: "the people" (Arikara), "real people" (Cherokee), "the flesh" (Zuñi), "men of men" (Pawnee), "allies" (Lakota), "first people" (Biloxi), and "people of the real speech" (Winnebago).[5] What has become abstractly distant for individualist-thinking Americans, "we-the-people" from the word Iroquois, is a specifically common definition of an Indian tribe.

Scott Momaday tells of the Kiowa arrowmaker who sat in an ordinary way working inside his tepee with his wife. The Kiowa fashioned and straightened arrows in his mouth, and the best arrows carried teeth marks. Once at night he saw a stranger looking in from the darkness. The arrowmaker said casually, in Kiowa, that if the outsider understood the tribal language, he should give his name. The stranger remained silent. Casually the arrowmaker bent his bow in one direction, then another, talking softly, and then killed the unnamed outsider with a single arrow.[6] Language defines a people. Words are penetrant as arrows, the finest shafts bearing marks from the mouths that shape them. The craft, ceremony, power, and defense of the tribal family depend on them. A well-chosen word, like a well-made arrow, pierces to the heart.

Oral tribal poetry remains for the most part organic, for tribal poets see themselves as essentially keepers of the sacred word bundle. Momaday calls these carriers of the language "men made of words."[7] They regard rhythm, vision, craft, nature, and words as gifts that precede and continue beyond any human life. The people are born into and die out of a language that gives them being. Song-poets in this respect discover, or better rediscover, nature's poems. They never pretend to have invented a "poetic" world apart from nature, but instead believe they are permitted to husband songs as one tends growing things; they give thanks that the songs have chosen them as the singers.

As with the land itself, the artists cannot presume to possess the living arts entrusted to them. Their caretaking marks these "poets" both unassuming and dignified, twice honored. They give the songs back to those powers that granted them voice, humbling themselves before nature's tribal circle; their visions enrich public ceremonies so vital to tribal health. Indian art is open, communal, of use to the people, even as it distinguishes individual artists. The song-poet's aesthetics are no less than useful, as the singer believes that tribal life needs beauty daily. Art is a function, then, of tribal necessity, and functional creativity is a daily staple. Among the Keres Pueblos "good" and "beautiful" are the same word.[8]

Tribal life centers in a common blood, a shared and inherited body of tradition, a communal place, a mutual past and present: the key concept is integrated relationship, as an individual within a family. Tribes gather ceremonially to observe cyclic continuities, sometimes imaged in the circle of life. Black Elk questions why the grass is kept penned up in squares along with city peoples, since the spirits have shown him the "sacred hoop" of the world: "You have noticed that everything an Indian does is in a circle, and that is because the Power of the World always works in circles, and everything tries to be round."[9]

Daily relationships, at once personal and ceremonial, preserve this continuity; all tribal members are considered close kin, as a parent to a child or a brother to a sister. Uncle, Aunt, Nephew, Niece, Brother, Sister, Grandson, Granddaughter, Grandfather, and Grandmother are still common forms of address on reservations. The older, idealized tribal values include sharing material and spiritual wealth, remaining loyal to the people at all costs, caring about one's place in relation to the encompassing world, maintaining an extended family as support for each individual, and being kind in the original sense of the word, that is, "of the same kind" and "kind" or generous within that bond. Ideally, to be giving and gracious is natural among kind people, even when the realities of contemporary Indian life, fractured between cultures too often, threaten tribal moralities premised on kinship.

Despite separate tribal histories, Native American literatures interconnect through a poetics resisting Euro-American literary conceptions: the artist as primal word- and world-maker (*poïetes*, "maker," in Greek), the printed word as fixed and finite, the poet's craft imposing order on nature, his creation making up orders unknown. Native American literatures, given their diversity, intersect in a common, organic aesthetics—a poetic kinship that unites the people, other earthly creatures, the gods, and nature in one great tribe.

ROOTED WORDS

Indian traditions place words organically in the world as animate, generative beings. Words are the roots of continuing tribal origins, genetic cultural sources within nature. Indian literatures are then grounded in words that focus being within a setting, detail by detail, as in the images of this Ojibwa song-poem:

> The bush is sitting under a tree and
> singing[10]

Secure in nature, the bush sings its own place "under" the larger tree. The poem is landscaped with care toward the ecology and interdependence that conditions singing, rather than the triumph of any one song ("bush" instead of "tree"). The language remains spare, neither more nor less than the evoked setting itself. Words carry their essential meanings, and the minimal perspective elicits the song-poet's attention to small detail, as it sharpens response to the larger world. In a Quechuan poem an insect orders the night's darkness, even death:

> The water bug is drawing
> the shadows of the evening
> toward him on the water[11]

The poems sing the origins of people, creatures, things, in local revelations, exactly where they exist. The people hear and glimpse truths unexpectedly, out of the corner of the eye, as nature compresses and surprises with rich mystery. All things are alive, suggestive, sacred, and in common.

A Sioux holy man reverently addresses a stone as *Tunkashila*, a word that also means *Grandfather*.[12] On the Great Plains, where everything finds being in vast emptiness, an isolate rock provides the world's cornerstone, a resting place for restless spirits, as in this fragment from an Omaha ritual:

> unmoved
> from time without
> end
> you rest
> there in the midst of the paths
> in the midst of the winds
> you rest
> covered with the droppings of birds
> grass growing from your feet
> your head decked with the down of birds
> you rest
> in the midst of the winds
> you wait
> Aged one[13]

Nature grants a base for wandering spirits—winds, birds, grasses that come and go, even droppings on the earthly origins. The rock's patience serves as the poem's refrain: "You rest . . . you rest . . . you rest . . . you wait / Aged one." Time is here a permanence of place.

Words do not come after or apart from what naturally is, but are themselves natural genes, tribal history in the bodies of the people. People are born into their heritage and tribal tongue. For the most part, they do not create words any more than they give birth to themselves or make up nature. Names can come from dreams, personal tics, external events, medicine people, or ancestors. Singers chant songs, drawing tonally on the voice as an interpretive human instrument for words living in the mouth and body; pitch modulates meaning; accent gives cadence to meanings drawing together. Instead of rhyming words (the poem as unifying technique), the songs rhyme perceptions, moods, natural objects, the world-as-word (the poem as unifying association). A lyric threads the story together through poetic time as chords tie the song together harmonically. The Tewa sing to Mother Earth and Father Sky, and the image of a weaver's loom appears:

> Then weave for us a garment of brightness;
> May the warp be the white light of morning,
> May the weft be the red light of evening,
> May the fringes be the falling rain,
> May the border be the standing rainbow.[14]

Formulaic repetition makes a ritual of the sky's interwoven lights, and resonances between rhymed events stretch the song taut over the sky loom ("fringes" "falling rain" and "border" "rainbow").

In a Navajo Night Chant, the singer's craft is discovered in a natural "house made of dawn":

> May it be beautiful before me.
> May it be beautiful behind me.
> May it be beautiful below me.
> May it be beautiful above me.
> May it be beautiful all around me.
> In beauty it is finished.[15]

The Navajo pattern the correspondences among natural things, as though tribalizing their kinships:

> cotton
>
>   motion
>
>   clouds

frog
    hail
        potatoes
            dumplings

cloud water
      fog
        moss

smoke
    cloud
      rain
        acceptance
          breathing in[16]

"Do you picture it," a Zuñi informant asked Dennis Tedlock as he was translating, "or do you just write it down?"[17]

MINIMAL PRESENCE

Native American literature suggests a philosophical awareness of all things, their resonances, their places in the sacred hoop. Space shapes objects, just as silence determines sound; objects in turn are defined at their circumferences, where they cease to exist. Shadows and echoes silhouette origins. "Listen!" the song-poets sing, invoking silence as the initial chord of a chant, the essential words depending on the silence from which they spring. The true poets listen as they sing. Momaday recalls:

> There is in the Indian towns also a sense of timelessness and peace. No one who has watched the winter solstice ceremonies at Jemez can have failed to perceive the great spiritual harmonies which culminate in those ancient rites. None who has heard the deep droning concert of the singers and the insistent vibration of the drums can have mistaken the old sacred respect for sound and silence which makes for the magic of words and literature.[18]

The strengths of young and old cross in the poet, who can sense words in the desert silence, pattern in the forest shadows, design in the falling stars, the return of the summer sun at the winter solstice.

Morality fuses with poetry in the telling of tribal stories, where an audience listens and learns customs, skills, and values. Morals are interwoven throughout the tales and in the seasons of telling, even with the Trickster tales that teach by comic mistakes. Sacred and profane stories are told according to seasons for telling. The participation of audience and teller, the performing context of the story, acts out the tribal interchange necessary to their collective well-being. In general, a storyteller does not interpret or gloss the tale or tell too much. Listeners imagine their participatory places in the story.

Just as silence speaks primally to the mind, so space is fertile without objects. Everything counts. "Nothing" can be suggestive presence, as echoed in the southwestern deserts or resonant on the Great Plains or shadowed in the northern woodlands. A tribal people learn to know richness in a sense of loss; they know through a necessary economy, tempered in poverty, that more is not always better. The tribe depends on natural growth cycles for survival; to go over or under what is necessary threatens the balance of nature and tribe. People in tribal cultures learn to give in order to live: witness the ceremonial "give-aways" and potlatches and rituals of sacrifice across Native America. Thoreau in *Walden* records that the Iroquois practiced a "busk" ritual of burning possessions every fifty years to begin anew. Nature is ever alive with spirits, powers, mysteries, sacred objects, and holy spaces—fertile in openness and creative emptiness.

SACRED PLAY

A truly sacred world allows for a sense of mockery and play that turns the weight of reality around. Tribal kinsmen joke to lift spirits, play to loosen an encumbering seriousness; their humor at once tempers and includes the serious world. Jerome Rothenberg observes that Seneca poetry "works in sets of short songs, minimal realizations colliding with each other in marvelous ways, a very light, very pointed play-of-the mind, nearly always just a step away from the comic (even as their masks are), the words set out in clear relief against the ground of the (Meaningless) refrain. Clowns stomp & grunt through the longhouse, but in subtler ways too the encouragement to 'play' is always a presence."[19]

Sioux *heyokas* sport sacramentally as clowns, just as the Trickster gods play with men. To become a heyoka, a Sioux vision questor dreams of lightning, the spiritual bolt between sky and earth; thunder is a cosmic form of laughter. Western Pueblo kachina gods (called "mudheads" by whites) use laughter to cleanse and purge the people. Iroquois "false face" priests mimic the wrong ways to do things. And in almost all origin myths appears the ancient bungler, Trickster, who in many respects turns out to be a culture hero: seeding edible plants with dessicated parts of his giant penis, stealing fire for the people, deciding life and death, and scaling man's pretentions down to a human level. Those touched by the gods at play—saints, clowns, priests, idiots, transsexuals, children, elders—become holy and foolish in one gesture. They carry the burden and distinction of their special powers. In like manner, the English word "silly" traces a double lineage back to the Old English "saelig," meaning holy and foolish.

Laughter, song, dance, and chant move the tribe through public ritual dynamically into nature's origins. Healing ceremonies and celebrations gather the people to dance and draw life touching the earth; they grieve to voice sorrow openly. "You have noticed," Black Elk says,

> that the truth comes into this world with two faces. One is
> sad with suffering and the other laughs; but it is the same face,
> laughing or weeping. When people are already in despair,
> maybe the laughing face is better for them; and when they feel
> too good and are too sure of being safe, maybe the weeping
> face is better for them to see.[20]

Tribal stories pivot on contrasts and reversals, releasing sorrow, sparking laughter, inspiring invention, purging primal fears. They give mankind a range of characters and settings from the animals and the earth to the gods and the sky.

A diverse sense of contradiction characterizes Indian storytelling. Black Elk laments that the sacred hoop of his tribe is broken and the flowering tree is withered after the Wounded Knee Massacre—"a people's dream that died in bloody snow"—and yet Black Elk dreamed the thunder spirits and all his life healed people as a heyoka or sacred clown.[21] A Nez Percé poem narrates how "coyote borrows Farting Boy's asshole, tosses up his eyes, retrieves them, rapes old women and tricks a young girl seeking power."[22] In a Cochiti story Coyote talks Beaver into exchanging wives, to Coyote's chagrin and his wife's pleasure.[23] In a Hopi tale Coyote Old Man deflowers the haughty tribal virgin, whom gods and men have courted unsuccessfully; he escapes and parades his genitals on a distant hill; then the rain god hunts him down and kills him.[24] The Maricopas tell how the Creator gave teeth of sun's fire to a gentle snake, as protection against a bullying rabbit, and the animals vengefully killed their Creator.[25]

In all these tales, gods and spirits walk the earth at one with plants, animals, and human beings. Powers of transformation interrelate both animate and inanimate creatures in a reverse kind of spiritual anthropomorphism: instead of projecting human forms on animals and the gods, men take their personal characteristics, family names, and clan names from the animal and natural world—Black Elk, Crow Dog, Lone Wolf, Eagle Heart, Crazy Horse, Two Moons, Sun Chief, Star Boy, Sweet Grass Woman.

The natural world speaks for itself without shame or self-consciousness, dancing its life and language. The Makah sing:

> Mine is a proud village, such as it is,
> We are at our best when dancing.[26]

Decorous senses blossom in the "orchidean" Mayan and Aztec cultures, eulogized by William Carlos Williams.[27] As the dance plays itself through, Aztec flowers bloom on the poet's lips, singing: a word is a flower is the dawn is a quetzal bird is a dewdrop is human life—beautiful, sexual, changing, perishable. In the words of a Nahuatl singer, "The flower in my heart blossoms in the middle of the night."[28] Passion. Human sacrifice. The terror of beauty.

No single mood corners nature's temperaments. No single curiosity exhausts the possibilities of surprise. Given a respect for nature's range, tribal peoples are free to experiment with natural rules, to discover inherent truths and error, to carry on their own investigation of traditions and moralities. Trusting tribal boundaries and a local sense of origin frees the people to explore their heritage and environment. The Pueblo moves over a space as small as a mesa top, down through kivas into the earth, among family and extended kin, back into a communal past working itself out in the present. A plainsman, in contrast, once roamed a thousand miles a season on horseback and felt at home in motion. The "traditional" freedoms, unconfined by space large or small, empower a tribal member to celebrate life beyond a sense of restriction, disregarding momentary hardship, unafraid of dislocation, and without self-pity. Plenty-Coups, chief of the Crow, told the white "Sign-talker":

> I am old. I am not graceful. My bones are heavy, and my
> feet are large. But I know justice and have tried all my life to
> be just, even to those who have taken away our old life that
> was so good. My whole thought is of my people. I want them
> to be healthy, to become again the race they have been. I want
> them to learn all they can from the white man, because he is
> here to stay, and they must live with him forever.[29]

MAGIC OF SENSE

The Indian poet sees the magic of the world through symbolic detail;
if attentive, he sees as a natural visionary. Lame Deer, the Sioux medicine
man, says:

> But I'm an Indian. I think about ordinary, common things
> like this pot. The bubbling water comes from the rain cloud.
> It represents the sky. The fire comes from the sun which
> warms us all—men, animals, trees. The meat stands for the
> four-legged creatures, our animal brothers, who gave of
> themselves so that we should live. The steam is living
> breath. . . . We Indians live in a world of symbols and images
> where the spiritual and the commonplace are one. To you
> symbols are just words, spoken or written in a book. To us
> they are part of nature, part of ourselves—the earth, the sun,
> the wind and the rain, stones, trees, animals, even little insects
> like ants and grasshoppers. We try to understand them not
> with the head but with the heart, and we need no more than a
> hint to give us the meaning.[30]

Seers feel the world "real" enough to be guided by and trust what they
sense, seeing from "the heart's eye," Lame Deer says.[31] Heeding intuition,
visionaries believe in a perceptual reality cognate with nature's reality. If
dreams seem unreal, Momaday's old woman spirit cautions him, then so are
the dreamers.[32]

A seer walks the *brujo*'s "path with heart," according to the anthropological fiction of Carlos Castaneda, whose popularity among millions
of Indians and non-Indians generally validates his writings as imaginative

literature, if not as anthropology: " 'The world is all that is encased here,' [Juan Matus] said, and stomped the ground. 'Life, death, people, the allies, and everything else that surrounds us. The world is incomprehensible. We won't ever understand it; we won't ever unravel its secrets. Thus we must treat it as it is, a sheer mystery!' " Castaneda, awkwardly the anthropologist and shaman's apprentice, must be surprised into knowledge. " 'We have exhausted nothing, you fool,' [Juan Matus] said imperatively. '*Seeing* is for impeccable men. Temper your spirit now, become a warrior, learn to *see*, and then you'll know that there is no end to the new worlds for our vision.' "[33]

"Go to a mountain-top & cry for a vision," the Sioux holy men counsel.[34]

The spirit world and the natural world interconnect through dreams, most intense in the traditional vision quest, whether a Papago on pilgrimage from the desert to gather sea salt, or an Eskimo shaman who drops to the bottom of the sea asking forgiveness from the earth daughter, or a Sioux warrior lamenting in a vision pit on a lonely mountaintop. Seers know the world with care, attune themselves with natural magic. Their healing aligns the people with the natural health and energy of the universe, the balance of all things. A medicine man ties the people's needs into the things of the world, releasing the spirits in things to move through the tribe. A thought is a spiritual act; a word has the magical power to actualize spirits.

Dreams relay visions from the spirit world. Sacramental songs ritualize the dream myths, bearing visions into the world (a shaman is midwife to the gods). A Sioux heyoka sings:

> The day of the sun has been my strength.
> The path of the moon shall be my robe.
> A sacred praise I am making.
> A sacred praise I am making.[35]

Song-poems are tribal conductors of dream power, and "sometimes dreams are wiser than waking," Black Elk says.[36] The spirits and ancestors speak to the living in dreams, giving their daily lives a sacred strangeness. Incantations, dream visions, totemic forces, and imitative magic set up conduits of well-being and power in energies beyond the limits of human beings. As noted earlier, the older Lakota reference to the creator Taku Skanskan, "What Moves-moves," implies the power giving living motion to all things.[37]

53

Dreams heighten the people's awareness, as does fear positively regarded, proving medicinal, therapeutic, and cleansing of the tribal spirit. A Navajo chant is word medicine to a supplicant asking health from the gods. The formula: chant, learn, be healed, remember:

> The singer stroked the patient's body
> and pressed his body to the patient's body.
>
> Have you learned? they asked him
> and he answered, Yes.
>
> They sang all night, and the patient learned
> and was well.
>
> Then he was told to be sure and remember all that
> he had been taught, for everything forgotten went
> back to the gods.[38]

The medicinal power of these words is inspired by the gods, yet remains communal; the sacred world is common to all in the mythic origins of religious thought. Black Elk's "great vision" does not heal until his people perform it tribally and locate it ceremonially in their daily life. The Navajo sing from the Night Chant:

> In beauty
> > you shall be my representation
> In beauty
> > you shall be my song
> In beauty
> > you shall be my medicine
> In beauty
> > my holy medicine[39]

A singer works at dreaming and seeing but does not dwell on the work. The work ethic can be transcended by a dream ethic, a natural magic and intuitive morality inspired by the spirit world. "Men who work cannot dream, and wisdom comes in dreams," warned the Nez Percé, Smohalla, of the Dreamer Religion. "You ask me to plow the ground. Shall I take a knife and tear my mother's breast? Then when I die she will not take me to her bosom to rest."[40]

TRIBAL SONG

I
the song
I walk here[41]

This Modoc chant must be imagined apart from any songmaker or audience, living a reality of its own. The people come to it for life, tradition, medicine, play. The tribe lives in the song's daily presence. The song is actually believed to "walk" the world speaking-singing itself. Tribal oral literature arises out of the common ceremonies of people talking day to day, joining in conversation and song. Many tribes speak of hearing the earth's heartbeat in their songs, as in the healing Brush Dance ceremonies of northern California.[42] The chanted rhythms rise with the heartbeat, drums, moving feet, and swaying body; through them the people dance to the earth's pulse and draw energy from their origins in the earth. Their singing lives in tribal time, in rhythm with nature's cyclic time—the seasons of planting, growing, harvesting, and returning to the living earth.

Oral poetry is kinetic ritual. The body dances and sings alive with the mind. Black Elk says of the grandfather stallion's song in his vision: "It was so beautiful that nothing anywhere could keep from dancing. The virgins danced, and all the circled horses. The leaves on the trees, the grasses on the hills and in the valleys, the waters in the creeks and in the rivers and the lakes, the four-legged and the two-legged and the wings of the air—all danced together to the music of the stallion's song."[43] This natural balance of wind and water, sky and earth, roots, leggeds, and wings harmonizes all living things in a commonly encircled existence. To know "in a sacred manner," Black Elk says, is to be moved by songs of interrelated life, to be alert, quick—as Castaneda's brujo speaks of native wisdom, "light and fluid."[44] Attentive to an environment in motion about him, a man of knowledge dances his wisdom. He animately *is* as he knows.

Song cadences balance one another and play in running rhythms; repetition and variation play on the multiple possibilities of any idea in relation to others. The song-poet groups words in parallel phrases and rhymes thoughts, letting associations gather tribally. A human condition rhymes with a natural phenomenon, man with animal origins, as in this Aztec poem:

> The divine *quechol* bird answers me as I, the singer,
> sing, like the *coyol* bird, a noble new song,

> polished like a jewel, a turquoise, a shining
> emerald, darting green rays, a flower song of
> spring, spreading a celestial fragrance, fresh
> with the dews of roses, thus have I the poet sung.[45]

The chanting returns without end to feelings and perceptions embedded over time, values that bear repeating and cannot be outworn or finally plumbed. A generative mystery lies within these songs, so far down and back in time that it startles the present alive.

A world ripe with associations spawns natural likenesses through rich overlappings of metaphor. In all this, as well, singers confront their individual limitations. A Tlingit laments, "It is only crying about myself/that comes to me in song."[46] A Nootka complains against the fog,

> Don't you ever
> You up in the sky
> Don't you ever get tired
> Of having the clouds between you and us?[47]

Or he sings to bring fair weather,

> You, whose day it is, make it beautiful.
> Get out your rainbow of colors,
> So it will be beautiful.[48]

The sensibility here, in Frederick Turner's words, lies "rooted so deeply in things that it goes through them and beneath them."[49] These songs sing themselves, given their natural orders and harmonies, as truths ancient in the world.

POETRY OF SURVIVAL

The Sioux physician Ohiyesa (Charles Eastman) says that Native American literature survives as "a perilous gift."[50] When the last native speakers of a language die, as with too many Indian cultures (Ishi the Yana most remembered), the literature of the tribe dies with them. The people keep the songs alive by necessity and choice; their words live humanly in the mouth, the torso, the heart, the limbs of the singers. As oral poetry, the song-poems

must compel listeners immediately, in the presence of performance, or they
will lose their audience, their right to be. The language is by definition,
Momaday says, one generation from extinction. A Wintu singer chants:

> Down west, down west we dance,
> We spirits dance,
> Down west, down west we dance,
> We spirits dance,
> Down west, down west we dance,
> We spirits weeping dance,
> We spirits dance.[51]

While the chant drops "down" to "weeping," it moves simultaneously
out toward life and against the descent of death. The lament works its way
toward healing, countering the downward thrust of dying. The poem ritualizes pain through repetition and accretion, stylizing grief in movements of
the dance, the pulse answering death's prone stasis.

A warrior prepares for death with philosophical counsel and bearing.
"Let us see, is this real, / This life I am living?" a Pawnee warrior chants, his
entry into battle a metaphysical question.[52] To a warrior, life comes as a perishable gift, the world his mystery and challenge. In the following song-
poem, fear inspires the Omaha singer to pray for life in humility before his
task:

> Wa-kon'da,
> here needy he stands,
> and I am he.[53]

Black Elk requests bravery and power from the spirit world, "the power to
make-live and to destroy." Second cousin to the warrior Crazy Horse, Black
Elk receives these interdependent powers from his Grandfathers in the western sky—a bow and a wooden cup of rainwater, the terror of a thunder-
storm and the gentle life force of its moisture.[54]

Indian literatures record how a warrior meets death directly, honestly,
with no illusions, confronting the defining fact of life, that is, not-life. His
bravery grows out of his chanted acceptance of smallness in the face of the
universe, realizing that the spirits one day will take back the life given him
for the moment. "Have pity on me," sings the Assiniboine warrior, crying
his need and vulnerability.[55] White Antelope, a Cheyenne war chief, stood

with folded arms and sang this death song, as he was murdered at the Sand
Creek Massacre of 1864:

> Nothing lives long
> Except the earth and the mountains[56]

Facing death with a chant is no less an Indian "literary" gesture, than
a ritual of peaceful life. An old Kiowa woman sings as she prepares the earth
for the Sun Dance in *The Way to Rainy Mountain*, and the older the woman
grows, the more ceremonial play frees her to live.

> We have brought the earth.
> Now it is time to play;
> As old as I am, I still have the feeling of play.[57]

Sacred processionals, ancient within the earth, ground the Sun Dance, as
Black Elk envisions the ancestors:

> But I was not the last, for when I looked behind me there were
> ghosts of people like a trailing fog as far as I could see—grand-
> fathers of grandfathers and grandmothers of grandmothers
> without number. And over these a great Voice—the Voice
> that was the South—lived, and I could feel it silent. And as we
> went the Voice behind me said: "Behold a good nation walk-
> ing in a sacred manner in a good land!"[58]

As old as the singer can dream, there are still older ancestors, and over them
the unspoken power of "What Moves-moves." It is a timeless and sacred
stream, a holy tribal way, through a "good land." All tribes come together
under such a vision.

TRIBAL CONTINUITY

The tribal Native American can find power in natural circles: sun and
moon, stars, nest, tepee, flower, rainbow, whirlwind, human contours, nature's seasonal cycles, and the "sacred hoop" of the world itself. The singers of a poetic tribal world live in the presence of spoken words, and their
words come back to them where they live with others. The mouth rounds

out in speech and song; the printed page by contrast remains fixed, rectilinear. Black Elk laments that Indians are penned up on "islands" of land, and Lame Deer questions the power of a society living in squares and plastic bags, ashamed of bodily openings.[59]

The vision quest is cyclic, requiring solitude, but not corners for hiding; the visionary leaves his tribe periodically in order to return with powers in common. "Help yourself as you travel along in life," the Winnebago, Crashing Thunder, counsels. "The earth has many narrow passages scattered over it. If you have something with which to strengthen yourself, then when you get to these narrow passages, you will be able to pass through them safely and your fellow men will respect you."[60] Like the warrior, the song-poet lives an individual for the sake of the tribe; his singing is a matter of life or death for the people. He does not celebrate himself separately, his vision apart from the natural world, but sings of kinship in the tribal circle. Native American cultures carry this old sense of interconnectedness, sacred among the people, down to the present time. A "49" line sung socially at contemporary powwows invites,

> When the dance is over, sweetheart,
> I will take you home in my one-eyed Ford.[61]

However they get there, whenever, going home again and rejoining the circle is the song that binds tribal Americans.

4

A CONTEMPORARY TRIBE
OF POETS

I weave the night, I cross the weft with stars
and the dark hollows of your eyes;
I plait the words you've said into my hair.

—ANITA ENDREZZE PROBST

Astounding: less than twenty years ago, there simply were no acknowledged, much less published, Native American "poets" in America. A
handful of exceptions proved the rule. Elémire Zolla discusses vestigial
Indian literature at the end of *The Writer and the Shaman: A Morphology of
the American Indian* (1969, 1973, originally written in French). Among the
few published Indians for over a century were John Rollin Ridge (Cherokee), Alexander Lawrence Posey (Creek), Bertrand N. O. Walker (Wyan-
dot), Mourning Dove (Okanogan), Will Rogers (Cherokee), Charles
Eastman (Sioux), and Luther Standing Bear (Sioux), who went unheralded
as American writers.

William Apes, a Methodist preacher and direct Pequot descendant of
King Philip, published his autobiography in 1829, *A Son of the Forest*,
followed by Chief Black Hawk's life story published in 1833, *The Life of
Ma-Ka-Tai-Me-She-Kia-Kiak, or Black Hawk*. From the turn of the century
on, there appeared several hundred as-told-to biographies dictated to non-
Indian ethnographers in translation, among them *Geronimo's Story of His*

Life by S. M. Barrett in 1906. The historian, Stanley Vestal (Walter Stanley Campbell), argued that Sitting Bull was a visionary poet in the epic sense, but the Wild West still framed Buffalo Bill's "American" Indian as primitive, and few readers took the poetic argument seriously in Vestal's *Sitting Bull: Champion of the Sioux* (1957).

Indian literature fell under the pall of ethnological field work, where the names of Francis La Flesche (Omaha), Ella Deloria (Sioux), and Archie Phinney (Nez Percé) were known among a handful of anthropologists. Still, poor translations perpetuated the stereotype of the unlettered savage, and tribal anonymity, bestowed on individual singers and tellers by many a careless ethnographer, shawled any personal sense of literary craft. Reliving Hiawatha's romantic myth in the nineteenth century, George Copway (Ojibwa) was befriended by Longfellow and Parkman; he acculturated, so to speak, as the White Man's Ojibwa visionary. Copway traveled Europe, lectured, and wrote five books between 1847 and 1851, including *The Life, History, and Travels of Kah-Ge-Ga-Gah-Bowh (George Copway)*, briefly edited a newspaper, *Copway's American Indian*, and died of alcoholism in 1863, the year of Black Elk's birth. Perhaps the first, and now forgotten, Algonkian novel was published by Simon Pokagon in 1890, *O Gi Maw Kwe Mit I Gwa Ki—Queen of the Woods*. Mourning Dove (Hum-ishu-ma) was the first Indian (Okanogan) woman to publish a novel, *Cogewea: The Half-Blood* (Boston: Four Seas, 1927).

For the most part, however, native singers, seers, and tellers were segregated from American literature. Changing all this, tribal oral materials are now shaping the written word; for many American readers, these are the first Native American voices to be heard. The present generation of postwar Indian writers now publishes poems, novels, plays, essays, and treatises in English as a first language. Their literary breakthrough gives voice to the present Indian renaissance.

I

The resurgence of "native" American consciousness in the 1960s spawned newly revised anthologies of old folkloric caches, John Bierhorst's *In the Trail of the Wind* (1971), William Brandon's *The Magic World* (1971) and Jerome Rothenburg's *Shaking the Pumpkin* (1972). These reworkings stirred old translation controversies.[1] Then Shirley Hill Witt, an Iroquois anthropologist, and Stan Steiner, popularist of ethnic rights, published *The Way: An Anthology of American Indian Literature* (1971) with a sprinkling of Ray Young Bear, Simon Ortiz, and James Welch, among a few selected others. More a cultural casebook, the anthology began with the powerful oratory of past tribal leaders, but soon bogged down in contemporary politics and the sociological jargon of the new Indian movement.

The next year Natachee Scott Momaday (the novelist's mother) released *American Indian Authors*, a young reader's survey of Chief Joseph to Vine Deloria in 150 pages. So, too, in 1972 Terry Allen's *The Whispering Wind: Poetry by Young American Indians* debuted 128 pages of verse from the Institute of American Indian Arts. Most of these fourteen young poets were known as painters, sculptors, weavers, potters, dancers, or actors, reflecting the integrated arts of tribal cultures. A representative young voice in this collection, Liz Sohappy felt like "a floating body," she related, until receiving her Palouse name, Om-na-ma, at the age of twenty-one in 1969. "My grandmother said that is how it was to be—no one is here on earth until he has an Indian name." And this fresh gathering of young Indian poems marked the beginnings of artists fusing old tribal names, new tongues, and adopted literary forms.

In 1973 Thomas Sanders and Walter Peek produced *Literature of the American Indian*, reprinting traditional materials (origin myths, song-poems, speeches) from Bureau of American Ethnology reports and older anthologies such as George W. Cronyn's *The Path on the Rainbow* (1918), Margot Astrov's *The Winged Serpent* (1946), and A. Grove Day's *The Sky Clears* (1964). These selections, though traditional, bore the archaic ring of talk-poetry; almost an afterthought, the collection appended a swatch of Ortiz, Welch, Russell, Momaday, and Emerson Blackhorse Mitchell as living Indian writers. The same year, Frederick Turner published *The Portable North American Indian Reader*, rich in historical, anthropological, and ethnological records. Turner's introduction forwarded close-to-the-bone arguments against stereotyping, with an insistence that readers read to understand the history of Indian literature, not proselytize about it. But again, a few recent Indian authors only tagged the collection.

Walter Lowenfels's *From the Belly of the Shark: Poems by Chicanos, Eskimos, Hawaiians, Indians, Puerto Ricans in the U.S.A., With Related Poems by*

Others (1973) attempted to crack the "White Poetry Syndicate" with ethnic proclamations. Yet the amassed single poems came off, too often, more as political cant than poetry; and Lowenfels, decrying "genocidal attack on people of color," inadvertently reinforced that attack in the collection itself with *more* total pages of "related poems by others" than work by contemporary Indians. Leslie Silko's "Old-time Indian Attack" on imitators of Native American poetry may have been seeded by such underrepresentation. Silko warned those culture-hopping writers, who assumed the "universal consciousness" to express the "Indian mind," that in the long run "translations," cultural borrowings, and liberal guilt signify "stolen property."[2] Eagle Wing spoke to his people in 1881: "We have been guilty of only one sin—we have had possessions that the white man coveted." Later and from the other side, Adrienne Rich asked sardonically in "8/1/68": "And you, Custer, the Squaw-killer, hero of primitive schoolrooms— / where are you buried, what is the condition of your bones?" Michael Rumaker protested from the bloody loam of his tormented "Poem": "Indians, stop interrupting my dreams—Let me sleep the white death." For too long a time, Indian place-names for mountains, lakes, rivers, streams, streets, and cities no longer echoed their tribal referents; the intruding culture fell deaf to original tongues. Dead campfires, fading petroglyphs, unraveling wampums, and weathered feathers left funereal testimony to America's losses. Again, the American renegade need to get out of one's self and a dubious history drew empathetic poets, from Thoreau and Longfellow to Merwin and Snyder, toward displaced native peoples.

> Blanketless
> I stand exposed, alone, outside,
> to think: Fine old tradition
> don't come cheap these days:
>
> And go.

As felt in these lines, John Milton had lived in the Dakotas long enough to know "El Turista en El Pueblo," in whatever corner of Indian country.

Out of this cultural miasma Dick Lourie sardonically elected to place "the Indian on the moon":

>   we are awarding them
> the whole moon: they will rebuild their ancient
> cultures in the gray dust   we will look up

to see the thousands of indians as
a spot on the luminous bright disc we
have loved in the sky:

And why all these dream words from would-be Indians? The myths and realities of white America's freedoms were bound up in contradictory myths of Indian culture and history: in the "free speech" of Native American oratory, freedom of movement in Native American migrations, freedom of definition within the thousands of years of Native American cultural tenure, freedom of religious expression protesting institutionalization, free verse in the nonrhymed Native American chants metered to the subject sung, and freedom of space in the "wilds," the "plains," the mystic forests, the forbidding mountains and almost impassable deserts. Native Americans lived here of their own volition, not wild but attuned with who and where they were. Native peoples lived at home in the American frontier. The pilgrims, homesteaders, pioneers, ranchers, city-builders, and now the poets watched at a distance in awe, fear, and envy.

II

Come to Power: Eleven Contemporary American Indian Poets (1974) first gathered Indian artists who realized "the timbre of the connections," in the words of Simon Ortiz from Acoma Pueblo. Gracefully selected and edited by Dick Lourie, these 127 pages were an entry into modern Indian poetry, as represented by Ray Young Bear, Norman Russell, Joseph Bruchac, Leslie Silko, and Duane Niatum, among the more well known. "They are out there," Bruchac introduced the collection, "they are speaking and they are being heard." This sampling was only a beginning, he continued. "For me, at least, a good anthology is always a reminder of how much more there is in store, like picking one berry at the edge of the woods and knowing from its taste that a whole summer full of berries is ahead."

Suzan Shown opened, "i breathe as the night breathes," and a new sense of color dawned in white America: "my heart's song is to the night." The beauties, moralities, and definitions of darkness were refracted in colors of night, a spectrum dispersed among darker 'Skins.

Joseph Bruchac spoke of giving back something, altogether different from art for art's sake, as the angel touched an artist's shoulder and the typewriter began "speaking in tongues." These reciprocal values have always characterized Indian cultures: give-away-and-receive. "I seek to make my life and my poems a part of the whole," Bruchac explained, "taking nothing without returning something in kind which will make the balance good." Duane Niatum found that such poetry meant to "live with mud on your shoes, ride out the flights of white owl in your sleep." He recalled the words of Andrew Joe, a Skagit in Washington: "when we can understand animals, we will know the change is halfway. When we can talk to the forest, we will know that the change has come."

The changes were moving through Leslie Silko, "a mixed-breed Laguna Pueblo," who said she wrote "because I love the stories, the feelings, the words." This poet edged into the publishing world critterlike, grinning and skeptical; she was hassled and hassling back all the white fuss. "But I keep trying it, like Coyote who keeps coming back for more—never quite learning his lesson." Trickster's contrary/wise fooling added twists to her tales. At heart Silko sang of the blended earth she wore as a mixed-blood.

> I am full of hunger
> > deep and longing to touch
> wet tall grass, green and strong beneath.
> This woman loved a man
> > and she breathed to him her damp earth
> song.

Gloria Levitas, Frank Vivelo, and Jacqueline Vivelo edited *American Indian Prose and Poetry: We Wait in the Darkness* (1974), cribbing Margot Astrov's revised anthology title. The volume offered the first significant cross-section of Native American poets now writing. Yet even here (thirteen culture areas "Before," "After," and in the "Present" white occupancy) the contemporary poems seemed overly selective, one poem per poet, and the quality of these isolated pieces was uneven. The editors badgered the reader through samplings from past and present Indian history, asserting literature *as* literature, though all in all the texts fell short of literary consistency. The awkwardness and hyperbole of the movement, with a dash of older noble savagery, strained through patchy prefaces, fractious and too often condescending.

In the same year came *Voices from Wah'Kon-Tah: Contemporary Poetry of Native Americans* (1974), culled from *Dacotah Territory, The Mustang Review, Pembroke Magazine, The Prairie Schooner, South Dakota Review,* and fully half from the Santa Fe Institute of American Indian Arts. Robert Dodge and Joseph McCullough sought to counter stereotypes through a casebook of thirty-five Native Americans who talked boldly in poets' voices. Vine Deloria's foreword saw these poets bridging "the gap between Chief Joseph and Russell Means," a "glorious past" dissolving into a "desperate present." Deloria characteristically struck to the core of things: a poet in "frightful solitude," he observed, can transcend chronology and take us down into the inner self, hence into Indian cultures, dreams, angers, despairs, and courages. These testimonies were not names and dates only, explanations after the facts of history, but languages of witnesses that most directly and deeply drew a reader close. The poets risked the personal voice. They trusted the heart's pain, the bitter dust of past and present betrayal. They struggled to fight back and resist, to define self and reality, to press for a better life. Arresting, challenging, complex, and diverse: Native American experiences spoke here with an ear to tradition, an eye to now, a tongue to one's own heart in voices, plural, many-minded, human, undiluted in social science.

> Coyote and this night
> be still.
> I wonder how a man can cling to life,

Paula Allen ended her opening lament over the death of a Lakota grandfather. Charles Ballard followed, quietly sure:

> But time was the trail went deep
> Into a green and vibrant land.

Emerson Blackhorse Mitchell traveled "this vanishing old road" vision-questing "within the curved edge of quarter moon," as the poetry angled distinctly modern. David Martinez's "Song for Yellow Leaf Moon" lay dreamlike on the page:

> Night blues as abstract as the ninth
> day of yellow leaf moon—
> the autumn season starts with September willows.
> Life slows to a complicated new dusk—

The American Indian experience for the artist was historically surreal: foreign and civil wars, roads and relocations, hard times and hardpan deserts, promises and reserves, a second language and a bullying big brother.

In all this the poets could carve visions of themselves still Indian, roads and ways of words to choose, a language of their own thirsting tongues. Fred Red Cloud told "A Tale of Last Stands" in Custer's Montana:

> I sit with eyes like brown wounds
>   and remember a yellow-haired laugh
> in a place where
> tumbleweeds blow.

Marnie Walsh walked reservations

> Where disease like a serpent slips from house to house
> And hunger sits in the dooryard

The deadly sins of poverty slipped through off-reservation towns run by "disgusted, busted whites," James Welch saw in a nightmare of reality, where "a slouching dwarf with rainwater eyes" administered government handouts. Christian missionaries, advance men of Manifest Destiny, dredged for converts. Ray Young Bear could hear near "Empty Streams of Autumn,"

> A bible opens then closes real hard
> down the dirt road.

The things Marnie Walsh's poems failed to say, what they stuttered out, numb in despair, tugged absently, mutely at America. "Emmet Kills-Warrior" of Turtle Mountain told of his mother

> in government hospital
> she get their funeral too
> my brother at their war
> my sister in their jail
> i come out to the prairie
> sit on old rock

What Emmet had to say came in what he could not say.

> well that what i got inside
> that my story
> the government can go shit

For "Vicki" at Fort Yates, "No. Dak. 1970," a gap in consciousness told all: "saturday night   whiskey night." Walsh registered an agony of voices speaking as they could, with no decoration, from open wounds, in the shock of pain. The poetry seeded a negative "style" that, in the twists of language and truth, created a new voice, naked and honest, true to people in their own places. A friend remembered "Bessie Dreaming Bear" of Rosebud, South Dakota, 1960:

> we all went to town one day
> went to a store
> bought you new shoes
> red   high heels
>
> aint seen you since

How could Indians learn again to listen "when the / rain falls and we do not hear," Ray Young Bear asked. Mother Earth answered in "The Listening Rock":

> earth heard them
> talking to themselves
> far away and always spoke
> back: you are home.

These "voices" from *Wah'Kon-Tah* began to carry American Indian poets home, less than a decade ago, to America.

III

America

> give me a color
> to step in,
> a color for my
> table, a color to thrash
> my hands in—
> my inner swirls
> are grey with yesterday's promises
> becoming today's raining wail.
>   —Wendy Rose

Harper and Row initiated a Native American Series in 1972 with Hyemeyohsts Storm's *Seven Arrows*. The series picked up Welch's first poetry and fiction, and in 1975 published a fifth volume, Duane Niatum's *Carriers of the Dream Wheel: Contemporary Native American Poetry*. The anthology was boldly illustrated by Wendy Rose. Practicing artists, teachers, and students were brought together here as literate poets, college educated, and published in scores of journals and chapbooks:

Jim Barnes	Choctaw	born Oklahoma 1933
N. Scott Momaday	Kiowa	born Oklahoma 1934
Duane Niatum	Klallam	born Washington 1938
James Welch	Blackfeet/Gros Ventre	born Montana 1940
Simon Ortiz	Acoma	born New Mexico 1941
Joseph Bruchac	Abnaki	born New York 1942
Gladys Cardiff	Cherokee	born Montana 1942
Lance Henson	Cheyenne	born Oklahoma 1944
W. M. Ransom	Cheyenne/Arapaho	born Washington 1945
Liz Bahe	Yakima	born Washington 1947
Roberta Hill	Oneida	born Wisconsin 1947
Wendy Rose	Hopi/Miwok	born California 1948
Leslie Silko	Laguna	born New Mexico 1948
Dana Naone	Hawaiian	born Oahu 1949
Ray Young Bear	Mesquaki	born Iowa 1950
Anita Probst	Yaqui	born California 1952

The average age of these seven women and nine men was thirty-one when the collection came out.

> And they carry the wheel among the camps,
> Saying: Come, come,
> Let us tell the old stories,
> Let us sing the sacred songs.

So Momaday offered the anthology's title in "Carriers of the Dream Wheel," and a new Indian image of the educated traditionalist began to emerge. Indians did not have to fail in mainstream America to define their Indianness. Separatism was not the essential criterion for tribal identity. To know workable talents and put them to use, whether potter, hunter, poet, businessman, carpenter, professor, or lumberjack, was *not un*-Indian, these cultural craftsmen argued, by their own example, against the American mainstream drop-out. Roberta Hill challenged in "Dream of Rebirth":

> We stand on the edge of wounds, hugging canned meat,
> waiting for owls to come grind
> nightsmell in our ears. . . .
> Groping within us are cries yet unheard.
> We are born with cobwebs in our mouths
> bleeding with prophecies.

No longer *a* poem to illustrate *an* author, but a serious and committed body of work coalesced here. These were not occasional acts of poetic insight, but life and work, true craft.

Going back to Oneida, Roberta Hill looked into "Night Along the Mackinac Bridge":

> What was once so distant
> breaks upon me now, while dark dark water crumbles the moon.

Wendy Rose went to touch her Hopi father, asking "who am I?" and pled with her Miwok mother, "please believe in me."

> Pottery shards, splintered and dusty,
> glued together by that which is spirit
> —may it someday hold water—

Under a "snow-fat" Montana sky, James Welch ran with words, fugitive from Delphi. His whip-snaking, cross-rhymed verse defied white winter torpor through Indians "Surviving":

> The day-long cold hard rain drove
> like sun through all the cedar sky
> we had that late fall. We huddled
> close as cows before the bellied stove.
> Told stories.

The poets honed a firm, lean language into stanzas with muscle. Hunters of themselves, they tracked with deft skill, the sure touch and go of symbolic attention. Gladys Cardiff saw her poems cut through the world: "My song scythes over wet fields." Roberta Hill looked back:

> I've grown lean walking along dirt roads,
> under a glassy sun, whispering to steps.
> Twenty years I've lived on ruin.

Hill's images flared over a prairie of severity and promise. "Bones flash like shells / in salt green grass," she obliquely recorded in 1973, occupying

Wounded Knee. "How can I mark this sorrow?" Wendy Rose stood her ground at Alcatraz in 1969: "Neither leader nor fullblood / how and why me?" The feminist poems unsettled with terrible promise. Anita Probst "thigh deep in pasture" warned, "I am gentle, but angry." This sorceress of bitter charms, night spells, and surreal images chanted in "Learning the Spells: A Diptych,"

> I am the beast she never knew or wished. I grieve
> with lust: I will split her like the water's reeds.
> That damp-backed woman's spell runs, wounded.
> It hides, a coiled snake, under silken leaves.
> Betrayal flies quietly on dark wings.

Anita Probst wrote in the shadow of Tezcatlipoca, the Aztec god whose name meant "smoking mirror" from the obsidian he saw by: lord of night and death, of sorcerers and warriors, of omens and terror. Such a god, the Aztecs said, reigned omnipotent and omnipresent, "like the darkness, like the mind."[3]

The traditional virtues in *Carriers of the Dream Wheel* still held, however tenuously, in a modern wasteland of imposed white values. The poets pushed back the nightmare, grounded the metaphor, sobered the vision-drunk questor, and called all home again to the family of the tribe. W. R. Ransom drilled a language of nights under figureless stars, waiting in "Critter":

> Sat up all night and lugged at the moon.
> Grunted. Nothing changed.
> Sun rolled up the mountain.
> I could tell about
> meadowlarks, finches
> or dogwood and poplar,
> madronas, cedar—
> no, it was Orion I waited for.

In upstate New York a mountain stream flowed on limpidly simple in Bruchac's "IV":

> I shall go there
> and wade into those clear ripples
> where the sandy bottom
> is spread with stones
> which look like the bones

of beautiful ancient animals
I shall spread my arms
in the sweet water
and go like a last wash of snow
down to the loon shadow
in the last days of April

Out west, Simon Ortiz instructed his children by way of "old water courses, in wind, / where your mother walked, where her mother walked." His story-poems brought back to life Coyote Old Man, the elders, the old ways, the new sorrows. Ray Young Bear found himself "Coming Back Home" to the touch of his grandfathers:

i pressed my fingers
against the window, leaving
five clear answers of the day
before it left, barking down the road.

In 1975 Kenneth Rosen edited *Voices of the Rainbow: Contemporary Poetry by American Indians* to complete his prose anthology, *The Man To Send Rain Clouds* (1974). R. C. Gorman illustrated the collection: a Navajo face, hand, foot, or an abstract line cast a woman's body, brushed with water-color, in shadow negatives. By now, the poets had grown familiar in print, some new names, some on leave. Eleven of the twenty-one poets initiated fresh voices. Phil George asked, "amerika's-whiteman-life makes me sad. / Am I alone?" Peter Blue Cloud chanted death songs for "Wolf" and hawk, buffalo and grizzly, the hunted and tracked-down freedoms of the past:

a wind of running leaves across the prairie,
a scent of pine in frozen north the muskeg
    lakes
        lent footprints
    cast in sandstone
grains rubbing time the desert's constant edge.

The native country of America had receded farther back, but still called through tribal voices. The meadowlark's nectared song reached Carter Revard's "notch of cement-bottomed sky" driving through Oklahoma. Oxford education led a Rhodes Indian scholar all the way back to

> . . . a wilderness big enough
> to find a vision in
> while quite alone.

But this modern Indian poet had moved into academia, as his immigrant father was once "taking up the city and losing at cards." In the modern malaise, artists like John Berryman, "hunchvoiced henry," took their own lives, carrying out the Western suicidal art of Hart Crane, Hemingway, Sylvia Plath, and Anne Sexton. So, too, Gerald Vizenor wrote of mixed-up mixed-bloods "hanging the wrong man / for raising the wrong flags." A passing Indian saluted with the wrong hand and committed suicide with young birds "on the wrong trees at dusk."

The women in *Voices of the Rainbow* pressed for existence beyond barren survivals: rebirth, rage, forgiveness. "Joy is tough like hide," Roberta Hill heard the frogs whisper from "Swamp." She asked the hunter in "Seal at Stinson Beach":

> Teach me
>
> your crisscross answer
> to the cackling of gulls.

Hill's "Winter Burn" bore a vision of rebirth:

> Let clear winter burn away my eyes.
> Let this seed amaze the ground again.

Leslie Silko's "damp earth song" proferred no end to searching the old or new ways: "the struggle is ritual." Memory would spill into the world at all times, as she made ritual "Preparations": "Let wind polish the bones."

IV

Joseph Bruchac (Abnaki) edited a second anthology in 1978, *The Next World: Poems by Third World Americans* who participated in 1970s workshops. "We are a nation of nations," Bruchac prefaced the poets, rising above American prejudice by making literature from it: "an era which is alive with exciting new poets, a new era in which voices which have been traditionally silent (or silenced) are being heard." Tempered understandings replaced the invective of *From the Belly of the Shark* five years earlier.

Indian poets could share a world with America; with common oppressors pan-Indians took a place among Third World movements. Karoniaktatie (Alex Jacobs, Mohawk) invented an upbeat language of get-down talk, a dialect away from black mumbo-jumbo, Puerto Rican hip, and Chicano hustle:

> california
> gold rush
> what a rush
> u need Pit River
> to wipe LA's ass
> u need Alcatraz
> to make tourist bucks
> u need Maidu graves
> for Reagans mansion
> california
> dats not a tan
> dats my caked blood
>
> what a rush

This tongue on the streets spoke English with a twist, variations on medicine chants, war songs, and hip obliquities. Dialect and dialogue, jargon and slang fed into the crafts of poetry, chanting "America" from the slant of native histories. These were the voices of outsiders who would fist and knuckle their own insider's talk, deep within the dominant culture.

All along, Simon Ortiz listened to older Acoma men talk as they stood by mixing troughs to build Pueblo walls:

> the men who keep up the traditions of our people, community,
> of our language. These are the people who insure that the lan-
> guage keeps being a way of *touching* among ourselves, the
> things we see and hear, the things that we all are enjoined
> with, those things around *all* of us.

Among "this cluster of tongues, this dark flying world / this trying-on of the whiteman's witchery," Wendy Rose saw herself a Hopi half-breed "between skins that think I'm too white, whites, that think I'm too Indian." She looked "for acceptance somewhere" and stood up in her poems, counting, crying openly, asking the hard questions of herself split in America.

Wendy Rose caught herself at the "Vanishing Point: Urban Indian," lamenting her cultural quest,

> It is I in the cities, in the bars, in the
> dustless reaches of cold eyes who vanishes, who leans
>
> underbalanced into nothing; it is I without learning
> I without song, who dies & cries the death time, who
> blows from place to place hanging onto dandelion dust,
> dying over & over.

Geary Hobson's *The Remembered Earth: An Anthology of Contemporary Native American Literature* (1979) mustered the broadest cross-section of living Indian writers today, 427 pages with 74 artists grouped by geographical kinship among tribes. What this literary powwow skitter-stepped, in terms of sustained technique, it compensated by bringing together talents, sentiments, causes, aspirations, and griefs, from reservation to off-reservation, urban to academic Indian. Elizabeth Cook-Lynn touched a common center in "The Bare Facts":

> The spirit lives
> when it moves and sings your name
> when grandfather and coyote keep warm
> together, and lizard gets damp
> from the earth, stays fast and hard to kill,
> when lark flies straight and high to clouds
> and you hear the buzzard weeping under blankets,
> when butterfly still talks to women,
> when ants will fight and die to carry stones,
> seedlike and shiny, from mound to rattle,
> when we hang by fingernails, remote and hidden,
> at the ridge of words.

Many, many voices of varying media and maturity in *The Remembered Earth* offered not only poetry and prose as "literature," but a collation of tongues. The writing ranged from folk, to politic, to journalist, to poetic. Multiple forms among diverse perspectives reawakened the young Indians, gathering in clans among their elders. "It is renewal, it is continuance—and it is remembering," Hobson introduced the gathering. Everywhere energies were breaking through these experimental forms, and they generated an American Indian renaissance in print: idiomatic Indian voices from all parts of

America, breed to blood, wrote prose essay, voice play, fiction, prose poem, novel-in-progress, free verse, rhymed and metered poetry.

Maurice Kenny defined the traditional art by way of cultural content, artistic intent, and tribal effect: "a touching, teaching, often practical, more often significantly religious, a gratefulness and, possibly, a warning." Witness the work of Peter Blue Cloud ("I too am Spring time" rattlesnake pled), Carter Revard (winter-counting Uncle Gus's memorial feast), Barney Bush (leaning across pool tables and jukeboxes), or Larry Emerson (cornered drunk in Gallup). Joseph Bruchac sensed "The Remedies":

> Half on the Earth, half in the heart,
> the remedies for all our pains
> wait for the songs of healing.

Native American women drew upon the courage of their waiting to ritualize personal sorrows. Paula Allen prayed in "Rain for Ke-waik Bu-ne-ya":

> like the old ones we sat
> gathering fragments of long since broken hearts:
>
> bring tomorrow.

And tomorrow does come, speaking, singing, writing, as Momaday defined the Indian "Man Made of Words": "Instinctively, and with great care, he deals in the most honest and basic way with words." Simon Ortiz insisted in a range of forms—short story, poetry, reportage—that "The story of a People is the history of what they are doing. It is the story of their struggle to continue."

These writers touched their native earth to remember themselves Indian. "No one has ever left" Okla-homa, Joy Harjo believed, land of the "red earth people." And furthermore: "That which has happened to the earth, has happened to all of us as part of the earth." The "cinnamon colored soil" of Linda Hogan's Oklahoma so too grounded Duane Big Eagle's song of a land, "as open as his shirt collar" in "My Father's Country." Whether Southwest desert, Oklahoma dirt farm, Pacific coastal wood, Southeast hill country, Northeast lake region, or Great Northern plain, "We are the land," Paula Allen stated simply, directly. And Indian identity is the land, not pre/positionally "in" or "of" or "on," but is: "the Earth is the mind of the people as we are the mind of the earth. . . . that perfect peace of being together with all that surrounds one."

Momaday held that "an Indian is an idea which a given man has of himself," according to region and tribe, beyond bloodline and cultural stereotype. Geary Hobson accordingly, and in strapping tones, put whites in their places coming to play Indian. He chastised the faddishness of shit-kicking white shamans, would-be "natives," branding some "the bastard children of Snyder." Less tendentiously, still with firmly informed lines of demarcation, Paula Allen's "The Sacred Hoop" argued native cultural views: "The great mythic and ceremonial cycles of the American Indian peoples are neither primitive in any meaningful sense of the term, nor are they necessarily the province of the folk; much of the material on the literature is known only to educated, specialized persons who are privy to the philosophical, mystical, and literary wealth of their own tribe." Wendy Rose carried the dream wheel another turn in her own life, chanting to "Some Few Hopi Ancestors":

> No longer the drifting
> and falling of wind,
> your songs have changed.
> They have
> become thin willow whispers
> that take us by the ankle
> and tangle
> us up with the red mesa stone,
> that keep us turned
> toward a round sky,
> that follow us down
> to Winslow, to Sherman,
> to Oakland—to the ends
> of all the spokes
> that leave earth's middle.

V

Alan R. Velie's *American Indian Literature: An Anthology* (1979) rounded a decade of anthologies full circle, from tales, songs, memoirs, and oratory to poetry and fiction by the now known writers, Welch, Revard, Ortiz, Henson, Momaday, and others (a disproportionate Oklahoman dose). Velie reprinted early century ethnology: Radin's Winnebago Trickster tales, Neihardt's retelling of Black Elk, Brinton's *Walum Olum* with the pictographs, Delaware oral narratives and translations, and Densmore's ethnomusicology. The anthology included musical notation, in an effort to trace the translations back to their origins in song, ceremony, music, and dance (John Bierhorst also acknowledged the song-poem translations in *A Cry from the Earth*, the annotated record album accompanying his collection of traditional verse, *In the Trail of the Wind*). Velie's assortment of contemporary "49" powwow social songs updated the older musicology. The collection stood serviceable, generally informative, but not significantly new; it tended to popularize ceremonial Indian texts and patronize modern artists, as an intrusive editorial voice slipped into analogies with classics and popfamiliars: Shakespeare, the Bible, Greeks and Romans, TV and mainstream movies.

The Modern Language Association went tribal with some added twists. In 1980 Dexter Fisher published *The Third Woman: Minority Women Writers of the United States*. "Just as the nations of the third world are 'emerging' in the sense that the Euro-American world has 'discovered' them, so is 'the Third Woman' revealing herself to us, though she has always been present," Fisher began. If there were revolutionary depths in America, this double minority of voices (by circumstance of sex and racial class) constituted an articulate feminist majority.

The American Indian section of Fisher's anthology led off with detailed introductory notes, vivid writing, and a full bibliography. The collection was expertly edited and paced; the readings from eighteen women rang refreshing. Keepers of family, culture, tradition, and their own integrity, these twentieth-century Indian women remained alive to old ways and new. Leslie Silko asserted relationships, personal accessibility, and coming to terms: "some kind of equilibrium with those people around you." Showing people "ways of seeing things" timelessly new, Silko spoke of her art organically: "There are those stories that just have to be told in the same way the wind goes blowing across the mesa." Elizabeth Sullivan looked back unflinching on the Creek Trail of Tears, Helen Sekaquaptewa told her Hopi life story, Mourning Dove related Okanogan Coyote tales, and Kay Bennett retold the Navajo origin myth of earth mother or Changing Woman, "A Woman She Becomes Time and Again." Janet Campbell remembered the snowfall in her Coeur d'Alene childhood, and Opal Lee Popkes, a Choctaw with eleven unpublished novels, wrote of a bonsaied

California Indian, Zuma Chowt, eating rats and surviving fifty years as a twentieth-century Ishi, stashed in a cave above a southern California beach.

These women poets stabbed at a history of racial oppression, cultural white arrogance, and male dominance. Wendy Rose, doctoral candidate in anthropology at UC Berkeley, found a 1977 catalog in which "collectors" still sold "Plains Indian Art" looted from the Wounded Knee Massacre:

> I expected my skin and my blood
> to ripen
> not be ripped from my bones;
> like green fruit I am peeled
> tasted, discarded; my seeds are stepped on
> and crushed
> as if there were no future. Now
> there has been
> no past.

Southwest child, decadent child, artifact child, child-bearing child, incorrigible woman, the Navajo Nia Francisco sang out,

> call me dine asdzaani
> i am child of winter nights
> growing in rhythm of summer thaw
> i am the one you will see walking before dawn
> and dancing after raindew has dried

Anna Lee Walters (Pawnee/Otoe) still heard that "no color" jr. hi boy cawing "squaw, squaw, squaw." Marnie Walsh followed Vicki Loans-Arrow into a bar toilet, checking on her cousin Charlene Lost-Nation, who could not kill herself in *The Blood of the Knife*:

> she looks at me
> and i see the knife
> sticking out between her teeth
> and remember what that means
> and i know shed like to die
> but cant
> so she killed her tongue
> instead

There were gentler moments in *The Third Woman*: Ramona Wilson's Colville grandmother washing her hair in willow water, Elizabeth Cook-Lynn hearing her Sioux grandmother tell stories, and Anita Endrezze-Danielson (formerly Probst) painting Yaqui "Still Life":

CONTEMPORARY TRIBE

> Oranges sleep,
> lazy alley cats, curled in the heat.
> With my knife, I slap thick oil on apples:
> red knees streaked with grass stains.
> Dried paint clots my nails;
>
> Pearls of oil cling to my hair.

Roberta Hill heard the Oneida "music of the voice that speaks through me," enough to brave a modern woman's "Leap in the Dark":

> I stand drunk in this glitter, under the sky's grey shelter.
> The city maple, not half so bitter, hurls itself
>
> in two directions, until both tips darken and disappear,
> as I darken my reflection in the smoking mirror
>
> of my home. How faint the sound of dry leaves,
> like the clattering keys of another morning, another world. . . .
>
> Truth waits in the creek, cutting the winter brown hills:
> it sings of its needles of ice, sings because of the scars.

Despite "Moonshot: 1969," Paula Allen considered a Laguna moon still female, the mysterious province of a woman:

> gazing into the moon reaches of the mind,
> searching with careful fingers of sense-memory,
> listening inside the ear for lost songs,
> almost forgotten footfalls,
> felling gingerly with the tongue-tip of the heart—

This poet translated blessing from the past in her "Medicine Song":

> I add my breath to your breath
> That our days may be long on the Earth;
> That the days of our people may be long;
> That we shall be one person;
> That we may finish our roads together.
> May my father bless you with life;
> May our Life Paths be fulfilled.

VI

Through words as aural signs, poets add breath to our breath. Of the hundreds of Indian poets anthologized and the thousands unpublished, the fifty or so discussed here make up an American Indian literary renaissance, perhaps better termed an emergence, as the Pueblos speak of coming up through layers of world-realities. The Homeric epics in sixth-century Greece, no less than the Bible, the Confucian Odes, or the Upanishads and Vedas of India, were set down in such transitional artistic fertility, as oral traditions found shape in print.[4] In Native America tribal ties shuttle to older wisdoms, as the artists weave identity through new word tapestries. "The past is always the past as it is always the present," Elizabeth Cook-Lynn observes in *Then Badger Said This.*[5]

So Indian artists shape and are shaped by a past that continues to inform them. Jim Ruppert notes, "The poet/singer draws his strength from the ceremonies and sacred stories, variations of secular materials, oral history, personal reminiscences, place-names, charms, prayers, lyrics and laments, and popular characterizations of places and animals, just to mention a few. It is essential that the writer gives back and enriches these. The dynamic between the writer and this varied, growing cultural material helps define the writer and his relationship to the community."[6] The bonds of Indian life should be restated, so there may be no mistaking. Always integrative, Native American arts correlate spirit and use in the beauty of concrete forms— words, pots, walls, baskets, blankets, carvings, or clothing. All things are serviceable in the common aesthetics of tribal life.

Poems chant sources of vision, as well as revelations of craft; they present *re*visions of Indian ways, looking, and looking again. A poetic awareness in and of the world serves to place artists communally among related life forms. What begins as a lump in the throat, or an event known as a name, or a dream that intensifies waking, patterns the world's common significances. Indians live among many cultures, hearing ancestral *and* contemporary voices. They make the best of diverse ways. Their dreams, angers, searchings, prayers, loves, and myths bow from one horizon to another, refracted in the prisms of Native American literatures today.

5

WORD SENDERS:
Black Elk and N. Scott Momaday

> He is a word sender. This world is like a garden.
> Over this garden go his words like rain, and where
> they fall they leave it a little greener. And when his
> words have passed, the memory of them shall stand
> long in the west like a flaming rainbow.[1]
>
> —BLACK ELK

In 1931 when John Neihardt approached Hehaka Sapa, or Black Elk, to tell his Lakota people's story, the holy man sanctioned the transcribed notes being published in an English translation. Literature as both men knew it changed. An Indian oral tradition of medicine, religion, winter count history, and tribal ceremony bridged from living ritual performance into the marketplace of print. Black Elk dreamed and lived a tribal "life-story" that Neihardt transcribed with poetic license and fixed in history. The oral "sending" of words came through a new voice, a printed text.

The Lakota had no word for poet or poem. They did not talk of secular aesthetics apart from religion. Art for them could no more exist for its own sake than a person separated from a tribe. Black Elk had to coin the term "word sender" and adopt the writer with the vision-name, "Flaming Rainbow," to insure their collaboration. The holy man's intention was clearly to extend himself for his people, and he appealed to the non-Indian world for understanding through Neihardt. Less autobiography than tribal history, then, his story was a collective telling of a tribe.[2] Black Elk lamented a "nation that was dying," beyond himself. He went on a new form of healing quest: a story in search of a people's renewal.

Olowan, the closest Lakota term to poem, means song. *Piyalowan* is to repeat a song from four to twenty-five times during a healing ceremony, and *piya* or "renewing" the song (by repeating) renews the patient. William K. Powers writes of ceremonial language among the Lakota:

> Given that music is part of the natural order, it is *there* occupying a niche in the natural universe, with a capacity, like human, to be born and die, to undergo changes, to be renewed, "cured" if you will (as the language suggests). Music is not so much composed from whole cloth, as it is, metaphorically, reincarnated, just as is true, so the Oglala believe, with humans. The term, *yatun* "to give birth to song," is perhaps the closest gloss to "to compose," but the connotation of "*tun*" is "to give rise to something *that has already existed in another form.*"[3]

A Lakota healer such as Black Elk is called *wapiye*, "one who repairs," Frances Densmore recorded in 1912.[4] The healer renews his people by singing the old songs, telling the tribal stories, as natural and necessary as breath to a culture's continuation.

Today, an Indian inherits the word-medicine of his ancestors, but at a distance from healing, religion, and ritual. An Indian artist furthers tribal culture in the written word. The transition at once opens new life to print and endangers the living touch of oral traditions. The contemporary Kiowa poet, N. Scott Momaday, moves into present history with a southern variant of Black Elk's plains vision. The two men are of different tribes and times, but the continuity of acculturating Plains Indian traditions stretches between them. Momaday hears old healing chants among pan-Indian "Carriers of the Dream Wheel":

> They shape their songs upon the wheel
> And spin the names of the earth and sky,
> The aboriginal names.
> They are old men, or men
> Who are old in their voices,
> And they carry the wheel among the camps,

WORD SENDERS

> Saying: Come, come,
> Let us tell the old stories,
> Let us sing the sacred songs.

Black Elk, in Lakota oral traditions translated by Neihardt, and Scott
Momaday, adapting older Kiowa ways to written forms of literature, align
as "word senders" or "carriers of the dream wheel" across the tribal
history of the Great Plains. *Black Elk Speaks* is most certainly a transitional
text into Momaday's poetry and prose; the two "word senders" represent
old and new Indian "artistic" voices.

The Lakota and Kiowa, across the northern and southern plains, were
warlords in powerful alliances with other tribes. They first encountered each
other during the Kiowa migration along the prairies east of the Rockies,
described in *The Way to Rainy Mountain* as "a long rain shadow on the sea
of grasses" (*WRM* 23). These buffalo-hunting, sun-dancing, vision-
questing peoples maintained territorial imperative over the Great Plains
from the eighteenth into the nineteenth century. Mounted on horses, they
saw themselves as centaurs. Black Elk's mysticism, as a visionary warrior,
secularizes into Momaday's naturalism, as a contemporary artist.

A plains holy man—healer, visionary, teacher, artist—is inspired by a
sacred, natural world through dreams. He converses with the energies of
plants and animals and the earth itself, and the core his identity is shaped
by vision questing. The holy man appears variously as shaman or priest,
healer or witch doctor, but this tribal role is to bind the people's spiritual
needs with things of this world, as an umbilical cord ties a child to a
parent.[5] The medicine man releases the spirits *in* things to move through
this world; in this integrated reality there is no split between ideas and
things. Religion and culture fuse with medicine and morality, art and history. The plains people respect this healer as a wise man, a seer of heart and
knowledge. He moves freely among the best and worst of the tribe, humbled
and empowered by the natural spirits of his vision, carrying a medicine
bundle with a sacred pipe.[6] He doctors and blesses, counsels and laments, in-
terprets signs and keeps alive stories, songs, and visions essential to the
tribe. Whether traditional or iconoclastic, he is distinguished as someone of
power and vision, chosen by the spirits to heal.

The traditions of these "old ways" lie *down* within the natural Indian
world. Through ceremony, discipline, sacrifice, and improvisation, a medicine singer opens himself for spirits to move through the world. Like the

conduit of the medicine pipe, the healer works as a medium from a deeper order of spiritual Reality to the corporeal reality people ordinarily live.

By way of Neihardt as intermediary, Black Elk envisions intersecting realities as the Red Road, north to south, and the Black Road, west to east. They come together at the heart of the world through a flowering tree. So, too, the words of sacred songs carry mysteries from places of silence into worldly harmonies, through the rhythms and tones of drumbeat, dance, and chant.[7] In coining the term "word sender" for a "poet," Black Elk imagines language in projective flight, as in the arrowed movements of spirits from one place of sacred origin into worldly form. This embodiment of the sacred or wakan may take place by way of a shaman's language today, imprinted on the page as poetic mystery. Momaday, in this "holy" sense, sees words as projectile and penetrant, to be regarded as sacred arrows.

Black Elk and Momaday, as "word senders" in different tribal times, seek a preverbal "Reality" down in the world. Some decades ago, Ernst Cassirer observed of Plains Indian visionaries in *Language and Myth*: "It is especially the cult of mysticism, in all ages and among all people, that grapples again and again with this intellectual double problem—the task of comprehending the Divine in its totality, in its highest inward reality, and yet avoiding any particularity of name or image. Thus all mysticism is directed toward a world beyond language, a world of silence."[8] In the old days on the plains, the Lakota would not speak a person's name in his or her presence; *Wakan Tanka*, or the "Mysterious Great," could not be translated into spoken words or logical concepts.[9] Talked, sung, or written language evokes this unnameable Reality, as a shadow calls on a distant object or an echo trails an original sound. "Now suddenly there was nothing but a world of cloud," Black Elk recalls his great vision, "and we three were there alone in the middle of a great white plain with snowy hills and mountains staring at us; and it was very still; but there were whispers" (*BES* 19). In the old days one did not even mention Wakan Tanka in ordinary conversation. There were "whispers" on the still white plains of a holy man's vision. The right word improved on silence only by respecting silence.

As Black Elk was receiving his visions in the Dakotas of the 1860s, John Ruskin, "across the Big Water," conceived of four orders of poets anywhere in the world: the first sees clearly, but feels too little; the second feels strongly, but thinks less and sees untruly: the third feels greatly, thinks deeply, and sees lucidly, to the maximum of human powers. But there are still languages of poetic vision beyond human control. Ruskin thought that the fourth, and highest, order of poet, the prophet, synthesizes all these perceptions, yet the vision so takes him over that he sees and speaks beyond himself.[10]

Orpingalik, a Netsilik Eskimo, told Knud Rassmussen in this regard:

> Songs (poems) are thoughts sung out with the breath when people are moved by great forces and ordinary speech no longer suffices. . . . And then it will happen that we, who always think we are small, will feel still smaller. And we will fear to use words. But it will happen that the words we need will come of themselves. When the words we want to use shoot up of themselves—we get a new song.[11]

Visionary humility before an awesome world and an organic sense of poetics —a "song" sings itself as people are stilled—intersect in higher traditions of prophecy and word-sending among poets the world over.

THE SHADOW OF A VISION YONDER

"I was born in the Moon of the Popping Trees (December) on the Little Powder River [Dakota Territory] in the Winter When the Four Crows were Killed (1863)." Fourth generation to bear his family medicine and name, Black Elk entered the world a holy man, wicasa wakan, second cousin to Crazy Horse. He was born into a time commonly known as the "Indian Wars," which dated from the Civil War to the massacre at Wounded Knee, 29 December 1890. During this period Congress closed the frontier and confined Indians to reservations, free to leave only with passes from agents. As his earliest memory, Black Elk recalled his father crippled for life at the 1866 Fetterman massacre; he died in 1890, the year of Wounded Knee. "It must be the fear," Black Elk says, "that I remember most" (BES 11).

Black Elk turned to the world of spirits. His first trance came at five years old, again in a fuller vision when he was nine. The tribe gathered to perform the "great vision" ritually when he was seventeen. "I looked about me and could see that what we then were doing was like a shadow cast upon the earth from yonder vision in the heavens, so bright it was and clear. I knew the real was yonder and the darkened dream of it was here" (BES 142).

WORD SENDERS

Visionaries from all times, Plato, to John of the Cross, to Black Elk, question whether they stand only on, inside, or beyond the world. Lakota traditions view the common world infused with mystic naturalism: the vision seeker opens to the reality all around him and commonly inside ordinary things. There is an imagined heart, wakan or holy, within all things. This natural sense of sacred power throughout the world is underscored from the careful statements of medicine people in Frances Densmore's *Teton Sioux Music*, through the J. R. Walker papers, *Lakota Belief and Ritual*, to collaborative and more contemporary biographies with Luther Standing Bear, Lame Deer, and Frank Fools Crow.[12] The conflict between Indian and white religions comes whether a person lives in or beyond this given world. A visionary can press for transcendence of the world, as in the Christian tradition; an Indian on a lifelong "vision quest" tries to live spiritually inside this material world, as Black Elk ideally imagines traveling the red, spiritual "road" simultaneously with the black, worldly road of life. Black Elk was baptized "Nicholas" by the Jesuit "black robes" on the sixth of December, 1904, and became a Catholic catechist. Fusing two religions as he tells Neihardt his life story, Black Elk vacillates between this world and the next, the Lakota sense of mystic naturalism and the Christian way of worldly transcendence. It is an uneasy shifting between shamanic power and Christian resignation.

John Neihardt remembers "half seeing, half sensing" the purblind healer's story, translated across languages, cultures, and time itself, "a strange and beautiful landscape by brief flashes of lightning" (*BES* xi). There seems to be a consensus among seers, scholars, and intermediaries the world over that the visionary truth of a higher reality enters the ordinary world through special concentrations: strange dream images, a language of many tongues speaking in one, a fleeting sense of witnessing more than the common mind can see, comprehend, or tell. The dreamer's language, wakan or "holy," is not to be understood in ordinary words. Niehardt functioned as intermediary to interpet Black Elk's vision:

> Then I was standing on the highest mountain of them all, and
> round about beneath me was the whole hoop of the world.
> And while I stood there I saw more than I can tell and I
> understood more than I saw; for I was seeing in a sacred man-
> ner the shapes of all things in the spirit, and the shape of all
> shapes as they must live together like one being. And I saw
> that the sacred hoop of my people was one of many hoops that

> made one circle, wide as daylight and as starlight, and in the
> center grew one mighty flowering tree to shelter all the
> children of one mother and one father. And I saw that it was
> holy. [*BES* 36]

A Lakota shaman sees the transcendence of "reality" into *Reality* as *wakan yan* or "seeing in a sacred manner." Mircea Eliade documents this entry into sacred reality among religions the world over as the "eternal return" to the origins of time, place, and being.[13] "This they tell," Black Elk recalls of the earth mother, White Buffalo Calf Woman, three centuries ago bringing the sacred medicine pipe to the Lakota, "and whether it happened so or not I do not know; but if you think about it, you can see that it is true" (*BES* 4).

Lakota traditions place value in the spiritual openness, or positive "Nothing," inside material things. The ideal, through ceremonial sweat and visionary ritual, is to purify by cleaning out and becoming selfless. So among his people, Black Elk "laments"—ceremonially lowers and humbles himself—as in continuously preparing for a vision quest. In dreaming the thunder spirits, he must act out the role of heyoka or sacred clown.[14] He assumes no control or credit for what powers move through him, rather he is a force of wind and spirit, sun and moon.[15] Virtually a breathing sacrament, the medicine pipe forms the core of a kinship system based on the circle open at the center. This spherical conduit opens infinitely into the spirit world of the "sacred hoop" or horizon that encompasses all tribes under the sky and within the earth.

> You have noticed that everything tries to be round. In the old
> days when we were a strong and happy people, all our power
> came to us from the sacred hoop of the nation, and so long as
> the hoop was unbroken, the people flourished. The flowering
> tree was the living center of the hoop, and the circle of the
> four quarters nourished it. The east gave peace and light, the
> south gave warmth, the west gave rain, and the north with its
> cold and mighty wind gave strength and endurance. This
> knowledge came to us from the outer world with our religion.
> Everything the Power of the World does is done in a circle.
> The sky is round, and I have heard that the earth is round like
> a ball, and so are all the stars. The wind, in its greatest power,
> whirls. Birds make their nests in circles, for theirs is the same
> religion as ours. The sun comes forth and goes down again in
> a circle. The moon does the same, and both are round. Even

the seasons form a great circle in their changing, and always
come back again to where they were. The life of a man is a
circle from childhood to childhood, and so it is in everything
where power moves. Our tepees were round like the nests of
birds, and these were always set in a circle, the nation's hoop,
a nest of many nests, where the Great Spirit meant for us to
hatch our children. [BES 164–165]

The circle remains a balanced form in motion, evincing unity among
the people. It runs continuously, fusing endings and beginnings in history,
so that time is projected as spatial curvature, rather than linear sequence.[16]
The circle lies equidistant from a still center, imaging equality among all
things. It is unsegmented, symbolizing the shared necessities in tribal life.
The pipe stem forms a spine to the body of the stone, the bowl a living
ancestor in the earth. The sacred smoke is the breath of Wakan Tanka entering the people. As with the *yuwipi* society of medicine men, whose name
means "to bind up," the pipe ties into the spirit world and reunifies worldly
with spiritual concerns. It links the individual to tribal necessity and aligns
the black road of material life with the good red road of spiritual life. There
is an emptying out and opening up in all this, to allow a place for wakan
within the world.

The Lakota see the natural world made sacred through powers of transformation. In Black Elk's vision the gift-bearing grandfathers or tunkashila
change back and forth from elders to stallions of the "four winds." The
grandfather spirits come from the cardinal directions, symbolized in the
primary colors dark blue (interchangeable with black), white, red, and
yellow. The healing of the black stallion's song—"the power to make
over"—lies in these symbolic transformations of direction ritualized among
hundreds of tribes. Black Elk envisions a world of interconnected, renewing
life forms in overlapping images, from grandfathers who turn into horses
that turn into elk, buffalo, and eagle. And reversing time, the bay stallion
or earth grandfather grows backward from old age into the young Black Elk
himself.

First, a black stallion rides out of the west, where fall rainstorms gather
to bring life to the plains. He gives Black Elk a bowl of water and a bow,
"the power to make-live and to destroy." These sacred common objects image the cup of the sky and the lightning bow, a natural joining of holy man
and warrior though the life-gift of rain and the striking power of storm.
Black Elk and Crazy Horse, Neihardt was told, were born cousins in a

genealogy of holy men, interrelating visionary and warrior in the black stallion's gifts. The white stallion from the north stands for the test of winter. This power of healing takes place through hardship. It is the medicine of endurance. The grandfather of *Wa*, the "white" of *Waziya* or the "snow" in the north ("white" men become *Wasicuⁿ*), offers Black Elk a sacred white herb and white goose feather. These empower him with holy medicine and winged flight. The sorrel from the east represents renewal and enlightenment, the sunrise of spring after winter's trial. It is a dawning spirit. In the east Black Elk sees the daybreak star of understanding and the

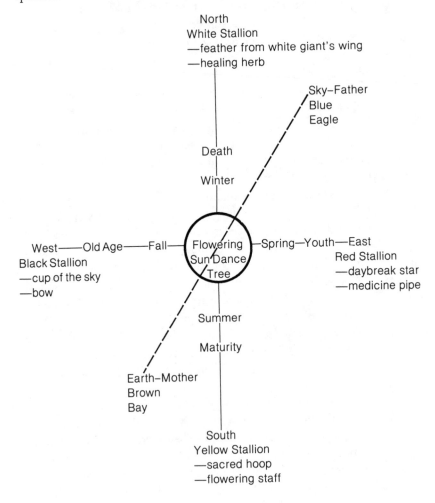

North
White Stallion
—feather from white giant's wing
—healing herb

Sky–Father
Blue
Eagle

Death

Winter

West——Old Age——Fall— Flowering —Spring—Youth—East
Black Stallion   Sun Dance   Red Stallion
—cup of the sky   Tree   —daybreak star
—bow   —medicine pipe

Summer

Maturity

Earth–Mother
Brown
Bay

South
Yellow Stallion
—sacred hoop
—flowering staff

sacred red pipestone (this ancestral bloodstone comes from a quarry several hundred miles due east of Pine Ridge Reservation in Minnesota). The fourth grandfather appears as a buckskin from the south. He represents summer's richness when the sun rises highest. This yellow stallion gives Black Elk a flowering staff and the sacred hoop. These image a tribal circle around a living cottonwood axis, the center of the annual Sun Dance.

The fifth ancestor is an eagle representing the "father sky," and the sixth a bay representing the "mother earth." Adding sky-blue and earth-green to the cardinal colors of the four winds, black-blue, white, red, and yellow, surrounds Black Elk with an ancestral nimbus: six elders before, behind, above, below, one side, and the other. The sacred hoop ideally encircles a person, wherever he is, extending a primal sphere around each tribal member. This encompassing is imaged in the daybreak star with six points clustered around a central seventh point, which stands for the sacred tribal self. The number seven, then, completes the integration of four and three, earth and sky, object and spirit. With this vision, Black Elk says, everywhere is the center of the earth.

Inside the "flaming rainbow teepee," and out of ordinary space-time, Black Elk's "great vision" reaches back through Lakota traditions. Some time ago, Siya'ka told Frances Densmore of an elk dreamer's sacred hoop: "Part of the rainbow is visible in the clouds, and part disappears in the ground. What we see is in the shape of a hoop. This word is employed by medicine-men and especially by dreamers of the elements of the air and the earth." Siya'ka then sang:

> Something sacred wears me
> all behold me coming.
>
> Something sacred wears me
> all behold me coming.
>
> All behold me coming.
>
> A [sky] hoop wears me
> all behold me coming.
>
> All behold me coming.[17]

The four winds of this sacred "sky hoop" are represented in the unifying four primary colors, the four annual seasons, the four times of day in sunset (west), midnight (north), sunrise (east), and midday (south), and the four ages of man in old age, death, rebirth, and maturity. In *The Sacred Pipe*, the second of Black Elk's narratives, the holy man explains,

> in setting up the sun dance lodge, we are really making the
> universe in a likeness; for, you see, each of the posts around
> the lodge represents some particular object of creation, so that
> the whole circle is the entire creation. . . . You see, there is a
> significance for everything, and these are the things that are
> good for men to know, and to remember.[18]

Lame Deer speaks of this attitude toward the natural world as "symbolic" in Indian ways of seeing "from the heart's eye."[19] Things *are* themselves and in themselves sources of meanings that tie the world together by association.

Cassirer posits that "before man thinks in terms of logical concepts, he holds his experiences by means of clear, separate, mythical images."[20] A formalist could "explain" these visionary images splitting reality into analyses between the language of experience, as in the natural "poetry" of things, versus the logic of cognition, as in rational discourse. Schiller states the dialectic simply: "the poet *is* nature, or he *seeks* nature."[21] Yet Black Elk's vision "wide as daylight and as starlight," or one phrase from Navajo ceremony, "house made of dawn," places the tribe within all the ecological beauty, continuity, and organic order alive in the earth household. The Indian world is not so much explained as witnessed, in preexisting harmony.

A language of natural signs carries over in Neihardt's translation of the holy man's story:[22] the six grandfather spirits "older than men can ever be—old like hills, like stars" (*BES* 21), the creation's "roots and leggeds and wings," the "bitten moon" waning, and the tribal clan name, Oglala, which means "scattering-one's-own" among the seven council fires of the Lakota or "allies." To Black Elk the Battle of the Hundred Slain, crippling his father, seemed "like something fearful in a fog" for a boy of three (*BES* 7). His older friend, Fire Thunder, says of the 1867 Wagon Box Fight, "they shot so fast it was like tearing a blanket" (*BES* 14).

As in the ancient winter counts sketched on animal skins and ledgers,[23] history is recorded in telling images, the visual words of pictographs. Black Elk "signs" his name concretely, drawing a man connected with a dark elk. In his day time was pictured seasonally, by moons:

Moon of the Red Grass Appearing (April)
Moon When the Ponies Shed (May)
Moon of Making Fat (June)
Moon When the Red Cherries Are Ripe (July)
Moon When the Black Cherries Turn Black (August)
  or Moon of the Black Calf
Moon When the Plums Are Scarlet (September)
Moon of the Changing Season (October)
Moon of the Falling Leaves (November)
Moon of the Popping Trees (December)
Moon of the Frost in the Tepee (January)
Moon of the Dark Red Calf (February)
Moon of the Snowblind (March)

Place-names derive from natural occurrences: Greasy Grass (Little Big Horn), White Clay (White Clay Creek), Wounded Knee, Pine Ridge, Rosebud. The state name, Nebraska, means "flat river" (for the Platte) from the Omaha, and Dakota, obviously, is taken from the tribal name for the allied nation of bands.[24] And in telling Black Elk's story the names of assisting narrators lend metaphoric presences: Standing Bear, Iron Hawk, Fire Thunder. There are mystic names as well. Neihardt is adopted as Flaming Rainbow; Black Elk is given the sacred name, Eagle Wing Stretches, in his vision; and Curly or Light-Haired-Boy grows up among the Lakota as Our-Strange-Man, according to his vision, Crazy Horse.[25]

In the animate language of Lakota oral tradition, silence lies fertile around spoken words; gesture, mime, and human interaction play out the meanings in words; things speak themselves, as the natural world comes alive in its own expression. The black stallion sings, and Black Elk remembers,

> his voice was not loud, but it went all over the universe and
> filled it. There was nothing that did not hear, and it was more
> beautiful than anything can be. It was so beautiful that nothing
> anywhere could keep from dancing. The virgins danced, and
> all the circled horses. The leaves on the trees, the grasses on
> the hills and in the valleys, the waters in the creeks and in the
> rivers and the lakes, the four-legged and the two-legged and
> the wings of the air—all danced together to the music of the
> stallion's song.

> And when I looked down upon my people yonder, the
> cloud passed over, blessing them with friendly rain and stood
> in the east with a flaming rainbow over it. [*BES* 35]

And yet sadly, with the Wasicu^n invading (Wa meaning, as noted, "white" of the snowy Waziya or north),[26] Black Elk says "a strange race had woven a spider's web all around the Lakotas." Eventually the web forced them onto "islands" of reservation life. "But there came a year when 'the sun died,'" Red Bird told Densmore. The Great Sioux Reservation was abstracted in 1868, only to be partitioned twenty-one years later, when nine million acres were ceded back to the Great White Father. Pine Ridge Agency became the Place-Where-Everything-is-Disputed. *Pahuska*, the "long-hair" Custer, forged the Bozeman Trail or "Thieves' Road" into the Black Hills and discovered gold in 1874, violating Red Cloud's Treaty of 1868. Custer "told about it with a voice that went everywhere," Black Elk says. "Later he got rubbed out for doing that" (*BES* 66). Named for the sunsets at his birth, Red Cloud led the negotiators to Soldiers' Town or Fort Robinson, and they became Hang-around-the-Fort Indians, coffee-coolers, "friendlies."

Here in 1877, accompanied by the legendary seven-foot Touch-the-Clouds and Little Big Man, Crazy Horse was betrayed and assassinated by bayonet: "And suddenly something went through all the people there like a big wind that strikes many trees all at once" (*BES* 119). Twelve years later the Sioux Act of 1889 halved the Lakota lands again; the government abortively set out to convert nomadic hunters into homesteaders who would farm poor grazing land. In 1883 the last Sun Dance was held and the last buffalo killed. "So the flood of Wasichus, dirty with bad deeds, gnawed away half of the island that was left to us" (*BES* 196).

"Well, it is as it is. We are prisoners of war while we are waiting here. But there is another world" (*BES* 166). Beyond the Wasichu greed for land, penning up grass and people in cities, the Lakota clung to their ancestral ground. Despite the "other Pahuska," or "long-hair" Buffalo Bill commercializing warriors in his Wild West Show, they maintained cultural dignity. Black Elk survived the despair of a conquered nation within a nation. The plains healer turned to the prophecy of reemergence, after "four ascents" or generations of his people suffering: "But I was not the last; for when I looked behind me there were ghosts of people like a trailing fog as far as I could see—grandfathers of grandfathers and grandmothers of grandmothers without number. And over these a great Voice—the Voice that was the South—lived, and I could feel it silent.''

"And as we went the voice behind me said: 'Behold a good nation walking in a sacred manner in a good land!' '' (*BES* 30)

Black Elk Speaks is possibly the single most well-known Indian story in America. By 1972 the book had been translated into eight foreign languages. Black Elk's "Great Vision" fascinated no less than Carl Jung, and the native healer's traditional regard for the "roots and leggeds and wings" continues to educate non-Indian readers in Native American ways that bind tribes together. The visionary "history" of Neihardt's translation is most significant, for this reader, because the book integrates spiritual and worldly necessities, without splitting the personal and traditional voices of a people. A "life-story" is the people's history. A healer's common "vision" is his daily ritual. This tribal "sender's" words voice the culture of "a good nation walking in a sacred manner in a good land."

Neihardt has captured the tenor, if not the actual text, of this holy man's story; a "strangely beautiful book," in Neihardt's words, is proof of the power of Black Elk's dream (*BES* xii). It is a vision partly intuited, partly translated. "Perhaps with his message spreading across the world," Neihardt wrote at the age of ninety, just before he died, "he has not failed" (*BES* xiii).

MOMADAY'S WAY

Across plains history, Momaday's influence from Black Elk recovers an impressionist reverence for the land, the elders, the traditions, and the spirits alive in all these. The modern writer translates older Indian ways through an idealism of the imagination: he believes traditionally in people *being* as they image and name themselves. "We are what we imagine," Momaday testifies in "The Man Made of Words."[27] Religious and cultural views of the past emerge as aesthetic faith in the present. Just so, Momaday in *The Gourd Dancer* relates the story of his grandfather honored with a black stallion: "And all of this was for Mammedaty, in his honor, as even now it is in the telling, and will be, as long as there are those who imagine him in his name" (*GD* 37).

WORD SENDERS

Words contain the remembered past, as the Kiowa writer selectively records from plains oral tradition; one powerful word, rightly recalled, gives the "word sender" access to details of experience that come into focus imaginatively through sound, just as his grandmother could "see" the Black Hills through Kiowa legends, though she had never been there. Names, in themselves, emerge at the heart of ritual language, the crafted word used as power, vision, and meaning. Such names put humans in touch with the spirits of the gods on earth. The "great Voice" Black Elk feels "silent" lies as a still muse immanent in things, a vision that "remembers itself" over the years. The vision rekindles as Momaday listens over centuries to his own grandmother, Aho, speak from plains "grandfathers of grandfathers and grandmothers of grandmothers." There is always a child to be brought to life among the old ones, always a descendant born out of an older age to listen and carry the voices on. In the quietness of natural things, the speakings of plants and animals, the presence of terrain and elements, the carry-over of the old ways, Momaday hears a poetry of natural order and beauty. He records this Kiowa heritage in a plain style that opens naturally to arts native in the world. The artist does not shape the world so much as place himself in touch with what lies down in things.

Momaday began publishing poetry in *The New Mexico Quarterly* (1959) as an undergraduate at the University of New Mexico. Several degrees, institutions, and volumes later, he may be the best known American Indian writer. His distinctions mark a new image of the Native American. He received a Stanford doctorate in American literature in 1963, a Guggenheim Fellowship in 1966, the Pulitzer Prize for Fiction and an Indian of the Year award in 1969, a teaching Fulbright to Russia in 1974, and since 1973 a professorship in English and comparative literature at his alma mater, Stanford University, after teaching at the University of California in Santa Barbara and then in Berkeley. In 1981 he joined the Native American Studies faculty, along with Leslie Silko and Vine Deloria, Jr., at the University of Arizona.

The Gourd Dancer (1976) gathers poetry over twenty years. As a lyrical imagist, Momaday attends to the musicality of words in the chimes and rhymes of couplets, the softly overlapping assonance and consonance of melodic cadences. He intones in "Plainview: 1"—

> There in the hollow of the hills I see,
> Eleven magpies stand away from me.

Low light upon the rim; a wind informs
This distance with a gathering of storms

And drifts in silver crescents on the grass,
Configurations that appear, and pass.

There falls a final shadow on the glare,
A stillness on the dark, erratic air.

These lines pair with regularity and poise, a learned formalism, in verse that keens and lulls. At times the poet listens more minutely than he sees. "The Burning," for example, opens viscidly:

In the numb, numberless days
There were disasters in the distance,
Strange upheavals. No one understood them.
At night the sky was scored with light,
For the far planes of the planet buckled and burned.

Reality for this poet is something to be evoked in the prairie-fire shadow of a "world yonder," to borrow from *Black Elk Speaks*. His attempts to draw nearer rarely concretize.

In the dawns were intervals of darkness
On the scorched sky, clusters of clouds and eclipse,
And cinders descending.

The tenets of impressionist painting and mythic shading govern here; varying angles of light and shadow tonalize objects, known more as presences than material things, through hours and over seasons. "The Burning" continues:

Nearer in the noons
The air lay low and ominous and inert.
And eventually at evening, or morning, or midday,
At the sheer wall of the wood,
Were shapes in the shadows approaching,
Always, and always alien and alike.

With a common strangeness Momaday scallops thin, hesitant lines, poised for revelation, surviving on small truths. By its ending, "The Burning" records a carefully diminished attention:

And in the foreground the fields were fixed in fire,
And the flames flowered in our flesh.

The lines strain in parallelisms, alliterations, rhymes, and near rhymes. The epigrammatic form almost erases the visceral world, as the poet's apprenticeship with nineteenth-century verse filters through: Frederick Tuckerman's minutiae, Emily Dickinson's shy touch, and Yvor Winters insisting on the crystallization of common things through aesthetic form.[28]

Momaday's position in *The Gourd Dancer*, as poet and sketch artist, seems one of waiting at the windows of reality. His own fine-line drawings agitate the margins of tangible images, tentatively approaching objects, busying the outlines of things, hesitant of their thingness.

> Desire will come of waiting
> Here at this window—I bring
> An old urgency to bear
> Upon me, and anywhere
> Is a street into the night,
> Deliverance and delight—
> And evenly it will pass
> Like this image on the glass.

All things pass, the countervoice reassures the poet's darker restlessness, just as his own image fades on panes of vision. This visionary transience is a reflection of a native life-spirit, Black Elk's "What Moves-moves" regenerate.

Momaday's prose, at the same time, shines with a fine musical tuning. Throughout *House Made of Dawn* and *The Way to Rainy Mountain*, a tensile voice speaks directly to things and ideas; the language rises out of a formal underlay within natural objects. Form is not imposed, but brought forth from within, the artist here a participant with natural events. Each line quiet to itself, one of Momaday's early love poems opens:

> Earth and I gave you turquoise
> when you walked singing
> We lived laughing in my house
> and told old stories
> You grew ill when the owl cried
> We will meet on Black Mountain

A reader notes Black Elk's sense of propriety here, down in things, just as Momaday the artist recalls an unnamed woman buried in an elegant buckskin dress east of his grandmother's house in Oklahoma. This art, native to the land, derives from a personal response to the "reality" within history. It is an organic premise: that art, less than made, is revealed in things.

Momaday's tone poem in eight parts, "The Colors of Night," adapts codings from the winds, sky, and earth out of older Indian traditions.[29] Three women haunt the movements of this white-to-black prose poem: one of sumac leaves, one awakening in moonlight, one wrapped in darkness. The first girl is a lost red beauty, abused and scattered like leaves over the plain. The second girl awakes and looks out onto a moonlit meadow—

> There appeared to be a tree; but it was only an appearance;
> there was a shape made of smoke; but it was only an
> appearance; there was a tree.

The shifting images of reality, no less than dreams, green and fade seasonally, as does all beauty. Finally, a woman "whose hair was long and heavy and black and beautiful" shawls herself in darkness and steals singing into the men's societies. "And always, just there, is a shadow which the firelight cannot cleave." This mystery embraces all the colors of the darkness of night, a dream that remains inviolable.[30]

Momaday writes intensely conscious of the art of words. A friend's child dies in the early poem, "Angle of Geese," and language falls from pure, still being. The imperceptible flight of silence drops like a bird downed with words.

> So much symmetry!—
> Like the pale angle of time
> And eternity.
> The great shape labored and fell.

This descent into mortality echoes Keats's self-questioning, as the artist contemplates design seize and hold life in "cold pastoral" on a Grecian urn.[31] Conversation buffers the mourners from deeper recognitions of time and death: "the dead firstborn" lag forever "in the wake of words." Custom and civility rescue the grief-stricken from shock, as they begin to stir through the motions of consciousness, trailing direct contact with things, bearing up, moving on. "More than language means, / The mute presence mulls and marks." This alliterative "presence" haunts the time lag between things and their articulations, murmuring discontent and loss, pleading the original silence of Black Elk's "great Voice." Agonized by expression, numbed by death, the poet sifts for relief in the spaces around things and words, yet: "I am slow to find / The mere margin of repose."

Momaday's more formal poems search for a language of events, as in "Crows in a Winter Composition."

> This morning the snow,
> The soft distances
> Beyond the trees
> In which nothing appeared—
> Nothing appeared—
> The several silences,
> Imposed one upon another,
> Were unintelligible.
>
> I was therefore ill at ease
> When the crows came down,
> Whirling down and calling,
> Into the yard below
> And stood in a mindless manner
> On the gray, luminous crust,
> Altogether definite, composed,
> In the bright enmity of my regard,
> In the hard nature of crows.

In the beginning, the poet broods on "nothing," which by its nature does not appear; but out of absences then gather the "soft distances" and "several silences / Imposed one upon another," mutually "unintelligible." Winter itself, muted, receding, layered, and indistinct, is evoked in this waiting time with "nothing." The poet seems almost at peace with no demarcations, no meanings, no edges in the snowy landscape, no words. "Sometimes you look at a thing and see only that it is opaque, that it cannot be looked into," Momaday reflects in *The Names*. "And this opacity is its essence, the very truth of the matter" (*N* 146).

But crows *crow*. The raucous cries come "whirling down and calling" on this quiet scene, as noisy words break the peace of silence and dark definitions intrude on a white expanse. The crows stand in the yard below, highlighting "the gray, luminous crust" of snow. The marginal tone sullies winter's calm by realizing things grayly into focus. To leave the scene blurred, no-colored, silent seems preferable—but obviously the poem proceeds, and gets written, by this tension and contrast. The "words"—dirty, staining, noisy, compared with untinctured silence—offer the only way a poem can get written, albeit in a fallen medium. Language stands forth "definite" and defining as "the hard nature of crows" crowing; words equivocate and here violate the poet's private impulses to speak softly, if at all, to stay out of things, to escape into the "great Voice" breathing "silent" in Black Elk's vision.

An unspoken poetry underlies Black Elk's vision of the "real" reality, a place unnamed, intangible, and out of reach here and now. To name something is an act of possession, traveling the Black Road of this shifting world; to touch and fix anything spiritlessly is potentially to lose it, demean it, finally not to touch it at all.

There seems another, older recourse, a preverbal language of things truly themselves. Down in the world, fossilized, lie powers of objects sacred with age. Only the ancient, hard edges of things, severely defined, rescue these spirits from a shadow-world of material confusions, half-perceptions, and failed languages. Momaday asks for objects "clean and precise in their beauty, like bone," or none at all—old natural artifacts, inviolate with age ("Forms of the Earth at Abiquiu," a poem for Georgia O'Keefe). Such art has endured the wreckage of consciousness and time, now ageless.

Only one hundred handmade copies of Momaday's first book were made. No title page, no pagination, no gloss, no footnoting—simply a rich calfskin binding with The Journey of Tai-me engrained in dark blue letters in the lower right-hand corner, followed by a one-page opening, thirty-three Kiowa tales, and seven woodcuts. Copy number 80, signed by the artist, is held in the special collections vault at the University of California, Santa Barbara, where Momaday began teaching and in 1967 handcrafted The Journey of Tai-me, collaborating with D. E. Carlsen and printer Bruce S. McCurdy.[32] This rare edition pays tribute to ancient and sacred art forms imprinted with human hands, "in the trail of the wind," Navajo creation myths say.[33]

The Journey of Tai-me merges the writer's grandmother, Aho, with her own mother's contemporary, Ko-sahn, in a storyteller commonly named "old woman." Inside the calfskin cover a loose-leaf, earth-toned woodcut images the silhouette of a shawled woman who holds something glowing before her face. The interplay of light and shadow, through dark browns and tans, suggests a presence felt, but not clearly seen. The art is a collective shadowing through shape and tone, rather than detail isolated in time, too old, too far back to bring into near focus. It is a creativity of blendings, mergings, the reciprocities of people and things melded through age, so that matter and spirit flow together like the silt of an old riverbed.

The Kiowa stories stand in and of themselves. Rather than making something of an object through stylization, the craftsman brings forth the art in natural objects—the richness of leather, the texture of paper, the imagery of idioms, the resonance of tribal heritage. Momaday combines simplicity and natural beauty here, passing on the Kiowa tales in the sacred spirit of Tai-me bringing life to the people. " 'Take me with you,' the voice said, 'and I will give you whatever you want.' From that day Tai-me has belonged to the Kiowas" (*WRM* 36). The book, like a still creature with wings, conveys something ancient, fragile, and yet alive. The pages are textured as parchment of an old woman's skin, her voice warm and thin as Oklahoma wind on a summer evening. Each small tale arcs from the upper right-hand page across a sepia openness, essential words placed in the expectancy of clear space. The natural paper is traced with fine black hairs, recalling scattered tracks of wildlife that once accented the open plains. A printing rarity, *The Journey of Tai-me* reaches back to redefine the nature of books, through ancient storytelling and craft.

The artist carries over twenty-three of the thirty-three Tai-me tales and dedicates *The Way to Rainy Mountain* to his parents, Natachee Scott and Al Momaday, themselves artists and writers. Scott Momaday's own name combines families of two relocated Oklahoma tribal ways. The one-eighth Cherokee on his mother's side, an Appalachian agricultural people, walked the long 1830s Removal from Georgia to forced acculturation on the Great Plains. They were leaders among the Five "Civilized" Tribes of the Southeast where Sequoyah devised the first native syllabary in 1821. By contrast, his father's Kiowas, a nomadic and comparatively "wild" tribe of buffalo hunters, migrated freely down from the northern mountains over three centuries, to roam the lower plains by the mid-eighteenth century. According to plains lore, the Kiowa owned more horses and killed more whites per capita than any other tribe; they are still suing for their share of the Black Hills.[34] So with Scott Momaday, several ways and cultures and pasts merge. Farmer and hunter, temporizer and renegade, earth-mother and sky-father (Mammedaty means "Walking Above") come together. The collection is illustrated by Momaday's father, told by his grandmother, peopled by his ancestors, landscaped in the heart of the continent, and informed by tribal and anthropological records.

If individual and collective tribal identities have fragmented into myth and legend, memory and imagination, Momaday's "way" to Rainy Mountain recomposes Kiowa "histories." Each facing passage in the book speaks across to the other. The collage of perspectives realigns four modes presenting the Kiowa story: the tribal or folkloric memory speaks through Aho, the grandmother muse; the pictoral or visual mode projects through the senior Momaday's drawings to illustrate his mother's stories to her grandson; the historical or public medium documents events through James Mooney's *Calendar History of the Kiowa Indians* (1898), borrowings from Elsie Clews Parsons's *Kiowa Tales* (1929), and parallels with Mildred P. Mayhall's *The Kiowas* (1962);[35] the personal or impressionist voice elegizes a journey through Momaday's own recreated pilgrimage from Montana to Oklahoma, occasioned by Aho's death.

The book's quest is to find Aho alive in her grandson's imagination and memory. As with the hundred-year-old Ko-sahn who ends the book, "there was no distinction between the individual and the racial experience, even as there was none between the mythical and the historical."[36] Rather than separating past and present cultures, or making something new in a modern form, Momaday's intention is syncretic—to tend and nourish a life passed through his own family. In this sense he becomes a keeper of tribal culture and adds to the composing mosaic of Kiowa history.

A set of directional axes emerge around Aho's house from Momaday's memories, corresponding with Black Elk's "sacred hoop" intersected by red and black "roads."[37] (See illustration on page 104.) These coordinates seem personally evolved from Plains Indian ways. They are less formally tribal than Black Elk's vision, perhaps even subliminal for the artist; but the cultural placement according to space, tone, and time, the balancing of personal life within Kiowa values and heritage, the observances of all these with regard to the "four winds" offers essentially a re-*member*ed Native American self-definition. It is a realization, through words, of what Momaday experiences and imagines as a tribal Kiowa.

Momaday's "way" moves through and toward "the history of an idea, man's idea of himself, and it has old and essential being in language" (*WRM* 2). The artist continues a pilgrimage begun over forty millennia ago, according to Bering Straits theories. A carefully structured personal history takes place within a whole narrative sequence of tribal life, imagining what it meant and now means to be Kiowa. The collection strikes a familial tone, in the particular and inclusive sense that Black Elk's life story includes all wings, leggeds, and roots sharing one mother and father.

Elsewhere in Momaday's personalized genealogy, *The Names*, the artist remembers simply as a child in Oklahoma, "There would be old men and old women in my life."[38] *The Names* rambles through "that past, pastoral time of my growing up" with Momaday's nostalgia for a mythic Indian world that he never felt fully or singly integrated with. "It was not our native world, but we appropriated it, as it were, to ourselves. . . ." (*N* 150).

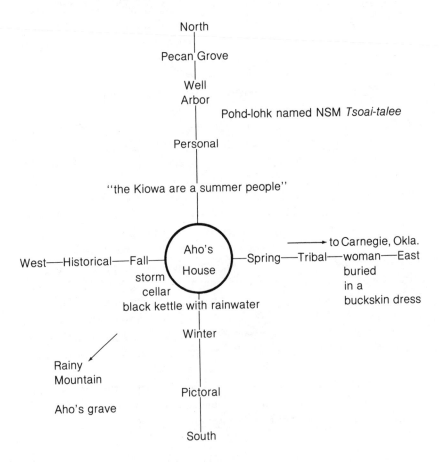

Momaday turns to words to palliate the loss. In its stream of consciousness evocation of childhood, *The Names* seems imitative of Joyce's *Portrait of the Artist as a Young Man*, here an Indian boy trying to discover himself through his ancestry: "an idea of one's ancestry and posterity is really an idea of the self" (*N* 97). This, too, suggests how the artist's mother may have reclaimed her own fragmented Indian identity, bearing a Kiowa-Cherokee child in Oklahoma and teaching in reservation schools across the Southwest.

The Momadays' house is "Indian" because Indian pictures hang on the walls, relatives talk Kiowa, and people laugh and sing in the older traditions. But the Indian child, in a non-Indian and mixed-blood setting, grows confused about his composite identity, no less than Joyce's young Irish Dedalus. Momaday's self-portrait reveals a child inside, looking out at "Indians," questioning how he can define himself as a bicultural American. This confusion, this challenge, *is* an Indian identity in America, as much as the call for harmonies in the old ways or tribal integrities.

Momaday remembers ancestors buried in the ground and "kinsmen in the sky," especially the seven star sisters whose origin myth takes place at *Tsoai* or "Rock-Tree" (Devil's Tower near Sundance, Wyoming, a laccolith Black Elk's people call *Mato-tipi* or "Bear-lodge"). The place-name yields Momaday's first Indian name, *Tsoai-talee* or Rock-Tree Boy, as celebrated in his name-poem, "The Delight Song of Tsoai-talee."[39]

> I am a feather on the bright sky
> I am the blue horse that runs in the plain
> I am the fish that rolls, shining, in the water
> I am the shadow that follows a child
> . . . .
> I am the glitter on the crust of the snow
> I am the long track of the moon in a lake
> I am a flame of four colors
> I am a deer standing away in the dusk
> I am a field of sumac and the pomme blanche
> I am an angle of geese in the winter sky
> I am the hunger of a young wolf
> I am the whole dream of these things
> . . . .

What began three centuries ago as a people's migration toward a homeland continues through the early 1960s: "There, where it ought to be, at the end of a long and legendary way, was my grandmother's grave. Here and there on the dark stones were ancestral names. Looking back once, I saw the mountain and came away" (*WRM* 12).

Momaday records details as art. He brushes things and trusts the grazed edges to speak the whole. *The Way to Rainy Mountain* maintains, directly and simply, "a going forth into the heart of a continent," as the artist's Kiowa ancestors came down from the mountains into their homeland (*WRM* 4). A hushed landscape is impressed upon the imagination, waiting for the right accent to cohere the design of things in the world.[40] At last facing the rising sun, Momaday ends the body of Aho's tales on a note of personal rebirth:

> East of my grandmother's house the sun rises out of the plain.
> Once in his life a man ought to concentrate his mind upon the
> remembered earth, I believe. He ought to give himself up to a
> particular landscape in his experience, to look at it from as
> many angles as he can, to wonder about it, to dwell upon it.
> He ought to imagine that he touches it with his hands at every
> season and listens to the sounds that are made upon it. He
> ought to imagine the creatures there and all the faintest
> motions of the wind. He ought to recollect the glare of noon
> and all the colors of the dawn and dusk. [*WRM* 83]

Everywhere is the earth's center in this vision, old as Anasazi petroglyphs, new as Monet haystacks. "It is a mood in the earth, I think, suffered here only, " Momaday writes of Oklahoma, the "red earth-people" land, "a deep, aboriginal intelligence in the soil, deeper than the intricate geometry that I see below, so deep as ever ran the roots of that single tree of the blood of the buffalo."[41]

The opening poem in *The Way to Rainy Mountain*, "Headwaters," suggests the detailed emergence of a people from life forms within the earth, "wild and welling at the source." The poem seems at least obliquely geological and evolutionary, as well as mythic, a lyric echo of native natural sciences embedded in folklore. Aho tells her grandson of the first Kiowas entering the world through a hollow log, hence named *Kwuda*, "coming out." An Indian knows these things through the "heart's eye," Lame Deer says, but equally, Momaday observes, through attention to the language of natural history. Things show forth analogically in "scant telling." The "smallest things" stand out of the depths of the plains, Momaday says,

"—and each of these has perfect being in terms of distance and of silence and of age" (WRM 17). This field of sight is consistent with a painter's near and distant fields of vision, attuned with a storyteller's "old sacred respect for sound and silence which makes for the magic of words and literatures."[42] Momaday's depth and range of perspective in the environment confers an *age* of being in time and space. He conveys a poet's indigenous sense of history and place.

The artist first singles out particles from masses, giving birth to oneself. The shaping environment here lends a sense of background and foreground: "All things in the plain are isolate; there is no confusion of objects in the eye, but *one* hill or *one* tree or *one* man" (WRM 5). And these details, isolated, take on natural significance reflected mythically in their names: "A single knoll rises out of the plain in Oklahoma, north and west of the Wichita Range. For my people, the Kiowas, it is an old landmark, and they gave it the name Rainy Mountain" (WRM 5).

But the near detail and far legend require the eye's depth of perspective, a sense of proportion, continuity, and placement in terrain and time. Early in *The Way to Rainy Mountain* Momaday returns to Aho's house in mourning, to see "for the first time in my life how small it was." He then notices, as if by synchronous accident, a cricket on a handrail that "filled the moon like a fossil" (WRM 12). And in the distant illumination "was its small definition made whole and eternal."

The same visual sense of small placement within larger context, tone against tone, object next to object, near and far occurs in *The Colors of Night* broadside: the cover frames a black dog against a full moon. Dark and light, object and spirit, here and there, now and then, real and imagined—the interplay reestablishes a balance among things and their correspondences. The artist realigns worldly and spiritual "roads," as Black Elk sees the sacred hoop in balance by noticing detail in the perspective of layered origins. Just so, native individuals find their place in an ancestry, an ecological setting, and a set of cultural definitions that inform tribal behavior through time.

Parallel to these aesthetics of composition and perspective, tribal themes of a split and reintegrated consciousness run through the text. After Kwuda or "coming out," the Kiowas took the name *Gaigwu*, evolving toward their modern name; it signifies differing halves, and by custom the warriors once cut their hair on one side, leaving it long on the other. A certain primal innocence of mythic origins falls into divisions of experience and history, only to be reintegrated by a tribal maturity that speaks across separations and losses. For example, a sun-child with a gaming ring doubles himself into twins who laugh at the procreative split, as their grandmother cries; a warrior captured by enemies is forced to dismount the centaur and pack his equestrian brother across greased buffalo heads; a child, who will grow up an artist, remembers the "glad weeping and waterlike touch" of his dying great-grandmother, Keahdinekeah.

A cautionary parable illustrates this singling out, dividing, and reconciling of self through composite perspectives. As a boy, Momaday swam in the Washita River on summer afternoons in

> a secret place. There in the deep shade, inclosed in the dense, overhanging growth of the banks, my mind fixed on the wings of a dragonfly or the flittering motion of a water strider, the great open land beyond was all but impossible to imagine. But it was there, a stone's throw away. Once, from the limb of a tree, I saw myself in the brown water; then a frog leaped from the bank, breaking the image apart.
> [WRM 31]

A fixated near attention, like the child's immediate sense of time and place, can block out the extended background of "the great open land beyond." The narcissistic near image is splashed apart by a frog, lowly, comic, and long an amphibious symbol for the necessary disruptions and adaptive transitions in growing up. Later in The Way to Rainy Mountain, the secretive child's world is completed by the open shelter of the summer arbor, a familial sunshade out-of-doors.

> Some of my earliest memories are of the summers on Rainy Mountain Creek, when we lived in the arbor, on the north side of my grandmother's house. From there you could see down-hill to the pecan grove, the dense, dark growth along the water, and beyond, the long sweep of the earth itself, curving out on the sky. The arbor was open on all sides to the light and the air and the sounds of the land. You could see far and wide even at night, by the light of the moon; there was nothing to stand in your way. [WRM 61]

Open to light, air, and sounds from the larger world, the arbor contrasts with the "secret place" of reclusive adolescence (the eye depends on a horizon, Emerson observed in *Nature*). The arbor also represents the openness of Momaday's own nameless infancy. Here he is given Kiowa definition, the ritual name Tsoai-talee, by Pohd-lokh, the ancestral arrowmaker.

New-born innocence one day will return in old age, the exchange signifies, as the cycle of life completes itself. Undifferentiated again, "old man" will give away his name, according to tribal custom, and go anonymously into death, one again with the land, as in the legends of the red medicine stone incarnating plains forebears.

> Now and then in winter, when I passed by the arbor on my
> way to draw water at the well, I looked inside and thought of
> the summer. The hard dirt floor was dark red in color—the
> color of pipestone. [*WRM* 61]

The earth holds spirits of ancestry, as the arbor contains summer down inside winter, and the well taps water deep beneath the parched plains. This depth of perspective plumbs sky to earth, the lessons of the past, and the old ways. It is a Kiowa equivalent to Black Elk's good red road.

Inversely epic, people and objects compress with power as they age, like Ko-sahn "so concentrated in the greatness of her age that she seemed extraordinarily small" (*WRM* 86). Small things in a spare landscape harbor meaning. The sacred "Tai-me bundle is not very big," Aho remembers, "but it is full of power" (*WRM* 80). As medicine, grandfather Mammedaty wore one of the ten small "grandmother bundles" on a string around his neck; "they are very powerful," Aho says, "and the Kiowas got them a long, long time ago" (*The Journey of Tai-me*, tale 25).

Elsie Parsons cites four Kiowa informants who translate "aho" as "thanks" in Oklahoma (though Momaday says the accent shifts from "a-hó," or "thanks," to his grandmother's name "Á-ho"). Feather-Standing-Inside sang this lullaby for Parsons in the 1920s:

> *Aho aho aho!*
> River flowing from the west,
> Baby floating down it
> One leg is like a floating stick,
> One leg is like the leg of a rabbit.
> *Wawaa wawaa.*[43]

Such a small woman, "Aho," such a small word for a universal concept—yet there is more power here, the book itself regenerate from Aho, than in Catlin's portrait of the seven-foot Kiowa warrior, Kotsotoah, who could run down and kill a buffalo on foot.

Most simply, Momaday thanks Aho in *The Way to Rainy Mountain*.

> Now that I can have her only in memory, I see my grand-
> mother in the several postures that were peculiar to her: stand-
> ing at the wood stove on a winter morning and turning meat
> in a great iron skillet; sitting at the south window, bent above
> her beadwork, and afterwards, when her vision failed, looking
> down for a long time into the folds of her hands; going out
> upon a cane, very slowly as she did when the weight of age
> came upon her; praying. I remember her most often at prayer.
> . . . The last time I saw her she prayed standing by the side of
> her bed at night, naked to the waist, the light of a kerosene
> lamp moving upon her dark skin. Her long, black hair, always
> drawn and braided in the day, lay upon her shoulders and
> against her breasts like a shawl. [*WRM* 10]

Words, too, seem small occurrences in diminished light; yet their power, in a grandson's memory, continues to speak through generations of tribal descendants born into and out of a racial tongue. James Mooney writes of Kiowa naming:

> All the names have meaning and are as much a part of
> the owner as his hand or his foot. Children are usually named
> soon after birth by one of the grandparents or other relative
> not the parent; the name is commonly suggested by some pass-
> ing incident, but may be hereditary, or intended to com-
> memorate the warlike deed of some ancestor. . . . Young men
> as they grow up usually assume dream names, in obedience to
> visions, and these are sometimes superseded in later life by
> names acquired on the warpath, the hunt, or in council. Fre-
> quently an aged warrior, who feels that his day is near its
> close, formally gives his name to some young man who seems
> to him to merit the honor; the older man then assumes a new
> name, being referred to and addressed simply as "old man."
> Sometimes the old warrior, having outlived the need of a name
> and not regarding any younger man as worthy to bear it,
> deliberately "throws it away" and is henceforth nameless.
> Should he die without having bestowed his name upon a suc-
> cessor, the name dies with him and cannot be revived. The

> name of the dead is never spoken in the presence of the
> relatives, and upon the death of any member of a family all the
> others take new names—a custom noted by Raleigh's colonists
> on Roanoke Island more than three centuries ago. Moreover,
> all words suggesting the name of the dead person are dropped
> from the language for a term of years, and other words, con-
> veying the same idea, are substituted.[44]

This taboo on naming the dead lies behind the elegiac silence in "Rainy Mountain Cemetery," Momaday's concluding poem. The close attention to speaking and remaining silent—the music of how words mean and their limits—is traditional for the Kiowa artist.

The women's names in Momaday's family ripple like water:[45] Aho, Keahdinekeah, Kau-au-ointy, Ko-sahn. The men's names burst softly in the back of the mouth: Mammedaty, Pohd-lokh, Guipahgo. The land, too, comes alive through sound. The mountains gather to an epic roll call of "wilderness names: Wasatch, Bitterroot, Bighorn, Wind River" (*WRM* 23). Rivers demarcate the land like roving sentinels: "For more than a hundred years they had controlled the open range from the Smoky Hill River to the Red, from the headwaters of the Canadian to the fork of the Arkansas and Cimarron" (*WRM* 6). The softly interlocking names of trees thicket Oklahoma creeks, "groves of hickory and pecan, willow and witch hazel" (*WRM* 5). The landscape flowers in character—"a mountain meadow bright with Indian paintbrush, lupine, and wild buckwheat" (*WRM* 23), the rain shadow of the Rockies "luxuriant with flax and buckwheat, stonecrop and larkspur" (*WRM* 7). Even the crawling "relatives" are named exact to what they are—"dung beetles and grasshoppers, sidewinders and tortoises" (*WRM* 27). It is a closer, but no less imaginative, focus on Black Elk's sense of "all living things with feet or wings or roots" as sky and earth children (*BES* 2).

Words convey identity through personal vision. They grant an ability to deal with the world on reciprocal terms. The peyote priest in *House Made of Dawn* speaks of an original language of events-in-things themselves,[46] the Word "*older than the silence and the silence was made of it*" (*HMD* 97). Momaday's own grandfather, a peyote man, was bound to Saint John's sacred text in the Native American Church: "In the beginning was the word." Momaday writes in *The Way to Rainy Mountain* that a "word has power in and of itself," giving origin to all things. Words defend, as well as confer being, and Aho wards off ignorance and disorder with the interjection, *zei-dl-bei*, a negative twist on Black Elk's holy witness in the expression waka^n.

The hundred-year-old Ko-sahn remembers when White Bear told the Gourd Dance Society, "I have the sacred arrow. I am very old and can no longer dance. I want to pass the arrow on. The man to whom I give the arrow must dance with it; he must never touch its point to the ground" *(The Journey of Tai-me*, tale 29). The transfer is made, one generation to the next, and "then the young man had the sacred arrow," Ko-sahn goes on, "and there was a great give-away. You know, the giving away of goods is an old, old custom among the Kiowas. It happens when a great honor comes to someone." Momaday today is a member of the Gourd Dance Society; as a "word sender" or modern poet he uses words as crafted arrows.

With the "time and patience to their craft," old men in *The Way to Rainy Mountain* make arrows straightened in their teeth; like old words well made, these arrows are penetrant as hunting weapons, powerful as tools of defense, and valuable as trade goods. They represent a culture passing from old to young carriers, and their ceremonial medium is a fluidly charged sense of space. Reminiscent of Pohd-lokh, the name-giving arrowmaker whose photograph opens *The Names*, Old Cheney goes out each morning near Rainy Mountain to chant the sun "up on the land. There, at dawn, you can feel the silence. It is cold and clear and deep like water. It takes hold of you and will not let you go" *(WRM* 47).

Momaday's focus on words at the literal center of twenty-four sections of *The Way to Rainy Mountain* moves from sunset in Section XII to sunrise in Section XIII. To move forward in narrative sequence, starting with sunset, is apparently to go backward in conceptual time; and yet in the larger picture of all the tales the sun's time is circular, from sunrise to sunset to sunrise again, traversing the horizon's curvature or "sacred hoop" of Black Elk. The end (sunset) moves toward the beginning (sunrise), as a mythic regression transcends linear history. It is going backward, looking forward.

At the end of a "golden dawning" of Kiowa history, 1740 to 1833, Momaday traces back to his tribal origins, reordering the sun's journey. So, too, the Navajo Night Chant ceremonies begin at sunset and end with rebirth in the sunrise eight and a half days later,[47] and Native American Church services take place after sunset to the morning sunrise. To remember imaginatively is to overcome time, to carry the past bodily forward, to journey into the present. And in all this, words carry resonant meanings through a still dawn of light returning to the land.

A traditional Kiowa tale, as told in Parsons under the title Red Horse or Cyclone,[48] reemerges in *The Way to Rainy Mountain*, when the people learn to speak with the storm spirit, a mythic horse embodying tornadic winds. Al Momaday images the storm's four primordial elements, earth, air, fire, and water, in inversions of land and sky.

The Storm Spirit[49]

The horse's earth body thrusts backward in a fishtail and diagonally downward in a wind-whip; these vectors are paralleled by a lightning bolt struck from the forelock, bridled to the mouth, and flaring over the head in a mane of flame; the serpent's tale of rainstorm and bridle of lightning converge in the tornado's vortex from sky to earth. The Kiowas talked to the storm horse, legend recalls, saying "Pass over me," just as the sun twins spoke to smoke in the giant's cave, "*thain-mom*" meaning "above my eyes." Now "they are not afraid of *Man-ka-ih*, for it understands their language" (*WRM* 48).

All things talk. By speaking *with* the world, the Kiowas tribalize their environment. The bridle of lightning, tying a mane of fire through the horse's mouth to its hoof, illustrates the striking power of crafted words and the concreteness of language-as-action. Correspondent with Black Elk's cup and bow from the storm winds, lightning and rain translate into the hunter's need for arrows and the food-gatherer's dependence on moisture. The storm finally brings the peace of rain and regeneration to the earth.

Momaday remembers a childhood of felt language, a literal touching of objects both sacred and usable. Next to Aho's south porch stood a great iron kettle that "rang like a bell when you struck it, and with the tips of your fingers you could feel the black metal sing for a long time afterward. It was used to catch the rainwater with which we washed our hair" (*WRM* 81).

The old stories serve as tribal parables that encode and transmit the culture. The Kiowas tell a folktale of a handsome young man blinded by the wind for his recklessness; the tribe ostracized the man, along with his wife and child, forcing the family to hunt their own food. The man's wife then betrayed and abandoned him, reporting that his arrows missed the buffalo; but even blinded, the hunter "knew the sound an arrow makes when it strikes home" (*WRM* 58). Eating grass to keep alive, the lone hunter was reduced to the level of the game he hunted. In seven days a band of Kiowas took him in. By firelight he heard a woman telling of her dead husband. "The blind man listened, and he knew her voice" (*WRM* 58). At sunrise the bad wife was "thrown away."

Aside from the "hard lives" of Kiowa women and men, the tale points up the integrity of tribal words and the penalty for breaking them, cognate, it seems, with the hunter knowing instinctually, as well as literally by sound, a true arrow or a true voice "when it strikes home." Family is the core of tribal values, and abusing these bonds threatens all the people. The young hunter was punished with blindness for his recklessness, and had to learn to see again. Through a rite of *humilitas*, he was given a second chance to tribal rights, and he proved that he heard the truth of tribal codes. The woman lied twice, and twice a betrayer, was "thrown away" like a bad name.

The Kiowas and Lakotas kept yearly calendars, and the circle of tribal time bound all things together continuously. The Kiowa Sett'an or "Little Bear" winter and summer counts, from 1833 to 1892, imaged time as circular, beginning in the lower right hand corner of an animal skin with images for the years and spiraling to the center.[50] In 1848 scarce game brought all the people together, hunting in a "great circle" that closed in on the center. "By necessity," Momaday says, "were the Kiowas reminded of their ancient ways" (*WRM* 19).

Completing a sacred circle with no beginning or ending, Momaday's return to Rainy Mountain in the springtime of Aho's death grants him rebirth as a Kiowa grandson. "Carriers of the dream wheel" turn and center their voices on tradition, just as Momaday turns again to childhood memories of Tai-me: "There was a great holiness all about in the room, as if an old person had died there or a child had been born" (WRM 32). The return is timeless. As a boy Momaday's father, too, went with his grandmother, Keahdinekeah, to make a cloth offering and pray at the *talyida-i* shrine:

> The holiness of such a thing can be imparted to the human
> spirit, I believe, for I remember that it shone in the sightless
> eyes of Keahdinekeah. Once I was taken to see her at the old
> house on the other side of Rainy Mountain Creek. The room
> was dark, and her old age filled it like a substance. She was
> white-haired and blind, and, in that strange reversion that
> comes upon the very old, her skin was as soft as the skin of a
> baby. I remember the sound of her glad weeping and the
> water-like touch of her hand. [WRM 35]

When all else is taken or given away, tribal peoples still remember and imagine, tell old stories and sing the sacred songs, filling the earth with familial voices. Not to do so is to die as a people.

> Botone was the last Tai-me man. He was the only man who
> could open the bundle. But he forgot about Tai-me. You
> know, the Tai-me man is not supposed to leave Tai-me after
> sundown. Botone forgot about that. Once he went chasing
> after women and left Tai-me alone at night. After that, Botone
> died. But before he died he told his daughter of a dream that
> he had had. While he lay asleep he heard a voice that said:
> "You forgot about me. Now I am going to forget about
> you." And sure enough, that was Tai-me. Botone died. [The
> Journey of Tai-me, tale 21]

Words live beyond their "carriers" or "senders" as visionary spirits and as medicine. A century later Ko-sahn remembers an "old, old woman" in her childhood bringing a "bag full of earth on her back" to start the annual Sun Dance. The remembering "long time ago" concentrates two hundred years in Ko-sahn, grandmother of grandmothers whose aged voice keens as she begins "to speak and sing":

> We have brought the earth.
> Now it is time to play;
> As old as I am, I still have the feeling of play.

There is another voice Momaday hears beneath the sacred play of words dancing. It is unspoken music attuned with the "silent" song Black Elk "feels" on the vision peak. At rest in her grave, Aho settles into Black Elk's "shadow of a vision yonder." In the beginning of the story, Momaday returns to his grandmother's burial, and at the end he stands beside her in "Rainy Mountain Cemetery."

> Most is your name the name of this dark stone.
> Deranged in death, the mind to be inheres
> Forever in the nominal unknown,
> The wake of nothing audible he hears
> Who listens here and now to hear your name.
>
> The early sun, red as a hunter's moon,
> Runs in the plain. The mountain burns and shines;
> And silence is the long approach of noon
> Upon the shadow that your name defines—
> And death this cold, black density of stone.

Momaday sees the engraved letters, "AHO," in stone, but by grief and custom he is unable to speak her name in death. Estranged in the name of the dead, the mourning grandson listens beneath the "wake" of words "here" and senses his grandmother's living spirit: her soul, like her name, spirits the shadows cast by a passing red sun (the ancestral "son" who carries her memory on). Momaday, Aho's grandson, is genetic evidence of her ongoing Kiowa life.

To image someone's shadow summons their soul, many cultures believe. Indians named Edward Curtis the "Shadow Catcher" for his photography, an art picked up by Horace Poolaw, "Kiowa George Poolaw" or Pohd-lohk's son, among the Kiowa.[51] People live on in silhouettes of darkness, temporal on the plain, Momaday's ending poem offers. All exist in passing under a running sun. The living continue to name themselves by way of open passages: a hollow log of tribal emergence, a mother's womb, an open mouth, a living breath, a space in stone. The "word" by which Kiowas imagine is thus more shadow than possession. Here on Rainy Mountain in Oklahoma, "Aho" is an engraved opening in the world's "density," a grandmother spirit alive in imaginative silence and space.

"IN BEAUTY IT IS FINISHED"

House Made of Dawn borrows its title from a Navajo healing ceremony centuries old.[52] The novel tells of a young Jemez Indian named Abel from the Pueblo where Momaday grew up, the age of twelve through high school. Its prose rhythms, complex narrative points-of-view, and flashbacks assimilate experimental techniques in modern fiction and New World romantic themes. Faulkner's interior monologue and multiple time shifts lend a contemporary cast to Lawrence's neoprimitivism.

Abel's dislocations as a contemporary Indian fracture a voice that searches for consciousness. His ancestors were exiled from the plains by plague and taken in at Jemez. His mother and brother died years later of pneumonia. Abel was "kidnapped" from his grandfather and put into a government boarding school, drafted into a world war, and sentenced to prison for ritual homicide, then *re*located in the urban ghetto of Los Angeles. Past, present, and future—Indian life as-it-was, then estranged among whites, followed by a prolonged return—disjoint the narrative. School, war, prison, and the city are white institutions where the martyred son of the earth, the biblical Abel, lives through the Indian nightmare of a machine come into the garden.[53]

> Then, through the falling leaves, he saw the machine. It rose
> up behind the hill, black and massive, looming there in front
> of the sun. He saw it swell, deepen, and take shape on the
> skyline, as if it were some upheaval of the earth. . . . Then it
> came crashing down to the grade, slow as a waterfall,
> thunderous, surpassing impact, *nestling* almost into the splash
> and boil of debris. He was shaking violently, and the machine
> bore down upon him, came close, and passed him by. A wind
> arose and ran along the slope, scattering the leaves. [*HMD* 25]

Natural rituals of the body offer Abel regeneration through Pueblo traditions—running in the annual Jemez dawn race as his grandfather ran generations before, dancing to the traditional drumming at feasts, purifying with ashes and water at Francisco's death, singing the Night Chants with his Navajo friend Benally in peyote services, making love and laughing with Milly the white social worker in Los Angeles. The ceremonies promise a reordered life through childhood visions, remembered vividly: eagles soaring with a rattlesnake, the cultural myth of Santiago and his curative sacrifice that feeds Indian stories into Roman Catholic ritual, Francisco's first bear hunt in the mountains, and Abel's participation in the stickball race to clear the spring irrigation ditches. The ancient chants embrace all times: "House made of dawn, House made of evening light, House made of dark cloud, House made of male rain."

Momaday grew up an outsider to Jemez Pueblo.[54] He spoke English and some Navajo, languages that surround the New Mexico Pueblos along with Spanish. He did not, however, converse in his father's Kiowa or his mother's distant Cherokee. So, too, Abel remains some distance from the Pueblo kiva, instinctual rituals among Jemez people, and the denotative meanings of the village chants. "The old men went in for the last time, and he heard them pray. He remembered the prayer, and he knew what it meant—not the words, which he had never really heard, but the low sound itself, rising and falling far away in his mind, unmistakable and unbroken" (*HMD* 13). Momaday listens lyrically beneath the designations of words. His art calls on the balances, rhythms, and tones shaping sentences as patterns of landscape:

> They were golden eagles, a male and a female, in their
> mating flight. They were cavorting, spinning and spiraling on
> the cold, clear columns of air, and they were beautiful. . . . He
> hit the snake in the head, not with the slightest deflection of
> his course or speed, cracking its long body like a whip. Then
> he rolled and swung upward in a great pendulum arc, riding
> out his momentum. At the top of his glide he let go of the
> snake in turn, but the female did not go for it. Instead she
> soared out over the plain, nearly out of sight, like a mote
> receding into the haze of the far mountain. The male followed,
> and Abel watched them go, straining to see, saw them veer
> once, dip and disappear. [*HMD* 17-18]

The novelist reaches beneath the words themselves, separately considered, down into the rhythmic cadences on which meanings ride. The prose contours the dipping and veering, the daring of the spectacle, its "magic and meaning," as though the undercurrent of the eagles' flight patterned the sentences themselves. The art is a perfected grace of imitative form.[55]

The albino, who flagellates Abel in the Feast of Santiago, rides through the Pueblo on a black horse as an embodiment of the machine of war, inhumanly efficient: "A perfect commotion, full of symmetry and sound. . . . And yet there was something out of place. . . ." (*HMD* 43). The Indian albino personifies a blank anonymity settling over all races in America, a white winter coldness of spirit and culture.[56] Genetically mutant and homosexually disturbing, this stereotype of the white oppressor in the Indian must be killed, Abel feels. He ritually castrates and disembowels Cain, reversing the Christian myth of Abel's murder: "it was there, in the pale angle of the white man's death, that Abel knelt" (*HMD* 83–84).[57] Momaday portrays the albino more as symbol than character, the ancient evil in human nature serpentining into the kiva by way of invading Christianity. "The white, hairless arm shone like the underside of a fish, and the dark nails of the hand seemed a string of great black beads" (*HMD* 84). The Indian "white man" threatens to suffocate Abel, wanting to seduce him outside a bar, where the plot lends some corroboration to Leslie Fiedler's argument that American men, estranged from mother earth, turn impotently and malevolently to their ethnic "brothers."[58]

A more insidious threat appears in the condescension of Angela Grace St. John, a Beverly Hills matron who journies to Jemez for the healing waters. Angela stays on to seduce the priest's woodcutter, Abel. A lukewarm Catholic mystic with priestly eunuchs (Fray Nicholas and the one-eyed "father" Olguin), Angela goes slumming religion and race to pursue "the last reality" beyond all things seen and known. She is an angel of condescending grace, bearing white woman's burden, an unborn child. "Beyond the mountain," she drones in her Anglo mantra for consciousless reality, "neither nothing nor anything."

The Cochiti corn dancers touch a mystery that whispers salvation, where Angela's own doctor-husband and tourist-priest fail: "Their eyes were held upon some vision out of range, something away in the end of distance, some reality that she did not know, or even suspect" (*HMD* 36). The divine trick, Angela fancies, is "to see nothing at all, nothing in the absolute. To see beyond the landscape, beyond every shape and shadow and color, *that* was to see nothing" (*HMD* 36–37). Perhaps, but if the dispossessed Abel must return from the dead and participate in the healing pain of ceremony to relearn his ancestors' vision of the sacred earth, Angela will find no easy redemption carrying the Indian's seed. Pregnant with the void of her doctor-husband, she seeks relief from the white man's world and escapes abortively and transiently with an Indian lover.

Angela's spiritual emptiness collates with predatory sexuality as imaged in the albino's death outside Paco's bar:

He seemed to look not at Abel but beyond, off into the
darkness and the rain, the black infinity of sound and silence.
Then he closed his hands upon Abel and drew him close. Abel
heard the strange excitement of his white man's breath, and the
quick, uneven blowing at his ear, and felt the blue shivering
lips upon him, felt even the scales of the lips and the hot slip-
pery point of the tongue, writhing. He was sick with terror
and revulsion, and he tried to fling himself away, but the
white man held him close. The white immensity of flesh lay
over him and smothered him. He withdrew the knife and
thrust again, lower, deep into the groin. [*HMD* 82–83]

Earlier in the novel, Abel makes love to Angela in the form of "the
great bear, blue-black and blowing," as Francisco works his cornfield and
the albino watches furtively.

He was too old to be afraid. His acknowledgment of the
unknown was nothing more than a dull, intrinsic sadness, a
vague desire to weep, for evil had long since found him out
and knew who he was. He set a blessing upon the corn and
took up his hoe. [*HMD* 66]

A toiling Adamic grandfather followed everywhere by water, Francisco suffers witches and fallen mothers and a stillborn child. Grandfather blesses his
corn-children, in the traditions of the Pueblos and his sainted namesake, and
continues the old ways receding from Abel. He is graced by plants and
animals with "tenure in the land" twenty-five thousand years old. In the
old man's instincts "silence lay like water on the land" (*HMD* 10). Francisco endures, conditioned in the earth, waiting and listening, as the stillness
of time itself outlasts the invasion. "They have assumed the names and
gestures of their enemies, but have held on to their own, secret souls; and in
this there is a resistance and an overcoming, a long outwaiting" (*HMD* 58).

Francisco's quiet death in a troubled world draws the ritual moments
of his life to a still edge: the bear hunt when he returned a warrior, his first
drumming with the kiva dancers when the heated drums passed in unbroken rhythms under his hands, the ritual spring race at dawn for the coming rains:

The moment passed, and the next and the next, and he
was running still, and still he could see the dark shape of the
man running away in the swirling mist, like a motionless

> shadow. And he held on to the shadow and ran beyond his
> pain. [*HMD* 208]

Abel is humbled with the ashes of his grandfather's death a century later. He takes his place among the runners beneath a "clear pool of eternity" embracing the mountains. Rain begins to lace the snow-covered, dawn-lighted desert: "He could see at last without having to think." And beyond his pain Abel sings silently, "House made of pollen, house made of dawn. *Qtsedaba*." The novel ends on this ancient, voiceless chant, at sunrise, with a man's body in motion on the vast plain.

It is an image that could well represent the moving oral traditions of Black Elk's visionary plains people and Scott Momaday's adaptive "way" into modern literary forms. It is an image of the native body as words-chanted-in-motion. It is a sunrise image of reintegration, of renaissance. The image places the contemporary Indian in alignment with "What-Moves-moves," the older natural powers and spirits of Native America.

6

TRICKSTER'S SWAMPY CREE BONES

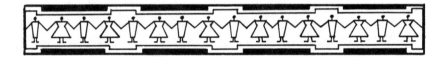

Reconciliation of opposites and adaptation to environment, the essential values which guide comic behavior, are
necessary both to biological evolution and to the full expression of mankind's highest talents. Humility before the
earth and its processes, the essential message of comedy, is
necessary for the survival of our species.

—KONRAD LORENZ in Joseph W. Meeker's
*The Comedy of Survival: In Search of an
Environmental Ethic*

OLD MAN

Coyote, hare, raven, crow, jay, wolverine, loon, or spider: a recreant
spirit masks as an animal wandering through hundreds of tribal Indian
myths. He resists the boundaries of any given species and is likely to appear
at any time in any image. Trickster goes his ways "undifferentiated," Paul
Radin observes, a makeshift, unregenerate figure fomenting reality.[1] He is
less divine than bestial, more mythic than animal. This figure, also known
as Old Man, scavenges in and out of the tribal world a gamesman, glutton,
amoralist, comic rapist, world transformer, and improvisational god.[2] He
steals wealth, devours game, breaks rules, seduces the princess, procreates

plants and animals, and makes up reality as people unfortunately know it, full of surprises and twists, contrary, problematical.

A trick misleads by duping others, perhaps in play. Trickster's divine demonism seems "agonistic," to borrow from Johan Huizinga's *Homo Ludens*: human needs conflicting, at stake, and still to be played out.[3] In the give and take of tribal tellings across time, Trickster's pratfalls emerge as comically inverse parables. He gambles with values in the breach; he stirs up original considerations, fringed with moral and epistemological concerns. Trickster acts out the serious play of hunting, eating, defecating, loving, gaming, fighting, civilizing, and surviving death. And all such Trickster storytelling illustrates, at least indirectly, what Jarold Ramsey sees as "man's place in that generous, unforgiving order" of reality, the world-we-know.[4]

Trickster is still kicking around tribal cultures. Most recently he grins through *The Wishing Bone Cycle* (1976), Swampy Cree narrative poems translated by Howard A. Norman. Cousins to the Great Lakes Ojibwa, the Swampy Cree or *Muska koo* speak a dialect among the Plains, Eastern, and Sandy Cree. They live traditionally around the Lake Winnipeg woodlands as hunters, trappers, and fishermen, from south-central Canada northeast to Hudson's Bay. Cree Indians adapt to variable necessities of their hunting-gathering ecosystem with a "contingent" sense of reality, Richard Preston argues in *Cree Narrative*.[5] Human equivalents of Trickster's necessary improvisation, the people live a mutually interdependent existence; they co-exist within the changing conditions of their northern environment; they tribally share both the hazards and the bounty of their lives. The Cree participate with nature, effectively, rather than assume patronage over it. They *are* nature, in a word. Preston shows how "the contingencies of the Cree world are not predictably patterned and directly apprehended in all their complexity. There is, in place of our sense of a system of natural laws, only a series of changing relationships, determined empirically, case by case, as practical and congenial ends are sought."[6] How a person sees, calls, and images the world in words, then, is premised on day-to-day evidence. What things are "called" seeds an explicative story. How they "sound" echoes in a song.

Though not genetically Indian, Howard Norman grew up among the Swampy Cree of Canada speaking Algonkian. Norman's father worked as an old-time geographer on Cree reserves, and his parents began raising an adopted Cree daughter, one year younger than Howard when he was seven. White and Indian acculturations took place reciprocally in terms of an older hospitality and sense of extended family. This adoptive kinship goes beyond tribal, territorial, and even genetic boundary lines. By the age of seventeen, Howard Norman was apprenticed to the Cree storyteller, Jacob Nibènege-nesábe, and culturally versed as a non-Indian "Indian" among many bands of Cree.

Through summer tramps and Trickster tellings, Norman remains in touch with the some one hundred villagers of Otter Lake, recording life stories, songs, tales, and exercising his skills as ethnologist, translator, and poet among the oral traditions of literatures current among neighbor Cree tribes.[7] Norman's naming poems of eighteen men and twelve women in *The Wishing Bone Cycle*, for example, are Cree friends' names. Their life stories and tribal personalities are encoded in these names. The ways Cree people speak to and of each other tonalize the primary level of what-they-are-called; a Cree premise toward language as improvisation, steeped in serious play, filters through the Trickster cycles. Such names as Many Talks, Eyebrows Made of Crows (Norman's own descriptive nickname), or Turned Weeping Over evidence a particularizing interest *in* the world around the Cree—notable, nameable, memorable things, events, peoples, and places. These tribal oral traditions, a function of a daily language of attentive living, compose a distinct and primary literature in translation. The Cree world is a delightful world, full of challenging contraries, when all is said and done.

The translation of Cree names and narratives and songs is dependent on a personalized voice. Norman conveys the living presence of a storyteller among his responsive people, or a singer culturally alive in performance.[8] With a personal twist, these Cree translations in *The Wishing Bone Cycle* present a Trickster repertoire and variant improvisations convincing as poetry in itself. The texts regenerate from voice into print, distinct yet not divergent from the sources. Rightly recreated, the translations reflect the collective and personal voices of a tribal culture that assumes, in Preston's account, "that men have only a partial grasp of their situation, and that things *do* look different from different perspectives."[9] Jacob Slowstream comments traditionally, "Everyone / had his own way / of putting it" (*WBC* 168).

The Cree language is rich in an organic lexicon where poetic detail reveals itself naturalistically. For example, the old storytellers occasionally speak in ventriloqual tongues that sound like their animate referents: *sh-ísh-is-te* for "snake." So, too, an eel could be referred to as a "confused snake," Norman explains in conversation; swirls of wind over winter drifts are called "snow snakes." A "loon" makes the sound of what it is called, *Mwoak*. "I'm always amazed," Norman says, "not at the complexity of the Cree language, but in its economy . . . the way the Cree talk about their language is that it's easy to use a lot of words, but it's hard to use a few words in a lot of different ways."[10]

Earlier this century, Edward Sapir observed that "single Algonkian words are like tiny imagist poems" in word-clusters.[11] Such a polysynthetic or "fusional" language gestates from eidetic energies down in people, animals, and locales. All these things, the Cree feel, are "artistically" taking place in the world. Norman believes that "the concept of diversity is very important, and so these translations are fairly literal, in the sense that it's a poetic language. I find it easier to be honest in Cree, because the language doesn't go up here first [points to his head], it just flies out of whatever you're talking about. There's no . . . something in between. So I see it as a very complex language, but it handles itself in very direct, simple terms" (discussion February 1980).

The etymology of events shows forth concisely, as the poetry crystallizes through economy.

> I can't travel
> away from you
>
> rolling pine cone
>
> Each time I go to leave
> my shoes hide
> in your dreams

The diction, tone, imagery, and mind-set of these natural lyrics generate reflection through suggestive detail and delightful insight, a curious story-in-a-name or surprising shift of events in *The Wishing Bone Cycle*. When anyone tries foolishly to seize or control this shape-changing reality, it dissolves. The best way is to approach things parabolically, in the "asking voice" of a suitor humbled by Trickster (*WBC* 168).

Very simply, Norman touches the details that narrate poems in themselves, as the natural world tells its own story—a technique of natural attentiveness, rather than style. "As far as the translations themselves,"

Norman wrote me, "the process is long, and often varied. I think I told Bill Merwin once, that the problem is not the Cree but finding equivalents in English—I need help with the English. And Cree *is* a vital lively language, and the translations *are* very very close to the originals, and the variety, range, and vibrance of Cree storytellers have always been dulled by poor translations, Anglicized versions, all the historical calamities" (correspondence September 1979). So the key to these translations lies in the spirit of the original transforming English, a second language, toward Cree distinctions.

As in traditional American Indian song-poetry, Norman's lines forgo meter, rhyme, and formal literary convention for a tone trusting the craft *in* things. The poet's attention turns on what Yeats termed, in Homeric art, "the swift and natural observation of a man as he is shaped by life."[12] Norman once heard a new parent sing softly,

> Little snail
> curled up
>
> leaving a snail shape
> in the blanket
>
> when I lift you

As in continual birth, all things live and leave their shapes in the world: shadows, memories, words and deeds, lyric stories. This mythic world, though coded, is "open" to reading, as Mircea Eliade shows.[13] It is possible that code or "cipher," particularly in Indian storytelling, suggests meaning through a certain latent richness of texture, down under the bald surface of things. The lure of such engrained meaning draws the participant-reader *into* the world he or she inhabits imaginatively.

Norman's translations then seem acts of essential selection. He edits detail, word, and event, placing the parts sparely in English to compose the whole in verse. The poems come into focus so succinctly and naturally that any other way of casting the insight would seem to blur as explanation.

FORKED HUMORS

The Wishing Bone Cycle opens with an origin myth improvised by Jacob Nibènegenesábe ("Slowstream"), a ninety-four-year-old teller of tales who always invoked his audience to "listen" (*Nutoka moo*), then began formulaically, "I go backward, look forward" (*Usá puyew usu wapiw*), "as the porcupine does." Just as the Cree word for "porcupine," *Kwakwu*, transmutes open vowels across two syllables, so the phrasing for "goes backward" and "looks forward" playfully rearranges phonemes in a kind of oral acrostic:

The same letter-sounds economically mutate and regroup in new combinations, so that the old is renewed in a variant on the pattern, just as Slowstream improvises freely within the Trickster cycle traditions. There is both continuity and change here, having things two ways at once. It is the inclusive contradiction of a culture that varies and stays the same through the passage of time. To back into the old tales, reversing and suspending historical time, is to reenter that protective burrow of tradition looking out on the future, as Kwakwu does.

Slowstream's humor flows through the currents and eddies of the story-poems, as he goes about making things up. His imagination follows the natural streambed of storytelling traditions, while improvising around the bends. The art is not so much in any one story, as in the ability to make one up. To wit, Slowstream begins: One spring a snow goose alighted on a smaller inlet near Lake Winnipeg, only to be stalked and eaten by a lynx; but just as the lynx got down to cracking the marrow bones, a man called out of the woods and scared him away. The picked-over bones left the man no meat, yet among the scraps he salvaged a metamorphic wishing bone: an improvisational tool born from his own hunger. Now, bones lie inside things, naturally, the last and sweetest meat to get to (the lynx almost got to crack the bones) and the last to go (outlasting flesh). The Cree regard animals' bones as sacred and magical, according to Boyce Richardson:

> Around all the camps hang bones of various kinds, the means
> by which the hunters show their respect for the animals. At
> one of the camps I visited, bear bones had been carefully
> wrapped in bark and tied around the trunk of two trees. No
> one messes around with bear bones. Beaver bones, particularly
> the head, arms and tail, are preserved, placed in a bag and put
> up in the bone tree.[14]

The trick in the bone, then, carries the secret of survival, in mythic regard for the animals that feed the Cree. Trickster's bones preserve a framework inside the culture with artifacts of ongoing tradition, tuning forks for the imagination, and daily hunter's tools. The Cree show particular respect to birds, especially the geese migrating in spring and autumn, harbingers of summer and winter.

> When the goose is killed, a special cake has to be made and eaten first. All of the first kill has to be eaten and shared, whether it is one goose or ten. Before the first meat is tasted, a piece must be put in the fire. None of the goose bones are thrown away; all are put up in a tree in a bag. The head is stuffed and ornamental beadwork made on it.[15]

The wishing bone protects the heart's dreams with a carapace of humor, and play around the "deep heart's core," as Yeats felt, taps the marrow of life. Hunger whets the art of this ritual magic; need hones its disciplined edge. This winged bone quickens the world with changes. It offers imaginative alternatives to reality's given rules, and people get what they "like" in metaphoric flight, unrestricted to what grounds them in the world. As Jarold Ramsey posits of Nez Percé orphic myths, here in a Trickster context, "We lend Coyote our dreams."[16]

Significantly forked, the wishing bone implies unified options and divisions, a delightful duality not uncomplicated in this world of changes. It is old as the Chinese ideogram for man the biped, 人, modern as Swift's description of "a forked straddling animal." The wishing bone images a divided yet continuous universe whose come-and-go pulses in the very rhythms of heartbeat and breath. It embodies the in-and-out, right-and-left complements of a binary reality that balances itself through enantiomorphic inversion: Usá puyew usu wapiw.

The Swampy Cree refer to these contrary dynamics in the world as *tipi-kochiyetim*, or "opposite thinking," inherent through the cyclic natures of reality and ritualized in an oral tradition of *tipiskoochtopawin*, or "opposite singing." For example, one wishing bone eye sees a porcupine, as the other sees a bird; the animals know north by the smell of Trickster running south; and there are two moons in the sky, "one moon for each of his eyes!" This thinking in opposites and fusions, Norman explains in notes to an elder woman's life story, "is best illustrated in Sarah Grey's speaking of her first husband's blindness, 'He often had summer birds in his eyes, even in winter.' "[17]

In the north, winter cold alternates with its absence, as there are basically two subarctic seasons.[18] One harsh possibility is latent in its tempering opposite, winter in summer, sorrow in joy, complexity in simplicity, death in life. Norman tells us that "in the north, if a person comes in from the cold shivering, you would, in the old way, speak only of summer things and rub broth into his/her temples and speak summer-talk to help this person thaw out."[19] Or, in a tragic belief associated with winter starvation, a chill is thought to enter a Cree from the opposite direction when a *Witigo* approaches to kill and eat him.

Like Kwakwu backing into its burrow "looking forward," to progress simultaneously on different planes of thought is to do two things at once, bridging incongruities, combining opposites. This doubling perspective runs basic to comic paradigms the world over, and Tricksters from Africa to the arctic act out the primordial tenets of comedy: the ritual scapegoating and slaying of reality's fool, his springing back from death, his integrating liminally into the tribe as sacred buffoon.[20] A humor of twists and turns, contraries and reversals remakes everything into something surprising. "I couldn't think straight so thought crooked," the wishing bone Trickster confesses, as he snakes through a world of lemniscate swirls and tracks that perennially double back.

A storyteller among the Cree can be called *a-kwee-mish-tes*, that is, "some-one-who-lies-without-harming-anyone," Norman says. In this spirit, Jacob Slowstream makes up a repertoire of trick poems that places him among Cree Trickster narrative traditions (thus, *The Wishing Bone Cycle* distinguishes between a man as a wishing bone "trickster" and *Wichikapache* later as the mythic Trickster of old). A storytelling tapestry in Norman's translations, from improvisations, to individual names, to private songs, to sacred texts, shows the Cree to be socially and aesthetically interwoven within their constantly evolving culture. Some sacred stories carry a "need-to-be-told" urgency, Norman says, renewed in the tellings that feed the spirits that keep the world going. As Job Walks says of "an old agreement" voiced between people and the animals who gave men speech, "If we stop speaking of them, they will leave."[21] Everyone involved, narrators through listeners, out through the animal and spirit worlds, participates in a process of tribal talk that of its own tells the tellings.

Slowstream began his wishing bone tales standing a tree, then a man, upside-down, treating poems as played inversions; they reveal the world in the surprise of opposites (Alexander Calder is said to have invented the mobile imagining a tree upside-down). "I try to make wishes right / but sometimes it doesn't work," Slowstream's Trickster admits, and even that's a story. These comic reversals relate to the shaman's or magician's ancient trick of reaching down a person's throat for a vestigial tail to yank inside out. The person ravels back through himself to a new self, while the old outer self sloughs back inside. So, down within this present world of quick changes lie mythic origins. Trickster says that once the salamander tried to worm down two holes at once, when a bird came along, so he wished it legs to scurry under a log. "But the worm / is inside them somewhere," to be remembered from a time of magic beginnings.[22]

William Smith Smith determined: "The best storyteller is one who lets you live if the weather is bad and you are hungry" (*WBC* 172). So first of all, a good story holds information necessary to live in the north. "Maybe it won't be easy to hear," William Smith Smith adds, "inside the story, but it's there. Too easy to find you might think it was too easy to do."[23] Consider this poem about seeing in fog:

> A snake lost his eyes once.
> Don't blame this one on me!
> It was the snowy owl.
> He was playing the moon.
> That owl closed his eyes
> and sat in a fog tree
> with his white face.
> The snake looked up through the fog
> and saw that round face
> and said, "Moon, show me a meal!"
> Then that moon came down and took his eyes.

A still hunt of natural masking lures prey to predator: owl *plays* the shut-eye moon. If the hunted are to escape the deadly patience of this wait-in-disguise, they must see through the fog of self-blindness. Snake's mistake, in a mutual plot of necessity, comes in assuming he will be *shown* a meal. He does not see what *is* there. The request for a free meal backfires and gives away his gullibility. Consistent with the natural, if severe, rules of the game of survival, snake loses his eyes to an appearance of the one-eyed moon.

Thus to misapprehend the environment means to go hungry, even to satisfy another's hunger. Duplicity, trickery, appetite, and craft fill up this world, like it or not. Best learn to deal with reality here in the play of words, the telling implies.

Trickster teaches that all creatures in the world-at-large are capable of all the negative virtues. Each can play wishes inversely. Slowstream dreams up a crying lake, for example:

> One time I wished myself
> into a moose deer.
> I was lying down and sleeping
> with my own shadow
> and then you came along
> saying the sun was in your mouth,
> saying you were thirsty!
> I wished you to where you drank tears.
> It was a lake
> everyone cried into,
> full of people's tears.
> At night
> some of the tears left
> to look for sad faces
> to fall down.
> Then the whole lake cried.
> Some said it was the loons.

Framed by the petulance of a shadow-sleeper wakened by sun-in-his-mouth, tears take on a life all their own in Loon Lake. To image sadness just so, freshly, as a lake thirsting with tears, graces sorrow. And beneath this elegiac art another voice of older counsel assures that a rarely imagined truth redeems even one's sense of loss. Long ago the Ojibwa sang,[24]

> A loon I thought it was
> But it was
> My love's
> Splashing oar.

If truly imagined, reality transcends and outplays any tunnel vision, single mood, or blocked temper that would fixate the world of experience. Reality to the Cree is, after all, most interesting.

131

To entertain living in this uncertain world, then, pivots on *not* knowing things for sure. People must stay alert to participating in events as they unfold. Preston observes that "the Cree do not acknowledge *intrinsic* inconsistency, but only possible misunderstanding of the way things 'really are.' "[25] So in Slowstream's trickster poems tone shifts quickly, from the nibble of a turtle laughing bubbles under a river, to a duck catching the "old" and "poorest" hunter's arrow for its nest.

> A goose caught my arrow
> and broke it
> in two.
>
> I am old, old.
> Don't bring me pity,
> but food
> yes.

Trickster's magic wields a temper all its own, consistent with natural truths he often forgets. One trick boomerangs and breeds another, and to play this mercurial game is to be played by it, if unwittingly or unwillingly. One time, because he got lost, trickster wished all the squirrels' tails pointing north to peg down direction. In nature and art, conformity buys trouble, unkindly uniform. Skunk the avenger is called in to reorder things in their true diversity. Trickster backs away north and. . . .

> Awgh! I ran south
> shouting, "He sprayed me!"
>
> For days everyone knew
> in their noses
> which way south was,
> because of me.

So trickster now knows north running the opposite direction. The others smell south where he has gone. The inverse unknowns in all this tricking, by way of narrative parable, make the Cree conscious of radically contingent variables to keep alive. They survive a deceptive world vital with critical play. Acted out dangers, comic or close to the bone, serve to wake listeners up with well-imagined fear. Skepticism grounds sympathy to keep the heart honest. The tales point toward a certain cautious empathy with an unpredictable, uncontrolled world.

All the world opens to people in the poems, for better or worse, as they walk in and out of dreams of themselves, taking on the environment, seasons, weather, the animals and plants around them. The Cree live continuous with animals, things, motions, and spirits. Preston notes that these Indians have no word translating as a generic term for "animal"; other life forms may be "other-than-human persons" inhabiting a "world populated by many kinds of persons."[26] In radical particularity each object or person or creature remains unique to itself. Simultaneously, each is bound up in an ecology of variable likenesses among things. Particularities in a common world compose homologues; specific beings make up species. Each shares a context with others, without compromising its own identity.

So, too, the world rhymes across differences, each linked part separately animate and associative: a grin on a storyteller's face, laughter thawing out in spring, a foot or arm acting on its own (Trickster's arms stab and kill each other fighting over moose meat), footprints sniffing around assorted feet, a name looking for a person to fill it up, a pile of story-shadows, noises crowding into a house, a wounded goose bearing "south in its neck," moss that drinks, winter as that "far north beast" with an ice heart, the shifting fog, a cantankerous wind, pond and stream floating away, sun and moon searching. In spring people even "rub winter" out of their feet!

Each animate being moves through the world on its own terms, sometimes finding a name to "live inside." Norman writes in *Who Met The Ice Lynx* (1978), "The Swampy Cree say stories live in the world, may choose to inhabit people, who then have the option of telling them back out into the world again. This all can form a symbiotic relationship: if people nourish a story properly, it tells things about life. The same with dreams. And names."[27]

In telling stories it is not so much the name, the tale, the trick, or the text itself that finally counts, as the spirit to invent things out of reality's parameters. The potential to do things means more than the thing itself, just as the "inside" of things implies more than "outside." What the people seem to want, most of all, is "inside" and to "be inside," where the action is. Among Cree tales, the imagining of plots down in the world tells more than surfaces; the outside tends to change shape in the "shut-eye" game of appearance and reality. By illustration, Slowstream says that once trickster wished up a coat wearing a man inside, analogous to the Cree finding a name to "fill up" with someone. It was summer, though, and the villagers asked "Why do you have that coat on?" The man cried back, "It has me in it!" Friends then tried to show the hapless man how to take "off" his coat. "Even that didn't work," trickster gloats; the coat wasn't "on" the man, he was "inside" it. "Things were getting interesting." It got on toward fall, the teller goes on, so someone thought to suggest that the coat should find a coat to wear through winter.

> Ha! I was too busy laughing
> to stop that dumb coat
> from leaving the man it wore
> inside.

There's always a wrinkle to be played back on Trickster, snaring him in his own cleverness when he is too sure. One time he wished up a foot-print tree. Bearprints would leap off the branches, smack the ground, and sniff around passing bears. Birdprints would fly off to catch birds!

> I tell you I was happy after wishing that tree up!
> Except, later, I had leaves
> from the mud and snow I'd walked in
> sniffing around my feet too.

So trickster can be tracked to the source of all confusion, humor, puzzlement and pain, riddles, problems, losses and gains—anything in the world that keeps on going on. It is just so with the resurrected goose eaten by the lynx found by the wishing bone man, who transforms back into a goose and migrates in season with gathered leaves and feathers:

> Then all the feathers leaped on us
> and we flew south. This is what happened.
> This is how I went to make wishes somewhere else.
> I brought my sack of old wishes with me.

And with the rising sap and warming winds of the next spring, Slow-stream's wishing bone trickster will fly back to improvise more mischief among the Cree.

NAME STORIES

The untitled wishing bone poems seed story-themes; conversely, the naming poems tell stories nascent in titles. The name *sticks* to Who Called the Mud-Places, out front of the others calling back, "MUD! MUD!"

Naming does not so much normalize behavior, as specialize characters along an art of differences. Always Surprised comically acts out the virtues of things-that-don't-fit-the-norm:

> Even if a leaf fell on his shoulder
> he jumped, JUMPED as if he was
> always being surprised.

Particular truths about people resist conformity. Oddities turn into assets. Who Tapped Frogs In "earns" a name that suggests how he "adapted to a sort of blindness," Norman relates.

> First thing to know is
> he was blind
> so he walked along the stream
> a different way

The *seer*-who-is-blind taps "all along the edge" of objects, hearing to see, seeing through not-seeing. He listens through specialized senses, related to narrative arts, to walk the edges of the physical world, guided by an innate sense of things down in the world. Just so, Walked Toward the Lynx learns to *hear* the lynx by touching his fingers to claw marks on trees.

In oral cultures, stories encode ways of remembering, thus preserving things taken into the tribe. Personal names activate daily visions, winter counts chart changing moons, seasons color landscapes with temporal designs, and place-names recall events that inhabit a region. To remember the stories engrained in names tells Cree history in a roll call of narratives, since the people reify tribal experience. "To say the name is to begin the story," Samuel Makidemewabe ("Turtle Wait") held as tribal historian, waiting patiently for "animal-persons" encrusted with their stories to crawl up the bank of a would-be tale.

To name something, first and finally, is to give it a place among the people. Names focus stories idiographically. A girl with long legs once slept among the water reeds and "Woke Into A Heron":

> This was the first time we saw someone
> do this, so we named her
> not to forget it.

For Listened to Birds Crack Out, memories inside words hatch like eggs. "He saved the shells / to remember how it went," as an archaeologist reactivates time from fossils that tell old stories. Like people, seasons, and places flowing amid the currents of time, names organically come and go, change, wear out, and give way to other names. Names are as shape-changing as people, their animate media.

In the common magic of memory, a generative and regenerative power infuses words. Remembered words are the twists in the lifeline to the past, carried forward humanly. Born Tying Knots came into the world with an umbilical cord around his toes; his birth name hints of words tied along the genetic cords of a tribal tongue, binding the people orally.[28]

> Later, he heard his birth
> story.
> It caused him to begin tying knots again.

So, Born Tying Knots acted out his name, tying up everything, even shirts and pants and a kettle to his feet, "so they wouldn't float away / in the river he dreamed." The dream keeps the name alive, as though spiriting the "named" dreamer (the Cree ask a visitor, upon first entering a village, what dreams he brings, Norman recalls). When the dream lives itself out, its twists straightened, the name-event goes too.

> After the dream stopped,
> he quit tying things,
> EXCEPT for the one night he tied up
> a small fire.
> Tied up a small-stick fire!
> The fire got loose its own way.

Swampy Cree song-poems in the third section of *The Wishing Bone Cycle*, "Far North Beast Ghosts the Clearing," go on to celebrate the lyrics of human improvisation. The mind's mimicry is revealed in the body's masquerade. Accurately imaged and mimed, the truth of things simply touches and releases a pure joy, as people play out the contagion of their delight in chosen masks.

> O-HA!
>
> so happy
> it was all I could think
> to do

What Norman, as zoologist, terms "mimicry" in the mirroring kinships of nature runs throughout the tales, cognate with all creatures adapting humorous guises. (Trickster traditionally goes by the fool's name, "Imitator.")

Here is an animal wit at play in human "nature," an improvisational alertness akin to protective coloration. Masking and mimicry keep creatures comically alive in a world that misleads the inattentive by natural laws of prey-predator relationships. Norman adds, "It's one of my primary sustenances—in the north—to combine the way a naturalist might look at concepts of animal behavior and the way a storyteller relates such behaviors. They are symbiotic—as a study, or simply a private way of thinking, of getting through the days up there" (correspondence September 1979).

The comic trickster imagination moves keenly through all this, inversing, reversing, mutating, and surprising; the tales crane our necks to see concealed sides to old truths about the natural interplay of danger and necessity and humors to survive. As witnesses to a world askew, we are "puzzled / but interested," like one of the poem's wolves, stalking a man, changed into a moose, farting in a hammock large as a valley—led on, curious with apprehension and delight, in a mercurial world. And we pursue a chimerical reality, the Cree poems suggest, because we can*not* catch it. At one point a magical duck lights up a swamp at twilight, masking the moon miming the sun swallowed in the dusk:

> But the duck said nothing.
> It lightened up the swamp.
>
> Then the men tried to capture the duck.
> They grew very quiet, and got close.
> Then they leaped toward the duck,
> but all they caught
> was mud in their mouths.
>
> "Look, over there!" one man called.
> Then they saw the duck sitting far away
> on the water.
> It was lighting up the swamp again!
>
> I just happened to be there.
> But in the morning we were both gone.

More than one elusive Trickster prowls the half-light in these poems, pursued endlessly by men who would break reality between their fingers.

A local Cree dialect speaks of *pecheyow* or "inwardly, into the body," and designates huddling with oneself, Norman explains, a sense of "being lowered down into yourself, past fears, until you feel safe."[29] One's totemic *Mistabeo* watches over this sanctum, the Cree believe; especially in critical times, this animal-overseer paces evenly and parallel to the guarded person, granting special presence. People inwardly envision themselves, totemically, from what they "see" outwardly; the energy of the totemic image shines back out through their features, interreflecting what they imagine and where they exist in illuminative mimicry.

> All the warm nights
> sleep in moonlight
>
> keep letting it
> go into you
>
> do this
> all your life
>
> do this
> you will shine outward
> in old age
>
> the moon will think
> you are
> the moon

The world, so tribalized by correspondences between inner and outer states of being, reflects a unity among all things, inner-penetrant and interdependent. Within the caprice and play of Cree Trickster traditions lies a sense of relational balance, quietly profound.

The memories in things speak reciprocally *with* people, where the very earth remembers the imprints of history. "The whole of the country is in effect an oral map," Norman says of naming stories in the Cree world, "for the specific place-names *should be spoken aloud* upon arriving at each one. This way you bring alive what happened, or still happens, there. When you arrive at a place, and live there in an attentive manner, you see where its name comes from."[30] Many Talks puts "something important" in the "many mouths" of baskets, to fill them with objects-that-talk of where she has been. The basket with the catfish skull, "GRINNING," reminds her of the first fish she ever caught, and Many Talks becomes the story-creature she narrates. The event shaped and still shapes her, grinning "all through / the telling."

The naming poems imagine and act out the animal in human nature. People's voices, masks, and bodies pantomime who-they-imagine-they-are as "other-than-human-persons," or animals. Sam Makidemewabe "saw a squirrel wake up / in his face'' each time Who Heard Squirrels listened for his namesake. Tree Old Woman impersonates a tree, until a woodpecker comes toward her menacingly, then a frog, before the largest turtle in the lake swims by hungrily. She continues to slip away from the fixity of ''human-persons,'' and her audience, captivated by her mimicry, pursues the counterimaging.

> This time we kept our eyes on her
> as she went to sit
> by an old man, the oldest
> in the village.
> She sat down next to him.
>
> Their two faces were close together,
> and hers began
> to wrinkle up again.

Physically interconnective, all beings take shape in shared lives with one another, consciously and subconsciously, by choice and chance alike. Trickster skitters in the shadows of these more serious perceptions.

Each story-name resists gloss. Each carries its own local revelation in the world. Turtle Wait (the teller's own signature among the names) exercises the patience necessary for the event to come and name him:

> Other turtle watchers gave up. But he would
> wait until *that* turtle came out
> to tell *him* things
> and no one else.

According to her own temper, Quiet Until the Thaw remained silent in winter (the Cree have ''many, many, many words for silence,'' Norman emphasizes):

> The first winter this happened
> we looked in her mouth to see
> if something was frozen. Her tongue
> maybe, or something else in there.
>
> But after the thaw she spoke again
> and told us it was fine for her that way.
>
> So each spring we
> looked forward to that.

Looking forward to spring in each person, tribally bound, is tested as well as sparked by trickster's delights. Thomas Johns Bear calms a stuttering pond with a song-poem, remarking, "Each of us does it differently" (*WBC* 93).

Hard domestic lessons stud the games too. Once a married man wanted to go and meet the misanthropic Wolverine, "tricky one, clever one," against the traditional advice of the village.

> So I started saying bad things
> about him, rotten things,
> all lies.
> I said, "Wolverine shits out whole hills."
> The next day my house was covered.
> Then I said, "Wolverine sneaks up on people."
> When I got home my wife was gone.

But Wolverine *then* shows up to offer the man a new wife!—*not* a fat one, this time, he adds. Confused and momentarily conciliated, the husband takes the bait, declining to fight with Wolverine.

> Suddenly, he threw off his face
> and fur skin. It was my wife!
> "Wolverine sent me! Ha!" she said.
> Then she ran back
> into the woods forever.

The story of the Wolverine-in-the-wife imparts a comic marital warning about infidelity. Apart from a lie coming round true, and reacquaintance with the Wolverine's legendary intractibility, the husband's prodigal curiosity leads to his abandonment, it seems. He conspires with dispositions better left alone.

The Swampy Cree concern for particulars down in things, termed "the science of the concrete" by Lévi-Strauss,[31] surfaces in epistemological stories: the lone old warrior hearing ancestors moaning from the trees, the callow youth leaving stilts standing in the shallows as he hides from a cloud, the aged men carving owl sticks to fly in the face of ridicule, the homeless hunter crouching in a bear coat "between" villages and human-animal identities, the boy balancing turtle shells to turn weeping into laughter around the village. The young girl, Saw Through to the Bottom, stayed alone near a murky lake everyone feared until she "*saw through the mud on top*." Sturgeon churned on the bottom! Others began to see through their muddy fears, and eventually all came round to the girl's discovery, "after *our* babies got fat / on sturgeon."

Like the bridging duality of the trickster wishing bone, names finally yoke opposites and wed contraries. Pollen Leggings rolled in the flower fields picking up yellow "leggings in the summer!" and,

> When she would come back to the village
> one old woman always asked her,
> "Do the flowers have pollen yet?"
> This girl would sit down on a blanket,
> then get up, leaving pollen from her legs
> as the answer! It was a game
> those two did just among themselves.
>
> That went on, too.
>
> Pollen leggings, yes. We saw the chance
> to hear a winter *and* summer thing
> in a name.
> So we didn't let that pass by.

In continuity with the seasons of life, a sisterly bond ties the old woman, waiting in the village, to the sensuous young girl, rolling in the meadows: winter to summer, age to youth, memory to experience, word to deed. Trickster's sap rises each spring. The two share an expectancy of the earth's perennial, sensual blooming. Words-as-questions elicit actions-as-answers, where people "speak" across differences many ways; they discover complementarity in dissimilarity, when the "game" is mutually played.

Changed His Mind ends the naming poems touching down gently in the-way-things-are. Not waywardness as an end, but "home," is the still center of these tales. The pragmatic aspect of Cree reality brings home an inverse sense of fantasy and play. The second group of poems grounds itself in a resolution that is the mirror complement to poems in the first group: a settling sense of reality, springing inversely analogous to the fall trickster, who was transformed by the wishing bone into a migrating snow goose and flew away. *What-is*, after all, is the object of these wishful, tricky lessons. Changed His Mind continually boasts what he *will* do unnaturally with his hands, only to right his wishes by what he *does* on his feet; finally rooted and upright, as well as mobile, "He walked on his feet / home." Daring, magic, and invention come down to earth where they begin, grounded in the truths-in-things coming home, all the while storytellers imagine the marvelous things possible in our common world. "It's better the way you are," a horizon voice tells an owl "thinking" it has changed into a grand pine.

The-way-we-are, tricking or naming or truth-telling, flying away or touching down in the earth, generates the tales, the traditions, and the people. "I hope you heard this clearly," Norman recalls how the Cree close a telling. "That's it for now."

TRICKSTER AFOOT

The Wishing Bone Cycle rounds off with an *atayohkawin*, or "sacred story," from the traditional Cree Trickster myths. The tale features Wichikapache, old "BORN OF OLD," tramping out of the past. "Nutoka moo" [Listen], "Usa puyew usu wapiw" [He goes backward, looks forward]. If a teller "talks" backward to look sensically forward, inverting things to right them, he also resolves the paradox of "old" history recurrent, the past present in things. And in the tribal codes, provisionally specific to each event, Trickster wanders around, from folly to foolery, instructing by recreant exaggeration. The sacred language of poetry reveals the world from the inside out. For the Cree, morality is not an issue objectifiable as "truth," but more how people come to know their world. They learn through the drama of presentation, the historical showing forth of trial and error.

Jacob Slowstream ritualizes the tales with self-conscious artistry: the third-person voice of mythic history speaks here, once removed from the personal mask of the wishing bone narrator in the beginning. That is, rather than conjuring up I-the-trickster or The-Trickster-in-all-of-us, Slowstream recounts the classical tales of Wichikapache, the Trickster of sacred origins. Here the Swampy Cree audience and teller commonly acknowledge their mythic genesis and comic continuations.

Trickster improvises out of hungers and humors. He is an original incarnation of the forked wishing bone:

> ". . . most things
> get at least two names,"

> Wichikapache said.
> "For instance,
> BORN OF OLD,
> which is me."

The first child and oldest father, BORN OF OLD embodies the generative paradox of an ancient reality that won't settle down or stay put: the base curiosity and restlessness in man, snaking him into and, by the same errant wit, out of trouble. It is an ancient observation among cultures. The Homeric trickster's name, "many-minded" Odysseus, is played upon analogously as "travel," special "talk," and "trouble" in *The Odyssey* (XIX, 409, as is still cognate in odometer, ode, and odium). Autolykos, in ill temper over his own travel and trouble coming to the birth, named his grandson "Odysseus," variously translated and punned upon as "man of all-odds" (W. H. D. Rouse), "Man of Wrath" (Albert Cook), and "distasteful" (Richmond Lattimore). Farther north, but in proximate mythic time, Wichikapache's inquisitiveness specializes and curses him, kills and renews him, takes him new places only to repeat "the old ways."[32]

"We-are-going-walking," say the Cree, a formulaic invitation to walk and watch, a kind of "let-us-go-and-see."[33] The Cree phrase Norman recalls most fondly translates as "focused wandering." It suggests taking the cognizant time necessary, knowing a destination, to travel alertly, registering the terrain, life systems, and events of the journey. Given the right attention, the Cree contend, the journier finds his "home" focused in the places he wanders, while moving purposefully. There is no sense of estrangement in the "wilderness," only relative aspects of being at home. The concept applies as equally to storytelling as to traveling. Such experience clothes the traveler in a story to carry back home, reuniting what Walter Benjamin sees as the oldest of tellers, wanderer and keeper of the hearth, seafarer and husbandman.[34]

In the beginning, BORN OF OLD packs his things and goes walking, hearing "animal noises" all around. Then in the distance, a moose deer runs away from him (the tales clearly serve to train younger Cree in the ways of a hunting-gathering culture).

> "Wait a minute," Wichikapache said, "Little Brother,
> don't run. Let's talk!"
> *Let's talk, yes, that's what he said.*

143

Slowstream opens his atayohkawin with the fabled wandering fool inviting an animal to stop and talk. The incident seems reflexive of his own audience: the artist offers a tale to capture his listeners' attention; the mythic predator entices an unwitting beast into conversation (as we say, "to chew the fat"); the ancient Trickster, in narrative disguise, plays the world-at-large for its very life. Audience to all, the animals stop and listen and watch, alertly suspicious of such invitations. "It got quiet." This stillness focuses a dramatic humor that begins things with mythic talk between spirits and commoners. Trickster asks for sympathy from the wary moose deer, who

> approached *carefully,*
> but not careful
> in its thinking

and ". . . died with this trick in its eyes." And so the teller seizes our attention, opens eyes, offers food for thought. A serious play informs Cree lessons to be learned here by all, the traditional premium on human attention and care, historically ritualized at the core of tribal values.

Appetite incarnate, Wichikapache dupes others by talking his tricks. Meanwhile, he plots to kill and eat them, always wanting more, always walking on. Creatures laugh at his machinations, trick him back when they can, and stay ever careful of his contrariness—not to be trusted, always skulking about—a mischievous thief whose presence is announced when anything goes wrong, backfires, or seems deviously other than it is, lies to boot. Trickster gets blamed for the things that timelessly go wrong. This onus makes him a comically rich, composite god, and Indian tales evince a resilient faith in this maker-bungler who can be parodied. The storytellings implicitly seem to trust the god's forgiving humors, to know when things are being played.[35] All offenses can be granted in good faith in these stories.

Wichikapache mirrors people's foolish conceits, their cussed inability to take advice and learn from error. Nonetheless, he acts out an appealing, if comic egoism, bragging when foiled, "*Who do you think made this world?*" Who, indeed, the audience asks. This mock god-child plays a sacred spirit, essentially human and animal in unregenerate ways. Trickster is a liminal more-and-less-than-animal-human-person, as Victor Turner would have it in *The Forest of Symbols,* covering the distance between home and the wilds.[36] Trickster mixes up characteristics of animal, human, and god, confusing distinctions within extended kinship systems. He is the foolish literalist. Masking as a deer, skunk, or goose, Wichikapache the "Imitator" burlesques the laws of mimicry in the natural order of things.[37] Always the egoist, he wants to change into "*A large fly!*" among his "little little brothers" feeding on a deer's head.

The Cree tacitly seem to value imaginative strategies of masking, from tale telling, to naming, to still hunting, but would caution, most assuredly, against confusing real particulars among orders of beings. Their direct simplicity does not betray any naiveté. Stories tell the world with varying successes, names mean for better or worse, and a bad hunter eventually goes hungry. There is, after all, a survivor's artistry in the play of disguise and identity, beyond the assumption, perhaps too easily cast, that a human can become a bear, just anyone a god, or a god ever would deign to be a skunk. Wichikapache thus parodies the blind seer, so honored as visionary singer among all tribes. He juggles and loses his eyeballs in the bushes, trying to exorcise a headache,[38] or he stumbles around blinded by a deer's head he wished to eat and fell into.

The Cree hold that animals gave birth to Trickster, then to people, for a sense of humor, just as they gave language to people for reciprocal exchanges. The northern Indians also believe that "other-than-human" Witigos prey terribly on "human-persons," as Trickster in turn comically stalks "other-than-human-persons." The ice-hearted Witigo darkens Wichikapache's foolishness and makes this comic fool prove himself necessary to Cree survival. Between these inversional figures of comedy and tragedy, Cree villagers work out their interdependences along an interlocking food chain not at all dominated by man. It is what Konrad Lorenz, in the epigraph to this chapter, calls "humility before the earth and its processes." To feed and be fed upon, no less, keeps a hunter or gatherer symbiotically aware of how to survive the natural scheme of things.[39]

Challenger to Witigo's tragic fixity, Wichikapache gambols to regenerate the world, to change, or to make over, or simply to underscore a reality ever in flux. Trickster teaches, by comic negative example, that this shifting world bears careful looking into. Masking and duplicity are naturally embedded in behavior, as every naturalist observes. The living survive through and despite trickery, perhaps even learning from its inventive, if untrustworthy ways.

So it happens that others come to count on Wichikapache, the Cree hold. They share a world of problems with this scoundrel, stay careful of him, and depend on him to keep them alert, laughing, and sharp to the rules of survival and play. The ice-hearted Witigo looms over their failures. Pitted against this winter monster is a failed wit, nonetheless a comic survivor.

As a Trickster, furthermore, Wichikapache is not even predictably duplicitous, but sometimes evolves from reality's fool to world transformer. Wichikapache is always capable of reversal, even for positive ends. His foolish mirror to man finally may be the most instructive lesson of all, as the aheroic foil to human pretention.

Trickster honors a promise to weasel, renowned for sharpening its teeth on icicles, who bites the cannibal's ice heart to death. Without humor or dreams, the Witigo lacks any wishing bone to protect its heart.

> There was
> *screaming*.
> But when she died
> Wichikapache was the only one still screaming.
>
> The weasel
> had done the job well.

Wichikapache thanks weasel with the "beautiful," not to say useful, gift of protective coloration through the changing seasons.

So this Born of Old, for better or worse, evolves comically toward a culture hero. His trials illustrate the survival of spring player over fall destroyer, summer's continuity over winter's end. It may be his most terrible joke of all to be left screaming in the arms of a cannibal monster, but he lives to scream, and tramp on. . . .

> Wichikapache looked for people.
> Just to be difficult.
> Just to be contrary he did this.

Switching sexes, mating with a vain young man, birthing wolf cubs, and ducking out, Wichikapache returns to mock and stir up more trouble. His since remarried husband, now less vain, prods the errantly tricky "wife" to go suckle their pups on "his" feet.

> "No!"
> Wichikapache said,
> "I leave!"
> He said this
> laughing to himself.

He kept walking.

Nibènegenesábe's tale ends on the regenerative refusal of the contrary to take his place in the tribe, lurking just outside the communal norms and alliances, always moving on. Comically dispossessed, for the most part disregarding interdependencies, Trickster stays on the prowl in the shadows of time, never satisfied, alert to whatever new original sin disrupts the world and keeps it going on going.

7

BLACKFEET WINTER BLUES:
James Welch

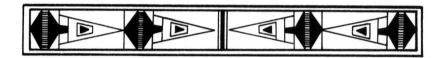

As we turned away,
A woman blue as night
stepped from my bundle,
rubbed her hips and sang
of a country like this far off.

—"Verifying the Dead"

Born in Browning, Montana, in the first year of the Second World War, James Welch (Blackfeet/Gros Ventre) was raised Native American and educated mainstream American, with a college degree from the University of Montana where he now teaches. He sifts the debris of two cultures in conflict. Indian ruins scatter amid the wreckage of Western materialism: junked cars, tarpaper shacks, blown tires, rusting radiators, discarded bathtubs, shattered glass . . . and the memories of traditions past. The haunting tribal names, Speakthunder, Earthboy, Star Boy, Bear Child, remind the Blackfeet of times-that-might-have-been, old myths half remembered and half made-up.

Times change, elders "look back" to worn "tracks," idealize a mythic past out-of-reach even in "the old days," and in despair "stumble-bum down the Sunday street." So records the poem, "Grandma's Man." Parts refuse to mix, and differences are the rule. All things tense in incongruity and incompatibility: "alone, afraid, stronger," the poems say paradoxically, in "a world of money, promise and disease."[1]

The present desecrates the sacred past, as Indian memories warp in fantasy and pain. Heart Butte, once a holy height for men in quest of vision, crumbles littered with dreaming drunks, Moose Jaw is winter-locked, Havre lined with bars and no-luck fishermen. Between boilermakers and too many fingers of scotch, lost men tell tall tales of epic catches. The white "airplane man" once bagged a thirty-pound Minnesota pike, he brags in *Winter in the Blood*. Stuck in Montana, the Indian narrator mutters,

> "You'd be lucky to catch a cold here."
> "Caught some nice little rainbows too. Pan size."
> "There aren't any rainbows." [*WB* 56]

There are no longer any covenants between Christian or Indian gods and these fallen sinners, wasting away in a hostile parody of Eden. All stands winter-still after a flood of white invasion. The narrator's understated dialogue puts a drag on artificial lures and big white lies, letting characters speak beyond themselves in low-keyed, delayed exchanges. "Not even a sucker" swims the polluted Milk River, the narrator flatly contends.

Welch resists any illusions that would meliorate pain: begin in earth with bone of *what is*, the "blood" definition by tribe, and ask no more. "Up there in Montana," Welch has said, "there are bones all over the place and the wind blows all the time. All of the towns that I write about, all of the country, is real."[2] The artist searches through "a dream of knives and bones" to piece together skeletons of the present, heard in the rattle of the old ways. "Only an Indian knows who he is," Welch argues in a second interview, "—an individual who just happens to be an Indian—and if he has grown up on a reservation he will naturally write about what he knows. And hopefully he will have the toughness and fairness to present his material in a way that is not manufactured by conventional stance. . . . What I mean is—whites have to adopt a stance; Indians already have one."[3]

The Indian stance may be native, but never easy. The Blackfeet were born into a winter that was always severe, a northern and western climate of mind. Seasons turn with exacting change, falling away: "A damned, ugly cold. Fall into winter" (*WB* 159). Even during the searing heat of late summer, northern Plainsmen know winter down in their bones. This knowledge meets the chill of necessity. It breeds a "hunger" that "sharpens the eye," says the blind grandfather, a Tiresian seer of *Winter in the Blood*, whose "fingers were slick, papery, like the belly of a rattlesnake" (*WB* 78). Estranged ancestors, such as grandfather snake and grandmother spider, "are best left alone," the old ones say (*WB* 171).

The Montana Blackfeet were long considered the fiercest "hostiles" on the Great Plains, the last northern tribe to negotiate a truce with Washington. The popular historian, George Grinnell, wrote in 1892: "Fifty years ago the name Blackfeet was one of terrible meaning to the white traveler who passed across that desolate buffalo-trodden waste which lay to the north of the Yellowstone River and east of the Rocky Mountains."[4] During 1883–1884, "the winter of starvation," more than a quarter of the remaining Blackfeet died of hunger as the Great White Father systematically eradicated the last of the buffalo herds. That fall of 1883, the men went hunting and there were no buffalo. All but a few hundred lay carrion on the plains. By 1894 the Indian Bureau thought to make reservation-settling, potato-farming, beef-eating, hymn-singing Christians out of once nomadic buffalo-hunters who worshiped the sun and now starved. The Indian Commissioner ordered:

> Sun dances, Indian mourning, Indian medicine, beating
> of the tomtom, gambling, wearing of Indian costumes
> . . . selling, trading, exchanging or giving away anything
> issued to them have been prohibited, while other less perni-
> cious practices, such as horse-racing, face-painting, etc.,
> are discouraged.[5]

Two generations later and no less "hostile" in spirit, James Welch inherits a resistance to the "Big Knives." Wielding a pen in place of a knife, he asks in "The Renegade Wants Words,"

> Were we wild for wanting men to listen
> to the earth, to plant only by moons?

The key to Welch's art seems an adversary's sense of reality—attitudes that resist, counter, and invert conventions. "I like to warp reality a little bit," Welch admits.[6]

The ethnologist, Clark Wissler, records one of the earliest Blackfeet creation parables, told and retold from ancient times, about Old Man (*Na'pi*) and Old Woman (*Kipitaki*). These original beings were wedded contraries, a combination of creator spirits and first people, personified on occasion as the sun and the moon (literally, the "night-red-light" or "night-sun," as among other plains tribes). In the beginning of the world, Old Man gets the first say, Old Woman the second, making things-as-they-are. Na'pi unwittingly plays a trickster, consistently the sacred clown. He thinks that people should have no hard work; Kipitaki, ever pragmatic, reverses the idea, to cull the good workers from the bad. Old Man next would have the eyes and mouth vertical on people; Old Woman changes the position crossways, as things are. Old Man figures people need ten fingers on each hand; Old Woman says that's too many, they'll get in the way. When Na'pi suggests placing genitals at the navel, Kipitaki argues that childbearing would be too easy, and people wouldn't care for their children. So the "order" of things interweaves divine nonsense and correc-tive sense, the gods playing against a "working" etiology. Old Woman sounds the worldly countervoice to Old Man's original naiveté.

This generative couple suggests a Blackfeet epistemology still operative for Welch. A "married" dialectic of absurd initial impressions distorts the world comically, then must be corrected by a firmer sense of why-things-are-what-they-are. The nature of things is contrary at the heart of any marriage.

The tale continues. Old Man and Old Woman are stumped by life and death. Old Man proposes a gambling solution. He'll toss a buffalo chip on the water; if it floats, people will die a few days, then live forever. If it sinks, they die for good. "No," Old Woman counters, "we'll throw a rock on the water."

So death comes to be, as it is, the draw in a fickle game of inversions, and the living lose. "If people didn't die forever," Old Woman reasons close to the bone, they wouldn't "feel sorry for each other, and there would be no sympathy in the world." Old Man must agree.

The parable ends on a reversing coda: Old Woman bears a daughter, who dies. She would recant the order of things, in mime of her husband's first-say folly. "No," Old Man stands on the last word, "we fixed it once."[7]

This Blackfeet myth illustrates the dialectic nature of a world where men and women are fated as counterfools. Reason meets its limitations, wedded to folly. Reality teeters on a fulcrum of absurdity. Things get "fixed" at cost. Human fantasy recoils from an exacting reality, and neither rules. People are destined to act out adversary designs, an interplay between men and women, first and last, life and death, humor and pain. The hard sinking stone of death is the only fixed point of life. Play here is for keeps, darkly comic, seasoned in grief.

BACK-TRACKING

> Meaning gone, we dance for pennies now,
> our feet jangling dust that hides the bones
> of sainted Indians. Look away and we are gone.
> Look back, tracks are there, a little faint,
> our song strong enough for headstrong hunters
> to look ahead to one more kill.
> —"Blackfeet, Blood and Piegan Hunters"

Welch's first novel, *Winter in the Blood* (1974), opens in a borrow pit, the ditch that drains the road to the deserted Earthboy homestead. "In the tall weeds of the borrow pit, I took a leak and watched the sorrel mare, her colt beside her, walk through burnt grass to the shady side of the log-and-mud cabin. It was called the Earthboy place, although no one by that name (or any other) had lived in it for twenty years" (*WB* 3). This windy, vacant space, once fertile and peopled, is now ghosted with weeds. The earth has been dredged to crown a highway over the prairie where Indians once lived in harmony with all things, or so the myths contend when men look back. The tenant farmers moved away, but their names haunt from the dispossessed past, as the borrow pit drains the white man's blacktop where an Indian empties his bladder. Words no longer speak integrally with the things they name, but are what things are "called."

The closest the narrator comes to a name is his drunkenly comic father in the borrow pit, "peeing what he said was my name in the snow," on the way to visit an unacknowledged grandfather (*WB* 182). Christian names with lost referents—Agnes, Teresa, John, Moses—and out-of-place Indian names like First Raise and Lame Bull drift among incongruous place-names—Malta and Moose Jaw, Havre and Heart Butte, State Highway #2 and the Milk River. The narrator confesses his lost identity, "I was as distant from myself as a hawk from the moon" (*WB* 4). His contrary mother, in turn, complains of his dead father, "He was a wanderer—just like you, just like all these damned Indians" (*WB* 26). On the fringes straggling home, these dislocated natives are the butt of Trickster's grim humor. They descend from "Old Man" and "Old Woman."

The thirty-two-year-old narrator remains nameless and faceless through the story. According to Gros Ventre tradition, a man at thirty-two (grown up through four-year groupings of age-graded societies) goes on a vision quest, looks for a wife, and qualifies for initiation in the Crazy Lodge: this on the basis of self-sacrifice, "crying for pity," "seeking a grandfather," and mystic cleansing whose insight leads to right conduct.[8] So, too, the persona of the alienated wanderer, martyred at thirty-two, is a modernist rhetoric of fiction for nameless invisible men on existential pilgrimage.

In this "No-Name" narrator of *Winter in the Blood*, ancient as Odysseus in the cannibal monster's cave, Welch ironically updates the Blackfeet tradition that forbids one to speak his own name to others (as with Kroeber's "Ishi," the last surviving California Yahi who, not allowed to speak his given name, could refer to himself only as "a man").[9] Still, to be here without kin or name grants a measure of anonymous freedom, among dislocated referents of dispossessed cultures. And "No-Name" first and finally serves as the reader's mask, a participant-observer in Indian storytelling tradition, who takes on the narrator's pain. The reader looks through this "first" person, akin in interior anonymity, rather than looking at and labeling him. It is all very confusing, as Indians well know.

Human sufferings and survivals distantly correlate in Welch's fiction, muted desperations of modernism from Eliot's *The Waste Land* to Pinter's *No Man's Land*. Indian crises of culture and history echo through an urban cold war, where red and white refugees cry out the need to simplify, to identify self, to uncover essentials, to trace an archaeology of traditional roots, to find a design down *in* things. "Lost, in this (and its environments) as in a forest," Williams wrote in *In The American Grain*, "I do believe the average American to be an Indian, but an Indian robbed of his world."[10] So in a sense this novel is Indian in subject, but modern and essentially human, an integration of red and white laments.

The narrator of *Winter in the Blood* stands before the family grave sites: "no headstone, no name, no dates. My brother. . . ." Only a white priest from Harlem would tax a person with a biblical given name affixed to an Indian surname—John First Raise, the mock adventist father, and Moses First Raise, the death-exiled brother.[11] Teresa First Raise, like her canonized namesake exhumed in the nineteenth century, is as coldly fresh as the day they buried her first husband. Brother "Mose" lies in bondage as the biblical Moses under the deserted Earthboy allotment on the Blackfeet promised land. "Earthboy calls me from my dream": the novel opens with a poem fragment, broken off from the whole, "Dirt is where the dreams must end." And Montana, like Canaan, belies the myth of milk and honey.

Somewhere behind Earthboy's fall lingers a pastoral memory of the creation, a Christian "Old Man" or Adam, whose Hebrew name once meant "red earth."

> Earthboy: so simple his name
> should ring a bell for sinners.

The Bible records a Christian origin myth: "And the Lord God formed man of the dust of the ground, and breathed into his nostrils the breath of life; and man became a living soul" (Genesis 1:7). Now exiled from Eden, face-down and "dirty," Earthboy Adamically suffers the fruit of "red earth" disobedience: the bruised snake (no longer grandfather) eats dust, women ruled by husbands conceive in sorrow, and men farm a dead land. Christian history weighs heavily on Old Man and Old Woman:

> cursed is the ground for thy sake
> in sorrow shalt thou eat of it all the days of thy life;
> Thorns also and thistles shall it bring forth to thee;
> and thou shalt eat the herb of the field:
> In the sweat of thy face shalt thou eat bread,
> till thou return unto the ground;
> for out of it wast thou taken;
> for dust thou art,
> and unto dust shalt thou return.

> [Genesis 3:17–19]

Back home, John First Raise stretches "dead"-drunk beneath a styrofoam cross, his grave fallen a foot into the earth, as though the dead kept dying in borrow pits sluicing white highways. Soiled family names scatter, estranged from the mother earth, and "white" kids taunt "dirty" dark Indians, "comic" in their losses.

> Bones should never tell a story
> to a bad beginner. I ride
> romantic to those words,
> those foolish claims that he
> was better than dirt, or rain

that bleached his cabin
white as bone.

In a disquieting mixture of surreal poetry and bone-dry prose, *Winter in the Blood* begins with Indians tilting off Turtle Island. "Riding" the Earthboy foreshadows an unending Indian fall, a descent from unregenerate quarter sections of land, drawn and quartered by the barbed wire of white allotment.

Welch's Milk River runs muddy, polluted purple from a sugar beet factory, fished out. The old medicine man, Fish, prophesied a century ago (just as the Fisher King vegetation myths looked to Christian trial in a desert wasteland, one day to be drained by Eliot's "tumid river") that white men would spoil the streams to gut women and fish for sport (see the narrator's *delirium tremens* opening chapter 16). When the game commission stocks the waters, the fish don't even die, but simply disappear, as does the game commission. The "airplane man" flies in to the promised angling land as a parodied white avatar on the lam from the F.B.I. "Took a little something that wasn't exactly mine—," he admits, fessing up to Western history (*WB* 103).

This fugitive Fisher King touches down to cast in sterile waters, barhops the banks of the tumid river, and recruits an Indian sidekick for the price of a faded blue Falcon to replace Tonto's twenty-three-year-old white swayback, "Bird." The two abort an escape under a full moon into Canada, where Sitting Bull with his renegade Lakota and Chief Joseph with his fleeing Nez Percé tried to outrun the cavalry in 1877. The historical irony of an Indian helping a white man flee America salts the narrator's disbelief: "I can't figure out why you picked me—maybe I should tell you, those guards like to harass Indians. They can never figure out why an Indian should want to go to Canada" (*WB* 104). The comic displacement of these scenes, the hilarity and disbelief, all serve to focus the narrator's pain and allow him to play out the nightmare of an absurd existence.[12] A purple teddy bear with a red felt tongue, or Doris Day with her toe stuck in a bottle on a matinee poster, grant the narrator enough distance on his own folly to endure, as the old jokes go, to grin and bear it and go on.

The comic clarity of the plot releases a lowly humorous poetry. Descriptions startle and quicken in flintlike strokes. John First Raise freezes "a blue-white lump in the endless skittering whiteness" of the borrow pit (*WB* 26). Grandmother's eyes burn "black like a spider's belly" (*WB* 43). A "zipless" lover's breasts spread "like puddings beneath the sheet" (*WB*

93). The imagery and idiom of working ranchhands, waitresses, bartenders, and day laborers are selectively compressed in a work of art not so much made up, as salvaged from the low-life reality just off reservations, t-shirts and Levis, Pepsi and potato chips, Fritos and vin rosé. In penetrantly common attention, the narrator records a world of working Western things: his stepfather in high rubber farming boots, his mother rubbing Mazola oil into a wooden bowl, a *Sports Afield* ad for a lure that calls to fish "in their own language," a John Deere tractor and Farmall pickup haying a fall pasture, an American Legion punchboard paying chocolate covered cherries, a girl friend's teeth crème de menthe green in a barroom, a "coarse black hair on the white pillow" in a one-night-stand hotel room where a vacuum cleaner hums "somewhere far away."

The unreal nonsense of bar banter tells the contrary reality about men and women. "Shit" ricochets up and down vinyl stools, chorus to a sexual come-on dropped as a put-down. The narrator winks at himself alone in the bar mirror; the barmaid glances and scowls back, catching the reflection of his misdirected pass; the two spar at cross-purposes in the half-light; and all of a sudden they wake from screwing in a hotel bed. The next chapter opens in *delirium tremens*.

Real details prove the accuracy of this fiction. A balking horse "crowhops" and "sunfishes" and "hunkers" beneath a stubborn rider (*WB* 73). The narrator watches a young tough pick lint from his black shirt and his girlfriend's brother blow a fleck of dandruff from a pocket comb. He sees a tuft of black hair in a bus driver's ear. This Indian No-Name describes a world of minute detail for the reader to see and hear, as older Blackfeet tellers drew an audience into the performing experience of a tale. The words snap. The morning after a drunk, "I drank a long sucking belly-ful of water from the tap" (*WB* 64). The narrative voice is edged and braced with the sting of a plains death chant.

> It could have been the country, the burnt prairie beneath a
> blazing sun, the pale green of the Milk River valley, the milky
> waters of the river, the sagebrush and cottonwoods, the dry,
> cracked gumbo flats. The country had created a distance as
> deep as it was empty, and the people accepted and treated each
> other with distance.
>
> But the distance I felt came not from country or people; it
> came from within me. I was as distant from myself as a hawk
> from the moon. [*WB* 4]

Getting through is the novel's staying power, taking courage from a direct language of words-as-things-are. The novel's chapters seem chiseled like petroglyphs, isolated in starkly precise planes. Scenes string out on a wire of pain just short of breaking, and the reader sees by glimpses, moment by moment, as the narrative almost fails to cohere and go on. Because and in spite of its fragmentation, its despair and loss, the story involves the reader in the struggle to survive.

The plot hangs together almost with a mock pretense of balance and unity. Edward Curtis documents that *seven* represents the Blackfeet mystic number, the traditional union of odd and even; the old warriors called Ursa Major "Seven," and all sacred things were painted with a red earth called "seven paint."[13] In Welch's novel, seven primary characters are doubled by seven incidental characters: nameless narrator, Teresa (Christianized mother), Agnes (Cree girl friend), Lame Bull (breed stepfather), the khaki "airplane man" (a white "brother"), unnamed Indian grandmother ("Old Woman"), and Yellow Calf ("Old Man," unknown as such, until the end). These seven are understudied by Long Knife (the one-day hired hand), Malvina and Marlene (bar girls), Dougie (the "brother"-in-law caricature), Ferdinand Horn and his wife in turquoise frame glasses, and Doagie (the absent half-breed "grandfather").

The narrator's girl friend deserts him, and his mother marries a squat, half-breed farmer. No-Name dredges local bars from Malta to Havre, to retrieve his stolen razor and rifle, tired totems of a man's virility in a worn-out medicine bundle, "my sack of possessions that I no longer possessed" (*WB* 69). The airplane man picks up No-Name to implicate the Indian in a bizarre escape. The plot falters.

Then, in quick sequence, the grandmother dies; the blind hermit indirectly admits to their blood union from that first "starvation winter" of 1883; the deaths of the father and brother, ten and twenty years back, surface from No-Name's tragic memory; and the novel ends on the death of Bird, farting in a muddy rain, following the gallows humor of "old woman's" burial:

> The hole was too short, but we didn't discover this until we
> had the coffin halfway down. One end went down easily
> enough, but the other stuck against the wall. Teresa wanted us
> to take it out because she was sure that it was the head that
> was lower than the feet. Lame Bull lowered himself into the

grave and jumped up and down on the high end. It went
down a bit more, enough to look respectable. [*WB* 198]

With comic futility and a dash of Shakespearean gravedigging, the survivors
plant corpses like potatoes, using a ''spud bar'' to break through the frozen
crust of the earth. The wasteland imagery calls on Nile regeneration myths
of Isis and Osiris, not to mention the long-awaited resurrection of Christ,
revived in the Ghost Dances that swept plains tribes in the late 1880s.[14]

No-Name's last gesture is to toss his grandmother's tobacco pouch into
her open grave. This anticlimactic, dark comic end is anticipated halfway
through the novel, when an old man in straw hat and green gabardines,
nameless in a cafe, laughs ''Heh heh'' three times, rolls his own smoke,
strikes a farmer's match on his fly, and pitches facedown in a bowl of
oatmeal. ''Deader'n a doornail,'' No-Name swears (*WB* 100). The plot tilts
in disbelief, absurdly off-balance within its realistic detail, as though reality
could be, in fact, a cartoon of itself. ''What do you say, sport?'' No-Name
quips, walking by Malvina's sullen son eating cereal. ''My name's not
sport,'' the boy sneers his mother's one-night lover out the door (*WB* 93).

If the novel registers as disjointed, the poetry dismembered by conflict,
Welch binds his art tenuously with a courage to face the truth. There is
ironic beauty in the pain of this fiction.

No-Name does not give up and he does not tell lies. Words splinter
the broken bones of his innocence in a language of hard bitter things, driving winds, a winter *in* the blood. The exacting elements that threaten life
give life.

The narrative rides on real talk that cuts abrasively: the bartender takes
a minute off ''to bleed my lizard,'' and Bird drops ''a walking crap'' on the
way to Yellow Calf's cabin. Trickster's realism here trades on the clownish
offense of *what is*, coupled with comic distance in the human disbelief
toward the truth of things. It is a sad and bad joke that people refuse what is
real.

Characters are detailed in action, against a natural setting, without
psychological flourishes. Grandma rocks and smokes, saying nothing, plotting to knife the Cree girl friend who reads movie magazines, dreams herself
Raquel Welch, and deserts with the narrator's rifle and razor. (The historian Grinnell wrote that in the old days a warrior's primary wife, ''sits-
beside-him,'' would be punished for infidelity by cutting off her nose or

158

ears, and a second offense would warrant death.)[15] When No-Name does find his girl friend, she won't go back with him; he can only advise her to get a skill. "Learn shorthand," he says. "It's essential" (*WB* 124).

Like speaking into a freezing rain, the art of survival in such a fiction depends on knowing less, not more. As Yellow Calf says of his cabin, "It's easier to keep it sparse than to feel the sorrows of possessions" (*WB* 77). With elliptical compression, the narrator's own brand of shorthand stays close to an elemental reality: homely witticisms, bar talk, street truths, country know-how, the common knowledge of ages—no more or less than Montana reservation life itself.

Northern Montana is a land, Grinnell notes, where field crops come through once in four or five years. Farming is still something of a bad Indian joke on a reservation that includes Glacier County. Winter temperatures fall fifty degrees below zero. Welch's seasons of birth, growth, and harvest, imaged in green, yellow, and red, are leached toward winter-snow shadows "blue like death" to a searing white. When "Christmas Comes to Moccasin Flat," the poet laments in lines outside *Winter in the Blood*, "drunks drain radiators for love / or need, chiefs eat snow and talk of change, / an urge to laugh pounding their ribs." In an environment polluted inside and out, Welch's fictional figures drink chintzy distillations of "white man's water"—whiskey boilermakers, crème de menthe, Coke, vin rosé, pop-top beer, and grape soda (the first alcohol sold to the Blackfeet in the 1870s was laced with snakebites such as black chewing tobacco, red peppers, Jamaica ginger, and black molasses).[16]

After a time the blues of *Winter in the Blood*—tones of distance, separation, and loss—blanch to a winter monochrome. The once symbolic balance of colors in the four winds is dominated by blue turning "that colorless allcolor" of melting-pot white, as Ishmael remarks of democratic atheism in Melville's *Moby Dick*. Just so, the women (Malvina, Marlene) and the men (Dougie, Doagie) smear into a half-shadow blurring away from the narrator. Small blue details code the background with ironic diminishment. The cows eat "blue-joint stubble" on the late fall prairie when "things grow stagnant, each morning following blue on the heels of the last" (so-called Indian summer is the illusion of a plains fall). Teresa's black hair turns "almost blue" with age. The Cree girl friend appears in a "short blue dress" exposing her thighs in a bar. The airplane man wears a blue neckerchief and blue-and-white striped sport coat. Marlene's faded blue jeans, panties loose inside, bunch on a hotel room floor. A touring professor's carsick daughter wears a blue-and-white beaded Indian headband. Ferdinand Horn's wife wraps a light blue hankie around her can of grape pop. And looming over these fall blues is the white blindness of oncoming winter.

A regional novel of local revelation, *Winter in the Blood* focuses on a Blackfeet sense of place. Observations are pointed and dispassionate in a lean, scoured environment. Distance tends to slur distinctions. Vast space hyperbolizes objects.[17] In such a homeland Welch's artistic principle is ironic displacement—the distance and disparity between things. These gaps set up an uneasy tension between distortion and truth, past and present, fantasy and realism, self and other in the dialectical terrain of Old Man, Na'pi.

"Then, toward the end of September (when everyone was talking of years past), fall arrived. . . . At night the sky cleared off, revealing stars that did not give off light, so that one looked at them with the feeling that he might not be seeing them, but rather some obscure points of white that defied distance, were both years and inches from his nose. And then it turned winter. Although it had not snowed and no one admitted it, we all felt the bite of winter in our bones" (*WB* 115). Such a way is this slant-rhyming land without perspective, "a country like this far off," set down in the poem, "Verifying the Dead"—directly before the eye, yet unreachable as the sky beyond. The narrator's tone, akin to his mother's "fine bitter voice," is laced with the irony of mystery without solution. One deadly Thanksgiving long ago, Teresa played Trickster's "shut-eye dance" with Amos the family pet duck, named after an apocalyptic prophet: and so mother proves "neither good nor evil yet she is responsible for both," like the first woman, Kipitaki.

The riddling mode of the absurd is Na'pi's reality, tricks and hard-edged doubling truths. "I began to laugh, at first quietly, with neither bitterness nor humor," No-Name says, faced with his blind grandfather coming into focus. "It was the laughter of one who understands a moment in his life, of one who has been let in on the secret through luck and circumstance" (*WB* 179).

The rule to understanding: never inflate. "I never expected much from Teresa," the son says of his mother, "and I never got it" (*WB* 27). This mother's face freezes in "a clear bitter look, not without humor, that made the others of us seem excessive, too eager to talk too much" (*WB* 154). The characters here divide between castrating mothers and orphaned sons of unknown fathers, symbolized from the sorrel mare and colt in the opening scenes; to the heifer and bawling calf at Mose's death; to the end where a white-rimmed, red-eyed cow cries for her lost offspring. As a coded inset, Belva Long Knife chews on calf testicles from the campfire and glares at the shamefaced men, overgrown bastards in a bitch of a world. "Poor sonofabitch," No-Name thinks of a lonely man shoveling an irrigation ditch in the rain (*WB* 48). By the novel's end he's cursing his broken-down nag, a mud-stuck red-eyed cow, "this greedy stupid country" of strangers, and Old Man's grim humor, "a joker playing a joke" on us all.

It is a world of bad jokes, but jokes nonetheless. "What are you looking up here for?" bar graffiti mocks No-Name above the toilet, "The joke's in your hand" (*WB* 102). Just so, the unwitting grandson ribs Yellow Calf about keeping a woman around. "Come on, tell me. What have you got in those pants?" The old man counters, "Wouldn't you like to know . . ." his mouth leering open and coughing a "spasm of mirth or whatever" (*WB* 78). This "old buzzard" secretly knows that the hundred-year-old joke in his pants engendered No-Name, who now stands unwittingly before him.

Bantering sexes know Trickster's amoral appetite and wandering needs. People laugh out of their mutual pain, the sadly intimate jokes that touch through loneliness. Men and women drink and make passes in smoky blue bars, groping toward one another. No-Name remembers, out of disorientation and desire, "me laughing on the bed" at the barmaid: "pants down around my ankles, her pulling off a shoe, laughing, protesting, reaching for her . . ." (*WB* 69). Out on the road, a tourist's anemic daughter vomits in the borrow pit bushes. "A piece of red hung from the point of her chin. I smiled back at her and a sudden pain shot up through my swollen nose" (*WB* 146).

These characters' funny bones break on the jagged edges of reality, as when Randolph Scott grins "cruelly" from a billboard to trigger No-Name's repressed memory of his brother's death. The fiction dares to joke with the pain and serious play of reality. The barmaid in Malta tells No-Name of her male customers, "you don't joke with them unless you mean business" (*WB* 60). The comic come-ons of need and hunger at public crossroads outlast people's suffering, humiliation, loss, and death itself. First and last, the oldest joker around fuses into Old Man himself, the original male deity and absurdist fool, who buried his first girl-child. Na'pi's sigh is another way to sing to Old Woman "fixing" things; Trickster's groan opens into a blue grin in the exchanges between them.

Confessing his winter of starvation with the narrator's grandmother, Yellow Calf's "lips trembled into what could have been a smile" (*WB* 176). Here is the Tiresian irony of a blind lover's "in"-sight into sex, registered in "silent laughter, as though it was his blood in my veins that had told me" (*WB* 181).[18] It is the laughter of knowing, admitting, touching down in the soiled earth, and going on going on.

Such realistic humor grounds the narrative vision and illusion in honesty and awareness. This countervoice to unreality breaks through the frozen crust of a parched earth, freeing Indian spirits under a choked sky. As in the ritual "fall" and "death" of the vision quest, a time of accepted disillusion is necessary to realize the "native" American truth about one's self. The plot makes this "visionary" point with low humor. On their first visit to Yellow Calf, old Bird "panted and rumbled inside, as though a thunder-storm were growing in his belly" (*WB* 74). The ancient horse still rumbles with flatulence on the second and final visit, where a farting "instant of cor-ruption" debases No-Name to know his namesake. In recognition of his grandson, laughter at last racks Yellow Calf, as his "bony shoulders squared and hunched like the folded wings of a hawk" (*WB* 179). Old totems of revelation, thunder and hawk, are still accessible, albeit through dark comedy.

Laughter in this novel is equated with a flatulent explosion of animal noise. It signals some advance over stunned silence, in a nonsensical world of chaos and imminent catatonia. Such earthy laughter is cognate with the thunder of approaching spring storms and the rumble of a horse's guts, the old voices of Trickster. At times confused with the distant rumble of a jet passing overhead, the thunder still speaks to "questors" who will listen for visionary voices scatologically comic in a farting old horse. Eliot heard "Da" over Lake Leman, translated through the first recorded language of Sanskrit in the Upanishads, as give, sympathize, and control ("What the Thunder said" in *The Waste Land*).[19] Even more lowly, Welch hears a grandfather reestablish kinship with his winter-blooded kin in the old sim-ple recognition, "You are kind" (*WB* 180). It is not a grand gesture, but a necessary one, tempered in realistic, understated humor.

Acts of dispossession pervade the novel: the narrator pissing in the bor-row pit where his father froze and brother fell to earth from a horse, to the last scene of throwing a tobacco pouch with an arrowhead, the old medicine, into grandmother's grave. If "planting" a hundred-year-old woman in the dead earth is the end, the agony of going home sets the pervasive quest—never easy, now tormented.

> Again I felt that helplessness of being in a world of stalking white men. But those Indians down at Gable's were no bargain either. I was a stranger to both and both had beaten me.
> I should go home, I thought, turn the key and drive home. It wasn't the ideal place, that was sure, but it was the best choice. Maybe I had run out of choices. [WB 135]

Yellow Calf carries this delayed homecoming a century farther back: "We had wintered some hard times before, winters were always hard," he remembers of 1883, "but seeing Standing Bear's body made us realize that we were being punished for having left our home. The people resolved that as soon as spring came we would go home, soldiers or not" (WB 174). A bifurcated reality serves both the ideal past and the necessary present: "The horse was killed because Standing Bear would need it in the other world; they ate it because they were starving" (WB 44).

Men press on to counter adversity and keep upright. The young now must learn to "lean into the wind to stand straight," the old man counsels (WB 79). The narrator feels ancient salt in the cut of time: to see and register the incontrovertible signs of reality, to know without fantasizing power to change things. "No man should live alone," the lone grandson says in ignorance of his blind grandfather's lineage (WB 78). Most men in this novel do.

In the end Welch adapts the adversary wisdom of Na'pi. "We fixed it once," Old Man said to Old Woman of death. The creator-fool's Blackfeet name literally translates as "dawn-light-color-man."[20] To the Gros Ventre on Welch's maternal side, the other tribe in this story, the sun was known as "Traveling-White-Man," second only to "One Above White Man." Thus, Yellow Calf's name translates from the original more literally as "Dawn-Light-Color Buffalo-Calf," according to William Thackeray.[21] The name ritually refers to Old Man rising again each day in the east, a grandfather who is the Grandfather of all, Na'pi or the sun himself.

There is divine comedy in the natural renewal of this old father-fool. Time's fiber lightens in the hair of all men and women, facing the sinking

stone of death, as age begins to see from the bottom of night, and the
returning sun silvers the dark horizon. The truth of things, says Yellow
Calf, the blind seer, has "no need to be flattered. I am old and I live alone"
(*WB* 76). Grandfather squats "on the white skin of earth," and like other
animals, who sense the thunder roll of Trickster's bones, knows a recur-
rence of seasons, a return of spring, in his arthritic joints. "Bird," his mis-
named equestrian counterpart in age, carries a questing grandson with no
name through the wasteland. "You have grown so old, Bird, so old the sun
consults your bones for weather reports" (*WB* 168). Time lodges deep as
winter in these bones.

HALF-BREED'S END

We need no runners here. Booze is law
and all the Indians drink in the best tavern.
Money is free if you're poor enough.
Disgusted, busted whites are running
for office in this town.

. . . .

Goodbye, goodbye, Harlem on the rocks,
so bigoted, you forget the latest joke,
so lonely, you'd welcome a battalion of Turks
to rule your women.
—from "Harlem, Montana: Just Off the Reservation"

The Death of Jim Loney (1979) opens under Montana fall rains that wipe
out a year's harvest and slog down a high school football game. As the
town boys lose 13–12, on a fumbled fake kick at the goal, no time outs left,
a local carps, "We're shit out of luck." The epigraph stands uncontested.
To men later drinking in the Servicemen's Bar, the "moral victory" of such
defeat adds up to an "Indian joke," the blue humor of living through loss.

Welch's second novel continues with "the sad same life of Harlem."
Boosting this wilderness ghetto, a twenty-year-old, warped billboard flaps
beside the highway, "WELCOME TO HARLEM, HOME OF THE 1958
CLASS B CHAMPS." The sorry plot is a search for home in no-man's-land,
ghosted by questions of glory from an unsettled past.

BLACKFEET WINTER BLUES

Rootlessness troubles Indian and white alike in this novel about a dead-end "breed." Slipping a few years and scattered places on from *Winter in the Blood*, Welch names his protagonist Jim Loney, a tease on the author's Christian name and a play on nicknaming an Indian "The Lone Ranger." Loney also puns (loon, lunar, lonely) on a "funny name," his girl friend Rhea muses, watching her sleepless bedmate doze like "a dark hummingbird at rest." Somewhere in the night, Jim's Indian mother is locked up in "that damn bughouse" for lunatics. In cartoon of feminine bondage, the local cop later handcuffs Rhea to the radiator in her classroom. "Loney, Loney," the green-eyed, blonde girl friend murmurs, staring at the moon waning over their lonely companionship: a half-breed isolato and a Texas millionaire's runaway daughter teaching high school English in Harlem, Montana. "Lucky" Loney, Rhea dubs him, "you can be Indian one day and white the next. Whichever suits you." Loney defers with a Hemingway twist, "It would be nice to think that one was one or the other, Indian or white" (*DJL* 14).

Jim Loney cries in his sleep, "I'm small," stunted from childhood abandonment. By day he's wolfish. Myron Pretty Weasel sees a "mongrel, hungry and unpredictable, yet funny-looking," once his basketball team-mate. Indians, too, are caught up in Indian stereotypes of "that quick animal glance, always alert, yet seeming to see nothing" (*DJL* 81). Loney lives the "breed" myth, half wild animal from the reservation, half poor white trash from Harlem. His prodigal mad mother, Eletra Calf Looking, though her ex-husband swears she's a Gros Ventre "whore," was "as good a goddamn woman as the good lord ever put on this poor earth." Loney's "scrawny" father, now a sixty-two-year-old barfly living on pasteurized American cheese, recalls Huck Finn's scurrilous Pap, "the worst type of dirt" any son knows. The narrative keeps the reader guessing and mildly alert to small things that seem to count, as well as people count on, like years. Loney remembers being nine or ten when his father left, then seeing Ike (the "I Like Ike" termination years) twelve years later, and telling of all this "fourteen years ago." So, again Welch's protagonist is roughly the artist's age, thirty-five or so now, but a fictional portrait *not* the artist.

Again genders cut between bitches and bastards: mothers and daughters run away like wild creatures, and fathers and sons hang around town, to no good. A distant sister and a transient lover want to hide Loney away in mirroring coastal cities, Washington, D.C., and Seattle, Washington, American capitals named for white and red "fathers." Sister Kate, "lean and striking as a dark cat," lives for the "present" alone, a dusky six-foot breed princess tired of telephones, travel, and male "fuck games." This maternal sibling flies into Harlem to rescue her little brother on the skids, as the green-eyed Rhea is making plans for her own Indian missionary work.

But Loney can't go anywhere. He has no place to leave, and exiled from the past, he has no future. "He thought of his earlier attempts to create a past, a background, an ancestry—something that would tell him who he was" (*DJL* 88).

> It always startled Loney that when he stepped out of his day-to-day existence he was considered an Indian. He never felt Indian. Indians were people like the Cross Guns, the Old Chiefs—Amos After Buffalo. They lived an Indian way, at least tried. When Loney thought of Indians, he thought of the reservation families, all living under one roof, the old ones passing down the wisdom of their years, of their family's years, of their tribe's years, and the young ones soaking up their history, their places in their history, with a wisdom that went beyond age.
> . . . He had no family and he wasn't Indian or white. He remembered the day he and Rhea had driven out to the Little Rockies. She had said he was lucky to have two sets of ancestors. In truth he had none. [*DJL* 102]

Loney lives as no man, nowhere, a kitchen drunk asking for "nothing" to end it all, as the first snow turns "blue in the dusk," running down the gutter next morning.

Nothing matters in this novel of small revelations. Everything, in detail, remains local, downplayed, and real to ordinary life. The brown-eyed basketball coach "never seemed to get upset, just sadder as his teams continued to break his heart" (*DJL* 40). Even the mountains here are diminished "Little Rockies." "It wasn't the end of the world," Rhea's grandmother in Texas would say, "but you could see it from here" (*DJL* 11). The two-engine Frontier puddle-jumpers skip in and out of dusty northwest towns, mostly off-schedule. The local cop from California wants a "safe, warm life," makes model airplanes and housewives, drinks beer with the football coach, arrests drunks, and eats TV dinners. The bartender drops mothball jokes. A North Dakotan carries a turd in his wallet for ID, Kenny Hart quips, in a state that claims the housefly as its native bird. And Hank

Williams twangs twenty-four of his *Greatest Hits* on Myron Pretty Weasel's car tape deck: "I'm so lonesome I could die."

With all this maudlin stir, Loney makes the best of a "plain" life in a kitchen musty with "the faint sourness of a man who lives alone": the day-to-day reliefs of a sometime girl friend, a glass of bourbon, fall rain, a losing Friday night game, the first snow on Saturday. It is a season when washing hangs frozen on the clothesline. "Loney hated the cold the way some people who had to live on it hated deer meat, hopelessly and without emotion" (*DJL* 49). These events anticipate worse things to come.

At the fall end of seasonal colors, the traditional green of regeneration darkens toward death. The promise of distance shades Rhea's eyes "the color of turquoise," Jim thinks, "and he wondered at their coldness, but in that morning light they were the warm green of alfalfa" (*DJL* 13). Kate sends a green-penned last paragraph in a typewritten letter about coming to save him from himself. Ike holes up in a green teardrop trailer. Loney notices last year's Christmas sweater never taken home from Rhea's place, "dark green with red deer marching across the chest" (*DJL* 42). The holiday pattern ties into a small point: Ike remembers Eletra "like a sleek animal" dressed in doeskin around "young bucks" (*DJL* 141). Loney ends his life plugging from "a green bottle" of Rhea's scotch, hunted like a deer in lands where mad red women run wild.

These mean characters average small-town American life, a tawdry common denominator. Happiness for Kenny Hart is "a bar full of good people having themselves a real good time" (*DJL* 93). Neither low enough for tragic depth nor high enough for insight, the monotony of common events picks away at these people's lives. Rhea makes it through another week, then another fall, cleaning Tampax from her gym locker, gossiping over the Trojan condom found in Colleen's desk after lunch. "It had been a long time; not a bad time, just a vaguely discontented time" (*DJL* 7). Time to move on. Like the cheap painting that hangs over her bed, Rhea slides through things, a mildly passionless woman "waiting for something to happen." She remains a Dallas blonde with a literary M.A. from Southern Methodist, munching English muffins, warmed through northern nights by her half-breed "Southern gentleman." The third party to this affair is a deaf old dog, Swipesy, who eats tomato soup, never barks anymore, and freezes to death in the mud on Thanksgiving, "his mouth open and his blind blue eye staring up at nothing" (*DJL* 53). Man's best friend foreshadows his suburban Indian end.

The Death of Jim Loney is more self-consciously interior than *Winter in the Blood*, less historically Blackfeet or Gros Ventre. There is little, if any, older ethnology. The Indian subject and background of the first novel seem to have been altered: here to write an American "breed's" novel, neither Indian nor white. Not quite so pointedly gutsy in detail, the second novel's focus is blunter, with a muted sense of place, ear for dialogue, and controlling narrative voice. Like a surreal play, much of the action and passage of time takes place offstage, in gaps between chapters. The corny bartender at Kennedy's serves as a low-comic stage manager. But the bar jokes aren't as bizarre in a novel whose plot and style seem warmed-over from the first. It takes two North Dakotans to eat a rabbit: "One to watch for cars." Street slang like tit, crotch, nuts, turd, poopface, and shithouse truncate the everyday data of small lives in small places, where Zane Grey and Mickey Spillane supply the male reading matter of bars, barbershops, and bathrooms, with a smattering of dog-eared *Argosy, Field and Stream, Reader's Digest, Hustler,* and *The Legion Magazine.*

This novel is almost too real. Unsubtle little ironies intersperse a poetry of inarticulations: "Their bodies touched on the narrow bed, yet they did not touch each other" (*DJL* 42). "He knew her but he didn't know much about her" (*DJL* 156). "She was a mother who was no longer a mother" (*DJL* 175). Such a language, dying of labels, could fall flat if pushed for effect; but Welch states things as the half-alive half-know them, or don't know. "I realized I didn't know anything," Loney says to his deaf dog. "Not one damn thing that was worth knowing" (*DJL* 18). The clichés about commercializing Christmas and eating white bread along empty Thanksgiving streets remain too easily spoken.

> There was something determined about Harlem as it readied itself for the Christmas season. Except for a few decorations—a red cellophane wreath with an electric candle in the Coast-to-Coast store, children's cutouts of snowflakes in the laundromat window, and a cardboard Santa pointing out Buttrey's holiday items (hard candy 59¢, tinsel 29¢, hot buttered rum batter 89¢)—and the fact that the stores stayed open until nine every evening, it was hard to tell that a season of joy had visited itself on the community. But the weekly *Harlem News* proclaimed the event with a notation beside the weather box: "Only 12 More Shopping Days Till Christmas, Joyeux Noel." And there were kids on the streets.

BLACKFEET WINTER BLUES

> Kenny Hart was shaking Christmas trees in the Lions Club
> lot beside the Texaco station. He had read somewhere that if
> you could shake the needles loose, then that tree was too dry.
> [*DJL* 92]

"Christmas makes for strange barfellows," Loney muses. To speak the smallness of the common malaise isn't quite enough, as realism reaches its limits.

The novel comes across more as ideas than execution. It tightens and quickens by midpoint, the plot congealing, prose toughening, but the overall sting does not penetrate the way *Winter in the Blood* does. Welch goes inside Loney's alcoholic mind to the extent of muffling his story, imitating a boozy reality with too much blur: "Loney felt nothing but the warmth of the wine and a mild regard for the country they passed. It was a shallow country, filled with hayfields, thickets, stands of willow, and leafless cottonwoods that marked the course of a river without movement" (*DJL* 113). In uneasy mix with pulp fiction, Joyce's Stephen Dedalus shadows the plot: the opening football game, Jim's mission school and boarding house adolescence, the dark bird foreshadowing the fall of Icarus in Loney's dreams. The novel may be Welch's portrait of the drunken artist as a not-so-young Indian. Thunderbird wine induces Jim's rotgut visions; Mogen David consecrates his holidays. An epigraph from *Under the Volcano* opens the story on a note of tragic sentiment from Malcolm Lowry, novelist of drunks, the slow suicides—a dream lover galloping "into the heart of all the simplicity and peace in the world." Jim lives without friends, just "cronies," screwing a forgotten girl, Colleen, in the car at a rodeo and leaving her sprawled in the backseat to go drink beer.

Real gaps slur conversations, real smears smudge a drunken consciousness, while Loney drinks to feel nothing, and numbness steals over him, "a general forgetfulness of all but the most whimsical detail, the most random thought" (*DJL* 109). His hands begin to shake from wine, cigarettes, and insomnia after thinking for a month to see "things strangely, yet clearly." "A real dream made of shit," Loney concludes (*DJL* 119). To Rhea he laments, "I want to make a little sense out of my life and all I get are crazy visions and Bible phrases. They're like puzzles" (*DJL* 105).

So as a stranger coming to a stranger, Loney confronts his derelict father with questions about a phantom mother. "What do I know that you'd want?" Ike challenges his son. "I'm an old man. I was born to buck and broke to ride. It's all over" (*DJL* 139). Jim toasts his "sonofabitch"

169

father with grainy pathos, "To the way we are," an epithet for the novel's realism (*DJL* 142). His tautological solution to sins of fathers is to commit a crime that will be exorcised by his own murder. "And Loney knew who the guilty party was. It was he who was guilty, and in a way that made his father's past sins seem childish, as though original sin were something akin to stealing candy bars" (*DJL* 146). So on an ostensible "pheasant" hunt, in truth for illegal deer, the "wolfish" Loney mistakes Pretty Weasel for a bear (bizarre totemic confusions) and shoots him. The Oedipal-bred Loney then blasts the window of his father's trailer and some of Ike's face with a shotgun old as Jim himself, makes love to Rhea one last time, and goes south to Mission Canyon on the reservation. Here he once picnicked with a preacher's family and seduced Rhea in a parked car.

Loney can't say he loves Rhea during the finale: "there was no place to take it." The half-breed clutches at a displaced self trying to run away. "I have to leave, he thought, but he held her as though to prevent her from slipping away" (*DJL* 154). This dispossessed man must run, but he can't leave a place not there; he fears others leaving as he drives them off. " 'Good bye,' he whispered, and he didn't weep and he didn't feel corny" (*DJL* 156). His tragedy is a loss of place, simply designated "home"—the Indian heritage of land, family, clan, tribe, and spirit turned nightmare. And the doubly tragic solution is ritual death, betrayed by "an old bastard" father.

With his father's "perfect bird gun" and Rhea's scotch in below zero weather, Jim arranges his own execution at the hands of a tribal cop, Quinton Doore, a "thug" edged into the reservation police. "He stopped and caught his breath and took one last look at the world. And it was the right light to see the world, halfway between dark and dawn, a good way to see things, the quiet pleasure of deciding whether the things were there or not there" (*DJL* 167). To die, definitively, ends a mean existence. "This is what you wanted," Loney thinks finally. "And he fell, and as he was falling he felt a harsh wind where there was none and the last thing he saw were the beating wings of a dark bird as it climbed to a distant place" (*DJL* 179).

The Adamic myth of a falling Icarus informs this Hemingway out, a denouement to end it all, with a touch of Cooper's *The Last of the Mohicans*. ". . . it was like everything was beginning again without a past. No lost sons, no mothers searching" (*DJL* 175). And still a reader questions why such "realism." Drawn from an American frontier fascination with regenerative violence, this suicidal culture hero perpetrates despair's sorry end, along with companion stereotypes of the bloodthirsty savage, noble redskin, cigar-store stoic, and vanishing American in the wilderness Harlems of Native America. An old American myth, repeatedly fictionalized, frays reality once more: a violent end to a life of trouble, death a "place" to go "home" to a lost mother. Richard Slotkin traces this psychohistory in *Regeneration Through Violence: The Mythology of the American Frontier, 1600–1860*. A. Alvarez tracks the self-violence of Western artists through a history of suicides in *The Savage God*. It is alarming how self-destructive heroes, native and near, appear in diversely related American contexts: Magua, Ahab, Jesse James, Crazy Horse, Joe Christmas, Gatsby, Dillinger, Berryman, and Plath, to name only a few from fact and fiction.

A reader can, if encouraged, consciously work away from these images toward reseeding such a modern wasteland of the psyche—the end of civil war on reservations, the control of alcoholism, the reversals of dispossession. To be sure, James Welch sees and gives voice to the truth of suffering. He takes the first moral step in a historical fiction whose muse is truth. "We're neither of us bad guys," Loney thinks of Indians drinking ill-humoredly in a bar, "just adversaries, that's all" (*DJL* 7). How shall this be played out?

Old basketball teammates end up shooting one another after twenty years of mainstream acculturation: "he used to be the best friend I ever had," Pretty Weasel jibes Loney. Jim replies, "Times have changed" (*DJL* 101). Myron's white "success" deep-ends Jim's breed estrangement; in an accident with subconscious intent, Loney kills "Super Chief," the Uncle Tomahawk who went to the University of Wyoming on scholarship and quit to modernize his father's ranch. And Doore, the second-stringer "standing right behind" Loney in the Class B championship photo, assassinates the lone wolf with a deer-hunting rifle. Welch's half-breed Jim Loney finds Thanks-giving in death, a suicidal prophet after the buffalo's end a century ago.

> Loney decided it must be very early because all the houses were dark. And he remembered the boy who had watched him chip Swipesy out of the frozen mud and he wondered which house was his. Amos After Buffalo, and he came from "out there." Loney saw him standing on the bleak Harlem street, pointing south to these mountains and his country. That had been on Thanksgiving Day, almost a month ago. Amos After Buffalo will grow up, thought Loney, and he will discover that

BLACKFEET WINTER BLUES

Thanksgiving is not meant for him. It will take him longer
because he lives in Hays and Hays is on the edge of the world,
but he will discover it someday and it will hurt him, a small
wound when you think about it, but along with the hundred
other small cuts and bruises, it will make a difference, and he
will grow hard and bitter and he might do something bad, and
people will say, "Didn't we tell you, he's like all the rest,"
and they will think Indians do not know the meaning of the
word "Thanksgiving."

Amos, if I could, I would take you with me, right now,
and spare you sorrow. I might survive. Oh, God, we might
survive together, and what a laugh. . . .

Loney turned to the dog. "You tell Amos that Jim Loney
passed through town while he was dreaming. Don't tell him
you saw me with a bottle and a gun. That wouldn't do. Give
him dreams." [*DJL* 166–167]

FOXY SHAMAN

They shook the green leaves down,
those men that rattled
in their sleep. Truth became
a nightmare to their fox.

He turned their horses into fish,
or was it horses strung
like fish, or fish like fish
hung naked in the wind?

Stars fell upon their catch.
A girl, not yet twenty-four
but blonde as morning birds, began
a dance that drew men in
green around her skirts.
In dust her magic jangled memories
of dawn, till fox and grief
turned nightmare in their sleep.

And this: fish not fish but stars
that fell into their dreams.

BLACKFEET WINTER BLUES

This poem, "Magic Fox," opens *Riding the Earthboy 40* (1971). To "ride" the earth, working an allotted farm section on surreal machinery, evinces precarious balance from the start. "And the rolling day, / it will never stop? It means nothing?" Welch asks in "Getting Things Straight." The poet's dreamed reality unsettles between likeness and things in themselves; truth becomes a foxy game refusing to make sense. The shaman's mystery, a source of poetic vision, is in trouble and in question. Day turns to nightmarish magic; love swirls among leaves falling through a nervous dance of memory; poetry shifts on a dangerously unstable set of images. The traditional death chant—to meet the rattling darkness—has secularized into old men snoring leaves off the Sun Dance tree of life. Even Trickster's cousin, fox, is not sharp-eyed or clawed enough to unravel what is here the unreality of reality. Welch's quick-witted totem pairs with the wheeling hawk, a vision of circling needs of hunger and the hunt. There are no fixed points, all is disquiet, falling.

In fact, the stars did slip and fall in a nineteenth-century nightmare sky. Following the 1833 Leonid meteor showers, smallpox killed two-thirds of the 20,000 Blackfeet in 1837, and there were successive plagues in 1845, 1857, and 1869.[22] Fatal pox marks erupted on Blackfeet skin, seeming to be further evidence of the falling stars. The horses were shot by cavalry or led away like so many bagged fish on a stringer, as the buffalo were slaughtered and reservations staked. The sacred Sun Dance tree was torn down, to be replaced by the cross and flag pole. And the poet-shaman today, haunted by nightmares of a past that skews the present, is left discredited with a "blonde" afterimage of his people's seduction and fall. He wakes delirious to the dangers of shamanic medicine that failed, the instability of magic and metaphor, remembering that in the old days a dishonored medicine man could be ostracized or even killed. The "all-face man," as the Blackfeet shaman was known, can find no tribal mask for the present, no patronage among his people; his power goes underground, a "holy ghost" ironically questioning itself along "Arizona Highways," or lost in the alcoholic anti-ways of "Blue Like Death":

> You see, the problem is
> no more for the road.
>
> . . . .
>
> the way is not your going
> but an end. That road awaits

> the moon that falls between
> the snow and you, your stalking home.

James Welch writes a poetry of startling half lines and broken forms, not unlike John Berryman's *Dream Songs* or James Wright's *The Branch Will Not Break*. Conversational syntax and diction tense against formal line lengths, so that verses enjamb or break at midpoint; fragments of images impact in commonplace rhythms, logics falter along broken lines of thought, and lines bang to abrupt full stops. And within the verse, ideas implode in identical rhyme: "Look away and we are gone. / Look back. Tracks are there. . . ."

Beginning with the off-rhyme idea that fox could be related to Native American tricksters such as coyote (but fox is more European import than traditional Indian trickster), the possibilities of slanted rhyme crisscross in "dance" and "fox" and "catch" and "fish" in the opening poem. Iconoclastic rhyme carries through as a binding technique, to the internal dissonance of the closing poem, "Never Give a Bum an Even Break":

> —instead he sp*oke*
> of a role so bl*ack* the *un*cle died
> out of l*uck* in a westend sh*ack*.

The near rhymes and sharp repetitions of explosive sound, a forced yoking of old and new ways, remind the reader of "a woman blue as night," stepping from the medicine bundle and singing of a slant rhyming world "like this far off" in the second poem, "Verifying the Dead." This blue earth mother, replaced by the blonde witch, sings of the old ways gone, but echoed on in Blackfeet chants. A Blackfeet child's bedtime Christian prayer, ironically assimilated in "Dreaming Winter," jars against the older native belief that shadows of departed souls go to the "Sand Hills" to rest on the Saskatchewan border.[23]

> Have mercy on me, Lord. Really. If I should die
> before I wake, take me to that place I just heard
> banging in my ears. Don't ask me. Let me join
> the other kings, the ones who trade their knives
> for a sack of keys. Let me open any door,
> stand winter still and drown in a common dream.

The Blackfeet poet's voice descends through winter count history from the shaman's tongue, mysterious and ritualistic. He chants "finicky secrets,'' as he hawks through the night of today in strangely dense phrases, wheeling on paradox and parable. Images seem refracted from ordinary associations, as visions-turned-nightmare shadow the dark side of day-to-day life. The shamanic poet's words are difficult, contrary, uncommonly common here in ''Counting Clouds'':

> A long way to come—
> this rain so old my bones
> crackle no before you speak.
> A way to come: downwind
> before the sudden clouds appear,
> turn you statue—no, I say,
> no to the north and no, no
> to your crummy mirror.

Grinnell notes that a Blackfeet medicine doctor was known literally as ''a heavy singer for the sick'';[24] and a century later Welch chants the lonely sickness of dispossession for Indians in search of healing.

Physician and patient share one voice, a common pain. This terribly familiar voice casts fearful insights into the shadows of people's lives, not just Indians. The poet-shaman says of the nighthawk's secrets, ''And another: man is afraid of his dark.'' Positively regarded, the truth of fear feeds a shaman's power; he can teach people how to live with the unknown and uncontrollable, how to use the threatening world as a source of courage, how danger quickens the mind. A traditional, now pan-Indian poetry of Native America records:

> There I run in rattling darkness
> cactus flowers in my hair
> in rattling darkness
> > darkness rattling
> running to that singing place[25]

At one with the courage of fear and sharpened senses, the poet-shaman well knows the alembic of anger. Welch calls for ''mountains to bang against,'' a concrete reality that pushes back when men intrude in ''The Versatile Historian.'' Rhythm rages tangibly through this naturalistic landscape, as in ''Surviving'':

> The day-long cold hard rain drove
> like sun through all the cedar sky

> we had that late fall. We huddled
> close as cows before the bellied stove.

The poems drum the people to arms against the self-defeat of acculturated poverty, as the old warrior songs moved the tribe into battle.

> With thunder-
> hands his father shaped the dust, circled
> fire, tumbled up the wind to make a fool.
> Now the fool is dead. His bones go back
> so scarred in time, the buttes are young to look
> for signs that say a man could love his fate,
> that winter in the blood is one sad thing.

> His songs—I don't explain. Desperate in my song,
> I run these woman hills, translate wind
> to mean a kind of life, the children of Speakthunder
> are never wrong and I am rhythm to strong medicine.

A contemporary Blackfeet "blood to bison" and "desperate in my song," Welch inherits the original voice of Speakthunder "In My Lifetime." Na'pi created man-the-fool ironically in his own image, while Thunder gave the tribe a medicine bundle and voices to pray for saving rain (the sacred bundle is still opened each spring after the first thunder is heard).[26] Welch drinks wind of the sacred run after wild game, chants the old earth rhythms, drums the sky for rain, and translates breath into the rhymes of poetry. He carries the running meter of "Speak"-thunder from rites of passage into the crafted modern meters of a poet's vision quest. "Today I search for a name," opens the poem, "Toward Dawn." And in "Getting Things Straight" the questing lamenter asks the traditional four questions of the circling hawk: Is hunger the life-need? Who feeds the hawk? Am I his prey? "Is he my vision?" Riding toward "Crystal" through a night of drunken insight, horses begin to sing, coyotes prowl under blooming moonlight, and places mean their names. The poet does not "try to understand," only to witness "Crystal's gray dawn."

Through the correspondence of ideas and objects, Indian songs traditionally ritualize the relationships of all things. Welch clusters images discordantly, jarring against the parallel phrasing of the old chant formulas. His insistent rhymes and rhythms rope straining lines together. He couples the eidetic imagery and tension of modern surrealist poetry, distantly related to the vision quest, with Blackfeet attention to the land and people in his blood.

176

BLACKFEET WINTER BLUES

> Once I loved this gravy land
> so famous in my blood
> my hair turned black
> with love. A way to think:
> so cold the sun could call me
> friend.

> ["Counting Clouds"]

This palimpsest of modernism and Indian tradition also appears in the northern plains art of Oscar Howe (Lakota), a painter who fuses the hallucinatory energy of Indian visions with cubist forms (see, in particular, Howe's "Medicine Man" and "Dakota Eagle Dancer," 1962). Under intense compression, there is just enough disquiet between old and new forms to stir the reader's involvement. Ideas call to a receding past, falter to rhyme, and grope for clarity.

The poems come off as densely imagistic conversations, surreal talk in stutters of the mind. An image suspends thought in midair; an ellipsis, colon, or hyphen trails an idea beyond recorded speech; a full-stop at midline drills rhythm to closure. In "Going to Remake This World,"

> Moose Jaw is overcast,
> twelve below and blowing. Some people. . .
> Listen: if you do not come this day, today
> of all days, there is another time
> when breeze is tropic and riffs the green sap
> forever up these crooked cottonwoods.
> Sometimes,
> you know, the snow never falls forever.

So, too, the old stories scatter as shards of ancient earthenware.

> We ended sometime
> back in recollections of glory, myths
> that meant the hunters meant a lot
> to starving wives and bad painters.

> Let glory go the way of all sad things.
> ["Blackfeet, Blood and Piegan Hunters"]

The myth of Icarus, immigrant from Greece, appears as a sign out of context to the drunken Indian envisioning "his future falling" in "Two for the Festival." The inebriate poet comes stumbling on "awkward rhymes," cradling a blind toad (the "all-face" toad associated with a medicine man, whose coiled hair was said to liken him to the horned toad). Attended by his magic fox of surreality, the poet fingers "thirteen lumpy stones" (a reduction of the sacred "buffalo stones" once considered powerful hunting medicine).

All this medicine power—totems, beasts, myths, and chants—in no way prevents the falls of Icarus or the lately descendant Indian. Fox hugs his stones in fear. One more drink and the acculturated drunk lurches home, "dreaming winter" of middle-class Christian keys to heaven. Material white salvation antiquates neolithic knives and bones.

Welch undercuts the fantasy of New World riches for the savage —opening "any door," standing "winter still" in Anglo-American prosperity, drowning "in a common dream" of melting-pot democracy whose self-help excludes the dark-skinned poor. In "Harlem, Montana: Just Off the Reservation,"

> Booze is law
> and all the Indians drink in the best tavern.
> Money is free if you're poor enough.
> Disgusted, busted whites are running
> for office in this town.

Deafy, the cigar-store stereotype of silence, can't hear the world anymore, behind his "drum-tight ear." He pretends he's "dumb" in "There Are Silent Legends."

> Though wind has shut his ears for good, he squats
> for hours at the slough, skipping stones, dreaming
> of a moon, the quiet nights and a not quite done
> love with a lady high in costly red shoes.

The "civilized" savage in "Plea to Those Who Matter" bleeds from a smile, nose smashed straight and teeth scrubbed away with stones. Acquiescent, head down, and penitent, he wears the mask of American camaraderie, "happy for the snow clean hands of you, my friends." And, back on the reservation, the still unregenerate Indians are "Surviving":

> That night the moon slipped a notch, hung
> black for just a second, just long enough
> for wet black things to sneak away our cache
> of meat. To stay alive this way, it's hard. . . .

Self-tormented by these double-edged ironies, Welch counters the American Myth of white plenty, giving thanks for Blackfeet seasons of loss. He writes from a mind of late fall into winter. The poet challenges "In My First Hard Springtime":

> Starved to visions, famous cronies top Mount Chief
> for names to give respect to Blackfeet streets.
> I could deny them in my first hard springtime,
> but choose amazed to ride you down with hunger.

An essential paradox of Indian tradition, and inversely now of tribal history in America, lies down in an old concept of *humilitas*, the power gained in loss.[27] "Pity me, for I want to live," the Sun Dancers cry in flesh-piercing ceremonies; "Listen," the vision seekers chant to the spirits. The ritual loss of self brings spiritual gain, just as winter warms the blood, hunger sharpens the eye, and the lonely vision quest leads a dreamer back into the tribe.

So in "Thanksgiving at Snake Butte," the Indians ride to the crest of a holy mountain and find petroglyphs left crudely, without pretense of control, by wandering ancestors "driven by their names / for time."

> On top, our horses broke, loped through
> a small stand of stunted pine, then jolted
> to a nervous walk. Before us lay
> the smooth stones of our ancestors, the fish,
> the lizard, snake and bent-kneed
>
> bowman—etched by something crude,
> by a wandering race, driven by their names
> for time: its winds, its rain, its snow
> and the cold moon tugging at the crude figures
> in this, the season of their loss.

The old ones lived out their words, imaged the needs of their seasonal losses, hunted for their lives, and depended on the animal in themselves to know when more is less under a "snow-fat sky." Bowed in rituals of blood sacrifice, "bent-kneed" bowmen climbed lonely buttes to lose themselves into their world's uncompromising truths.[28]

"Thanks"-giving, then, cuts two ways at once, like the double-edged knife Welch uses as his pen: the seasonal and positive ritual loss in the old ways, designed to meet necessity, finding strength through abstinence; and the history of cultural loss ensuing from the first Algonkins giving thanks with the pilgrims in 1621. "No one spoke of our good side, / those times we fed the hulking idiot, / mapped these plains with sticks / and flint," the poet recalls in "The Renegade Wants Words." Algonkian speakers who migrated westward before the invasion, the Blackfeet stood at odds with the "Big Knives" from their initial plains contact.

During a winter blizzard in Moccasin Flat, "a quick 30 below,"

> Christmas comes like this: Wise men
> unhurried, candles bought on credit (poor price
> for calves), warriors face down in wine sleep.
> Winds cheat to pull heat from smoke.

Blackfeet children beg legends through the long winter, "a myth that tells them be alive." Medicine Woman, spitting at her television to predict the end of day in five o'clock news, translates the old Christian and Indian stories as one "peculiar evening star" bringing light to people in need, "something about honor and passion, / warriors back with meat and song." Outside mainstream Christian America, the original Savior is perhaps more mythically alive to "warriors face down in wine," hungry friends awaiting commodities, children leaning into grandmother's stale breath, and Charlie Blackbird feeding his fire against the dark cold of winter. In the late 1880s Ghost Dancers joined hands, danced in circles, and chanted Christ's return until they fell down in visions:

> The whirlwind! The whirlwind!
> The new earth comes into being
>   swiftly as snow.
> The new earth comes into being
>   quietly as snow.[29]

In "Legends Like This" Welch sees the crucified Savior as a renegade poet flanked by two other hostiles, "dying in the sight of God," who never bothered to learn their true names. Resurrected among renegade poets of the lost northern plains tribes, they "burned His church / and hid out for a long, long time."

Welch's interwoven Christian, Indian, and Homeric fragments of myth, then, seem archaic historical dreams, broken relics for exiles suffering the losses of the present. "Our past is ritual, / cattle marching one way to remembered mud," the poet sees bitterly in "Spring For All Seasons."[30] The old ways taught survival in a severe northern climate. Hunters learned to grow stronger in seasons of loss. Accurate translations of these ways in poetry and prose steel a modern warrior through an imposed winter of white dominance, eschewing the "sentimental crap" of country-western songs in junction bars.

> Some looked away; others in their throats
> began to laugh, not loud, but blue,
> a winter blue that followed
> mongrels out the door
> ["The World's Only Corn Palace"]

The last section of *Riding the Earthboy 40*, "The Day the Children Took Over," tempers the hand-to-hand struggle of the opening "Knives" section, pulls back from the "renegade" bitters of the second section, and moves beyond the third section's image of the poet weaving styptic spider webs (the old medicine for wounds) "to bandage up the day" in "Snow Country Weavers." With winter down in their blood, the children redefine a season of cold beauty "in their own image" as a time of counterplay "to create life," while a cultural storm surrealistically locks conventional mothers, lovers, statesmen, and priests in the arms of their losses.[31] These closing poems register a spirit of reaffirmation and comic rebirth in the warrior's serious play with the odds against his people. Militants, like Montana weathers, move the tribe to action in "Call to Arms":

> The eyes were with us,
> every one, and we were with the storm.

Welch brings a warrior's courage forward, out of the sentiment of defeat, under pressure of necessity, to battle today's clear and present dangers: "None looked behind, / but heard the mindless suck of savage booted feet." The old ones die "Gravely": "we watched her go the way she came, / un-envied, wild—cold as last spring rain."

Na'pi's mask reappears in the final poem, "Never Give a Bum an Even Break." The poet borrows from a W. C. Fields movie title to thaw the grip of winter. If Thunder gave the original medicine bundle to invoke spring rain for the Blackfeet, Welch's contrary bundle of chants opens in the "fall" of Indian time and closes drumming a spring "comic rain." The "hostile" poet still stands contrary to white society. He adversely leaves middle-class mirrors and waits with a fellow bum to blow up "one of the oldest bridges in town," perhaps an old sense of extended kinship underground to the *other* side of town. In 1960s protest the armed joker severs il-

181

lusory goodwill pretending to tie Red and white cultures together.[32] Or, the less militant option still remains: the poet can create new "comic" roles in his writing.

The old scores of history must be settled—broken treaties, lands stolen by "a slouching dwarf with rainwater eyes," present poverty and despair, condescending acculturation policies, termination threats—or Indians must create their own alternatives. Just so, the poet tries to adapt to a changing America, shifting to new forms of tribal medicine. The emergent roles may transcend a history of grief and anger.

As for now, the "all-face" poet remains the contemporary shaman, warrior, and vision seeker in a white freezing desert, chanting his angers, nightmares, laments, and conflicts through verbal "masks / glittering in a comic rain." This is Welch's Native American art, purged of losses, regenerating, reintegrating in the world-as-it-is. So, too, a tribal coalition of elders addressed the United States Congress in 1977, protesting the threatened abrogation of treaties by walking for half a year from the West Coast to the East. Their traditional voices are sources of James Welch's vision and art:

> We are the sovereign and free children of Mother Earth.
> Since before human memory our people have lived on this
> land. For countless generations, we have lived in harmony
> with our relatives, the four-leggeds, the winged beings, the
> beings that swim, and the beings that crawl. For all time our
> home is from coast to coast, from pole to pole.
>
> We are the original people of this hemisphere. The remains
> of our ancestors and of our many relatives are a greater part of
> this land than any other's remains. The mountains and the
> trees are a part of us. We are the human beings of many
> nations, and we still speak many tongues. We have come
> from the four directions of this Turtle Island. We are the
> evidence of the Western Hemisphere, the carriers of the
> original ways of this area of the world, and the protectors of
> all life on this earth.
>
> Today we address you in the language of the oppressor, but
> the concepts predate the coming of the invaders. The injustice
> we speak of is centuries old. We have spoken against it in our
> many tongues. We are still the original people of this land.
> We are the people of *The Longest Walk*.[33]

8

"THE NOW DAY INDI'NS"

EPILOG

Drop a kernel of corn on a rock
and say a prayer. It will shoot up
proud and green, tassel out,
pull the next crop from the thunderheads.
That's the Hopi way.
If the corn doesn't grow
you eat the rocks,
drink the clouds
on the distant plains.

Silko and Allen and Harjo and me:
our teeth are hard
from the rocks we eat.
—WENDY ROSE, *Lost Copper*

"If you have an idea in mind of what 'Indian literature' is, I suggest that you reconsider," Wendy Rose (Hopi/Miwok) cautions against archaic stereotypes of "Indian" writers, however recent:

> If your idea is based on the Indian-authored works you have
> read, consider the fact that it is often chosen according to
> editors' stereotypes. If your idea is based on a solid academic
> background about tribal literatures, consider that many of us
> do not speak our native language, were not raised on our
> ancestral land, and have no literary tradition other than what

we received in some classroom. If your idea is based on the observation of certain themes or images, consider that there is no genre of "Indian literature" because we *are* all different. There is only literature that is written by people who are Indian and who, therefore, infuse their work with their own lives the same way that you do.[1]

The new Indian poets are children of the old ways, students of historical transitions, teachers of contemporary survivals. In the last two decades, seminal writing has come from young Native Americans as they emerge out of tribal settings, go to American schools and study formal literatures, then go back to their own people, in country or city, to write personal versions of native experiences. The multiples and mixtures of Indian life are countless. These writers, many from matrilineal cultures, by and large balance the treatment of women and men equally in their work. Their families have been attenuated, severed, and relocated from country toward city concentrations, as America itself has shifted demographically. History has recombined racial lines, mixed cultures, and pushed tribes to the edges of urban limits at the bottom of the American dream. Recent social movements have politicized the artist's sensitivity over centuries of Indian dispossession, and many have newly broken through history's "primitive" and "savage" Indian labels into the caucus of the printed word. Native American writers have been honored by a Pulitzer Prize for Scott Momaday's novel, *House Made of Dawn* (1969), front page reviews in the New York literary magazines for Leslie Silko's novel of Laguna Pueblo, *Ceremony* (1977), and critical enthusiasm for the poetry and fiction of James Welch as a new Indian Steinbeck. Leslie Silko and Alfonso Ortiz have received the prestigious MacArthur Foundation awards. Over one hundred more young Indian writers have gathered around these leaders to participate in a Native American renaissance in a first generation of published Indian poets, novelists, and scholars.

INDIANS TODAY

The twists of history today place the majority of American Indians off the reservation. Only some thirty-eight percent of perhaps a million and a quarter Indians now live on tribal lands. This twice displaced majority of Indians, removed to reservations a century ago and subsequently *re*located by the government (or *re*-relocated), is for the most part composed of mixed-blooded peoples, dark-to-light, who adapt to the American mainstream and exist biculturally, at no small cost and with sharp self-questioning. California, housing a migrant plurality from everywhere in the world, has the highest Indian population today, officially counted in the 1980 census at 201,311. Most of these transplanted peoples have been federally removed from other states, Navajos from Arizona, Pueblos from New Mexico, Lakota from the upper Great Plains, Apache from the lower. Oklahoma, or "red earth-people" land, ranks second with 169,000, originally the 1830s Indian Territory west of the Mississippi. Arizona is third in Indian population with 152,000, mostly Navajo and Hopi; New Mexico fourth with two Apache and nineteen Pueblo cultures totaling 101,000; and South Dakota fifth with the Lakota.

Los Angeles alone quarters some 80,000 urban Indians. Oakland is pocketed with outriders of Lakota, Hopi, Pueblo, Navajo, and related Southwest cultures, among many others. Chicago, Minneapolis, Denver, Albuquerque, and Seattle support suburbs for off-reservation Indians, as well as countless small border towns around the 315 reservations in the United States. Some 150 Indian communities more are pressing for federal reservation status. This means that many Indians, earlier defined by geographies, histories, genetics, and cultures indigenous over centuries, have moved or been "removed" to off-reservation villages, towns, and cities. They seek job opportunities, better standards of living, higher education, and medical facilities. They worry about trading older Indian ways and values for short-term benefits in a modern world. Many try to escape the disadvantages of being Indian—to cite a few, redneck prejudice, unemployment, malnutrition, and abject poverty. Some want to get away from intolerable conditions on reservations, like the Lakota civil war smoldering on the Pine Ridge Reservation since the 1973 militant Wounded Knee occupation.

So "being Indian" today, what my Lakota brother, Mark Monroe, calls a "now day Indi'n," can mean living uneasily among white people, in poorer sections of WASP-founded towns, south of the tracks, or in city ghettos; holding a job, going to school, even to college; staying sober enough to function like anyone else in white society, where alcohol is the social anodyne; and mixing white ways with Indian ways. George Lone

Wolf remembers Jennie Lone Wolf, the Oglala Sioux medicine woman from Pine Ridge Reservation and northwest Nebraska: "You take Mom, now, she was a good Catholic, an' she had her Indi'n medicine, ya know, some of both." Indians can be Roman Catholic or Episcopalian, Baptist or Mormon, yet still pray with a Lakota medicine pipe in a plains ceremony or take peyote to see Christ in the Native American Church. They can ride the Manhattan subway and go to an Iroquois sweat lodge for purification; run a small business in Phoenix and attend a Navajo Beautyway ceremony with medicine people, families and clans, sand painting, chanting, a spirit hogan on the desert, and eight and one-half days of ancient ritual. All this ceremony, with or without credit cards in a man's wallet, is rich with dancing, feasting, fasting, and praying. The ceremonies offer a healing suspension of ordinary time, out of the everyday sense of things. "We must remember well that all things are the work of the Great Spirit," a banner in the Holy Rosary Mission chapel quotes Black Elk, the healer, who was both a Lakota wicasa wakan and a Catholic catechist, christened "Nicholas" in 1904. Jesuit priests on Pine Ridge Reservation today pray to the Great Mystery both with the medicine pipe and the Catholic sacraments.

These new mixtures of being "now day Indi'n" (or American) are no less "native" than changing conditions ever left people in North America. Scandinavian farmers on the Great Plains, Greek steel mill workers in East Chicago, black field hands in Louisiana, and Russian Jewish shopkeepers in Los Angeles do not surrender ethnic definitions over a few generations. Indians are even more ethnically self-contained, in many instances, since they have lived on separate and traditional land bases, apart from the American mainstream, and they consider themselves "Native" Americans, distinguished from all others.

The Navajo adapted with newfound horses in the sixteenth century, as they moved into the Southwest to trade, borrow, and plunder the Pueblos. The Lakota, somewhat earlier, migrated west from the Great Lakes woodlands out onto the Great Plains. Renamed the "Sioux" by French trappers among the Ojibwa (also known as Chippewa), the Lakota emerged from the forests as buffalo hunters with the horse, or "holy dog," replacing man's best friend 30,000 years native to North America. The Mohawk of New York translate older codes of courage into high steel work on construction sites, just as firefighters are recruited from reservations in many parts of the West. A Cherokee nowadays uses Carnation milk cans as leg rattles in a stomp dance; he or she is no less "Indi'n" than ancestors one hundred years ago, removed fom Appalachia to Oklahoma, who used turtle shells instead. There are simply fewer turtles where the people live now, more milk cans.

Degree of Indianness is not measured, de facto, by any refusal to adapt, or by scarcity of organic materials for a ceremony, but is distinguished more by the spiritual significance of the ceremonies, as witnessed and infused among tribal peoples, performing the old ways wherever they are, whatever their implements. If Cheyenne or Winnebago or Chickasaw or Papago relocate in Los Angeles, where 5,000 "Gabrielino" natives once camped, they bring their Indianness with them into the city, redefining themselves. Good medicine is good medicine.

Being Indian, then, may mean adjusting the definition to the tribal reality at hand, rather than living nostalgically in a mythic past. People move from one place to another, or conversely, live in areas that change as other cultures move in. Human time, place, and culture are carried through cyclic evolutions that never stand still. For the September Feast of San Esteban, an Acoma can climb 600-year-old cliff stairs 400 feet above a 7,000 foot New Mexico valley of squash, beans, and fruit orchards. There in the Sky City, the Acomas traditionally dance Pueblo rituals in ancient costume, pray for the balance of rain and sun and crops, eat old-time bread from beehive ovens, and drink water at one time carried on the heads of elder women in beautiful, old potteries. Next day they can drive to the modernized Pueblo suburb of Acomita in the valley below near Interstate Highway 70, where the people farm, run markets, work livestock, or even commute into Albuquerque. These Indians talk by telephone, as well as dance with rattles and drums; they drive cars and fly in airplanes, as well as ride horses; they hold jobs, vote, and pay taxes, as well as draw, paint, compose songs, tell stories, and make pottery in new applications of the old ways.

It is the threat of discontinuity that challenges Indianness today: how far the changes will go, how drastically they will alter Indian ways. "You can't relearn nothin' you never learned," says the Lakota, Mark Monroe, heading the Indian Center in Alliance, Nebraska. The young people, in large part, do not speak the Indian languages of their elders. Many of the ceremonies have gone underground or been abandoned. The medicine people are disputed. Sometimes the old people are ignored. The land has been mapped, allotted, subdivided, fenced, tracked with rail and road rights-of-way, and "developed" in non-Indian commercial ventures, as in South Dakota cattle leases or Four Corners coal mining or Southwest water rights.

The wolves, buffalo, eagle, deer, migrating birds, bear, moose, elk, and antelope have been killed back or off, the forests cut down, the prairies plowed
up, the rivers dammed and diverted. Indian people, along with all this, are
pitied and shunted to out-of-the-way places as endangered species, left to
their own demise and relieved of their natural resources. But the vanishing
American just won't die off, Russell Means charges as a twentieth-century
Sioux warrior in the American Indian Movement, though for white
America the Indian "lives out of sight, out of mind."

For the majority of some million and a quarter variously defined
Indians in America, being Indian involves not just the traditions or catastro-
phes served up on a buffalo chip of history, but a conscious set of choices.
The central issue is what to fuse of the new and the old, improvisations and
continuations from the past. In synchronous time, Indians shear sheep and
drive the sick to Public Health Service hospitals, plant corn and collaborate
on native language curricula, attend powwows and go to college, make
native art and learn modern planning techniques for economic growth
necessary to survival. These present-day people believe in themselves as Indians and act on that belief, within their own definitions. They realize
themselves within a sense of Indian community. Their Indianness is not individually seized, but tribally granted and personally carried out, as the old
ones carried time down to where it is on their backs. In the older traditions,
time is not passing around the people; we are time.

Being Indian, from Acoma to Pine Ridge, Tahlequah to Tacoma,
Wounded Knee to the Hopi mesas, upstate New York to down-home
Ohio, would seem, finally, to be *doing* something about seeing or being or
defining oneself Indian. It can be working with Headstart children from
farming communities to urban poverty areas. It can include bringing goods
and concern to the old ones, staying to listen to their memories and wisdoms. Being Indian is as much behavior and attitude, life style and mind-set,
as a consequence of history or bloodline. It may mean placing people above
the possession of things. Such an Indian life checks individual gain against
the communal well-being, not taking too much, not tolerating degradation,
the energies of new minds tempered with the tested patience and care of the
old. Being a "now day Indi'n" would seem, as with most positive human
values, more active than passive, although the past obviously informs
tribalism through cultural continuity and a sense of common heritage.

Dawson No Horse told his people, gathered in a Lakota yuwipi ceremony the summer of 1981 at Wakpamni Lake, Pine Ridge Reservation:

"NOW DAY INDI'NS"

"We're gonna make it as we go along, generation to generation, addin' on an' addin' on."

A LANGUAGE OF COMMON WALLS

> All these, working in the mind,
> the vision of weaving things
> inwardly and outwardly
> to fit together, weaving stone
> together, my father tells me
> how walls are built.
>   —Simon Ortiz

Simon Ortiz, a traditional Acoma Pueblo, teaches writing at the University of New Mexico and travels the world over reading his work. Wendy Rose, an urbanized blend of California coastal, Southwest Indian, and immigrant Americans, was born in Oakland and teaches American Indian literature at the University of California, Berkeley. These poets bridge modern theory and ancient practice, from Charles Olson's poetics to Pueblo crafts; present acculturation and past tradition, from academia to native ritual; contemporary politics and regional particulars, from Karl Marx to New Mexico elections. Simon Ortiz and Wendy Rose articulate the concerns of the new "Indi'ns" and voice continuations of tribal definitions.

In a southwest land of ancient syllables and stone monuments—Lukachukai Mountains, Ocotillo Wells, Chuksa Mountains, Many Farms— Simon Ortiz writes poems to teach his children, Rainy Dawn and Raho Nez, the old, time-trusted regards and ways of home. He says in *A Good Journey*, "Like myself, the source of these narratives is my home." What his father taught him of names, values, attentiveness, kinship, gentleness, respect, and building walls, this father as a poet now teaches his own children. "Be patient, child, be kind and not bitter." And again, another time: "Sing a bit, be patient. Wait."

This word-sender, hitchhiking to Colorado, offers up traveling song-prayers in natural acts of attention:

> Look, the plants with bells.
> Look, the stones with voices.

So, too, attend here: "Be patient, child, / quiet," as a Navajo woman "in the calm of her work at the loom." Simon Ortiz sings an inclusive poetry of walls and looms, carpentry and pottery, interwoven with teachings and observances, remembrances and prayers. His language appeals to the traditional moralities of "home" for any people—land, family, the elders, the clan, kin, animals, plants, stones, and the gods. These walls adjoin, rather than separate.

Ortiz cares for all things in a natural religious regard, unscaffolded with theology or a monotheistic deity. This poet's religion calls upon a sense of the world as greater than man, multitudinous, spiritually alive, if Indian people ritually prepare and conduct themselves in a sacred manner. But "sacred" here infuses the "common" world, so that *this* world, the ordinary things now, come forward speaking of significances related to, yet apart from, man. The Indian world is reciprocal with people.

Walls testify to such kinship. Ortiz appeals continuously to the "good" life, as in the Navajo concept of *hózhó*, discussed by Gary Witherspoon: "*Hózhó* expresses the intellectual concept of order, the emotional state of happiness, the moral notion of good, the biological condition of health and well-being, and the aesthetic dimensions of balance, harmony, and beauty."[2] The poet says it this way in "Apache Love":

It is how you feel
about the land.

It is how you feel
about the children.

It is how you feel
about the women.

It is how you feel
about all things.

Hozhoni,
in beauty.

Hozhoni,
all things.

Hozhoni,
for all time.

190

"NOW DAY INDI'NS"

Hozhoni,
through all journeys.

For Simon Ortiz, poetry lyricizes experience. It is not so much a function of the words in themselves, poetry or prose, as a choice of subjects, and ways to see, and attitudes to think about things. He voices a complete act of seeing-in-saying-in-being. Ortiz recalls his father's songs as he carved wood: "I listen carefully, but I listen for more than just the sound, listen for more than just the words and phrases, for more than the various parts of the song. I try to perceive the context, meaning, purpose—all of these items not in their separate parts but as a whole—and I think it comes completely like that." For Simon Ortiz, then, language completes itself in the process of listening-and-speaking, not just in each word as product. He speaks toward and from a mind integrated within its culture: "that is, when a word is spoken, it is spoken as a complete word . . . not spoken in any *separate* parts."[3]

Ortiz perceives and articulates, in his own contemporary language, what it means to be Acoma Pueblo, among the "Acumeh" at "Acu," a people with a two-thousand-year-old sense of themselves. "Acoma" means, according to the elders, a "place that always was." Tribal legend records occupation of the "Sky City" on Acoma Mesa before Christ. Archaeologists conservatively agree that Old Acoma has been peopled from at least A.D. 1200 to the present.[4]

All this is a past continuous in the present, as in the poet's own family. "My father is a small man," Ortiz begins his essay, "Song/Poetry and Language—Expression and Perception." "My father carves, dancers usually. What he does is find the motion of Deer, Buffalo, Eagle dancing in the form and substance of wood . . . his sinewed hands touch the wood very surely and carefully, searching and knowing."[5] Before his death in 1978, Ortiz's father worked as a wood sculptor, a stonemason, a carpenter, a welder, and "one of the elders of the Antelope people who are in charge of all the spiritual practice and philosophy of our people, the Acumeh. He and his uncles are responsible that things continue in the manner that they have since time began for us, and in this sense he is indeed a 1,000 year old man."[6] Among his last acts at Acoma, Ortiz's father manually rebuilt the Antelope Society House, his son remembers.[7]

As the father shaped wood and layered stone, so the son fits words. These are the traditional arts of natural and useful objects. A concrete language of necessary elements joins and particularizes the world. It makes experience both communal and special. Ortiz, in turn, fashions poems as a part of things and apart from things. Language co-joins the world, and is a medium in itself.

In ''A Story of How a Wall Stands'' the poet speaks of a four-hundred-year-old wall on an incline holding an ancient graveyard of ''dirt and bones,'' the past interred and shored up through the craft of stones. The Pueblos listen back to ''the old rocks, millions of years old,'' all the way back to Mesa Verde and Four Corners. The *Anasazi*, or ''ancient'' stones with voices, still carry inflections in ochre and sienna sandstone. The sun's light weathers these earth bones like a palette of sunset tempering the desert below. The poet's mason father tells him that

> ''Underneath
> what looks like loose stone,
> there is stone woven together.''

The hand that shapes the wall is so shaped itself, as the layered stones are knitted in the manner of bones inside the stonebuilder's hands.

> He tells me those things,
> the story of them worked
> with his fingers, in the palm
> of his hands, working the stone
> and the mud until they become
> the wall that stands a long, long time.

Here stands a wall ''built that carefully'' to last.

The poet's own young son, as well, will be ''tasting forever'' the dust of stones in his mouth at Canyon de Chelly, the oldest continuously inhabited ''home'' in the contiguous United States (''Canyon de Chelly'' in *A Good Journey*). And in Rainy Dawn's birth, ''You come forth / the color of a stone cliff / at dawn,'' so in her continuing life,

> relish
> the good wheat bread your mother makes,
> taking care that you should think
> how her hands move, kneading the dough,
> shaping it with her concern,
> and how you were formed and grew in her.
> [''To Insure Survival'' and ''Forming Child'']

The key is to discover the fit. A person's body, tools, and spirit in making the world so, *are so made.*

> Essentially, it is how you fit
> into that space which is yourself,
> how well and appropriately.
> ["Four Dheetsiyama Poems"]

Breathing native prayers, working among the people, dancing ceremonial songs: poetry then is organic. Verse is consistent with carving the designs *in* ("into" and "from") the grains of wood; rebuilding and rebinding ancient village walls; coiling, molding, firing, and decorating pottery. It is so with the stones interleaved and mortared in Anasazi walls; there is a continuity of flowing parts.

A wall transcends its own parts in the harmony and wholeness, hózhó, of separate stones that interlock. And, too, words complete their "sentence" when spoken, ritualized sequentially in song. They gather not as separate phonemes, but complete as whole syntactic movements. "For example, when my father has said a word—in speech or in a song—and I ask him, 'What does that word break down to? I mean breaking it down to the syllables of sound or phrases of sound, what do each of these parts mean?' And he has looked at me with exasperated—slightly pained—expression on his face, wondering what I mean. And he tells me, 'It doesn't break down into anything.'"[8] It is so, as well, with the people, the stones, and the mortar made of earth—these elements that comprise a culture *are* earth. The flesh itself, made of dust, comes from the body of mother earth, and *is* her body.

In *A Good Journey* the earth-body extends even farther, to interconnect interior and exterior conditions of the tactile world. "This Occurs To Me" speaks of "how useful" Ortiz finds "dirt and stone," by way of his father's instruction, "what you can do with them." *Working* with the mystery of making things, *watching* light and shadow and animal movement and the strata of sediment, *touching*

> with foot and hand
> the tamp of sand
> against cliff wall,
> noting the undershadow
> of stone ledge.

The verb in the title, "This *Occurs* To Me," implies the natural, participatory context of these observations. These things are. They register as "ordinary" perceptions, intrinsic, unassuming, almost conversational in import, but essential as poetry. Maria Chona, the Papago, told Ruth Underhill half a century ago: "My father went on talking to me in a low voice. That is how our people always talk to their children, so low and quiet, the child thinks he is dreaming. But he never forgets."[9]

The Pueblos have always known walls, from Anasazi origins in cliff-dwellings within nature's own embracing walls, to adobe multiple dwellings with adjoining man-made walls, to earthpit kiva chambers down in the ground-wall itself. Tabletop exposure left the Anasazi cliff-dwellers vulnerable, and the mesa walls dropping into deep valleys offered protection sheltering the old ones from the elements and their enemies. These majestic walls cradled whole villages at Batatakin or Cliff Palace or White House. Families shared adjoining walls like clusters of nesting children. These walls did not divide, so much as fit form to function, like protective layers of durable cloth that contour to the body; indeed, weaver and mason both mold their materials to human needs. Ortiz then learns from his father the traditions of "weaving stone"—not piece work individually, no more than words exist separately, but a tapestry of stones, a pattern that connects. It is a mortaring, too, of son to father, inner to outer being, stone to spirit, concrete particle to organic design. Such a craftsman releases the intrinsic pattern in his materials.

"The words are the vision," *The Good Journey* opens in dedication to the poet's children, "by which we see out and in and around." The poems grow out of the natural language of daily prayer, memory, and thought.

> In the morning, take cornfood inside,
> say words within and without.
> Being careful, breathe in and out,
> praying for sustenance, for strength,
> and to continue safely and humbly,
> you pray.
> ["A San Diego Poem: January–February 1973"]

Gary Witherspoon writes of Navajo language, art, and religion that "speech is the outer form of thought, and thought is the inner form of speech."[10] Knowledge (inner) is to language as thought (inner) is to speech. The whole rests on a religious philosophy of the "in-standing wind soul" breathing life through all people and things. In short, words breathe the inner wind-soul into the world: "It was the wind that gave them life. It is the wind that comes out of our mouths now that gives us life. When this ceases to flow we die. In the skin at the tips of our fingers we see the trail of the wind; it shows us where the wind blew when our ancestors were created" (Navajo origin myth).[11]

Simon Ortiz is not Navajo, but scholars note how the Diné culture grafted on beliefs from older Pueblo traditions; the Navajo expanded and made conscious what their ancient brothers left unsaid and implicit.[12] So the father of Ortiz's sketch, "Something's Going On" in *Howbah Indians* (1978), "breathed in and out upon the cornmeal, motioning to the children that they were to follow along, giving it life so life would continue."[13] Or as Ortiz himself speaks consciously of artistic processes, "The song is basic to all vocal expression. The song as expression is an opening from inside of yourself to outside and from outside of yourself to inside but not in the sense that there are separate states of yourself. Instead, it is a joining and an opening together."[14]

Just as touching flesh-to-flesh, skin being the body's wall, acknowledges mutual need and separation, so the pueblo wall and the tribal word serve to bond the people, at the same time granting them privacy. A walled pueblo allows for communal distinctions where people share common, yet distinct places—compartments, clans, kivas—within the whole. Walls permit cohabitation. Inside to one family is outside to a neighbor, and vice versa. Once recognized as such in a *commun*-ity, neighbors acknowledge their mutual concerns for freedom within adjoining walls, reciprocal lives "inside/outside" across a continuum of time and space. These social dynamics are fusional in positive tensions, kiva circles fronting apartment rectangles, the old riddle of squaring the circle, the one and the many, the whole fitting *into* the natural wall of the earth.[15]

Rooted in sandstone and clay, the old ones hugged the mesa walls and scaled, stone by stone, toward their fields and common sky overhead, never forgetting their spiritual origins down in the kiva *Shipapuni* or "place of emergence." So the old stories say. Pueblo ceremonial life took place underground in the kivas, and the people descended down a "water ladder" into the "water-filled" ritual chamber. The drama of this spiritual descent must be inferred, not at all obvious, through the small hole in the earth's surface wall.

"NOW DAY INDI'NS"

What is said for his father's stonemasonry and ancestral dwellings could as well be carried over to Ortiz's mother and sisters making pottery. Foods and liquids contained *in* traditional vases are determined by the walls of their containers. Both walled container and contained space form the jar, with a functional inner surface adjoining an artistic outer design. And his father's wood carving, to turn the concept once again, exactly inverses this dynamic of pottery making, without losing the principle of common surfaces. In bringing forth the immanent design *in* the grain, the sculpted wood reveals the intrinsic spirit embedded in the grain. Surface both reflects and is substance here. Decoration and function lie contiguous in one "wall" of wood, as it were. "Indeed," Ortiz remarks of an Indian language of common walls, "the song was the road from outside of himself to inside —which is perception—and from inside of himself to outside—which is expression."[16]

HORIZONS HOME

The brown people losing trails
and finding trails and losing them
and finding again—

the horizons
and rains
in the far distance.
—Simon Ortiz

Outside the walls of family and past today, a horizon planes into the future. Will the walls hold? Across America, Ortiz's poetry journeys painfully through the ruins of the present, the despair and challenge of contemporary acculturations. Coyote, reality's credible fool, makes up an origin story to begin things in *Going for the Rain* (1976):

"First of all, it's all true."
Coyote, he says this, this way,
humble yourself, motioning and meaning
what he says

and then the old Trickster lopes off to another page. A gently attentive humor binds Ortiz's poems humanly together, acknowledging and partly

"civilizing" the animal-who-wanders-in-man. This Indian poet declares
"The Significance of a Veteran's Day":

> that I am a veteran of at least 30,000 years
> when I travelled with the monumental yearning
> of glaciers, relieving myself by them,
> growing, my children seeking shelter
> by the roots of pines and mountains.

The trickster-poet's moon-singing laughter temporizes our "b.s.-ing"
human affairs, forgiving and reminding the people of their base natures,
directing them on toward

> the continuance of the universe,
> the travelling, not the progress,
> but the humility of our being there.

"Are you really a poet?" someone asks this hitchhiker. "Shore," Ortiz replies, like a cricket *is* simply a cricket. Along that road where coyotes
prowl and crickets scrape, no more nor less than poets, the wandering pil-
grim stops over at "Washyuma Motor Hotel" where "The ancient spirits
tell stories / and jokes and laugh and laugh." These things keep things going. They make up the cycles, the "ups and downs," the jokes and pains,
the continuities, as time warps back into the circle of all things. This poet
centers on "continuance": laughter's survival, the old ways persisting, a
journey toward being, a joke, a tale, a song-poem always unfolding before
the people. "Why do you write?" an anonymous voice asks in the preface
to *A Good Journey*. "The only way to continue is to tell a story and that's
what Coyote says," the poet returns, then considers further, "your children
will not survive unless you tell something about them."

"Once, in a story, I wrote that Indians are everywhere. / Goddamn
right." But a park ranger at the Florida state line tells Ortiz, "This place is
noted for the Indians / that don't live here anymore" ("Travels in the
South"). The poet must scavenge for Indian survivals, "fugitive" in San
Diego, Chicago, Hollywood, and New York. He hangs on desperately with
bourbon and beer, gutting out hitchhiking hungers, loneliness for home, a
*sub*way blues.

The contemporary Ortiz in *A Good Journey* writes throwaway lines,
fragments of notes, shards from "The Poems I Have Lost": "a long ram-
bling / letter, called it a poem, from Nashville."

> Memories, I guess they are,
> crowd me because of all the signals
> I've missed, the poems that keep
> coming back in pieces.

Prose voices and local Indian views come back to him, as Eagle skips flint stones off Highway 66, sparking a summer night long ago in *Howbah Indians*. It is an eidetic image for the Indian poet: ancient stones flaring off a white man's *high*way penciling the Southwest. A billboard fills the horizon over an Indian gas station, "WELCOME HOWBAH INDIANS."

Ortiz travels Interstate 40 from Albuquerque to Gallup in "Horizons and Rains"—

> witness to the brown people
> stumbling Sunday afternoon
> northwards—

seeking a life-source on the desert. "Where's the rain that feels so good?" The question means "rain," yes, but more than rain: where is the good "way" gone? In this drought of modern times, where are the native gods who wed earth and sky, promising the futurity of spring?[17]

"Where it has always been," Ackley says; the poet asserts of a distance he journeys *into*, "The horizons are still mine" (" 'And The Land Is Just As Dry' " in *A Good Journey*). It is a time, then, to journey home.

The "good journey" to the horizon, "going for the rain," voices a traveling-prayer. The way of words becomes a lifelong pilgrimage, a road one travels away from, and back toward Acoma. "There are things he must go through before he can bring back what he seeks, before he can return to himself." Whatever word assigned—home, family, clan, tribe, history, time itself—the Pueblos seek a place of origin, still alive in the "place where the spirits enter the world." The underground *Shipapuni* is traceable from the Rio Grande basin to the mesa tops and down into the beginnings of the world, the primal Shipapu back with the Anasazi. In "Passing Through Little Rock,"

> The old Indian ghosts—
> > "Quapaw"
> "Waccamaw"—
> > are just billboard words
> in this crummy town.

"You know, I'm worrying a lot lately,"
he says in the old hotel bar.

"You're getting older and scared ain't you?"

I just want to cross the next hill,
through that clump of trees
and come out the other side

and see a clean river,
the whole earth new
and hear the noise it makes
at birth.

A Good Journey records the coming back home of a poet after *Going for the Rain*. "One step at a time to return," even if viewing dioramas of Pueblo "history" among Anasazi ruins, "I have to buy a permit to get back home" ("A Designated National Park"). Coyote Old Man, "Pehrru" the hungry one, goes tramping and shouting his head off, "bragging" around Western-style as "the existential Man":

Coyote, old man, wanderer,
where you going, man?

The poet comes home to his children, packing conversations, anecdotes, advice, recipes, and traditions. His plain speakings risk a prosaic voice; his homilies merge in common concerns.

This father-artist advises his daughter, first "learn how to make good bread." Here rest the old values—domestic virtues, homely moralities, humilities of prayer, laughter and weeping among blooded kin—still appropriate for a settled life and stable culture, no matter how apparently archaic by contemporary standards. The quest, for Ortiz, is always "a full life," a good journey, a bellyful of good food. He even jots down a prose poem, "How to make a good chili stew."

In the ongoing struggle with moneyed "foundations," who offer tractors and gas for mining rights to a culture, Indians thirst for trust,

We are hungry for the good earth,
the deserts and mountains growing corn.

While "Apache Red" and "Mericano" wrestle on one TV channel, and astronauts walk the moon on another channel, a *Howbah Indians* family talks across generations:

"NOW DAY INDI'NS"

"That's some story, Nana, but it's a dream.
It's a dream but it's the truth, Faustin said.
I believe you, Nana, his grandson said."

Somewhere in a bar in Cuba, New Mexico, the people come together to speak German, French, Navajo, Spanish, Acoma, and English all at one time: "We were a confluence of separate languages / and the common language of ourselves" ("Place We Have Been"). The word and the prayer, the struggle and the deed, register in the "continuances" of Simon Ortiz's children expressed in "A Birthday Kid Poem":

It shall end well.
It shall continue well.
It shall be.
It shall.
It shall.
It shall.
It shall.

FLAKES FROM THE MATRIX

Buckeye endures on this land
where oak and screwbean bend
blackened into human hands.
—WENDY ROSE, "Buckeye,"
from *Lost Copper*

According to the mythic bestiary and botany of her poetry, Wendy Rose issued from a badger father (Hopi) and a buckeye mother (Miwok) interfused with Euroamerican bloodlines. This "native" American, born in 1948 in urban California, lives off the reservation, with two-thirds of the Indians today. She sketches as a professional artist, writes poems and essays, studies anthropology (M.A. from Berkeley in 1978), and speaks out for "now day Indians" rejecting pureblood notions of noble savagery.

Almost-Indian, Indian-ghosted, an identity older than language waits to speak through Wendy Rose. Her origin is a spirit-being more instinctive even than a name, as voiced in "The well-intentioned question" from *Lost Copper*:

"NOW DAY INDI'NS"

> my Indian name listens
>
> for footsteps
> stopping short of my door
> then leaving forever.

She sees herself orphaned, a butterfly made to grow another way, a spoke of the sacred hoop sprung away from the middle. "I have chosen to sit at the stiffened edge / of autumn." The poet, fated a breed, will choose native differences.

Rose lives as a marginal woman on the lines between races, cultures, and languages. She is "foreign and familiar at once," the poet confesses, suffering and surviving on the limits of city and country. She stands her ground, however, in trenches of racial alienation, where mixed-bloods can exist neither Indian nor non-Indian, both and none. As Paula Gunn Allen (Laguna) writes about estranged half-breeds: "a white world that rejects him, an Indian world that abandons him. . . . To be sure, American Indians are not the only people who suffer alienation in the modern world, but they are among the most beleaguered, the most wounded by it. For, like the protagonists in their novels and like the speakers in their poems, they live in a land that is no longer their home, among strangers who determine, senselessly, the patterns of their lives, and they are, for the most part, powerless to do much more than determine the cause of their deaths."[18]

Allen and Rose and other Indian women, born "breeds," decide to fight for their Indianness and to write about that choice. Like Indian meal leached from California buckeye on the Sierra slopes, acrid and poisonous until processed, Wendy Rose's art tempers the native sting in a daily staple. She nurtures herself on her own struggle.

"And so my origin is one," Rose relates in "The day I was conceived,"

> of rocks and badgers; I sing
>
> but do not carve. My origin is one
> of moondust and medicine;
> I dance but do not pray.
>
> My origin is one of maize and mesquite;
>
> I grow but do not live.

Wendy Rose writes with a contrary's come-and-go, the "backwards-forwards" clowning that steeled northern plains warriors, men and women, in a world of inversions. It is Old Man Coyote's instinct for survival, as well, on the edges of village and wilderness. Rose dares reality with Trickster's nip-and-tuck, playing the serious game of life-and-death. She is a poet who barks and scudders for cover, who won't keep quiet or give in to oppression. She battles for native rights with a brave's honest sense of ambivalence toward the cost of life, without forsaking an artist's sensitivity. Hers is an old Lakota formula for a visionary leader, a sacred "word sender." She meets the world, too, with a skin "seven thumbs thick," as counseled among the eastern Iroquois when they spoke of strong leaders.

This poet-activist teeters in battle, rocklike, on the cliffs of vertical city walls: she opposes the violence of American city culture. She makes use of the energy of imbalance, a doubling self winding through the torque of Indian redefinition in contemporary society. The war, for her, is often fought in anthropological archives to defend Indian culture and still preserve, by way of her native and academic "twisted-twin birth," what otherwise would be lost. This woman's lineage traces to the mythic Hopi genatrix, "Hard Beings Woman" or *Huruing Wuhti*. "Hard Beings Woman" existed in the beginnings of all things, along with Grandmother Spider, her variously named twin granddaughters, and Southwest matrilineal deities. To this day, Indian women have learned to survive on rocks, as stated in the "Epilog" to *Lost Copper*.

> Silko and Allen and Harjo and me:
> our teeth are hard
> from the rocks we eat.

Rose etches herself "maverick" in America, as she says, "urban half-breed, burro-faced," in reference to broad-nosed, bold-lined, densely animate "orphans" sketched among her poems. "Chasing the paper-shamans" in *Lost Copper* asserts,

> I believe in them,
> these hard-lined flat people
> who are given life under my hand.

The artist's black-and-white images of Indian women defy convention and portray herself grinning back scampishly from her verse, where the idiosyncratic flatness of her water-color/ink art speaks with two-dimensional clarity.

"NOW DAY INDI'NS"

Here I go drawing pictures again.
I illustrate a different world
as I chase the shamans who watch each day

There is a firmness of attack and lack of pretense, as in the poetry, and no doubt where Rose draws the line.

Trickster, who traditionally feeds on bitter rind among the old tribal ways, steals the poet's words and leaves behind offal, garbage, rags, carrion, and cartoons. Rose collects her collage of poetic imagery from this strewn detritus, the latest book opening with a "Frontispoem" for *Lost Copper*:

This then my harvest

squash-brown daughters
blue corn pollen,
lost copper.

Among these earth-and-sky-stained offspring, she rolls like a wild mustang in the dirt of the aching earth. Food-gatherer and hunter, Rose farms her losses. She gallops from the archaeological catacombs of UC Berkeley down Telegraph Avenue, a renegade anthropologist turned centaur to roam the mountains and deserts. She mixes metaphors and ideas and inks and emotions in bicultural compost, a living poetic mixture unlike any other. She calls to her ancestors down city streets and academic corridors, summoning a native America within America—the songs, tales, flesh, bones, stones, and spirits in things here at home.

Sensitivity blossoms among the rocks of her loss and anger, as Rose's imagination graces the politics of have-nots and the poetics of estrangement: "touching ourselves / we touch everything," she claims in the poetry of *Academic Squaw*. We are, red and white, black and brown, clothed in earth bodies, bound in the immediacy of flesh, composed of things themselves. The many Indian religious beliefs of immanent souls in natural objects, from the Navajo concept of an "in-standing wind-soul," to the Yurok concept of an earth heartbeat, to the Lakota invocation of the creator-spirit in the wind, "What Moves-moves," reappear in this woman's pan-Indian poetry. Spirited bodies, we are moved, psychically and physically, as the spirit of the world lives through our touch, the poetry holds. So the older native beliefs contend, and so the poems demonstrate, at odds with the mechanistic indifference of modern society. There are no accidents in the ways things happen, Indian traditionals are known to say.

Wendy Rose is also, in her own words, "a woman who judges." She would protect living Indian cultures and their ancestral ties in ancient burial grounds from ignorance, greed, rapacity, and most of all, from a senseless belt of asphalt that is always going somewhere, fast, out of fear of the land itself, the land's history, the land's settlements, the land's ancient inheritors. The "developers," whether in real estate, movie making, energy resources, tourism, or anthropology, drive beyond their own bodies, divorced from their mother earth. As a doctoral student in anthropology, Wendy Rose has known the irony of trying to conserve "native" America from within the ranks of the invaders, the traders, the collectors, and the curators. From the curious to the avaricious, passers-by prey on Indian America. Rose protests: she must "promise again / to protect what's left," as in "November: San Joaquin Valley" from *Lost Copper*.

Indians are not artifacts. Wendy Rose knows the agony, confusion, bitterness, and blues of native bondage in a land whitewashed and blacktopped away from its natural sumac and oak, creek bed and watershed, abalone and egret, grizzly and pelican. The greed for gold, land, bones, beads, oil, copper, silver, coal, uranium, water, and entertainment in America stokes the engines of "progress," as it chokes this Indian woman's voice. "I suckle coyotes / and grieve."

The poet would talk back bitterly, even militantly, to this injustice: challenging big businessmen, redneck racists, Christian crusaders, prying academics, art-for-art's-sake aesthetes, and her own giving-in to middle groundings. As Vine Deloria, Standing Rock Sioux, argues in *Custer Died for Your Sins*, Indians would settle for a cultural leave-us-alone policy from tourist America.

Never soft on her audience, Rose is hardest on herself, this woman of stone courage. She lives an intensity and commitment to being "Indi'n." She has had to work for her self-definition, asking neither empathy nor solace. She speaks in fine resistance to wrong. She fists poetry out of Indian self-determination, as her lines concretize Indian feelings. And so Wendy Rose would harden into being, again as granddaughter to the Hopi creator, "Hard Beings Woman," against the white abstractions of Indians vanishing in the wake of the invaders' ignorance.

Since Indians have grown by a multiple of six, from the all-time low of a quarter million in 1900, Rose argues in "The endangered roots of a person" that

"NOW DAY INDI'NS"

Becoming strong on this earth is a lesson
in not floating, in becoming less transparent,
in becoming an animal shape against the sky

Her wild silhouettes push against an empty horizon and resurrect the totemic spirits and animal guardians of the old days.

Over at "The Anthropology Convention," the stiffening poet listens inside her scars to "trowel-ticked bones" of ancestors,

And some part of this world
old and pagan as the ticks on my skin
just holds on.

There are splinters in her tongue, critters on her skin. Her poems hold on, trading in traditional/contemporary surrealisms, dream visions, lonely chiseled images, impacted meanings that jar a reader. "I have learned to expect nothing," the poet says in "Looking Back from the Mud." She speaks through fragments, shards, ruins, no less than the wasteland poets of the twentieth century in Western literature:

These words must be remembered
as butchered things, as bits of life
thrown down;
["Aging into death: Petrify then dissolve"]

This poet of a twisted throat knows her art to be a language of "mutation," by conventional white standards. She sings beyond semantics, out of the agony of being Indian/white. She risks unaccepted syntax, irregular form, and ideas that bite in "Looking Back from the Mud":

I must look fine as I stomp & stride
through the salt-marsh university halls.
That long-ago theme of "Indian power!"
is an old echo now; at the university
we pretend we are deaf.
After all, we're *in* now—

. . . .

Was it all "to be somebody,"
to "know the enemy," to be a "Skin, man"
urban kin to the ones at home?

Not one seed
has sprouted from my sweat.
Not one prophet
has thundered from my books.

But through irregularities of original voices, all poets stutter toward revelation, and no lines come easy. In the wake of stunned witness and a vision of things, some remain more open to their pain and awkward art than others. Wendy Rose chisels her confusion powerfully, organically; her stone-sharpened poems run nicked on truth, never glazed simply in beauty. As here in "Politic," the fragments gather like scruffy coyotes in the rough music of many voices:

Freeing the song
from the music
is my poet's task;
the words
must be flaked
from their matrix.

This artist, finally said, works with her hands with words. She chips away at America's intractable rocks of ignorance regarding Indians.

If the word "stone" were a stone, we could stand on it, and indeed imagine ourselves rooted in the earth. If "bone" *were* bone, we would flesh ourselves around it and remain firm. If "sage" were only sage, we could say it blessed and wise. If "copper" were copper, we would touch our hands and temper our voices to it. Wendy Rose, an alchemical Indian poet, has incarnated her words with native integrity. If "lost" were forever lost, then we would have no memory ringing in our language, no words to live by, no books of poetry leading up to this most recent *Lost Copper*. Here is an Indian woman who mines the losses and makes alloys of native experience in American poetry.

RENEWALS

Being Indian is in part an idea of self, Scott Momaday believes, beyond bloodline, tribe, government roll number, or pan-Indian politics.[19] If so, it is an internal, even spiritual, self-definition that is registered in daily acts. It is the taproot into an ancestral past deep in the land.

To date, Indian poets and novelists are generally unknown outside tribal circles. They write in eclectic voices, draw from given languages and tribal backgrounds, overlap with other tribes and American culture at large, and focus the specialized vision of modern artists. The new Indian writers are children of the old ways and students of historical transition; they begin to serve as teachers of contemporary survival. In the universal particulars of their works, they write as disciples of visionary traditions that distinguish artists over all ages and cultures.

Indian poets, gathered since 1975 in the UCLA Native American Series, help to correct the image of lost, forgotten, or silent native voices contemporary in America: Norman Russell's *indian thoughts; the children of god* (1975); J. Ivaloo Volborth's *Thunder-Root* (1978); Barney Bush's *My Horse And a Jukebox* (1979); William Oandasan's *A Branch of California Redwood* (1980); and Paula Gunn Allen's *Shadow Country* (1982), published with funding from the National Endowment for the Arts. In 1983 the UCLA Indian Studies Center will publish Linda Hogan's *Eclipse* with an NEA matching grant.

In their varying styles and subjects, these poets facet a cross-section of Indian writing that could be reflected in other samplings, groupings of the seventy-four Indian writers, for example, anthologized in Geary Hobson's *The Remembered Earth*. The assorted poets represent the rank-and-file of artists across Indian America, backwoods to academia. It is from such a community of working poets that Momaday, Silko, Ortiz, Welch, and Rose draw their tribal sense of contemporary Indian arts.

> Crazy Horse dreamed and went into the world where there is
> nothing but the spirits of all things. That is the real world
> that is behind this one, and everything we see here is
> something like a shadow from that world.
>
> [*Black Elk Speaks*]

J. Ivaloo Volborth is a young American woman drawn to finding her personal identity in Native America. Her father of Apache descent, her mother Comanche, she grew up on the eastern industrial seaboard, severed from Indian communal life. As a school dropout in New York City, "far from Mescal Mountain," she still heard the bullroarers, the water drums, and the rain-making Sky-Boys whisper in the rubber and steel pulse of the city. Her poems are essentially personal transformations, in this regard, rediscoveries of a magic native in this earth—traditions rooted in indigenous peoples, their tongues, their lands, legends, and gods. The poet's needs tie into an imaginative tribal family, powerfully alive, at the heart of this Turtle Island; she sings the mix of cultures and tongues in her own gathering identity. *Thunder-Root* taps into the Sky-Boys' lightning, deep within the earth, deeper than concrete and the confusions of bloodlines, tribal dislocations, dispirited acculturations.

Volborth's *Thunder-Root* begins with dream songs to mark the night: abalone horses circling the moon's rim, sleeping beetles and a wet-nosed coyote about to sneeze, Coyote the dreamer out collecting fragments along a shore. Three movements—translucent image, comic disruption, dream quest—pattern the collection of poems.

The poetry occurs at quiet times, the dusk of need and desire and stirring dreams. In "Native Winter" the water spiders have gathered the lake shadows, the crows have ceased their gossip, and

> The-One-Who-Scatters-Leaves-
> Across-The-Snow
>   has departed

Here, essentially *without*, Volborth hears her muse, "the flute-player / rising in my ear." Everywhere there is the poet's stillness, a waiting and listening for images that focus the day's confusions into lunar clarity, from the traditional "rattling darkness" to the poet's own

> fluid pools
>   where Moon-seeds have fallen.

The poems register as acts of a tenuous courage drawn from darkness; the night, shadows, and edges of reality lay the ceremonial grounds for poems, as though the afterimages of daily life spirited the poet's imagination. "In the great night my heart will go out," chanted Owl Woman, the Papago healer, "Toward me the darkness comes rattling, / In the great night my heart will go out."[20] Volborth's songs to the night ceremonialize each day a good day to die, so the old warriors celebrated their mortality. Native American death chants arise in pulses of the heart, affirmations of life, mysterious and fearful.

The poetry takes us to poetic sightings where images dawn fresh and luminous. Says Don Talayesva, the Hopi, "I studied clouds and paid close attention to my dreams in order to escape being trapped by storms too far from shelter" (*Sun Chief*).[21] The process is both accurate in the world and deeply interior; the poems set up continuities between objective reality and imaginative recesses, the outside world and inner vision.

As in a dream, Volborth speaks of seeing the shape and texture of poetic detail, then listening for the tones of the image. The word "abalone," she told me, began to glow when she looked carefully at the iridescent, mother-of-pearl layers in a seashell—and then suddenly, as if by some natural magic, she could *hear* the opalescent ripples in "ab-a-lo-ne." And to sing of abalone horses circling the moon's rim is surely an act of creative vision.

Volborth's songs are consistently the chants of Moon-Rim-Runners, creatures on the lunar edges of things; they sing of thresholds, pilgrimages, magical transformations. Old Shadow Woman lifts her painted breasts in a dusk chant, and Grandfather goes "home, / back to his Mother, / to sit in the shadows / of her painted breasts." The poems often rest on the edges of not being there; the images appear, flare, and recede as the concrete world fades into the breath of songs, tonal images coalescing from the mists of words.

The poet works by the slender line, sculpted in the manner of Japanese haiku and northern plains song-poetry; she sees in patterned fragments, sketching line by line as the images gather.

> Old Woman bent by heavy snow,
> in the weight of her breath
> a Sky-Loom appears.

Her single-tone poems reveal a rare craft. A word strikes a note, then another, and the poet holds still for resonances, overtones, echoes.

> Iron-Door-Woman,
> behind downy plumed clouds.
> Crows await your eyes.

The waiting time is essential, consonant with the wordless canvas around each image that takes shape. All is dependent on a suggestive minimal stroke, and in the distance, a sky-clear terrain.

Volborth moves by instinct to the beginnings of things. She lets images surprise and shape her dreams in lyric terraces. And in such dream-poetry, the reader peers through a water-glazed lens, "a moon domed sea," at the calligraphy of a finely tuned imagination.

"NOW DAY INDI'NS"

There is another facet to Judith Volborth's poetry—an animal wit, a subtle play, a sneeze about to disrupt the need for meditative rest. The refrain for these poems might be the mad dogs' laughter:

> "Enough!" cried Coyote jumping in circles on his hind.
> But the mad dogs of four-quarters
> continued to yelp and laugh at Coyote.
> "Coyote dared dream on Red Ant Hill."
> "Coyote dared dream on Red Ant Hill."

Coyote lends the poet a mask to sing native places in a dreamworld where everything that goes wrong is right, matching wit with the gods, fabling our bestial selves through extended animal kin—Lone Hare, Dancing Bear, Night Otter, even Black-Coat, the pestilent missionary. Volborth has charmed the traditional Coyote Trickster, an inspired clown and libidinal god, into a lyric singer whose howl, rightly heard, is the music of wild, gentle things.

> Molten Moon
> drips down into the pine needles.
> Coyote tracks embers
> all along the embankment,
> "Yipyip-Eeeeooowww!"

The poet finds patterned release in Coyote's antics, melody in his yelp, design in his running, whirling, and spinning. Attuned with the wheeling moon, this lyrical Coyote is not simply an animal fool of license or comic exaggeration—but a singer and player, clever and sensical in his own tangents, ludicrous often, yet appealing as a "native" American, kin with all creatures. Still brother to the poet in her shy retreat, Coyote tells Turtle Medicine, "I've waited this long already"—for the world to quiet down so he can get some sleep, for the lice to go away, for Black-Coat to shut up. And yet he waits. Coyote can be patient, chanting shadows while the molten moon drips into pine needles; the goal is a mind of liquid illumination, the ideal a poet's incandescent clarity of vision.

A lean scavenger, the drone of fat-bellied flies, an empty buffalo head "makes a lean Coyote impatient." The lessons show going without in a world of changes, the landscape scoured, the poet a child alone, her "furry reach too small." Volborth sings her own "Animal Thirst," crouching below, looking up to visionary life with prosaic need:

"NOW DAY INDI'NS"

> Empty wind,
> milky tit
> in hollow sky:
> my furry reach
> too small.

The attitude is one of supplication, loss of self, the humbling of the vision quest. "Pity me, for I want to live," plains Sun Dancers chant, staring into the sun, helpless figures of pierced flesh in a vast plain. "And here I stand / with an empty bridle," the poet calls to the circling abalone horses on the moon's rim.

> Pass the whirl of Moon-Rim-Runners,
> journey into the den
> where The-Hump-Backed-Flute-Player
> has left his notes in cold stone,
> past soaring graves and dust hawks
> where clinks of bone rattles are heard.

"Come," she calls to us,

> enter where the ghost of my tongue
> seeds out skeletal words,
> where Bull-Roarers rage
> the windless cries
> of your frothy tears.

INDIAN HONKY-TONK

Barney Bush, a Shawnee/Cayuga in his early thirties, comes out of southern Illinois, Oklahoma, and New Mexico. Poet, teacher, and speaker, Bush is gifted with a first-person lyric voice, and he roams all over America. He sings the contemporary Indian blues—bars, loves lost, Indians in cities, powwows, booze, drugs, cops, suicides. He lives on the edges of a Native American pain, chanting through the broken bones in our lives.

Commenting on Richard Wright's "blues" and the ethnic American experience, Ralph Ellison has written in *Shadow and Act*: "The blues is an impulse to keep the painful details and episodes of a brutal experience alive in one's aching consciousness, to finger its jagged grain, and to transcend it,

211

not by the consolation of philosophy but by squeezing from it a near-tragic, near-comic lyricism."[22] To lament and to laugh at once, out of the pain of being Indian—and the pride—is Barney Bush's trickster talent. He lives with the holy humor of the Lakota heyoka or Southwest kachina. According to Vine Deloria, this humor is the binding "cement" of a contemporary Indian consciousness (*Custer Died for Your Sins*).[23]

In a generation of rough-cut Native American realists— James Welch, Leslie Silko, Simon Ortiz, Wendy Rose, Ray Young Bear, Joy Harjo— Barney Bush is a narrative chanter of the conversations that make up our everyday lives.

> —we both know—
> about how nights turn cold
> the leaves fall too soon
> and the grey mystery
> of glancing at each other
> over pool tables and
> jukeboxes

His poetry is distinctly contemporary. Rather than identifying in the older traditions with a single tribal origin and fixed sense of place, Bush works toward an Indian consciousness of tribes and places that would bind Native Americans together. He seems, first of all, a human being who reaches down for definition as an Indian—but with a present-tense twist, a traveler's knowing of the way things are in country and city nowadays. He carries a bedrock awareness of what it means to live "off" the "res," as most Indians now do, and long to go home again.

> I thought about how
> you walked
> cowboy boots, chokers
> Oklahoma, Pine Ridge,
> and an eagle feather
> I don't remember promising
> you

There is a lamenter's song here, in an updated ritual of the vision quest, "the long ride home" to Indian self-definition; it is longing and wistful at times, and other times gently sad or comic.

Bush writes of his own Indianness *in* the heart of America. His ancestral visions are clouded by urban despair, waste, a sense of something lost, though distantly recoverable. His traditional past is set against city time and the descents of history, nascent in tribal names, family ties, Indian places, powwows in "Milwaukee, Chicago, Minneapolis," city names all in their origins Indian.

The prologue to these poems speaks of a rock breathing and blowing leaves, while Bush's artist friend "Richard is laughing / with the otter / foaming whirlpools." Although the way is difficult, stone-broken in pain, a horizon from home, the poet still senses a whirling energy of correspondences and animal-human freedoms in the natural world of Native America; this imaging of likenesses throughout the creation is akin, in spirit, to the pleasures of pure laughter. The energy of delight, motion, transformation, and renewal allows Indian people to endure the pain of being alive: "laughing all the way / out to Volcano Cliffs about / Indians 49ing in the rain."

And in refrain there's the going home again: "By bits and pieces I made / it home," hitchhiking on Christmas Day, "back-tracking," James Welch has it, to a place and people always there by the side of the asphalt road. Barney Bush finds his way back with a mind of fall, a seasonal anticipation of hard, exacting times and the need to return home before winter sets in. Among cousins and at beer parties, the poet lives through the lean seasons beadworking and playing cards all night, warmed by piñon fires and a shared blanket until the wind calls. He writes poems to some lost one in the north country, voicing the human side of the contemporary Indian story, recalling wild, good times. He lives as Lame Deer, the Lakota stand-up holy comedian, saw himself alive, "An *ikce wicasa*, a common, wild, natural human being."[24] Barney calls a friend, mending broken bones in a hospital and hungering for breaded porkchops, "You goddamn crazy Indian." *My Horse And a Jukebox* comes alive with Coyote's Oklahoma bark, loping gait, scruffy hide, and midnight laughter. And while Coyote yaps in the half-shadows, Bush sings with the wind, "I been out drinking / all night long, way-ya hey-ye."

In all this coming and going, loving and parting, shadows sinking into the lake, the reader hears a drumming pulse, water-muted. It is an unspoken Indian accent, felt in the spaces between people—the wistful distances that separate things and memories and places we want to carry with us. "You heard it's tough to be an Indi'n," Lame Deer once said in his backyard, "but the whole world is a tough thing for ever'body."

My Horse And a Jukebox reaches down to a buried image, an interior Indian, coming to life through daily trust in songs and poems and stories:
"Feel that crazy / Chippewa sitting inside / my heart." Given the disparity between time (present) and times past, the tenuous correspondences between the young and the old-young, this poet straddles history. Across the
new and the ancestral, the past and the present-past carried with us, Barney
Bush talk-sings his Indian ways going home in the fall of America.

> for we know we are
> part of the shadows
> that sink deep into the
> lake after the sun
> has gone.

SOUTHWEST SHADOWS

Laguna mother, Lakota grandfather, Lebanese father, life on the
margins of mainstream and Indian: Paula Gunn Allen lives somewhere between American norms and Native American closures. She writes in the
shadows of visions, "fingering silence and sound" with a poet's touching
measure. She sings of desire and grief, confusion and rage over a horizon
note of loss. *Shadow Country*: that marginal zone of interfusions, neither the
shadower, nor the shadowed, both and neither, in liminal transition. "I
looked about me and could see that what we then were doing was like a
shadow cast upon the earth from yonder vision in the heavens, so bright it
was and clear," Black Elk remembered. "I knew the real was yonder and
the darkened dream of it was here."[25]

Paula Allen grew up in the halfway house of mixed ancestry. This
woman lives not so much in a given tribe as working to articulate her sense
of the tribal, without rhetorical claims. She chooses Native American definitions, defining Native American *in* her life. Her Laguna origins come mixed.
Ruth Underhill sees the Laguna Pueblo in *First Penthouse Dwellers of America*
as "a refugee town of Spanish days" back many centuries, a mixture of
Keresan, Shoshonean, Tanoan, and Zuñian influx with Navajo, Spanish,
and immigrant Anglo settlers.[26] Edgar Hewett elsewhere describes this

settlement as "an old aggregate of tribes and clans brought more or less together by acculturation and intermixes" (*Indians of the Rio Grande Valley*).[27]

Both part of and apart from Laguna, Allen knows only too well the tribal sense of alienation, the corresponding necessity for mutual assimilation. She lives America *and* Native America. And fall is always back of the country, under dreams of spring. Allen sees a changed America, unknown to her now, remembered lyrically as "native" for indigenous peoples. In "Tucson: First Night" she recalls,

> "the Road," we said,
> implying that time had no changing.
> (Like Plato in our innocence)
> clouds that were there
> are here. Now. My mind and the sky,
> one thing on the edge of surmise (sunrise).

Paula Allen rediscovers old traditions and records new Indian adaptations. Her poems shatter stereotypes of blood warriors and demure squaws. *Shadow Country* gives voice to the polychromatic shock of Indian modernism as, for example, visualized in Fritz Scholder's paintings: cowboy Indians slouch with cigarettes and dark glasses, Coors beer cans and American flag shawls, ice cream cones and flared umbrellas on horses. Scholder's "Portrait of a Massacred Indian" portrays an image of bow and plains buckskin, the warrior's head a blurred acrylic palette. "Indian Power" silhouettes a naked red torso on a lunging purple pony, Kafka not far away.

Paula Allen experiments with personal quests through poetic forms and subjects. A mood or technique carries her an uncharted distance through open forms; on the way she sets her own standards of honesty and love. The poet's body is her receptor, mind her tool, spirit her courage. Allen's *impression* leads toward thought; she follows a sentiment diversely, wherever it goes, without compulsion to answer or solve the problems encountered. Her poetry accepts a common "negative capability": the aloneness, irresolution, even tragedy a person lives out honestly and struggles to voice.

Allen explores a woman's self-images and self-esteems, with a girl-child's sensitivity to pain. Men stand in the distances, women foregrounded. In "Off Reservation Blues" she dreams the Lady of Laguna, locked in a tower of defeated fantasy, earth-fearing, behind glass and above a white-skinned figure who waves but cannot hear:

> night was coming
> and I had to speak
> raise my hand and hit the glass
> I groaned
> sound too soft to hear

The grief language of her body registers in mute acts. She braves see-through barriers of sex, race, class, education, language, "civilization," even consciousness itself in its many definitions—out of that breed no (wo)man's land of pained articulation, potentially revolutionary on the poet's tongue. Existing wholly neither Indian nor non-Indian, Allen assimilates both as best she can, through the racist fractures of native history.

Euro-Americans pull back from a dark-light otherness in mixed bloods, who are left peoples without a people when dark skins reject them too. In "A Stranger in My Own Life" Paula Allen states simply, "The breed is an Indian who is not an Indian." "That is, breeds are a bit of both worlds, and the consciousness of this makes them seem alien to Indians while making them feel alien among whites."[28] Realistically, more than half the native peoples in America today are neither Red nor white; the majority of Indians are mixed bloods living off the reservation. Fuller bloods reject these breeds on paling racial lines and broken cultural origins.

Artist of this crossed setting, Allen uses what-is to push toward her own self-definition, however painful and complex:

> If my language is oblique
> misunderstandable—
> if I confine myself
> within demands of imaged time—
> I saw true one night:
> the keeper and the kept,
> saw myself,
> how I must
> be—not in the forests of *should*—
> but actually:
> this narrow pass,
> this sharpness of tongue,
> this blade to cut your heart out
> and offer it to the sun
> must stay quiet awhile.

"NOW DAY INDI'NS"

She will wait, meditate, assimilate her own life, another day to speak.

On the diagonal, such a poet can write of "Relations" from the under-side: Trickster's contrary perceptions, knowing the world from bottom up, inside out, as Peter Blue Cloud says, asshole to grin-hole. Cast out and down, Trickster knows a ground sense *in* things, as poets plead and cajole, a study of thought in its origins, and felt thought

> of dead poets, dead buffalo, dead coyotes, dead waters, dead ground
> where understanding hangs in the balance,
> precariously.

Not-knowing, knowing forbidden or dangerous things, knowing obliquely, keeps this woman desperately alive, a chill in her courage to look down under words.

> cántas encantadas, wondering, de la luna, del sol, del muerte,
> de la vida
> (forgotten and lost) where song is a one-time shot, where
> pain and bearing in blood make the herbs of understanding bloom
> on this once new earth that is dying once again:

Dying also wakens the poet, her agony a birthing resurrection, her loss a new awareness. She knows by the shadows where we are: like memory in an afterimage, but more presently tense, absently and darkly with us.

> There are no shadows
> to tell us where we are,
> but memory of yesterday's
> perfect songs, when tomorrow was sure,
> a time of met images and kept fires:
> winter dreams that almost disappeared
> in scattered light.

Here, in canceled lines from "The Return," the price of knowledge is shaded by loss, the gap between being and knowing-of-being.

Allen's clarity, within confusions openly embraced, comes by way of her need to regain that still place of earth-integrated acceptance.

> This winter or next
> we will go home again
> back to our own time and earth
> and know the silence of change and bone,
> of easy disappearance and of flight.

217

"NOW DAY INDI'NS"

"The Trick is Consciousness," she says in the chapbook, *Coyote's Daylight Trip*, but an inverting trick at times, unpredictable.[29] Backtracking romantic and traveler of memory, betrayal, secret love, the night that covers and forgives all in mystery, Coyote reminisces dreams of truths in all lights, day or night. To know is painful too often, not to know can be innocent wonder.

> The key is in remembering, in what is chosen for the dream.
> In the silence of recovery we hold
> the rituals of the dawn,
> now as then.
>
> Watch

The "silence of recovery" reconciles: that looking back to witness, without questioning, without pain, momentarily.

This poet asks questions of human beings needing one another. Her poems speak of desiring out of the passion to touch and bridge distances; yet she realistically accepts this love as longing, bred out of failures and infrequencies of romance. Allen's true peace comes in accepting our common losses. She writes in "Moonshot: 1969" of a

> heart, a quiet cool house;
> children breathing dreams,
> whimpering sometimes to their visions;
> moon: a light softly centering inside my eyes:

But the moon's light illuminates a pale distance *between* people and things. Even light absorbs a time of loss traveling, the stars tell us; recollection falls away from immediate sensation. "The moon is still more imagination than rock," Allen argues a vision *of* reality, perceiver and perceived consciously interpenetrant.

> the moon reaches of the mind,
> searching with careful fingers of sense-memory,
> listening inside the ear for lost songs,
> almost forgotten footfalls,
> feeling gingerly with the tongue-tip of the heart—
> this gazing, steady, frightened, is the scape of moon madness,
> the certain consequence of remembering
> what is best forgot.

"NOW DAY INDI'NS"

At cost, there is clarity in looking back, by way of an inner moon of re-
membrance. This is not the "real" world of things imposed on the poet,
but a lyric counterstressing of freedom and will, the mind re-imagining its
own world.

Paula Allen admits and accepts places/things/peoples *un*known. She writes
in the shadows between "here" and "there," crystalline in "Snowgoose":

> North of here where
> water marries ice,
> meaning is other than what
> I understand.

Love recedes and proves abstract for the dislocated poet, unfulfilled on Indian relocation, a dreamed need more than a comfort. Surreal ache slaps her
conscious in "Paradigm":

> I dreamed
> of making love, of needing
> to make love, of
> not being able to. Of touching your face
> in awe, of seeing the rose of life on it,
> your skin a matin in a moister place.
> I dreamed of a dead cat they skinned for the party,
> a striped-grey cat that decided not to die
> but got up from its skinning and began to eat.

The losses of love reflect dreams and disappointments back on this woman's
desire, tensing her to search herself.

Paula Allen writes with the complete and myriad sensitivities of a
woman with children, with a husband, in love, out of love, marriage,
divorce, redefinition: old women with weavings and potteries, new women
with separations and self-definitions, "He na Tye Woman" chants the
waters of the ever fertile earth mother, in "recognition and remembering,"
through the "Long shadows of afternoon" now in the poet's life:

> (Lady, why does your love so touch me?
> (Lady, why do my hands have strength for you?
> (Lady, how could I wander so long without you?

Often, a woman's opaque teasing tints the poems, refusing linear logics
and singular openings of meaning. Shared American questions place the

poet, many-minded and multiplexly emotional, among her true "native" shadows, with echoes of Whitman, not to mention his descendants Pound, Williams, Olson, Creeley, and Snyder. "No you can't use me," an Indian mother defies abuse,

> but you can share
> me with me as though
> I were a two-necked wedding jar
> they make, over in Santa Clara—
> some for each of us
> enough

The poetry is feminist in an older sense. A woman's work lies at the heart of this poet's living, food and water, clothing and shelter, birthing and continuation:

> some make potteries
> some weave and spin
> remember
> the Woman/celebrate
> webs and making
> out of own flesh
> earth

In a land of sacred rain, where the Laguna *kashare* priests merge with storm clouds, often the only lasting reservoirs have been women's bowls. Pueblo potteries catch the spirits of the dead coming back in rainfall. Over centuries Pueblo women re*member* the old pots that cradle and carry water. These forms prove reusable with a sense of continuous ancestry, answering the people's daily needs:

> brown hands shaping
> earth into earth
> food for bodies
> water for fields
> they use
> old pots
> broken
> fragments
> castaway
> bits

"NOW DAY INDI'NS"

to make new
mixed with clay
it makes strong
bowls, jars
new
she
brought
light
we remember this
as we make
the water bowl

9

GRANDMOTHER STORYTELLER:
Leslie Silko

The Indians, first seeing in us their lost white brothers
who would establish the universal pattern of Creation,
had then projected on us the causes of our mutual
failure. We in turn projected on them our own fears of
the mysterious spirit-of-place of the new continent and
of the inimical forces of nature within us. So it was
that we both, the red and white, projected upon each
other the repressed dark shadow of our dual nature,
bringing forth the tragedy of America.

Once more we must go to them, not as invaders
despising them as primitive savages but as their lost
white brothers, without prejudices and projections.

—FRANK WATERS, *Pumpkin Seed Point*

    Indian storytelling, old and new, is drawn from living history. Its angle
of truth derives from a belief in families telling their lives directly. Its sense
of art turns on tribal integrity.

    To tell a story the Indian way, no less than to write, means not so
much to fictionalize, as to inflect the truth of the old ways still with us
("novel" may suggest making up new, even unreal events, considering the

second definition for storyteller is "liar" in the Oxford English Dictionary). The Indian storyteller weaves a narrative less as a point-of-view, detached on the crosshairs of art, more as a human presence, attended by an audience taking part in the story. It is not a question of the "rhetoric of fiction," in Western terms for the novel, but of historical witness to human events.

Why do cultures tell stories? Storytelling personally brings people together; it engages them collectively in giving and receiving the events of their lives. In such storytelling times, people occupy space with focused attention; they enter their common world more fully. In the tribe, people share and pass on information, values, and beliefs through stories. They are entertained while learning their culture's crafts, skills, and means of survival. They historically mark and recount events worth remembering, so that culture extends history as a collective experience, across the spaces between peoples, over time that separates living and dead.

Religious stories or "myths" put people in touch with powers beyond themselves; they may plumb a deeper, or more interior, sense of reality through what Black Elk calls "the wonder and strangeness of the greening earth." The artistry of storytelling draws people as well into a world playfully heightened and crafted through language. An Indian "word sender" or "carrier of the dream wheel" *characterizes* reality: peoples, landscapes, seasons, tonalizes, lightens, spiritualizes, brightens, and darkens human experience, all the while working with the reality that is.

In our common language, story once meant history. It connoted learning by inquiry. *Histo-* derives from the Greek for "tissue." The writing by younger Indians today is infused with this connective tissue—elders talking "stories" knowledgeably, to relatives who care. Simon Ortiz, for example, regards a storied native language as "a way of life," not just a writing tool, "a trail which I follow in order to be aware as much as possible of what is around me and what part I am in that life. I never decided to become a poet. An old-man relative with a humpback used to come to our home when I was a child, and he would carry me on his back. He told stories. My mother has told me that. That contact must have contributed the language of myself" (*The Man to Send Rain Clouds*).[1]

A story-backed old man gives the child eyes and voice, narratives that touch and are carried for life: words incarnate, flesh-and-blood ties, an embodied imagination. And the tribal backbone extends through ancestors who carry history in their bodies, natural and immediate as a boy's remembered "language of myself." Scott Momaday perches on his Kiowa grandmother's back in a family photograph of Aho (*The Names*). Alfonso Ortiz personally speaks of his San Juan Pueblo childhood leading a blind grandfather through standing rainwater. Among her first memories, Leslie Silko recalls her great grandmother, Maria Anaya, watering morning glories and telling Laguna tales. Grandmother's stories today give "form in bone and muscle" to *Ceremony*, Silko's first novel.

The concept of a true, living story, the personal inflection embodied and embraced in communal history, bedrocks Leslie Marmon Silko's fiction. She describes her people: "My family are the Marmons at Old Laguna on the Laguna Pueblo Reservation where I grew up. We are mixed blood—Laguna, Mexican, white—but the way we live is like Marmons, and if you are from Laguna Pueblo you will understand what I mean. All those languages, all those ways of living are combined, and we live somewhere on the fringes of all three. But I don't apologize for this any more—not to whites, not to full bloods—our origin is unlike any other. My poetry, my storytelling rise out of this source."[2]

ICE WOMAN

> I have slept with the river and
> > he is warmer than any man.
> At sunrise
> > I heard ice on the cattails.
> > > ["Indian Song: Survival"]

Silko's "Storyteller" cuts an ice-clear channel. The short story unfolds with an economy so lucid that nothing is lost. "It had come down suddenly, and she stood with her back to the wind looking at the river, its smoky water clotted with ice. The wind had blown the snow over the frozen river, hiding thin blue streaks where fast water ran under ice translucent and fragile as memory." Detail, tone, character, dramatic pacing, message: all are firmly placed and finely drawn, with the precision and certainty of crystals freezing on a dead man's face. Silko's "favorite" among her works, including the award-winning "Lullaby," the story carries no names, but works through "the interior landscapes of the characters."[3] Presences, sounds, and shapes are shagged with ice and snow; people huddle around the warmth of an oil stove, a woman's body, or an old man's story, as the sun freezes white in the sky. This northern cold is the analogue to southwestern desert heat, the climate where Silko grew up and then left to write some of her finest prose in Ketchikan, Alaska.

"Storyteller" opens with an Eskimo woman in jail, listening. The lowering, pale yellow sun, "worn thin by winter," stands still, trapped in the frozen river. She knows it is time. The story begins and closes with this prophetic sense of end: inevitable cycles of temporality enclose human action, inexorable fates trap man in a vast and intricate scheme of things.

The Inuit or Eskimo tell an old myth of a hunter's daughter who fell into the sea. When she reached for the gunwale of her father's boat, he cut off her fingers and let her drown. Takánakapsâluk now sits in a cave at the bottom of the sea, guarded by a dog "gnawing on a bone and snarling." She is keeper of the game, key to Eskimo survival. When times come hard, the people dying of starvation, a shaman or "one-who-drops-down-to-the-bottom-of-the-sea" must go to propitiate this tragic goddess known as Mother of the Sea. Negotiating the watch dog and the girl's father, who waits to seize dead souls, the shaman faces Takánakapsâluk. She is turned away in anger from the light and animals in her pool. Knud Rasmussen recounts the scene:

> Her hair hangs down loose all over one side of her face, a
> tangled, untidy mass hiding her eyes, so that she cannot see. It
> is the misdeeds and offenses committed by men which gather
> in dirt and impurity over her body. All the foul emanations
> from the sins of mankind nearly suffocate her . . . he must
> grasp Takánakapsâluk by one shoulder and turn her face
> towards the lamp and towards the animals, and stroke her
> hair, the hair she has been unable to comb out herself, because
> she has no fingers; and he must smooth it and comb it, and as
> soon as she is calmer, he must say:
> "Those up above can no longer help the seals up by
> grasping their foreflippers."
> Then Takánakapsâluk answers in the spirit language:
> "The secret miscarriages of the women and breaches of taboo
> in eating boiled meat bar the way for the animals."

The shaman shoots back up a tube, held precariously open by his tribal namesakes, and addresses the assembled people:

> "I have something to say."
> "Let us hear, let us hear."
> "Words will rise."

The women, quiet until now, recite the names of their household and confess their miscarriages. They fear that all the "soft things"—skins, clothing, animal hide coverings—must be thrown away because they have been poisoned by the women's blood secrets.

"I seek, and I strike where nothing is to be found!" the shaman chants. "I seek, and I strike where nothing is to be found! If there is anything, you must say so!"[4]

This myth, still ritualized, shadows Silko's "Storyteller," without necessarily structuring the narrative. Years back the Gussuck boats fired "big guns at the walrus and seals," and with nothing left to hunt, the girl's parents traded their rifle for a storekeeper's red can of "alcohol" that poisoned them. The memory of their death returns in the girl's menstrual nightmare of "something red in the tall river grass." A scabrous yellow dog now sleeps before the returned storeman's display case of knives and ammunition, where the reticent young woman, many times sexually defiled, unzips her parka and shakes "her long hair loose" by the stove. The lecherous white storekeeper, like a false shaman, will be sucked down into the river's current, never to rise.

The nameless girl's life shapes the narrative by way of her grandmother's prophecy: "It will take a long time, but the story must be told. There must not be any lies." It is a story of time's stern and just law—blood will out—told without contrition or forgiveness, no names, no slack, no dates, no sentiment. The figures are elemental: a girl, her grandmother, an old man, a sodomist, a drowned rapist. The story cuts to death's quick, sharp as a hunter crossing marshy tundra in early winter.

Before we begin to destroy a culture, Edmund Carpenter observes, we mistranslate it.[5] In Silko's story, English is a penal language. Words are mistranslated by people in lies, vilification, false promise. The girl's Eskimo jailer will not speak Yupik to her, only English; she remembers boarding school, downriver from her village, when the "dormitory matron pulled down her underpants and whipped her with a leather belt because she refused to speak English." From her cell the girl yells out "swear words she'd heard from the oil drilling crews last winter." The "Gussucks" swear to speak—pale, guttural men with oil rigs and bestial obsessions. Gussucks hate natives for "something of value" they could never have, the old man says. They despoil the land and import cultural genocide. Their oil rigs scar the fragile tundra, and the Eskimo forget "how to set nets in the river and where to hunt seals in the fall."

Takánakapsâluk turns her back on the people. "The ice was crouching on the northwest horizon like the old man's bear." So famine and unending winter darken the whitened land, and the game disappear. Dead sounds fall on the frozen snow: the rattling of snowmobile boot buckles as the jailer walks away, bursts of laughter and yelling from the girl, the snarling and howling of the dogs, the red-haired man's teeth rattling in postorgasm, the "occasional sound of metal jingling against metal" in the final deadly chase onto the river. And at the last: ". . . the sound of the churning gray water was set free. She stopped and turned to the sound of the river and the rattle of swirling ice fragments where he fell through."

Essentially two seasons divide the far north, endless day and endless night; the cold of winter permeates everything. Set in the tundra of Bethel, Alaska, "Storyteller" opens in a soundless freeze, "fifty below zero, the temperature which silenced their machines." The girl smiles coldly at lights run by generators, "flat yellow holes in the darkness." The Gussucks try to stop the cold with wads of yellow stuffing, but it is futile as their swearing and slovenly as the matted hunks of dog hair on the store floor. Nothing obstructs ice "prowling the earth" in this "final winter." The sun pales in a sky the color of iced river. Finally there will be no divisions. The prophecy will be fulfilled: no boundaries, no definitions, no taboos.

This catastrophic loss of distinction is reduced to "man" violating "woman." As the shriveled driller leads the girl to his trailer, "the whine of the big generators at the construction camp sucked away the sound of his words." Over the bed he tapes a photograph of a dog mounting a woman. Then he sexually abuses the girl. "They tell us we are dirty for the food we eat—raw fish and fermented meat," the old man later snarls, hearing her story. "But we do not live with dogs."

The grandmother tells her grim story and a nominal "Grandfather" speaks his dying prophecy, as timeless backdrop to events in the Gussuck camp. Grandma physically withdraws and ages into silence, frozen in her

227

rage, "eyes hard like river stone." The girl asks what hardens her arthritic body.

"The joints," the old woman said in a low voice, whispering like wind across the roof, "the joints are swollen with anger." Sometimes she did not answer and only stared at the girl. Each year she spoke less and less, but the old man talked more—all night sometimes, not to anyone but himself; in a soft deliberate voice, he told stories, moving his smooth brown hands above the blankets. He had not fished or hunted with the other men for many years although he was not crippled or sick. He stayed in his bed, smelling like dry fish and urine, telling stories all winter.

The night her parents died, the girl heard "sounds" outside. " 'Grandma,' she said, 'there was something red in the grass that morning. I remember.' " Grandma stops splitting fish bellies for the willow drying racks to tell of the storekeeper's tin of poison and her parents' deaths. "The old woman's voice sounded like each word stole strength from her," and her "telling the story was like laboring to walk through deep snow." In such coldness of the soul, the storyteller wastes no words, motions, or breath. "The wind came off the river and folded the tall grass into itself like river waves. She could feel the silence the story left, and she wanted to have the old woman go on."

The revenge-murder to expiate a parental crime crystallizes in images that follow: Grandma stabs the belly of another whitefish, snaps that the Gussuck storekeeper abruptly went downriver after the deaths, pulls out whitefish entrails, and speaks no more. "The old woman's voice flowed with the wind blowing off the river; they never spoke of it again." Grandmother dies silent. The plot crystallizes.

The old man grows more garrulous and lecherous as his time approaches. An avenging and visionary glacial bear drags an apocalypse of ice across the Northwest in his hallucinations. Old omens, migration myths, archaeologists' accounts, and ecologists' warnings merge in one storytelling: the blue bear descends with an ice sky that once froze the Bering Sea solid. The days of origin return. All "boundaries" white out, brought on by the lawlessness of Gussuck men, disregard for cultural differences, the deaths of plants and animals and native peoples. The last winter falls.

She felt a chill when she saw how the sky and the land were already losing their boundaries, already becoming lost in each other. But the red tin penetrated the thick white color of earth and sky; it defined the boundaries like a wound revealing the ribs and heart of a great caribou about to bolt and be lost to the hunter forever. That night the wind howled and when she scratched a hole through the heavy frost on the inside of the window, she could see nothing but the impenetrable white; whether it was blowing snow or snow that had drifted as high as the house, she did not know.

The old man hears the "rasp" of the giant bear as his breath falters. It is the death of the ancestral past in the ignominy of the slop bucket by his bed, the dessicated salmon and caribou under his stinking blankets, his bony old body. Yet the "grandfather" is terribly graced in his storytelling. "On and on in a soft singing voice, the old man caressed the story, repeating the words again and again like gentle strokes." His chanted story recalls a night the girl's parents died, "sounds like someone was singing" outside (the only occasions of song in the story, aside from the phonograph in the driller's trailer). It is crying the end of things.

Time in the narrative is boundless, known only by registering actions ("It was time to. . . .") and by snow tinctures: frozen white, creamy in thaw, or raw with "jagged yellow stains" of men's urine. Days pass imperceptibly in the weather. "The sky was gray like a river crane's egg; its density curved into the thin crust of frost already covering the land." Time cuts and splices narrative events like splinters of ice in a river of stories: the girl's past in the village with Grandma and the scandalous old man, her present in the Gussuck camp seducing the red-haired oil man and baiting the blue-eyed storekeeper, her framed present in jail for homicide. Her crime is not so much murder, as a fatalistic design she participates in and tells.

The traditional Indian colors of the four winds are soiled with vengeance, as time registers in primary colors that splotch against the night. Darkness encroaches on a white expanse: a pale *yellow* sun, "big yellow machines," jagged, dirty urine marks in drifts, blond matted dog hair, stringy yellow insulation, vacant oil lights that leave "flat yellow holes in the darkness," and the blinking kerosene flame in a mica stove window; the pale *blue* river and thin ice streaks, sky-frozen earth, bear the color of glacial

229

ice, and the Gussucks' thin lips and bluebottle eyes; the braided *red* tassels to the girl's pants, her crimson boot linings, blood, "red sweet wine," the sodomist's red hair, and red oil barrels flattened against cabins; all this to block the "impenetrable *white*" of the snow cold under the "heavy white belly of the sky," forecast in Grandma's gutted whitefish. In the Gussuck store spills a detail as telling as the old man's toenails, "long and yellow like bird claws": "On the bottom shelf a jar of mayonnaise was broken open, leaking oil white clots on the floor."

The girl's nominal "grandfather" is, in fact, her first seducer. This male violator is imaged reductively in the red-haired oil man, then in the storeman whose "blue eyes moved like flies crawling over her body." He becomes "the man" hunted in the dream-story, whose phallic jade knife shatters on the ice. The glacial bear, the girl's mythic protector, faces "man" at the story's end. The girl seems the only woman left in the frozen north. A young/ancient child of late spring blood, she is hounded by chilled seducers who rut in her body warmth. Her consciousness does not lie or shame itself, only avenges an old and ongoing crime. Death to the "man" is gestate from "something red in the tall river grass," the colors of spilled wine and blood, flowing to the red waste oil barrels nailed flat against the cold. And the stillborn soul of this primordial orphan must live out the telling of the story. "Lies could not stop what was coming."

"But she had a story now, about the red-haired Gussuck." It is a story to drive men mad, to trap a storekeeper: scandal of a red-haired man in a trailer who dreams himself a dog mounting a woman, as he thrusts inside a young girl's heat. "Grandfather" is not surprised. His lechery predates this compulsion: "the old man, whose hands were always hunting, like ravens circling lazily in the sky, ready to touch her." From a foul bed he accuses her in a hunter's tongue of smells, tastes, and touches: "I can smell what you did all night with the Gussucks." The old storyteller brags of touching her first: "He told her one time that she would get too old for him faster than he got too old for her; but again she had not believed him because sometimes he lied. He had lied about what he would do with her if she came into his bed. But as the years passed, she realized what he said was true. She was restless and strong. She had no patience with the old man who had never changed his slow smooth motions under the blankets." This hopeless sexuality smolders against a deadly winter cold.

And in the camp, the girl stalks her parents' murderer. "She laughed out loud again, and kept walking. She was thinking about the Gussuck oil drillers. They were strange; they watched her when she walked near their machines. She wondered what they looked like underneath their quilted goosedown trousers; she wanted to know how they moved. They would be something different from the old man." The girl's sex burns her, as it serves a weapon of revenge; her sensuality courses back to the orgiastic image of "something red" in the grass, stained by her parents' deaths. From bare-bottomed whipping for not speaking English in boarding school, to the "bright red flannel linings" of her mukluks and the "braided red yarn tassels around her ankles," sexuality braises the girl like Hardy's Tess for bleeding. She draws blankets "up around her chin, slowly, so that her movements could not be seen," as she touches herself in the motions of the old man, reaching for warmth in the solitary pathos of masturbation.

Rapacity sears this land of eternal cold. The girl's piercing laughter makes dogs howl and snarl and men suck in their breath. Oil wells pump the ground incessantly, generators pound out conversation, the tundra is broken and imprinted by machines that leave graves in the moss. Drilling men seize and possess land and women as they will. It is the polar variant of Conrad's tale of blackness, *Heart of Darkness*, the rape of native place and people in a heart of whiteness. All this is reduced to oily mayonnaise in the Northern Commercial store that breaks open and clots in the cold.

"The Gussucks did not understand the story. . . ." A failure of understanding marks the failure to hear, to attend and see. The invading Gussucks utter "noises" that make language a crime and negate translation: not to listen, not to care, not to recognize boundaries or necessities, not to heed the native place, the peoples, or the cold bear of the north. These failures are subsumed in the ominous voice of the river beneath the surface of the north. "She stopped and turned to the sound of the river and the rattle of swirling ice fragments where he fell through." On this last frozen run the girl knows to breathe through her mitten, in a gesture of knowing muteness, with tragic overtones of refusing words. Like Grandma she bears witness to the storeman's lie and says no more. She protects what is essential to her within her body. Knowing how to breathe, and to speak of necessity, relates to Silko's own narrative style, minimal and essential. In larger compass it is a Native American style of language, life, and survival.

The Gussuck storeman possesses "stores," but no story to save him. He pursues the girl blindly, breathing heavily, without mittens or parka, out onto the river, whose animate ice couples sexually with the girl to destroy the assailant. "She was familiar with the river, down to the instant the ice flexed into hairline fractures, and the cracking bone-sliver sounds gathered momentum with the opening ice until the sound of the churning gray water was set free." Momentarily stunned and distracted, she feels "for sinews of ice to hold her." She looks up into the dense white darkness and finds a spot of red, the target of a memory holding her tragically focused through all the years: it is a driller's oil barrel flattened against her cabin beyond the east river bank.

The girl's blood chant continues. " 'It began a long time ago,' she intoned steadily, 'in the summertime. Early in the morning, I remember, something red in the tall river grass. . . .' "

" 'I killed him,' she said, 'but I don't lie.' " The syntactic twist in her confession is telling. She did premeditate the murder, luring the storekeeper with her body, mocking laughter, long hair, and sexual license, *but* he killed himself, inattentively, his blue-eyed lust for "valuables" drowning him in icy darkness. His death is a true and necessary ritual through her eyes, an old myth of natural revenge working itself out in story. As Abel insists under oath in Momaday's *House Made of Dawn*, "A man kills such an enemy if he can." There are no accidents in the Indian world, some say, only accountabilities. The stories must be lived out, remembered, and told.

The old man rasps the story's end with his last breath. The spirit of his voice passes on to the girl, now the village storyteller. The Eskimo jailer must stay in the girl's cell to "translate" for the uncomprehending attorney who swears from evidence that she did not kill the storeman. Children witnessed the "accident." The story closes where it begins, icing the irony of failed translation in a simple word, the "lie." The girl's acculturated jailer, prompted by the attorney, is now "forced by this Gussuck to speak Yupik to her." And still, the "Gussucks did not understand the story; they could not see the way it must be told, year after year as the old man had done, without lapse or silence." The narrative circles into itself, without beginning or end.

"But she did not pause or hesitate; she went on with the story, and she never stopped, not even when the woman got up to close the door behind the village men."

" 'The story must be told as it is.' "

GRANDMOTHER STORYTELLER

CEREMONY
"Let us two go"

"The white men who came to the Laguna Pueblo Reservation and married Laguna women were the beginning of the half-breed Laguna people like my family, the Marmon family," Silko says. "I suppose at the core of my writing is the attempt to identify what it is to be a half-breed or mixed blooded person; what it is to grow up neither white nor fully traditional Indian. It is for this reason that I hesitate to say that I am representative of Indian poets or Indian people, or even Laguna people. I am only one human being, one Laguna woman."[6]

The 18 Pueblo cultures of New Mexico arc in a several hundred mile crescent along 130 miles drainage of the Rio Grande River, opening south on to the desert. The lower valleys receive scant rainfall of about 10 inches a year, flooding the arroyos, the mountains 24 to 30 inches in mixed rain and snow. Pueblo ceremonies cluster around a cyclic balance of rain and sun for growing corn, beans, squash, melons, and life forms essential to culture on the desert.

In the lower left-hand corner, near Acoma and away from the main river, lies the most recent and twice the most populous Pueblo of Laguna, along the San José tributary. Although the original settlement probably dates to the early 1500s, and the tribe in existence since 1300 (before that back to Mesa Verde), in 1699 Governor Cubero of Mexico named what many thought to be a splinter from Acoma, San José de la Laguna, for a two-mile lake now dry. Since its modern founding during the Spanish reconquest of the Pueblos, the community has assimilated a cross-section of the Southwest.

Laguna has evolved adaptively, as its sister village, Acoma, remains conversely rooted in an ancient site and ways. All the four language families of the eighteen Pueblos, Zuñi, and Hopi villages are represented by intermarriage in Laguna, plus Spanish, Navajo, and English. Elsie Clews Parsons, the first major ethnologist of the Pueblo, notes in *Laguna Genealogies* (1923): "Its position rendered it a place of passage for its neighbors to the west and to the east, even before the days of the railroad, and in many cases travelers or visitors came to stay."[7] Laguna may be regarded as a Pueblo of transitions—geographically, genetically, linguistically, culturally, and historically.

Sixty years ago, Parsons listed "House 61. Occupied. Not on the map. Frame, tin-roofed house, about 1/6 of a mile northeast of town. Owner, Robert G. Marmon, a white man who came to Laguna in 1872. He is married to a Laguna woman, and they have one daughter and five sons."[8] Also off the map and to the northeast live the *kurena* spirits of Laguna, represented in one of two *cheani* or medicine societies, the kurena and the kashare, who alternate ceremonies between the corn harvest and the winter solstice, or "south corner time." The kurena in the northeast are associated with sunrise; all their songs end with a single word, "sunrise."

Ceremony begins, turns in the middle, and ends with "Sunrise," an invocation that dawns on the page. Beginning the novel, the reader's eye opens over lighted space, and the sun lifts above the prose horizon of Tayo's story. At the novel's center Tayo meets a spirit sister of Yellow Woman, *K'o·'tc'inⁱina·'k'o*, whom the Laguna call "the mother of all of us," and he chants an old Laguna sunrise song: "The power of each day spilled over the hills in great silence. Sunrise. He ended the prayer with 'sunrise' because he knew the Dawn people began and ended all their words with 'sunrise'" (*C* 182). The Laguna gesture "sunrise," Franz Boas notes, touching the thumb to points of the fingers, then stretching the fingers and thumb to open the hand (as an artist might imagine the gestures of writing).[9] "They migrated northeastward," Boas reports of the mythic kurena, "leading a people called She-ken who carried flowers in their hands that withered and bloomed alternately."[10]

Traditionally, only kurena songs are chanted in Laguna from harvest to the winter solstice. The masked spirits once led the Laguna people back from the cacique's corn harvest, singing:

> Let us two go,
> let us two go;
> north outside
> field
> let us go.
> Corn
> yellow
> let us go for;
> Laguna there inside
> let us put it
> in below
> for ever.
> Sunrise![11]

The dualism so characteristic of Pueblo winter-and-summer, east-and-west, or north-and-south thinking comes through the invocation of "two" going to harvest, the stanzaic parallelism and verse repetition, the corn moved "outside" to "inside," and the storing of temporal grain "for ever" among the bodies of the people. Edgar Hewett would isolate two fundamentals here, the concept of "everything both ways" that interlocks Pueblo dualism: "belief in the unity of life as manifested in all things, and in a dual principle of all existence, fundamentally, male and female."[12]

The Pueblos regard life and death interfused. Laguna Pueblos tier cotton over the head of the deceased so the spirit will return as a rain cloud. Believing that the dead come back bringing rain, "each village needs its dead and needs to know that they are able to find their way to the homes of the living," Hamilton Tyler writes of spirit ceremonies. "In this way a perfect cycle is maintained, working back and forth between the two worlds, between the living and the dead. So that no one may be lost, and so that the dead will remember, the road must be kept open for them each year in this ceremony."[13]

This cyclic patterning halves each Pueblo, physically and ceremonially; strophic rhythms intersect, for better and worse, in *Ceremony*'s protagonist. Tayo lives half-breed marginality between Indian and white; he straddles the worst and best of the division. His name may amalgamate from a kashare song when the spirits came out of Shipapu, the Place of Emergence, migrated east to live with the *kopishtaya* or "angels" in the house of the sun, and the sun bird sang:

> I came out
> first early morning
> yaa ayo
> there in the east
> at sunrise the sun's house;
> the sun's (bird)
> T^YOWI T^YOWI he sings;
> KAYO KAYO he is singing.[14]

Tayo's name-story rises from the sun bird's dawn song, "T^YOWI T^YOWI KAYO KAYO," to reintegrate a split Laguna personality and cultural schism.

Twins personify an image of unified dualism, just as Pueblo moieties synchronize tribal life in complementary divisions. In *Ceremony* the blood "cousin-brother," Rocky, killed in the war, and the returning mixed-breed, Tayo, reenact a contemporary variant of old twin myths, reasserting the need for idiosyncratic pairing: a full-blood who imitates and dies for whites, a half-breed who gaps the two, accepted in neither, surviving. Tayo tries to come back home during a drought when veterans of foreign wars are POWs in their own land. It is a time when the cows eat charred cactus and a marble-eyed mule wanders in blind circles around the water tank. The agony and promise of Tayo's rain-seeking pilgrimage sets up an old quest home, now facing a new breed.

Within this structure, Leslie Silko reimagines Laguna reemergence through the hybrid fractures of contemporary Pueblo life: a hazel-eyed, catatonic, dark-light, illegitimate orphan of Laguna and white blood is shocked from one state of war to another. This divided culture hero is caught in the continuing journey of the past—legends of parentage, home, curing, and rain still shaping the needs of the present. "A'moo'oh, a'moo'ohh," Tayo's blind, cloth-slippered grandmother shuffles across the linoleum on "old bones that were stems of thin glass." She comforts his crying: "He cried because he had to wake up to what was left: the dim room, empty beds, and a March dust storm rattling the tin on the roof. He lay there with the feeling that there was no place left for him; he would find no peace in that house where the silence and the emptiness echoed the loss" (C 32).

CHILD OF SUN AND RAIN

> man of Sun
>> came to riverwoman
>> and in the sundown wind
> he left her
>> to sing
>>> for rainclouds swelling in the northwest sky
>>> for rainsmell on pale blue winds
>>>> from China.

> —"When Sun Came to Riverwoman"

In *Ceremony*, Silko enters a half-breed's fractured consciousness to bridge Western transitions between male and female, adult and child, history and myth, dark and light, Indian and white. "The major influence has been growing up around here," Silko says, "and listening to people and to the way the stories just keep coming."[15] As recorded fully in Boas and still told at Laguna, Thought-Woman, or grandmother spider, sits and thinks, names, weaves her web of stories, and the world takes shape. Thought-Woman, the matrix, deifies an old integrated regard for ideas, actions, being, plots, and things. She is the first being, *Ts'its'tsi'nako*, and her words spin healing webs of rain, as the shroud of darkness unravels from Tayo: "Then he could see the rain. It was spinning out of the thunderclouds like gray spider webs and tangling against the foothills of the mountain" (*C* 96).

Spider-Old-Woman's conflation of Indian, white, and Spanish grandchildren fuses in Tayo: thirsty, hungry, sick, unable to remember, only to hallucinate confused voices in the wake of a war. Tayo hears only "tangled things, things tied together"—Laguna conversation, a Spanish love song, Japanese military orders, a loud country jukebox in a bar. This bastard Laguna breed goes painfully in need of "a good ceremony" to unwind the twisted genetic, cultural, and historic confusions warring among estranged peoples.

Silko's novel is a word ceremony. It tells Tayo's story as a curative act. She writes out of an old medicinal regard for word-spirits powerful to make things happen.

> You don't have anything
> if you don't have the stories.
>
> [*C* 2]

Tayo's Old Grandma knows these things within the story, blind in her black shawl by the corner stove. She grandmothers her children by proximity, when her own daughter rejects a younger sister's illegitimate son.[16] "Everywhere he looked, he saw a world made of stories, the long ago, time immemorial stories, as old Grandma called them. It was a world alive, always changing and moving; and if you knew where to look, you could see it, sometimes almost imperceptible, like the motion of the stars across the sky" (*C* 95).

All names embody stories and confer identity in the Laguna world. They form connections with others, ties with the past. And so an old tribal myth centers the prose narrative in verse lines. Hummingbird and Bluebottle-Fly go to Old-Turkey-Buzzard for tobacco purification to release the *shiwanna* or rain clouds trapped by the Gambler.

He asked the people
"You people want to learn some magic?"
and the people said
"Yes, we can always use some."
Ma'see'wi and Ou'yu'ye'wi
the twin brothers
were caring for the
mother corn altar,
but they got interested
in this magic too.

[C 46]

Tayo, Silko's double, lives on the prosaic fringes of Laguna, and so the ceremonial verse of the ritual past draws the breed in toward the middle, the
once-standing Laguna kivas of Squash and Turquoise. Just so, the reader's
eye is drawn in to the vertical center of the verse on each page. Frayed family
lines still cohere around the traditional emergence of continuing Pueblo
peoples, just as sand paintings spiral inward from an outer perimeter.[17]

The novel's writing is naturally elegant, a prose so direct in naming
things-as-they-are that technique remains in the background. Silko crafts
a tensile plain style, her mind taut on desert roots and northern wind (*Ceremony* and "Storyteller" were written together in Ketchikan, Alaska). The
story unfolds organically, without chapter divisions, in a continuum fluid as
time itself. Her style is not so much plain, then, as true, placing us in the
narrated experience, without holding the reader audience to the art. The
novel is knowing of its subject, rabbit weed and wind devil, cow pony and
longhorn cattle, fencing pliers and GMC pickup, Coors beer labels in rat-
hole cantinas and the powder-dust thirst of desert drought. This prose
modulates to the ritual past by way of interspersed poetry and myth that give
form to the dismembered present. Finally, the narrator *is* the story, position-
ing, interweaving, toning, speaking for the characters—Tayo, his nameless
bastard double in Gallup, his feminine shadow, Helen Jean, the Apache
or Ute wanderer—listening to them speak, following their struggles to pattern their lives again, according to the old, never-ending Indian "balances
and harmonies."

A dry sickness grips the postwar land. Drunks grovel for wine "in the
mud on the sidewalk"—"people crouching outside bars like cold flies stuck
to the wall" (C 107). These walking Gallup dead are the drought war

counterparts to Tayo's international nightmare in "jungle green rain" of the Philippines, where he cursed the clouds and flies swarming over his brother, Rocky, only to come back with a coffin to tribal peoples dessicating in the desert. The times demoralize Indians. The kinships of rain and sun, human twin to human, have lost touch, it seems, at least for people's immediate needs. They forget the cycles of balance that synchronize flood and drought, hummingbird and bluebottle fly. They forget that skin colors do not exclude people their common humanity. It is not the weather going wrong, but people forgetting: cursing others and other things for their losses, forgotten ceremonies that would answer age-old necessities, a sense of origin and place, a narrative of survival. The old stories instill an acceptance of hard times in the larger patterns of sun, moon, stars, and darkness. "Nothing was all good or all bad either," Uncle Josiah says, brother 30,000 years back to the Asian enemy Tayo is ordered to execute—"it all depended" (C 11).

So Tayo takes on the scapegoat's role for the death of all soldiers, the men in his family and long-ago Asian ancestors, now enemies; he suffers the absence of the dead personified in the shiwanna rain clouds. Laguna was once a place of water, and like the Place of Emergence is presently an arid wasteland.

Tayo's role as orphaned culture hero concurrently parallels the sun twin who goes to find rain and fertility, trapped with the cloud spirits in the possessive Gambler's house. His dark-night journey finds its analogue of despair in Gallup Indian vagrants: "by the time they realized what had happened to them, they must have believed it was too late to go home" (C 115). For some it is too late. The whores and their tragic changelings hide in the arroyos under cardboard and tin lean-to shelters near the Gallup Ceremonial Grounds. Here the dead offspring are buried by hand, alone, without ceremony: "The sand she had dug with her hands was still damp on the mound. He circled the mound and stared at a faded blue rag partially uncovered, quivering in the wind. It was stiff with a reddish brown stain. He left that place and he never went back; and late at night when his mother was gone, he cried because he saw the mound of pale yellow sand in a dream" (C 111). Silko witnesses this suffering, as she hides it through powerful discretion, registering pain and loss without directly staring at the kneeling mother or her stillborn infant, or ever naming the child who mutely observes such grief. The strength of the novel's sensitivity lies in knowing tragedy, even while the story looks away toward the living.

Warring divisions between people's spirits and bodies beg reconciliation, the more positive blending of opposites traditional to the Pueblos. Two realities are at odds, divided languages and peoples in the old controversy over moieties, twin or twain. "But the fifth world had become entangled with European names: the names of the rivers, the hills, the names of the animals and plants—all of creation suddenly had two names: an Indian name and a white name" (C 68). The old Laguna belief offers that both these Red and white brothers, and all others, were created by Thought-Woman, the ancient grandmother who still makes them up in her stories. The new disbelief festers out of racist bitterness over stolen land, genocide, despair, and dark, defenseless peoples obstructing white Manifest Destiny.

So Tayo rides a gunnysack saddle on a blind gray mule, itself a sterile breed, roped to the other half-breed Harley's burro, plodding "up the line" of off-reservation bars for a cold beer after the war. It is a pathetic caricature of the water pilgrimage to *Shipap*. "He was thirsty. Deep down, somewhere behind his belly, near his heart" (C 56). An outsider in his own step-family, Tayo suffers between Auntie who "wanted him close enough to feel excluded, to be aware of the distance between them" and Grandma shawled in the corner (C 67). Tayo is born the breed Indian/Anglo, first generation of a mixed line that for centuries now has peopled Mexico; his Uncle Josiah's Chicana lover, the exotic Night Swan, "an old cantina dancer with eyes like a cat," recognizes their hazel-eyed kinship in a transitional green fertility that moderates the sky-blue of the white intruder's eyes and the earth-brown of the dispossessed native's. Her sexuality permeates a room like locust blossoms in a rainstorm, a gentle and powerful arousal, felt more than seen. She attracts Tayo toward life again, rain, generative stories, love between men and women, and finally the spirits of these living things centered in the sacred mountain, "Tse-pi'na, the woman veiled in clouds." The holy Mount Taylor draws the Night Swan to Cubero and Tayo to regeneration.

Blue shades the transition between night and day, making the darkness visible through light. The Night Swan's bright blue door over Lalo's place (the name echoes "Laura," Tayo's mother), blue armchair, open-toed blue satin slippers, blue kimono, painted blue flowers bordered on the walls, blue sheets tight across the bed—all lead toward the mountain spirit-woman herself, Ts'eh Montaño. "Ts'i-" is Keresan for water and "montaña" Spanish for mountain, hence "Water-Mountain" spirit-woman, perhaps, in the two languages, translated into English, that fuse Silko's own linguistic-genetic heritage.[18] Blue traditionally ties sky to water, the heavens to the seas, rain to earth. Ts'eh gathers blue-flowering herbs in a blue shawl to bring rain to the desert, making medicine the old way, aligning "blue-gray mountain sage with the blue stone" (*C* 184). It is, again, an old equation of rain and fertility under a sky of "Jemez turquoise, edged with thin quartz clouds" (*C* 230), as though the narrator, descendant of the surveyor, Robert Marmon, paused periodically to chart the story against the ceremonial blues of the heavens. In traditional ways she would consider the nourishment of blue cornmeal *piki*, a sacred staple, and the powder to cerulean to cobalt blues of turquoise, the "sky stone" that Indians believe crystallizes water in the Southwest and heals poor vision.

BLUE MEDICINE

"the struggle is the ritual"
"Deer Song"

Early in *Ceremony* Old Ku'oosh, a Laguna elder, comes to Tayo with "his bag of weeds and dust" to counter Emo's rattling Bull Durham bag of Japanese teeth (a story heard in Silko's childhood when some reservation lands became internment camps). Old Ku'oosh speaks the ceremonial language of a dialect that enacts meanings, revealing thought by natural action, all with the gentle care of growing things: "He smelled like mutton tallow and mountain sagebrush. He spoke softly, using the old dialect full of sentences that were involuted with explanations of their own origins, as if nothing the old man said were his own but all had been said before and he was only there to repeat it" (*C* 34).

This Pueblo medicine leads Tayo to a more arcane healer, Old Betonie, the contemporary Navajo/Mexican breed. Betonie also is known by hazel eyes, and he lives above the Gallup dump in an ancient hogan dug halfway (again, fusional) into the foothill. Betonie collects times and places, calendars and phone books, from his travels among Indians all over America: "all the names in them. Keeping track of things" (*C* 121). "All these things have stories alive in them," Betonie claims. Tayo recognizes calendar pictures from 1939 and 1940, predating his war sickness. The scene implies that healing involves the right triggering of memory, a health within things, natural to body and mind. And, similarly, to name things rightly is to make medicine through memory, to heal and give strength. This right naming connects inner with outer forms, the *ianyi* ("breath") or spirit with matter, by way of living words. So, to remember and breathe, according to traditional memory, places one naturally in a naming ceremony, aligned with the things that are and always have been. "You should understand the way it was back then. Because it is the same even now," Silko has said of mythic storytelling.[19]

In Gallup, Betonie tells Tayo to look "east to Mount Taylor towering dark blue with the last twilight," where the story finally will heal him. "It is the people who belong to the mountain," Betonie corrects Tayo's white misconception, not the mountain to the deed holder behind barbed wire (*C* 128). And the people belong to the names they bear, the language they are born into and grow through, the stories they are known by. "That's how you know, that's how you belong, that's how you know you belong," Silko reasons, "if the stories incorporate you into them. . . . In a sense, you are told who you are, or you know who you are by the stories that are told about you."[20] The sickness, then, is to forget and blame others for the loss, to fall silent, not to remember the ceremony of the natural world. "It is that town down there which is out of place. Not this old medicine man," Betonie nods toward the infernal Gallup arroyos and Ceremonial Grounds, where whites parade storefront Indians for tourists (*C* 118).

Not all "ceremonies" heal. Some are manipulations of the "witchery" started long ago, evil spirits showing off and competing their horrors. So it is recorded in the ritual legend of the shadow witch, who invented whites by telling a story of terror that came true.

> They fear
> They fear the world.
> They destroy what they fear.
> They fear themselves.
>
> [*C* 135]

But Indians cannot rule out whites, Betonie considers, for Thought-Woman created them all. Hating whites mirrors and feeds the Indian's own misery, as the white fears his own fear: "you don't write off all the white people, just like you don't trust all Indians" (*C* 128). For a mixed blood to condemn all whites is tantamount to historical parricide.

242

"The changing" always changes, in people and ceremonies they live by, and Tayo must complete the old rituals in order to "create new ceremonies." So the culture has always continued. It is not just the way things *were*, but how they *are*, evolving from the past; the past informs a living present, just as Spider-Old-Woman's web spins reality out of her aged abdomen. It is not object, but the life moving through things that matters most (*C* 135).

Betonie would have Tayo take responsibility for what is: his own life mediating several cultures, races, tongues, and times. The ceremonies of the stars and mountains and woman and rain, even rounding up the speckled wild cattle, account for everything without dehumanizing or denaturalizing any one part. They unify all people, bloods, breeds, bastards, whites, darks, animals, plants, spirits and stones in patterns of cyclic continuity. The witchery starts opposedly, displacing one's own pain on others, "me" against "them," castigating, warring, killing, dividing the people.

So Tayo must make a healing pilgrimage north into the Chuksa Mountains under "a sky so blue and vast the clouds were lost in it" (*C* 139). Betonie and his helper, Shush ("bear," Pueblo animal-spirit ally of warriors, because of its courage, and of healers, because it digs for roots), take Tayo through an old-time Scalp Ceremony for returning warriors. They call the bear-child back from the "whirling darkness" of neither man nor animal, body nor spirit, lost "in between forever."

Like Grandmother Spider behind the story, and Auntie by *Ceremony*'s end, a hundred years ago Betonie's grandfather knew that "it never has been easy" to bridge transitions. In grandfather's time, a "blue lace shawl" was one day found under a tree, and Navajo traders brought Descheeny a Mexican outcast for his bride. A century of plotting began here to offset the "witchery" of warring American racisms. The curing requires three generations of transition between dark and white, native and immigrant: "It will take a long long time and many many more stories like this one. . . ." (*C* 150). To counter racial divisions, the Navajo medicine man, Descheeny, and his Mexican bride a century ago made love and medicine and children, planning by the stars the ceremony that Tayo must one day complete: "He gazed into his smoky quartz crystal and she stared into the fire, and they plotted the course of the ceremony by the direction of dark night winds and by the colors of the clay in drought-ridden valleys" (*C* 150, 151).[21] All need "a safe return," the novel's cohering theme, as Rocky prays before going to war. Gallup survivors hunger their return home, as the desert thirsts for rain: the people turn again to the old ceremonies.

Old and new adaptations of ritual accommodate transitional change. The Night Swan's Mexican cousin sells Josiah "wild-eyed" longhorns, animals of mixed breeding and hazel eyes, more deer than cattle. "If it's going to be a drought these next few years," Josiah plans, "then we need some special breed of cattle" (C 75). And so the totemic stock range as Tayo's brown and white misfits, magically wild and mottled á la Faulkner's "Spotted Horses" and Iyetiko of the Laguna Fire Society: "Tayo watched them disappear over the horizon, their ivory hides shining, speckled brown like a butterfly's wing" (C 78). Tayo must round up these speckled mavericks, plunging through barbed-wired barricades with home "lodged deep in their bones" (C 188), headed "always south, to the Mexican desert where they were born" (C 197). He journeys south after the cattle, west to Old Betonie in Gallup, *down* east in a police car to Albuquerque after trying to gut Emo with a broken beer bottle ("east" here also in reference to his Oriental war duty and Rocky's death), *up* north to Ts'eh Montaño on Mount Taylor—the ceremonial six directions of Indian myth—and finally back to the middle in the Laguna kiva with the old cheani. Finding the cattle not south, but north on Mount Taylor (toward shipap origins and the land of the dead), at last Tayo realizes the significance of inverse transitions over the last hundred years: "Gathering the spotted cattle was only one color of sand falling from the fingertips; the design was still growing, but already long ago it had encircled him" (C 196).

Tayo's quest north to the Keres place of mythic origin with Ts'eh, attended by her consort hunter on the sacred mountain, offers a mythological and somewhat mystical place of healing. This retreat grants him a measure of natural calmness and strength to resist the witchery ending a century-old transition between dark and light skins. The positive transition is coded chromatically: sunrise yellow highlights the blue emergence of night into day. The Keres see Yellow Woman, possibly Ts'eh's matrix, as goddess of the game, giver of women's dress, baskets, and place-names; she is attended by Arrow Youth, a brother or husband, friend of the Great Star. She is sometimes seen as Moon Mother of the War Twins, *Masewi* and *Oyoyewi*, who search for the sun, their lost father.[22]

The issue whether Ts'eh derives from the Pueblo goddess complex of Yellow Woman (K'o˙tc'in^Yina˙'k o), a mountain spirit with yellow face, as well as the generic term for mythic heroines of Laguna stories, or whether Emo and the others are possessed by witchery, stands secondary to the curative effect of the "plot" on Tayo. He comes to believe in the story of his life. The narrative resolves and heals. Silko layers one level of contrary events—love with a beautiful woman of the old ways, warring sadism among men crazed by their displaced Indianness in white America—with a second level of mythological overtone.

One culture's religion may register as another's superstition; between cultures, without ceremony, Tayo negotiates between belief and disbelief to purge his own schizophrenia. Instead of proving or disproving Ts'eh, then, Tayo simply witnesses her presence. Tayo's love is, after all, a giving of spirit, no less than religion. To believe in Ts'eh, to remember her healing effect on him, resists the despair that destroys young Indians through alcohol, drugs, car wrecks, suicide, and violence all across America. This love strengthens, whether a reader testifies to gods or witches, old medicine or new psychology. Belief, when it heals, contains good medicine, in any culture. "But as long as you remember what you have seen, then nothing is gone," Ts'eh tells Tayo. "As long as you remember, it is part of this story we have together" (C 231). The curative memory of love calms Tayo's nightmarish voices: his abandonment, dislocation, rejection, and battle fatigue. The orphan can then come home.

The mountain setting tonalizes Ts'eh's character and speaks for her in natural landscapes. Everywhere around this woman blooms a sky, clouds, stones, horizons, flowers, plants, and cloths of blue: the sky "a bright blue intensity that only autumn and the movement of the sun from its summer place in the sky could give it" (C 184). Blue signifies the traditional Laguna color of the west and the first of four worlds under ours, yellow the color of the north and the second world; bear lives in the blue west, mountain lion in the yellow north.[23] Mount Taylor rises northwest of Laguna, balancing the two directions, and from there Tayo scans the blue Pueblo crescent below, his people's homeland for some thousand years: "Years of wind and no rain had finally stripped the valley down to dark gray clay, where only the bluish salt brush could grow. Beyond the Rio Puerco, to the southeast, he could see the blue mountains east of the Rio Grande" (C 184). The land's blue threads tie back through the story: Josiah's blue-lined notepaper sends Tayo to the Night Swan's blue door and bed during the rain, and he goes on to find a third hazel-eyed outcast in Betonie, who wears a blue cotton workshirt in a hogan arched with "thick bluish green glass of Coke bottles" (C 120). Even the empathetic cowboy who wants to let Tayo go free on Mount Taylor is graced by a blue bandanna.

At Tayo's last meeting with Ts'eh, "blue-bellied clouds" hang "low over the mountain peaks," and he gathers "yellow pollen gently with a small blue feather from Josiah's pouch" (C 220). Ts'eh walks toward him through sunflowers, with her curved willow and "blue silk shawl" (recalling a century ago when the "blue lace shawl" lay under the Mexican outcast's tree). She collects blue-flowering roots of rain plants: "This one contains the color of the sky after a summer rainstorm. I'll take it from here and plant it in another place, a canyon where it hasn't rained for a while" (C 224).

Tayo and Ts'eh kneel at an ancient she-elk rock-carving, "a dark blue shadow on the cliff" (C 231), where they recognize the ceremony in the stars. They imagine themselves mythically and realistically to be characters in a story, as though somehow the living creations of this storytelling could stand outside looking in on themselves. Traditional to Indian myth, the storyteller's sense of ceremony frames the people's lives from within, casting the participant audience in tales that have always been tribal. Silko's personal relation as artist to her materials, both in and out of her novel, induces a similar kind of empathetic magic in the reader; Tayo's return to life initiates the reader's own sense of homecoming in the plot's resolution.

This lovely medicine woman, with relatives all over the Southwest, comes and goes like a spirit. She has a traditional Indian name stringing out so long that she goes by the nickname "Ts'eh," or water (a tie with *Tsi'ty'icots'a* or Salt Woman, the pan-Pueblo spirit of pure water). Ts'eh Montaño, or "Water Mountain," seems a coded and composite reference to the spirit-woman who returns vitality to the arid desert for Indians, Mexicans, and whites alike, all embodied in Tayo, all sharing in the sickness and health of one another, many as one with the land.

Like the kurena, whose songs are sung from the corn harvest at the end of summer until the winter solstice, Ts'eh leaves going "uphill to the northeast" (C 234). Tayo witnesses a convergence of his mixed lifelines at the autumnal equinox, the celestial fusion of light and dark, analogous to this mixed blood, when summer and winter solstices balance zenith and nadir. Pueblo mythology is rich in this sense of changing balance.[24] In the four directions, plus the diagonal "south corner time" and "north corner time" (solstices) fusing up and down, appear the axes of the ceremonial six directions:

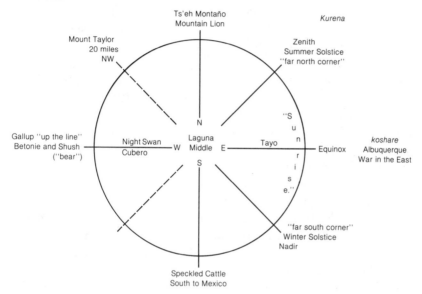

"The cloudy yellow sandstone of Enchanted Mesa was still smoky blue before dawn, and only a faint hint of yellow light touched the highest point of the mesa. All things seemed to converge there: roads and wagon trails, canyons with springs, cliff paintings and shrines, the memory of Josiah with his cattle. . . . Yet at that moment in the sunrise, it was all so beautiful, everything, from all directions, evenly, perfectly, balancing day with night, summer months with winter. The valley was enclosing this totality, like the mind holding all thoughts together in a single moment" (C 237).

A hundred years ago, Betonie told Tayo, the Indian holy men saw that "the balance of the world had been disturbed," when whites came buying land, logging, mining, killing bears and mountain lions for sport, not need. There would be "droughts and harder days to come" (C 186). So by Tayo's day, young Indian war heroes die "defending the land they had already lost" (C 169), and Emo wears a bronze star on a blue ribbon for blowing up Japs (C 164), while whites run cattle on Indian lands: "the lie was destroying the Indian people" (C 204). Tayo cuts open the barbed wire fence to retrieve his stolen cattle on Mount Taylor, and Silko intrudes: "If the white people never looked beyond the lie, to see that theirs was a nation built on

247

stolen land, then they would never be able to understand how they had been used by the witchery; they would never know that they were still being manipulated by those who know how to stir the ingredients together: white thievery and injustice boiling up the anger and hatred that would finally destroy the world: the starving against the fat, the colored against the white" (C 191).

What is the lie? In the contemporary imagery of *Ceremony*, it is the pretense that peoples fenced apart can live by "the plastic and neon, the concrete and steel." More personally, the lie comes in forgetting ceremonial regards for all life forms growing in transitions. It is thinking to possess human as nonhuman, to kill for "things"; the destroyers "destroy the feeling people have for each other" (C 229). The Indian traditionally counters in offerings of corn pollen and turquoise, rain clouds and sandstone, squash and melons, myth and ritual—a ceremonial life beyond owning things, free of possessing land or other people. But Josiah and Betonie, surrogate fathers, remind Tayo of a simple Indian belief: everything that is *is*. Indians cannot abnegate responsibility for their own lives maligning whites. To hate whites for their hatreds will destroy Indians.

All peoples stand accountable to all other peoples, the old ways hold; the mixed breed is living testimony to the transitions, the changes, the old ways evolving constantly into new variables. The ceremonies promise renewal out of the "end" of temporary life forms: continuity from one generation to the next, rain one day to end the drought, water to complement sun, a restoration of health after sickness, balance over time. The ancestral belief in natural benevolence through time orders the-way-things-are, even when life seems lost in the moment.

The fear of destruction is real enough, witchery or not. As the Pueblos only too well know, uranium gorged from the Cebolleta land grant was first exploded over White Sands to the south. The threat of atomic annihilation unites all peoples again into "one clan," if nations are to avert "witchery's final ceremonial sand painting." Even grandma's "old clouded-up eyes," thinking she was seeing the sun rise, could see the initial holocaust over Trinity Site when the desert sand burned to glass under a nuclear cloud (C 245).[25] Nuclear devastation is witchery's inversion of the "sunrise" that begins and ends the story.

Back home, the "destroyers" manipulate Indian people's despair. Tormented veterans drink cheap wine by night tumbleweed fires near the first uranium mine, blame and forget and wound their own brothers. Self-tortures stun them into destroying others, martyring the half-breed Harley over barbed wire fencing, cutting the whorls from his toes. The Indians' hatred of themselves and their oppressors fuels "witchery." This is a way of voicing a realistic state of fear, not just paranoia or superstition. It generates from an ominous sense of *un*reality and cultural dissociation that divides oppressed peoples among themselves.[26]

Nearing the autumnal equinox, then, Tayo at last knows his marginality must engender a courage to trust that "the pattern of the ceremony was in the stars": "The sun was nearing its autumn place in the sky, each day dropping lower, leaving more and more of the sky undilute blue" (C 238). He returns to a belief in himself, consistent with a belief in the world that tells his story. His mixed blood fuses peoples divided over time: "He cried the relief he felt at finally seeing the pattern, the way all the stories fit together—the old stories, the war stories, their stories—to become the story that was still being told. He was not crazy; he had never been crazy. He had only seen and heard the world as it always was: no boundaries, only transitions through all distances and time" (C 246). The equinox is his ceremonial confluence: "A transition was about to be completed: the sun was crossing the zenith to a winter place in the sky, a place where prayers of long winter nights would call out the long summer days of new growth" (C 247).

A sense of ceremony, restored to Tayo, also instills positive abstinence, knowing what *not* to do. The curing for the poison in people's bellies comes in *not* countering bitterness bitterly, in gathering Ts'eh's rain root seeds to end the drought. By extension, Tayo's positive nonaction is not to kill Emo: the wise patience, the discipline, the informed waiting counseled by the care of ceremonial design. The alternative to violence rests where it always has: "They were taking him home." The stars group in patterns, the land grows in cycles, all peoples gather as families in a house made of pollen, rain, sun, earth, darkness, and dawn. "The transition was completed. In the west and in the south too, the clouds with round heavy bellies had gathered for the dawn. . . . The ear for the story and the eye for the pattern were theirs; the feeling was theirs: we came out of this land and we are hers" (C 255).

K'o⸴⸴tc'in^Yina⸴⸴k o shines among kachina spirits in the dawning sun's "yellow light across the clouds," the "yellow river sand," and in the "pale yellow" leaves of the cottonwood by the river (C 255). Just as his mother,

Laura (from laurel for the victory of the century-old ceremony), returned naked at sunrise to cross the river, seeded with Tayo, so her son now comes home, across the river at dawn, to right her supposed waywardness. The kiva elders gather to confirm Tayo's story of the spirit-woman's fertile return. Inside the Pueblo now, the breed is acknowledged as one of "the people," a storied warrior who helped bring native life back into balance.

The novel moves from sunrise to sunrise, spring through a complete seasonal cycle to fall, on the promise of a new day returning. The threads of the web must be tied up: Harley and Leroy dead in the wrecked pickup, Emo killing Pinkie and ostracized to California. A reader feels something hasty in this ending, the stars wheeling round while young men die pointlessly: but these names serve less as characters in the story, more as signs of the destructive self-hatred in young Indians encased in shells, veterans sucked empty over a century of foreign and civil wars.[27] Grandma is no longer interested in the gossip of these war stories. Her grandson has been taken into the reconstructed kiva. The "Whirling Darkness" has turned back on itself.

If words, truly regarded from Indian beliefs, act out their beings-as-they-are, witchery witches itself, devouring its own belly in the centripetal motions basic to Pueblo world views. Like comes from like, as Alfonso Ortiz observes.[28] "It is dead for now." Anticipatory of winter storytelling, the people face a new day, scatter pollen trails for spirits to travel, and chant blessings in the old ways at the end of the novel:

> Sunrise,
> accept this offering,
> Sunrise.

✖ NOTES ✖

Introduction: "Sending a Voice"

1. Frances Densmore, *Teton Sioux Music*, Smithsonian Institution Bureau of American Ethnology, Bulletin 61 (Washington, D.C., 1918; reprinted, New York: Da Capo Press Reprint, 1972), p. 131.
2. James R. Walker, *The Sun Dance and Other Ceremonies of the Oglala Division of the Teton Dakota* (New York: The Trustees, 1917). Rev. and rpt. as *Lakota Belief and Ritual*, ed. Raymond J. DeMallie and Elaine A. Jahner (Lincoln: University of Nebraska Press, 1980), p. 35. See also William K. Powers, *Yuwipi: Vision and Experience in Oglala Ritual* (Lincoln: University of Nebraska Press, 1982).
3. N. Scott Momaday, "I Am Alive. . . ." in *The World of the American Indian*, Vine Deloria, Jr., and William C. Sturtevant, consultants, National Geographic Society (Washington, D.C., 1974), p. 13.
4. Michael Dorris, "Native American Literature in an Ethnohistorical Context," *College English* 41 (October 1979), 156.
5. Dell Hymes, *"In Vain I Tried to Tell You": Essays in Native American Ethnopoetics* (Philadelphia: University of Pennsylvania Press, 1981), p. 5.
6. Ibid., p. 382.
7. Mary Austin, "Aboriginal American Literature" in *American Writers on American Literature*," ed. John A. Macy (New York: Liveright, 1931), p. 427.
8. Emma Hawkridge, from "The Painted Desert" in *Poetry: A Magazine of Verse* 15 (January 1920), 194. More recent modern poets have shaped works with "native" improvisations: Ted Hughes's *Crow*, Jarold Ramsey's *Love in an Earthquake*, David Waggoner's *Who Shall Be the Sun?*
9. Marianne Moore, from "When I Buy Pictures" and Mary Austin, "Zuñi Folk Tales" in *The Dial* 71 (July 1921), 33, 112.
10. Austin, "Zuñi Folk Tales" and T. S. Eliot, "London Letter" in *The Dial* 71 (October 1921 Reprint edition. Lincoln: University of Nebraska Press, Bison paperback, 1967), 112, 452–53. It is historically significant to the interactions of literature and anthropology that in 1922, the year of T. S. Eliot's *The Waste Land* and James Joyce's *Ulysses*, Elsie Clews Parsons edited a volume of anthropological fiction culled from the Bureau of American Ethnology projects, *American Indian Life* (New York: B. W. Huebsch, 1922). Parsons collected twenty-seven portrait "stories" of tribally specific "native American life," as A. L. Kroeber described the method "of the historical novel," ostensibly borrowed from Walter Scott. These anthropologists-turned-artists included no less than Elsie Clews Parsons, A. L. Kroeber, Robert H. Lowie, Clark Wissler, Paul Radin, Frank G. Speck, M. R. Harrington, John R. Swanton, P. E. Goddard, Leslie Spier, Herbert Spindon, Edward Sapir, and Franz Boas, the godfather of Western anthropology.
11. William Butler Yeats in "The Municipal Gallery Revisited" (1937) and "The Lake Isle of Innisfree" (1890).

12. Walter Channing, "Essay on American Language and Literature," *North American Review and Miscellaneous Journal* 1 (1815), rpt. *American Indian Culture and Research Journal* 1 (1976), 6.

13. Gary Snyder, *The Old Ways: Six Essays* (San Francisco: City Lights Books, 1977).

14. William Butler Yeats, "A General Introduction for My Work" (1937), rpt. *Yeats: Selected Criticism*, ed. A. Norman Jeffares (London: Macmillan, 1964), p. 265.

15. Donald Wesling, *The Chances of Rhyme: Device and Modernity* (Berkeley, Los Angeles, London: University of California Press, 1980), p. 6.

16. Andrew Welsh, *Roots of Lyric: Primitive Poetry and Modern Poetics* (Princeton: Princeton University Press, 1978), pp. 23–24.

17. Ernest Fenollosa, "From *The Chinese Written Character As a Medium For Poetry*" (1918), rpt. *The Poetics of the New American Poetry*, ed. Donald Allen and Warren Tallman (New York: Grove, 1973), p. 16. John T. Irwin writes on art-as-sign during the "American Renaissance" of 1850–1855 (as first surveyed by F. O. Matthiessen in *American Renaissance*, the writings and thought of Emerson, Thoreau, Whitman, Hawthorne, and Melville) in *American Hieroglyphics: The Symbol of the Egyptian Hieroglyphics in the American Renaissance* (New Haven: Yale University Press, 1980). Almost a century later came a decade of "Native American Renaissance": from Scott Momaday's Pulitzer Prize-winning *House Made of Dawn* (1968) through James Welch's *The Death of Jim Loney* (1979), including Leslie Silko's *Ceremony*, poetry by Simon Ortiz and Wendy Rose, the reissued Black Elk texts, Howard Norman's Cree translations, some two dozen new anthologies, and over a hundred young Indian writers.

18. Fenollosa, *On The Chinese Written Character*, 31. The new poetries of the early twentieth century, imagism and vorticism specifically, were certainly fed by the discoveries of primitive "signs" sculpted into palpable things, the aboriginal "arts" that inspired Fauvism ("wild beasts") in France around the turn of the century and the major break-throughs of Picasso, Miró, Klee, and Kandinsky. See Max Kozloff, *Cubism/Futurism* (Charterhouse Books, 1973; reprinted, New York: Harper and Row Icon, 1974).

19. Charles Olson, "Projective Verse" (1950) in Allen and Tallman, p. 156.

20. Charles Olson, from *Human Universe* (1951) in Allen and Tallman, p. 165.

21. D. H. Lawrence, *Mornings In Mexico* (1927; reprint ed., London: William Heinemann, 1956), p. 45.

22. D. H. Lawrence, "Preface to the American Edition of *New Poems*" (1919) in Allen and Tallman, p. 73.

23. Dylan Thomas, "The Peaches," *Portrait of the Artist As a Young Dog* (1940; reset ed., New York: New Directions, 1968), pp. 11–12.

24. Paula Gunn Allen, personal conversation, May 1982, Los Angeles. Professor Allen came to UCLA in 1981–82 for postdoctoral work on American Indian women writers through the American Indian Studies Center. Openings for Indian artists in academia and the arts came with postwar recognition of such poets as Williams the medicine verse nativist, Pound the cross-cultural daemon, Olson the visionary archaeologist, and Lawence the sensual prophet. These more radical literary godfathers inspired a second generation: Creeley, Duncan, Snyder, Levertov, Ginsberg, Merwin, Kinnell, Bly, McClure,

Wakoski, Rich, and others in the direction of a new tribal poetics. Robert Penn Warren, senior American novelist and poet now in his late seventies, has just published a forty-four page poem, "Chief Joseph of the Nez Perce, Who Called Themselves the *Nimpau*—'The Real People'" (*The Georgia Review*, Summer 1982). The poem is made up of Penn Warren's tragically heroic sense of America, as voiced through Chief Joseph, Indian speeches, newspaper clips, military reports, and Penn Warren's own lyric sense of narrative verse. The artist's documentary method corresponds with Arthur Kopit's play, *Indians*, and looks back to John Neihardt's epic sense of Indian America in *A Cycle of the West, Black Elk Speaks*, and some twenty-seven other volumes.

Paula Allen studied poetry with Robert Creeley at the University of New Mexico in the mid-sixties, when she first read the new American poets and began writing. Creeley opened the door for her to write poetry, Allen feels. She also says that Joyce's experimental novel about a heroic "half and half," Poldy Bloom, the wandering ethnic of *Ulysses*, prepared the way for such stream-of-conscious, ethnic novels as Momaday's *House Made of Dawn*, as well as her own experimental fiction, *The Woman Who Owned the Shadows* (manuscript). "I hope he hasn't long greasy hair hanging into his eyes or standing up like a red Indian," Molly Bloom fantasizes Stephen Dedalus the "poet," in a 1904 parody of Oscar Wilde. James Joyce, *Ulysses* (1922; new ed., New York: Random House, 1961), p. 775. The Irish, to some, represent the "red Indians" of old Briton. Indeed, the American reservation system derives in part from English Parliamentary debates over what to do with the "wild Irish" several centuries ago. The color stereotype of a "Red Man" derived not from exotic genetics, but ritual face paint used by the natives of New England. In the Western mind, it is no secret that the color red suggests passion, lawlessness, violence, and bloodshed—negative images superimposed by immigrants on native peoples of the "wilderness."

25. See Charles Olson, "Projective Verse," pp. 147–158; Robert Duncan, "Ideas of the Meaning of Form," pp. 195–211; and Denise Levertov, "Some Notes on Organic Form,"pp. 312–317 in Allen and Tallman. Plato in *Phaedrus* quotes Socrates on organic parts in the patterns of discourse; Goethe in "Essay on Nature" speaks of the relation of parts to whole in living art: Coleridge in *Biographia Literaria*, "On the Principles of Genial Criticism," is attributed with introducing the term "organic" into Western poetics, via Schlegel: "The organic form, on the other hand, is innate; it shapes as it develops itself from within, and the fullness of its development is one and the same with the perfection of its outward form. Such is the life, such the form." See G. S. Rousseau, *Organic Form: The Life of an Idea* (London and Boston: Routledge and Kegan Paul, 1972); Philip C. Ritterbush, *The Art of Organic Forms* (Washington: Smithsonian Institution Press, 1968); G. N. Giordano Orsini, *Organic Unity in Ancient and Later Poetics* (Carbondale: Southern Illinois University Press, 1975); and Meyer Abrams, *The Mirror and the Lamp* (London: Oxford University Press, 1953). Gordon Brotherston shows how these organic concepts, words "flowering" on the Aztec poet's lips, for example, are embedded in Native American literatures many centuries old. See his *Image of the New World: The American Continent Portrayed in Native Texts* (London: Thames and Hudson, 1979), especially chapter 9, "Singer and Scribe," pp. 260–288.

26. Paula Gunn Allen, April 30, 1982, UCLA seminar though the English Department and American Indian Studies Center, "Contemporary American Indian Women's Literature," Spring 1982.
27. Jarold Ramsey, "The Teacher of Modern American Indian Writing as Ethnographer and Critic," *College English* 41 (October 1979), 169.
28. Four Zoas Press will publish *Song of the Sky* in 1983. Portions of the anthology, including Paula Gunn Allen's Foreword, were published in the special issue, "American Indian Writings," *The Greenfield Review* 9, 3–4 (1981), 106–142.
29. The Wintu shaman, Jim Thomas, sang this "Dream Song" in 1929. D. Dematracopoulou, "Wintu Songs," *Anthropos* 30 (1935), 483–494. The reworking and accompanying notes appear on pages 211 and 216 of Brian Swann's manuscript, *Song of the Sky*.
30. Jim Barnes, "Autobiography, Chapter XII: Hearing Montana," Native American Literature Issue of *Denver Quarterly* 14 (Winter 1980), 32.
31. Victor Turner, UCLA Department of Anthropology panel discussion, October 1977.
32. Claude Lévi-Strauss, *Tristes Tropiques*, trans. John and Doreen Weightman (1955; reprint ed., New York: Atheneum, 1974), pp. 47–60.
33. "Walum Olum," *American Indian Literature: An Anthology*, ed. Alan R. Velie (Norman: University of Oklahoma Press, 1979), p. 100. Velie draws on Daniel G. Brinton, *The Lenape and Their Legends* (Philadelphia: D. G. Brinton, 1885).

Chapter 1: "—Old Like Hills, Like Stars"

1. Knud Rasmussen, *Across Arctic America: Narrative of the Fifth Thule Expedition* (London and New York: G. P. Putnam's Sons, 1927), p. 164.
2. John Neihardt, trans., *Black Elk Speaks* (1932; New York: Pocket, 1972), p. 21.
3. I use Vine Deloria's figure of 315 culturally functional tribes in the United States today (*Custer Died for Your Sins: An Indian Manifesto*, [New York: Macmillan, 1969], p. 13). As a Standing Rock Sioux, former president of the National Congress of American Indians, and legal counsel for Indian affairs, Deloria is in a position to arbitrate figures that vary from two hundred to six hundred extant "tribes." *Wassaja* 7 (January–February 1979) published a Federal Register list of 280 "tribal reservation entities" having a government-to-government relationship with the Unites States and another 40 Indian groups petitioning for federal acknowledgment through the Bureau of Indian Affairs (February 1979).

   The statistics for aboriginal population are even less firm. Harold E. Driver cites Kroeber (1934, 1939) with the lowest estimate of 4,200,000 for North America in 1492 and Dobyns (1966) with about 60,000,000 for America. Driver revises the figures to estimate perhaps 30,000,000 for the continent. *Indians of North America*, 2d rev. ed. (1961; Chicago: University of Chicago Press, 1969), pp. 63–64. Dobyns's most liberal estimates are ten to twelve million people north of the Rio Grande, roughly two thousand cultures speaking a thousand languages. Henry F. Dobyns, "Estimating Aboriginal American Population: An Appraisal of Techniques with a New Hemispheric Estimate,"

Current Anthropology 7 (1966), 414. In response to this controversy over numbers, Alfonso Ortiz, the Tewa anthropologist, wrote me that "no responsible anthropologist known to me believes that there were several thousand aboriginal cultures in Native America north of the Rio Grande, nor were there a thousand languages spoken. Five hundred languages and as many cultures is a commonly agreed estimate. On population eight million is the most liberal estimate with any following at all. True, the figures keep getting revised upward slowly as retrieval and sampling techniques improve, but until they do even more, anything beyond what I cite is at best conjectural" (25 January 1979).

4. Jorge Luis Borges, "The Oral Poetry of the Indians," in *Literature of the American Indians: Views and Interpretations*, ed. Abraham Chapman (New York: New American Library, 1975), p. 277.

5. Barre Toelken speaks of "sacred reciprocation" in "Seeing with a Native Eye: How Many Sheep Will It Hold?" in *Seeing with a Native Eye: Essays On Native American Religion*, ed. Walter Holden Capps (New York: Harper and Row, 1976), p. 17.

6. Niehardt, *Black Elk Speaks*, p. 1.

7. Octavio Paz, *In Praise of Hands: Contemporary Crafts of the World*, published in conjunction with the first World Crafts Exhibition held at the Ontario Science Center in Toronto (Greenwich, Conn.: New York Graphic Society, 1974).

8. Constance Rourke, "The Indian Background of American Theatricals" in Chapman, p. 257.

9. Lawrence C. Wroth, "The Indian Treaty as Literature" in Chapman, p. 327. Peter Nabokov's *Native American Testimony* is the best anthology of American Indian speeches (New York: Harper and Row, 1978). Michael K. Foster examines Iroquois "speech events" still current in *From Earth to Beyond the Sky: An Ethnographic Approach to Four Longhouse Iroquois Speech Events* (Ottawa: National Museums of Canada, 1974).

10. Margot Astrov, ed., *American Indian Prose and Poetry*, originally published in 1946 as *The Winged Serpent* (New York: Capricorn, 1962), p. 87.

11. Dee Brown, *Bury My Heart at Wounded Knee* (New York: Holt, Rinehart, and Winston, 1970), p. 424.

12. D'Arcy McNickle, *Native American Tribalism: Indian Survivals and Renewals* (1973; reprint ed., New York: Oxford University Press, 1979), p. 51.

13. Neihardt, *Black Elk Speaks*, p. 112.

14. McNickle, *Native American Tribalism*, p. 72.

15. See Francis Haines, *The Buffalo* (New York: Crowell, 1970); Tom McHugh, *The Time of the Buffalo* (New York: Knopf, 1972): and Jerry N. McDonald, *North American Bison: Their Classification and Evolution* (Berkeley, Los Angeles, London: University of California Press, 1981).

16. Edward S. Curtis, *The North American Indian: The Indian of the United States and Alaska*, 3 (New York: Johnson, 1970), p. 11.

17. Howell Raines, "American Indians Struggling for Power and Identity," *New York Times Magazine*, 11 February 1979; Edgar S. Cahn, *Our Brother's Keeper: The Indian in White America* (Washington, D.C.: World Publishing, 1969).

18. Francis Jennings, *The Invasion of America: Indians, Colonialism, and the Cant of Conquest* (Chapel Hill: University of North Carolina Press, 1975), p. 30.

19. William Brandon, ed., *The Magic World: American Indian Songs and Poems* (New York: Morrow, 1971), p. 115.

20. T. J. Morgan, Commissioner of Indian Affairs, to the Secretary of the Interior, 1 October 1889 in Chapman, p. 16.

21. Malcolm McFee, *Modern Blackfeet: Montanans on a Reservation* (New York: Holt, Rinehart, and Winston, 1972), p. 64.

22. See Vine Deloria's argument for a pan-Indian political coalition based on a separate land base and tribal sovereignty in *Custer Died for Your Sins*.

23. Ibid., p. 2.

24. D. H. Lawrence, "Fenimore Cooper's White Novels" in *Studies in Classic American Literature*, 2d ed. (1923; New York: Viking, 1966), p. 36.

25. Williams first wrote on American violence as a mythic act of regeneration soaked into "the bloody loam" of the country's history (*In the American Grain*, 2d ed. 1923; New York: New Directions, 1956). Richard Slotkin has developed a "myth-poeic" reading of American cultural archetypes through a study of colonial and frontier literary history (*Regeneration Through Violence: The Mythology of the American Frontier, 1600–1860* [Middletown, Conn.: Wesleyan University Press, 1973]). New studies on Indian stereotyping and image-making are revising old myths about civilization and savagery: among many recent statements see Hugh Honour, *The New Golden Land: European Images of America from the Discoveries to the Present Time* (New York: Random House, 1975), Wilcomb E. Washburn, *The Indian in America* (New York: Harper and Row, 1975), Frederick W. Turner III, Introduction to *The Portable North American Indian Reader* (1973; New York: Penguin, 1977) and *Beyond Geography: The Western Spirit Against the Wilderness* (New York: Viking, 1980), and Fredi Chiappelli et al., eds., *First Images of America: The Impact of the New World on the Old*, 2 vols. (Berkeley, Los Angeles, London: University of California Press, 1976).

26. Frederick W. Turner III, *The Portable North American Reader*, p. 9.

Chapter 2: Crossings

1. Knud Rasmussen, *Across Arctic America: Narrative of the Fifth Thule Expedition* (London and New York: G. P. Putnam's Sons, 1927), p. 195.

2. Peter Nabokov, "American Indian Literature: A Tradition of Renewal," *ASAIL Newsletter* 2 (Autumn 1978), 31–40.

3. Jeffrey F. Huntsman, "Traditional Native American Literature: The Translation Dilemma," Native American Issue of *Shantih* 4 (Summer–Fall 1979), 6.

4. John G. Neihardt, trans., *Black Elk Speaks; Being the Life Story of a Holy Man of the Oglala Sioux* (1932; New York: Pocket Books, 1972), p. 160. For issues surrounding Neihardt's translation see Robert F. Sayre, "Vision and Experience in *Black Elk Speaks*," *College English* 32 (February 1971), 509–535, and Sally McCluskey, "*Black Elk Speaks*: and So Does John Neihardt," *Western American Literature* 6 (Winter 1972), 231–242. I first sketched this paradigm on a paper towel in a sauna. Over three years of rethinking, the model has evolved through several designs, some imprinted with other hands.

5. Huntsman, "Traditional Native American Literature," p. 6.

6. Charles Olson, "Projective Verse" in *Selected Writings*, ed. Robert Creeley (1951; New York: New Directions, 1966).

7. Walter Benjamin, "The Task of the Translator" in *Illuminations*, trans. Harry Zohn (1953; London: Collins, 1973), p. 80.

8. See Special Issues on Translation of *The American Indian Culture and Research Journal* (UCLA) vol. 4, nos. 1–2 (1980); vol. 4, no. 4 (1980).

9. Benjamin, "The Task of the Translator," p. 79.

10. W. S. Merwin, *Selected Translations 1968–1978* (New York: Atheneum, 1979), p. xi.

11. William Carlos Williams, *In the American Grain*, 2d ed. (1925; New York: New Directions, 1956), p. 137.

12. D. H. Lawrence, "The Hopi Snake Dance" in *Mornings in Mexico* (London: William Heinemann, 1956), p. 79.

13. Huntsman, *Shantih*, p. 6.

14. Hugh Honour, *The New Golden Land: European Images of America from the Discoveries to the Present Time* (New York: Random House, 1975), p. 12.

15. See William K. Powers, "The Archaic Illusion," review of *Hanta Yo: An American Saga* by Ruth Beebe Hill, *American Indian Art Magazine* 5 (November 1979), 68–71, and Alan Taylor, "The Literary Offenses of Ruth Beebe Hill," review essay in UCLA's *American Indian Culture and Research Journal* 4 (1980), 75–85.

16. H. S. McAllister, " 'The Language of Shamans': Jerome Rothenberg's Contribution to American Indian Literature," *Western American Literature* 10 (February 1976), 293–309. Jerome Rothenberg, "Total Translation: An Experiment in the Presentation of American Indian Poetry" in Abraham Chapman, ed., *Literature of the American Indians: Views and Interpretations* (New York: A Meridian Book, New American Library, 1975), pp. 294, 298.

17. McAllister, p. 296.

18. Ibid., pp. 297–298.

19. Brandon abraded ethnologists and linguists by wanting to see Native American literature as literature, apart from anthropological contexts, and taking liberties to rearrange and in some cases reinvent texts. See William Bevis, "American Indian Verse Translations" in *College English* 35 (March 1974), 693–703. Reprinted in Chapman, pp. 308–323. Also see Gretchen Bataille, "American Indian Literature: Traditions and Translations," *MELUS* 6 (Winter 1979), 17–26.

20. McAllister, p. 299.

21. William Carlos Williams, *Selected Poems*, 2d ed. (1949; New York: New Directions, 1969), pp. 69–70.

22. Howard A. Norman, trans., *The Wishing Bone Cycle: Narrative Poems from the Swampy Cree Indians* (New York: Stonehill, 1976), p. 127.

23. Neihardt, *Black Elk Speaks*, p. 41.

24. Margot Astrov, ed., *American Indian Prose and Poetry: An Anthology* (New York: Capricorn, 1972), p. 201. Astrov originally published the book as *The Winged Serpent* (1946). Maria Chona's statement was first published in Ruth Underhill, *The Autobiography of a Papago Woman*, The American Anthropological Association, *Memoirs* 46 (Menaska, 1936).

25. William Butler Yeats, "Why the Blind Man in Ancient Times Was Made a Poet" (1906) in *W. B. Yeats: Selected Criticism*, ed. A. Norman Jeffares (London: Macmillan, 1964), p. 153.

26. Ezra Pound, trans., *Shih-Ching: The Classic Anthology Defined by Confucius* (Cambridge: Harvard University Press, 1954), p. 111.

27. Rainer Maria Rilke, 11 August 1924, quoted in Martin Heidegger's "What Are Poets For?" in *Poetry, Language, Thought*, trans. Albert Hofstadter (1971; New York: Harper and Row, 1975), pp. 128–129.

28. Charles Olson, "Projective Verse" in *The Poetics of the New American Poetry*, ed. Donald Allen and Warren Tallman (New York: Grove Press, 1973), p. 156. First published in *Human Universe* (1951).

29. "Improvised Song of Joy (Iglulik Eskimo)" in Astrov, *American Indian Prose and Poetry*, p. 295. The song first appeared in Knud Rasmussen, *The Intellectual Culture of the Iglulik Eskimos* (Copenhagen: Gyldendalske boghandel, 1929), p. 27.

30. Ezra Pound, "Warning" in *A B C of Reading* (1934; New York: New Directions, 1960), p. 14.

31. Frances Densmore, *Teton Sioux Music*, Smithsonian Institution Bureau of American Ethnology, Bulletin 61 (Washington, D.C., 1918; New York: Da Capo Press Reprint, 1972), p. 88.

32. Astrov, *American Indian Prose and Poetry*, p. 3.

33. Albert B. Lord, *The Singer of Tales* (1960; reprint ed., New York, 1965), p. 13.

34. John (Fire) Lame Deer and Richard Erdoes, *Lame Deer Seeker of Visions: The Life of a Sioux Medicine Man* (New York: Simon and Schuster, 1972), p. 127.

35. Ibid., p. 163.

36. Vine Deloria, Jr., *Custer Died for Your Sins: An Indian Manifesto* (New York: Macmillan, 1969), p. 95.

37. N. Scott Momaday, "The Morality of Indian Hating," *Ramparts* (Summer 1964), p. 30.

38. Deloria, *Custer*, p. 82.

39. Jarold Ramsey, ed., *Coyote Was Going There: Indian Literature of the Oregon Country* (Seattle: University of Washington Press, 1977), pp. 38–39.

40. Norman, *Wishing Bone*, p. 172.

41 Ibid., p. 4.

Chapter 3: Ancestral Voices

1. D'Arcy McNickle, *Native American Tribalism: Indian Survivals and Renewals* (1973; reprint ed., New York: Oxford University Press, 1979), p. 11. See George D. and Louise S. Spindler, "American Indian Personality Types and Their Sociocultural Roots," *The Annals of the American Academy of Political and Social Science* 311 (May 1957), 147–157.

2. Gordon Brotherston, *Image of the New World: The American Continent Portrayed in Native Texts*, translations prepared in collaboration with Ed Dorn (London: Thames and Hudson, 1979).

3. A literary scholar is accountable to certain works of folklore, ethnology, anthropology, and biographical history outside the boundaries of "literature": Paul Radin's *The Trickster* (1956) and *The Autobiography of a Winnebago Indian* (1920, 1963), Theodora Kroeber's *Ishi* (1961), Ruth Underhill's *The Autobiography of a Papago Woman* (1936), Luther Standing Bear's *My People the Sioux* (1928) and *Land of the Spotted Eagle* (1933), Frank Waters's *The Book of the Hopi* (1963) and *Pumpkin Seed Point* (1969), Charles Eastman's reflections on Lakota childhood, especially *The Soul of the Indian* (1911), and Hyemeyohsts Storm's *Seven Arrows* (1972), to name only a few not cited elsewhere. An entire field of American literature, written by non-Indians, focuses on American Indians, from hundreds of captivity narratives and explorers' accounts and artists' impressions to Fenimore Cooper's Leatherstocking tales, frontier and Western sagas, Mari Sandoz's *Crazy Horse* (1942) and Stanley Vestal's *Sitting Bull* (1932), Thomas Berger's seriocomic *Little Big Man* (1964), Claire Huffaker's *Nobody Loves a Drunken Indian* (1967), Dan Cushman's *Stay Away Joe* (1952), a favorite on reservations, and Arthur Kopit's nightmarish play, *Indians* (1969), a surreal drama of the history and show business in Buffalo Bill's "Wild West." Leslie Fiedler's *The Return of the Vanishing American* (1969) offers a lively discussion of these materials. Richard Slotkin lays the mythic-historical groundwork for the colonial Indian period in *Regeneration Through Violence* (1973).

Daniel F. Littlefield, Jr., and James W. Parins list over 4,000 Native American authored entries in the second volume of a Native American Bibliography Series, *A Biobibliography of Native American Writers, 1772–1924* (Metuchen, N.J.: The Scarecrow Press, 1981). Wendy Rose is compiling a Native American authors bibliography that numbers over 7,000 entries, as announced May 1982 at the UCLA symposium on Native American Arts, "Sharing a Heritage," American Indian Studies Center 6th annual symposium on American Indian Issues in Higher Education.

An annotated bibliography on American Indian literature will appear in an anthology of traditional song-poetry translations edited by Alfonso and Margaret Ortiz, *To Carry Forth the Vine* (forthcoming, Columbia University Press). See also Arlene B. Hirschfelder, *American Indian Authors: A Representative Bibliography* (New York: Association of American Indian Affairs, 1970). The Studies in American Indian Literature *Newsletter* (SAIL) publishes updated bibliographies, the most recent by A. LaVonne Brown Ruoff, a 1978–1980 bibliography in two parts: *Sail Newsletter*, N.S. vol. 5, nos. 2 and 3 (Spring and Summer 1981). Other bibliographies appear in the many anthologies of American Indian literature and in special issues of literary journals, for example *Book Forum*, Special Issue, "American Indians Today," ed. Elaine Jahner, vol. 5, no. 3 (1981). See "Notes on a Bibliography" by Joseph Bruchac III.

4. A. Grove Day, *The Sky Clears: Poetry of the American Indians* (1951; reprint ed. Lincoln: University of Nebraska Press, 1964), pp. 4–5.

5. Vine Deloria, Jr., *God Is Red* (New York: Grosset & Dunlap, 1973), pp. 365–366.

6. N. Scott Momaday, *The Way to Rainy Mountain* (1969; Albuquerque: University of New Mexico Press, paperback ed., 1976), p. 46.

7. N. Scott Momaday, "The Man Made of Words," in *Literature of the American Indians: Views and Interpretations*, ed. Abraham Chapman (New York: New American Library, 1975), pp. 96–110.

8. Paula Gunn Allen, UCLA, May 1982. Octavio Paz argues that beauty in art remains "good" and useful in pretechnological cultures where the arts are functional crafts; pottery, weaving, wood and metal work, song-poetry and storytelling carry the touch of human hands. Octavio Paz, *In Praise of Hands: Contemporary Crafts of the World*, published in conjunction with the first World Crafts Exhibition held at the Ontario Science Center in Toronto (Greenwich, Conn.: New York Graphic Society, 1974). W. H. Auden felt that cooking was the only functional art, both necessary and aesthetic, left to Western technological cultures.

9. John Neihardt, trans., *Black Elk Speaks: Being the Life Story of a Holy Man of the Oglala Sioux* (1932; New York: Pocket, 1972), p. 164.

10. William Brandon, ed., *The Magic World: American Indian Songs and Poems* (New York: Morrow, 1971), p. 96.

11. Ibid.

12. John (Fire) Lame Deer and Richard Erdoes, *Lame Deer Seeker of Visions: The Life of a Sioux Medicine Man* (New York: Simon and Schuster, 1972), p. 185.

13. Brandon, *Magic World*, p. 83.

14. Margot Astrov, ed., *American Indian Prose and Poetry* (1946; New York: Capricorn, 1962), p. 221. Originally published as *The Winged Serpent*.

15. Ibid., p. 186.

16. Jerome Rothenberg, ed., *Shaking the Pumpkin: Traditional Poetry of the Indian North Americas* (Garden City, N.Y.: Doubleday, 1972), pp. 310–311. I have adjusted the line spacing to bring out the stanzaic cadence of each poem.

17. Dennis Tedlock, *Finding the Center: Narrative Poetry of the Zuñi Indians* (1972; Lincoln: University of Nebraska Press, Bison, 1978), p. xxxi.

18. N. Scott Momaday, lecture at UCLA, May 1970.

19. Jerome Rothenberg, "Total Translation. An Experiment in the Presentation of American Indian Poetry," in Chapman, *Literature of American Indians*, p. 295.

20. Neihardt, *Black Elk Speaks*, pp. 159–160.

21. "The Wisdom of the Contrary: A Conversation with Joseph Epes Brown," *Parabola*, Special Issue on The Trickster, 4, 1 (February 1979), 54–65.

22. Rothenberg, *Shaking the Pumpkin*, p. 105.

23. Brandon, *Magic World*, p. 54.

24. Ibid., p. 44.

25. Astrov, *American Indian Prose and Poetry*, p. 267.

26. John Bierhorst, *In The Trail of the Wind: American Indian Poems and Ritual Orations* (New York: Farrar, Straus and Giroux, 1971), p. 45. Originally published in Frances Densmore, "Nootka and Quileute Music," *Bureau of American Ethnology*, Bulletin 124 (1939), p. 81.

27. William Carlos Williams, "The Destruction of Tenochtitlan," in *In the American Grain*, 2d ed. (1925; New York: New Directions, 1956) p. 27.

28. Brandon, *Magic World*, p. 32.

29. Shirley Hill Witt and Stan Steiner, *The Way: An Anthology of American Indian Literature* (New York: Knopf, 1972), p. 16. The quote is from Frank B. Linderman's *Plenty-Coups, Chief of the Crows* (Omaha: University of Nebraska Press, 1962).

30. Lame Deer and Erdoes, *Lame Deer Seeker of Visions*, p. 108.
31. Ibid., p. 39.
32. N. Scott Momaday, "An American Land Ethic," *Sierra Club Bulletin* 55 (February 1970), 9.
33. Carlos Castaneda, *A Separate Reality: Further Conversations with Don Juan* (New York: Simon & Schuster, 1971), pp. 105, 187, 264.
34. Rothenberg, *Shaking the Pumpkin*, p. 197.
35. Neihardt, *Black Elk Speaks*, p. 160.
36. Ibid., p. 38.
37. James R. Walker, *Lakota Belief and Ritual*, ed. Raymond J. DeMallie and Elaine A. Jahner (Lincoln: University of Nebraska Press, 1980), p. 35. Walker letter, 13 January 1915.
38. Brandon, *Magic World*, pp. 64–65.
39. Ibid, p. 62.
40. Astrov, *American Indian Prose and Poetry*, p. 85.
41. Thomas E. Sanders and Walter W. Peek, *Literature of the American Indian* (Beverly Hills: Glencoe, 1976), p. 47.
42. Richard Keeling, "Songs of the Brush Dance and their Basis in Oral-Expressive Magic: Music and Culture of the Yurok, Hupa, and Karok Indians of Northwestern California," (Ph.D. diss. University of California, Los Angeles, 1982). The first chapter of the dissertation was published as "The Secularization of the Modern Brush Dance: Cultural Devastation in Northwestern California," Special Issue on Translation, *American Indian Culture and Research Journal* 4, 4 (1980), 55–83.
43. Neihardt, *Black Elk Speaks*, p. 35.
44. Castaneda, *A Separate Reality*, p. 16.
45. Day, *The Sky Clears*, p. 176.
46. Sanders and Peek, *Literature of the American Indian*, p. 47.
47. Ibid., p. 48.
48. Ibid.
49. Frederick W. Turner III, Introduction to *The Portable North American Indian Reader* (1973; New York: Penguin, 1977), p. 15.
50. Astrov, *American Indian Prose and Poetry*, p. 128. The quotation is from Charles Alexander Eastman, *The Soul of the Indian* (Boston and New York: Houghton Mifflin, 1911).
51. D. Demetracapoulou, "Wintu Songs," *Anthropos* 30 (1935), 483–494.
52. Astrov, *American Indian Prose and Poetry*, p. 109.
53. Ibid., p. 135.
54. Neihardt, *Black Elk Speaks*, p. 22.
55. Astrov, *American Indian Prose and Poetry*, p. 95.
56. George Bird Grinnell, *The Fighting Cheyenne*, 2d ed. (1915; Norman: University of Oklahoma Press, 1956), p. 178.
57. Momaday, *The Way to Rainy Mountain*, p. 88.
58. Neihardt, *Black Elk Speaks*, p. 30.
59. Lame Deer and Erdoes, *Lame Deer Seeker of Visions*, p. 121. Black Elk speaks of traveling with Buffalo Bill's "Wild West" show to New York and "across the Big Water":

"Afterwhile I got used to being there, but I was like a man who had never had a vision. I felt dead and my people seemed lost and I thought I might never find them again. I did not see anything to help my people. I could see that the Wasichus did not care for each other the way our people did before the nation's hoop was broken. They would take everything from each other if they could, and so there were some who had more of everything than they could use, while crowds of people had nothing at all and maybe were starving. They had forgotten that the earth was their mother" (p. 221). Black Elk had gone with the show "because I might learn some secret of the Wasichu that would help my people" (pp. 218–219), but the quest failed. "Well, it is as it is. We are prisoners of war while we are waiting here. But there is another world" (p. 200).

60. Paul Radin, *The Autobiography of a Winnebago Indian* (1920; New York: Dover, 1963), p. 80. First published in University of California Publications in American Archaeology and Ethnology, vol. 16, no. 7.

61. Alan R. Velie, ed., *American Indian Literature: An Anthology* (Norman: University of Oklahoma Press, 1979), p. 176. Songs collected by Raymond Tahbone from Anadarko, Oklahoma. A "49" song tradition in modern times is said to have originated when all but one of 50 Indian soldiers returned to Oklahoma after World War I. Others say it is a reference to the 1849 gold rush days.

Chapter 4: A Contemporary Tribe of Poets

1. See *Word Senders*, Special Issue on American Indian Translation, *American Indian Culture and Research Journal* 4, 1–2 (Spring 1980), UCLA American Indian Studies Center.

2. Leslie Silko's "An Old-Time Indian Attack Conducted in Two Parts" first appeared in *Yardbird Reader* (Berkeley: Yardbird Publishing Co., 1976); reprinted in the Native American Issue of *Shantih* 4 (Summer–Fall 1979), 3–5; reprinted in Geary Hobson, ed., *The Remembered Earth: An Anthology of Contemporary Native American Literature* (Albuquerque: Red Earth Press, 1979). See Geary Hobson's "The Rise of the White Shaman as a New Version of Cultural Imperialism," first appearing in *Yardbird Reader*, reprinted in *The Remembered Earth*. Also see Wendy Rose's poem, "For the White Poets Who Would Be Indian," in Dexter Fisher's *The Third Woman: Minority Women Writers of the United States* (Boston: Houghton Mifflin, 1980), first appearing in *Academic Squaw: Reports to the World from the Ivory Tower* (Marvin, S.D.: Blue Cloud Press, 1977).

3. Elizabeth Carmichael, *Turquoise Mosaics from Mexico* (London: Trustees of the British Museum, 1970), p. 12.

4. Andrew Welsh examines the connections between "primitive" poetry and modern poetics in *Roots of Lyric: Primitive Poetry and Modern Poetics* (Princeton: Princeton University Press, 1978).

5. Elizabeth Cook-Lynn, *Then Badger Said This* (New York: Vantage, 1977), p. 19.

6. Jim Ruppert, "The Uses of Oral Tradition in Six Contemporary Native American Poets," UCLA *American Indian Culture and Research Journal* 4, 4 (Winter 1980), 88.

Chapter 5: Word Senders

Page numbers cited in the text refer to John G. Neihardt, trans., *Black Elk Speaks: Being the Life Story of a Holy Man of the Oglala Sioux* (1932; New York: Pocket Books, 1972), cited as *BES* in the text; N. Scott Momaday, *The Way to Rainy Mountain* (1969; paperback ed., Albuquerque: University of New Mexico Press, 1976), cited as *WRM* in the text; N. Scott Momaday, *The Gourd Dancer* (New York: Harper and Row, 1976), cited as *GD* in the text; N. Scott Momaday, *House Made of Dawn* (New York: Harper and Row, 1968), cited as *HMD* in the text; N. Scott Momaday, *The Names* (New York: Harper and Row, 1976), cited as *N* in the text.

1. *John G. Neihardt, Flaming Rainbow.* Three long-playing records of Neihardt readings (Los Angeles: United Artists Records, 1973).

2. See Arnold Krupat, "The Indian Autobiography: Orgins, Type and Function" in *Smoothing the Ground*, ed. Brian Swann (Los Angeles: UCLA American Indian Studies Center, 1982).

3. William K. Powers, "Oglala Sioux Terminology," *Selected Reports in Ethnomusicology*, ed. Charlotte Heth, 3, 2 (Berkeley, Los Angeles, London: University of California Press, 1980), 33.

4. Frances Densmore, *Teton Sioux Music*, Smithsonian Institution Bureau of American Ethnology, Bulletin 61 (Washington, D.C., 1918; reprint ed., New York: Da Capo Press Reprint, 1972), p. 245.

5. Some Lakota still practice the custom of preserving the infant's umbilical cord in effigy, a physical sign of the tie between generations. See John Fire (Lame Deer) and Richard Erdoes, *Lame Deer Seeker of Visions* (New York: Simon and Schuster, 1972), p. 145.

6. As Lame Deer remarks, a *wicasa waka^n* among the Rosebud Sioux soars high as the eagle and sinks low as the bug. Ibid., p. 79.

7. The eighty-year-old Red Weasel at Standing Rock said of learning the Sun Dance rituals from his uncle, "In regard to the songs, Dreamer-of-the-Sun told me that I may pray with my mouth and the prayer will be heard, but if I sing the prayer it will be heard *sooner* by *Wakan' Tanka.*" Frances Densmore, *Teton Sioux Music*, p. 88.

8. Ernst Cassirer, *Language and Myth*, trans. Susanne K. Langer, 2d ed. (1946; New York: Dover, 1953), p. 74.

9. Citing the taboo on speaking a person's name in his presence, Densmore insists that the "sacred" power, Waka^n Ta^{n}ka or "Mysterious Great," remains untranslatable: "That which remains unspoken must be considered in the study of any deep sense of Indian thought. . . . Thus there is a 'sacred language' used by medicine-men in which familiar words take on an occult meaning." Densmore, *Teton Sioux Music*, p. 85 n.2; see also p. 120 n.1.

   In all religious thought, Cassirer says, it is "not the object of attention, but the sort of attention directed to it" that becomes crucial (p. 66). Black Elk prays thanks to the spirits on the sacred mountain, Waka^n Ta^{n}ka, for showing forth the "goodness and the beauty and the strangeness of the greening earth, the only mother" (*BES* 233). Waka^n

Taⁿka is revealed through things or events, but never reveals "it"-self; so at the origin of reality lies an original formlessness, a darkness before darkness and light. "As used by the Siouan Indian," Cassirer insists, "*wakaⁿda* vaguely connotes also 'power,' 'sacred,' 'ancient,' 'grandeur,' 'animate,' 'immortal,' and other words, yet does not express with any degree of fullness and clearness the ideas conveyed by these terms singly or collectively—indeed, no English sentence of reasonable length can do justice to the aboriginal idea expressed by the term *wakaⁿda*" (p. 69).

10. John Ruskin, "The Pathetic Fallacy" in *Modern Painters*, vol. 3 (1856; reprint ed., New York: E. P. Dutton and Co., 1923).

11. Knud Rasmussen, *The Netsilik Eskimos, Social Life and Spiritual Culture* (Copenhagen: Gyldendal, 1931), p. 321.

12. The most recent of these "as-told-to" biographies is *Fools Crow* by Thomas E. Mails (New York: Doubleday Avon, 1980), the life story of a contemporary Pine Ridge Lakota medicine man.

13. Mircea Eliade, *Myth and Reality*, trans. Willard R. Trask (New York: Harper and Row, 1963). According to Michael Castro's doctoral dissertation studying the transcripts, the cited passage was more written by Neihardt than dictated by Black Elk, though it is written as Black Elk would have spoken, Castro feels. See n. 22.

14. Joseph Epes Brown states that Black Elk was a heyoka. "The Wisdom of the Contrary: A Conversation with Joseph Epes Brown," *Parabola* 4, 1 (February 1979), 54–65.

15. Chased-by-Bears told Densmore at Standing Rock: "When a *man* does a piece of work which is admired by all we say that it is wonderful; but when we see the changes of day and night, the sun, moon, and stars in the sky, and the changing season upon the earth, with their ripening fruits, anyone must realize that it is the work of some one more powerful than man. . . . We often wish for things to come, as the rain or the snow. They do not always come when we wish, but they are sure to come in time, for they are under the control of a power that is greater than man" (Densmore, *Teton Sioux Music*, p. 96).

16. See Barre Toelken's "Seeing with a Native Eye: How Many Sheep Will It Hold?" in Walter Holden Capps, *Seeing with a Native Eye. Essays on Native American Religion* (New York: Harper and Row, 1976).

17. Densmore, *Teton Sioux Music*, pp. 295–296.

18. Joseph Epes Brown, *The Sacred Pipe*, 2d rev. ed. (1953; Baltimore: Penguin Books, 1971), p. 80.

19. Lame Deer and Erdoes, *Lame Deer Seeker of Visions*, p. 39.

20. Cassirer, *Language and Myth*, p. 37.

21. See Johann Schiller's essay, "On Simple [or Naive] and Sentimental Poetry" (1795) in *Criticism: The Major Texts*, ed. Walter Jackson Bate (New York: Harcourt Brace Jovanovich, 1952), p. 411. Also see the opening chapter of Eric Auerbach's *Mimesis. The Representation of Reality in Western Literature*, trans. Willard R. Trask, rev. ed. (1946; Princeton: Princeton University Press, 1953; 1974).

22. On the issue of Neihardt's role as editor-translator, see Sally McClusky, "*Black Elk Speaks:* and So Does John Neihardt," *Western American Literature* 6 (Winter 1972),

231–242 and Robert F. Sayre, "Vision and Experience in *Black Elk Speaks*," *College English* 32 (February 1971), 509–535.

Michael Castro has just completed a dissertation on American poets attracted to Indian consciousness (Washington University, St. Louis, 1982). His third chapter, "Translating Indian Consciousness: Lew Sarett & John G. Neihardt," discusses the "translation—or rather the transformation," Neihardt said, from Black Elk's spoken Lakota history to the published book. Castro concludes from a study of the stenographic notes and extant manuscripts, "When he makes changes, Neihardt almost always uses or develops Black Elk's imagery or thought rather than create something totally new" (p. 120). Thus, Castro argues, any changes "tend to read like extensions of his informant's consciousness, reflecting less the white writer's independent and impressionistic judgment than a hard-earned mutual understanding and trust" (pp. 120–121).

It should be noted that, aside from Neihardt's Indian experience, Black Elk had come a direction toward Neihardt's culture and consciousness many years before their meeting, and that the old holy man said he expected the poet to show up and collaborate with him. Lucy Looks Twice told Paul B. Steinmetz, S.J., that her father was baptized "Nicholas Black Elk" on December 6, 1904, at Holy Rosary Mission. Father Steinmetz has worked some twenty years as a priest at Pine Ridge, and he discusses Black Elk as a Catholic catechist in *Pipe, Bible and Peyote Among the Oglala Lakota: A Study in Religious Identity*, Stockholm Studies in Comparative Religion (Motala, Sweden: Borgströms Tryckeri, 1980).

23. See Amos Bad Heart Bull, *A Pictographic History of the Oglala Sioux*, ed. Helen H. Blish (Lincoln: University of Nebraska Press, 1967). Ben Kindle's Oglala Sioux oral winter count is reproduced in *The Portable North American Indian Reader*, ed. Frederick W. Turner III (1973; New York: Penguin, 1977).

24. It is commonly acknowledged that over half the state names in America derive from Indian words. *The World of the American Indian* (Washington, D.C.: National Geographic Society, 1974), p. 153.

25. Mari Sandoz, *Crazy Horse, The Strange Man of the Oglalas* (Lincoln: University of Nebraska Press, 1942; Bison 1968).

26. James R. Walker, *Lakota Belief and Ritual*, p. 109.

27. N. Scott Momaday, "The Man Made of Words" in *Literature of the American Indians: Views and Interpretations*, ed. Abraham Chapman (New York: New American Library, 1975), p. 103. For a careful reading of Momaday's work see Roger Dickinson-Brown's "The Art and Importance of N. Scott Momaday," *The Southern Review* 14 (January 1978), 30–45.

28. Professor Momaday plans a critical study of Emily Dickinson. With Yvor Winters as his doctoral advisor at Stanford University, he edited *The Complete Poems of Frederick Goddard Tuckerman* (Oxford: Oxford University Press, 1965).

29. Arion Press published *The Colors of Night* as a broadside of 500 copies in 1976, with Momaday's own sketches for each of the eight parts.

30. Lame Deer describes a yuwipi ceremony: "Imagine a darkness so intense and so complete that it is almost solid, flowing around you like ink, covering you like a velvet blanket. A

blackness which cuts you off from the everyday world, which forces you to withdraw deep into yourself, which makes you see with your heart instead of with your eyes" (p. 183).

31. In the opening to *House Made of Dawn*, repeated in the closing, the novelist etches a runner into an eternal landscape: "Against the winter sky and the long, light landscape of the valley at dawn, he seemed almost to be standing still, very little and alone."

32. The oldest human bones in the Americas, an archaeological skull from southern California coastal cliffs estimated to be 48,000 years old by amino acid testing, are housed in the San Diego Museum of Man. Thomas Y. Canby, "The Search for the First Americans," *National Geographic* 156, (September 1979), 332–333.

33. See John Bierhorst, ed., *In the Trail of the Wind: American Indian Poems and Ritual Orations* (New York: Farrar, Straus and Giroux, 1971).

34. Mildred P. Mayhall, *The Kiowas* (Norman: University of Oklahoma Press, 1962), pp. 110, 184.

35. Momaday quotes Mooney extensively in *The Way to Rainy Mountain* and is heavily indebted to Mayhall's first chapter in *The Kiowas*. The openings to the two books by Momaday and Mayhall are similar in tone and evocation of landscape. Parsons's older *Kiowa Tales* (1929) opens with the "Split Boys" tale, a sacred origin myth much the same as Aho's tale of the sun twins. Momaday has cut the excesses of Parsons's versions, tightened the serial structures, and spliced the various parts of his collection with personal and ethnographic materials that frame the storytelling and give it clearer lines. *The Way to Rainy Mountain* reflects this poetic shaping and placement in a grace that illuminates the tales simply. The synthesizing of oral and written record leaves the impression of a mosaic composition. The carefully shaped and structured parts interplay to make up the whole from history. The artist is not so much responsible for making up something new with his materials, as composing the given elements of Kiowa heritage and carrying on those traditions.

   Most recently, Momaday has been etching Kiowa shields, inscribed with legends as calligraphy around them, and reworking more of the tribal stories that inspired his early prose. N. Scott Momaday, "Tsoai and the Shieldmaker," *Four Winds* 1 (Summer 1980), 34–43. Again, there seems to be an integration of his mother's verbal and his father's visual media in Momaday's art.

36. N. Scott Momaday, "An American Land Ethic," *Sierra Club Bulletin* 55 (February 1970), 11.

37. The archetype of a circle in quadrants, ⊕, symbolizes the earth in ancient astrology.

38. N. Scott Momaday, *The Names* (New York: Harper and Row, 1976), p. 97.

39. Momaday's name-song bears some relation to formulaic Indian chants such as the Navajo "War God's Horse Song," reproduced in Margot Astrov's *American Indian Prose and Poetry* (1946; New York: Capricorn, 1962), and more recently retranslated by David P. McAllester, " 'The War God's Horse Song,' An Exegesis in Native American Humanities," in Charlotte Heth's *Selected Reports in Ethnomusicology* 3, 2 (Los Angeles: UCLA Department of Music Program in Ethnomusicology, 1980). "The Delight Song of Tsoai-talee" also carries distinct overtones of Douglas Hyde's translation from the Old Irish of "Amergin's rhapsody on landing in Ireland," a legendary poet, one of three

Druids with the invading Milesians, who came to Ireland somewhere between 1700 and 800 B.C.

> I am the wind which breathes upon the sea,
> I am the wave of the ocean,
> I am the murmur of the billows,
> I am the ox of the seven combats,
> I am the vulture upon the rock,
> I am a beam of the sun,
> I am the fairest of plants,
> I am a wild boar in valour,
> I am a salmon in the water,
> I am a lake in the plain,
> I am a word of science,
> I am the point of the lance of battle,
> I am the god who creates in the head the fire,
> Who is it who throws light into the meeting on the mountain?
> Who announces the ages of the moon?
> Who teaches the place where couches the sea [if not I]?

Douglas Hyde, *A Literary History of Ireland* (London: T. Fisher Unwin, 1910; 1899), pp. 243–244. Lady Gregory, W. B. Yeats's friend, retranslated this song in *Gods and Fighting Men*, and Alwin Rees and Brinley Rees examine the poetic traditions among early Celtic Druids in *Celtic Heritage* (London: Thames and Hudson, 1961; 1975). Professor Momaday, as a comparative literature scholar and teacher, seems responsive to many tribal oral traditions coming into print, from story to song, Euro-American to Native American sources.

40. See Momaday's co-authored *Colorado* with photographer David Munsch (Chicago: Rand McNally, 1973).
41. N. Scott Momaday, "To the Singing, to the Drums" in *Ants, Indians, and Little Dinosaurs*, ed. Alan Ternes (New York: Scribner's, 1975), p. 251.
42. N. Scott Momaday, "The American Indian in Conflict: Tribalism and Modern Society," lecture at UCLA, 13 May 1970.
43. Elsie Clews Parsons, *Kiowa Tales* (New York: American Folklore Society, G. E. Stechert, 1929; reprint ed., New York: Kraus Reprint, 1969), p. 133. "The Kiowa (and Crow; incidentally, in an archaic form) word for thanks is aho, a short 'a' and stress on the second syllable. My grandmother's name was Aho, with a long, accented 'A' " (N. Scott Momaday, 21 January 1980).
44. James Mooney, *Calendar History of the Kiowa Indians*, Bureau of American Ethnology, 17th Annual Report (Washington, D.C., 1898), p. 180.
45. Southwest Indian cultures depend on rainfall for their existence in the desert and image the gods as rainmakers. During sacred ceremonies Pueblo kivas are imagined as water-filled, entered by water-ladders, and celebrants are blessed with baptismal water upon re-emergence. From the "water-like touch" of Keahdinekeah's hand, to the water that fills Francisco's footprints and the runners imitating the rain gods beneath a "pool of

eternity" in *House Made of Dawn*, to the liquid silence at sunset and sunrise in *The Way to Rainy Mountain*, the artist draws symbolically on water as the life source of the world.

46. Tosamah's sermon is a mixture of "conviction, caricature, and callousness," at one point even quoting Momaday himself on his own grandmother. Trickster is at play here. Momaday's second Indian name is "Tsotohah" or Red Bluff, he relates in *The Names*. In *House Made of Dawn* Tosamah, a name that mimics Tsotohah, is known as Rev. John "Big Bluff" Tosamah, a parody of the artist as peyote priest, who quotes Momaday's reminiscences as though they were his own. The comic self-image relieves some of the high seriousness in the novel. Raymond J. DeMallie, an anthropologist, wrote me: "The name Big Bluff has, I think, two connotations in English: a land formation and a faker. But to get at it from a Kiowa perspective would require two more, I think: it is a place name for a specific land form which I believe is near Fort Sill, and in the form Little Bluff it is the name of one of their most famous chiefs (Dohasan). See Mooney" (11 March 1980).

47. See John Bierhorst, ed., *Four Masterworks of American Indian Literature* (New York: Farrar, Straus and Giroux, 1974) and Mircea Eliade on "conquering time" in ceremonies of myth, *Myth and Reality*, trans. Willard R. Trask (New York: Harper and Row, 1963).

48. Parsons, *Kiowa Tales*, p. 15.

49. Momaday, *The Way to Rainy Mountain*, p. 51.

50. See Mayhall, *The Kiowas* (p. 15) and Mooney (pp. 254–364). Mooney lived with Sett'an. His *Calendar History* includes a full-page plate of the Sett'an calendar.

51. Jim Cooley, "A Vision of the Southern Plains: The Photography of Horace Poolaw," *Four Winds* 3 (Summer 1982), 66–72.

52. See Bierhorst, *Four Masterworks*, pp. 279–351. Bierhorst edits Washington Matthews's original translations, *The Night Chant: A Navajo Ceremony* (1902).

53. See Leo Marx, *The Machine in the Garden: Technology and the Pastoral Ideal in America (1964)* and Henry Nash Smith, *Virgin Land: The American West as Symbol and Myth* (1950).

54. The Kiowa language may be related to the Jemez and Taos Pueblos as a Tanoan dialect. Edward Sapir thought Aztec-Tanoan, coupled with Kiowa, to be one linguistic family, but the theory is disputed. Mayhall, *The Kiowas*, Momaday writes of Abel's adoptive Bahkyush as stragglers from the plague-infested plains, taken in by the Jemez Pueblo long ago (*HMD* 15–22).

55. Momaday's art is primarily musical and visual in its use of descriptive and imitative language. A reader feels a marked contrast between the stylist in this case and the realist, say, in James Welch's fiction, hitting the meanings of things with hard, inviolable understandings. These two leading Indian writers may be said to countervoice each other. Whereas Welch selects particular words in end-stopped, declarative sentences, Momaday gathers rhythms of phonemes and phrases to build a sense of the movements beneath exact renderings of things. Momaday's words balance and suspend in a parabolic release of meaning. Welch's words knife home. Welch wants to know his world free of sentiment; Momaday gets caught up in his world impressionistically to know it.

56. Albinism is common among the Jemez Pueblo people. Momaday wrote in an early *Ramparts* essay: "The Indian has been for a long time generalized in the imagination of the

white man. Denied the acknowledgment of individuality and change, he has been made to become in theory what he could not become in fact, a synthesis of himself. . . . None but an Indian knows so well what it is like to have incomplete existence in two worlds and security in neither." "The Morality of Indian Hating," *Ramparts* 3 (Summer 1964), 29–40.

Vine Deloria states that "White solutions fail because *white* itself is an abstraction of attitude of mind, not a racial or group reality." *Custer Died for Your Sins: An Indian Manifesto* (New York: Macmillan, 1969), p. 189.

57. Abel's homicide is drawn partly from a historical court case in the 1950s. Simon Ortiz ("The Killing of a State Cop") and Leslie Silko ("Tony's Story") have also written fictions from the killing of Nash Garcia, 11 April 1952, a New Mexico state policeman murdered by Acoma Pueblo brothers, William and Gabriel Felipe. They pled guilty on the grounds of religious murder, since they were convinced that Garcia was a witch trying to kill them. Dr. George Devereux of the Menninger Foundation School of Psychiatry examined the brothers and found them temporarily insane at the time of the murder. See Devereux's *Reality and Dream: Psychotherapy of a Plains Indian* (New York: International Universities Press, 1951).

Momaday talked about his novel before viewing the film, *House Made of Dawn*, directed by Richardson Morse (Redbird Films, 1972), at the sixth annual American Indian Studies conference on Indian arts, "Sharing a Heritage," held at UCLA, May 28–29, 1982. He did not necessarily have the Nash Garcia case in mind, Momaday said, though the murder of a witch was one aspect of the plot; nor was he thinking in strictly biblical terms about his protagonist's name, though he was certainly "aware of symbolic associations." The facts were in front of the novelist: there was a man named Abel in Jemez, a postwar drifter, symbolic of dislocation in Indian men at the time when Momaday was a boy. There was common albinism in the Pueblo. There was a shooting. One Indian man confessed a point-blank killing because another threatened to turn himself into a snake. "And so of course I shot him," Momaday remembers of the assailant's defense in court. "Wouldn't you?" The author then quoted his "favorite character" in the novel, Tosamah, "profoundly cynical, very bright," to the effect that due process is a hell of a remedy for snakebite.

58. Leslie A. Fiedler, *The Return of the Vanishing American* (New York: Stein and Day, 1969).

Chapter 6: Trickster's Swampy Cree Bones

All unfootnoted quotations in the text appear in Howard A. Norman, trans. and ed., *The Wishing Bone Cycle: Narrative Poems from the Swampy Cree Indians* (New York: Stonehill, 1976), cited as *WBC* in the text. Ross-Erikson Press (Santa Barbara, 1982) has just issued a second edition expanding the collection with "Who Met the Ice Lynx" and "Why Owls Die With Wings Outspread." Howard Norman's comments quoted in the text come, for the most part, from class discussions and personal conversations, January–April 1981, when he taught a seminar on translation and Algonkian culture at UCLA. My gratitude to the American Indian Studies Center and English Department at UCLA for sponsoring Professor Norman's visiting appointment.

1. Paul Radin, *The Trickster: A Study in American Indian Mythology* (1956; reprint ed. Shocken: New York, 1972), p. 164.

2. Ibid., p. 155. "And so he became and remained everything to every man—god, animal, human being, hero, buffoon, he who was before good and evil, denier, affirmer, destroyer and creator. If we laugh at him, he grins at us. What happens to him happens to us" (p. 169).

David M. Abrams and Brian Sutton-Smith have developed a Trickster inventory for folklorists: *appearance*, comparatively small next to adversaries, animal-human, physically abnormal, changing in body; *locale*, living on the periphery; *behavior*, oral, narcissistic, taboo-violating, amorally ignorant, uncaring of others, individualist and isolationist, clumsy, magically powerful, tricky, capable of good deeds, dualistic in character; *playful dimensions*, humorous, exaggerating, pretenseful, playfully competitive, adventurous and curious, reversely behaving, fearlessly daring, constructively playful, vitalistic, variable, impulsive and regressive; *outcome*, humiliation both of Trickster and villain. "The Development of the Trickster in Children's Narrative," *Journal of American Folklore* 90 (1977), 29–47.

3. Johan Huizinga, *Homo Ludens: A Study of the Play Element in Culture*, 2d ed. (1950; Boston: Beacon, 1972).

4. Jarold Ramsey, *Coyote Was Going There: Indian Literature of the Oregon Country* (Seattle: University of Washington Press, 1977), p. xxi.

5. The Cree, for example, have no word for "owning," Norman says.

6. Richard J. Preston, *Cree Narrative: Expressing the Personal Meaning of Events*, National Museum of Man Mercury Series, Canadian Ethnology Service Paper No. 30 (Ottawa: National Museum of Canada, 1975), p. 141. The Cree hunter views "himself *as a part of events*," Preston observes, "not as master of them" (p. 257).

7. Norman has lived several years of an *achimoo*, or storyteller's apprenticeship, in the village and winter hunting camps with Samuel Makidemewabe, now in his eighties. Norman is translating this tribal historian's life-story from his northern Ojibwa dialect. Norman is also working with the elder, Sarah Greys, on her Swampy Cree life story. Sarah Greys is in her mid-nineties, and Norman has known her from childhood. "I have been up in Swampy regions, on & off now, for twenty-three years—mostly springs & summers, but also about six winters. Some of the time spent there was because of work my father was doing in Canada (surveying) but later, after I was seventeen, I simply returned on my own because I felt most alive & useful in the north. The first of the wishing bone poems, for instance, were worked on between Nibènegenesábe and me in 1966—until his death, and then until the book came out. As far as Nibènegenesábe, I've been working on some long sections of storytelling apprenticeships—mine with him, & others—and it's a long process to talk about really" (personal correspondence, September 1979).

Norman received his M.A. from the Folklore Institute of Indiana University in 1975. He finished his doctorate in zoology from the University of Michigan in 1981. The Academy of American Poets awarded him the Harold Morton Landon Translation Prize in 1978 for *The Wishing Bone Cycle*. His translations parallel the work of Dennis Tedlock with the Zuñi and Dell Hymes reexamining ethnographic texts from the standpoint of the original languages, with this addition: the key to translation, both linguistically and epistemologically, would ideally be a bilingual and cultural native expertise in *both* languages involved. In this regard, Norman's work places next to Alfonso Ortiz's Pueblo anthropology and forthcoming translations of Tewa Pueblo materials, *To Carry Forth the Vine* (New York: Columbia University Press, 1983). Continuing on with his ethnography, natural science, translation, and own creative writing, Norman was awarded a research fellowship at Princeton University for 1980–81, as well as a Guggenheim Fellowship. He has also published contemporary Trickster materials from Haiti, via "Ananze" African tales, in *The Woe Shirt: Caribbean Folk Tales by Paulé Bartón*, as translated by Howard A. Norman with drawings by Norman Laliberté (Lincoln: Penmaen, 1980). He is currently teaching at Tufts University.

8. The Cree songs and tales, to cite the Parry-Lord model for oral formulaic literature, preserve "tradition by the constant re-creation of it," taking shape not as a script but in performance. Albert B. Lord, "Singers: Performance and Training" in *The Singer of Tales* (1960; reprint ed. New York: Atheneum, 1974); p. 29.

The classic Trickster text has long been Radin's *The Trickster* (1956), Winnebago culture and tales within a folkloric context. But folklore as a science, directed toward the literate specialist, grinds oral performance to its own structural ends. Most academic texts are not, on the whole, consistent with the artistic and cultural origins of Indian literatures. As the Nez Percé, Archie Phinney, wrote his teacher, Franz Boas, in 1929, there has always been a certain "loss of spirit" in translating and recording Native American stories (Ramsey, *Coyote Was Going There*, p. xxv). Richly documented folklore, Radin's *The Trickster* seems one-dimensional as literary performance. In this author's opinion, the narrator's craft and tribal presence are backgrounded from a text of partially translated plot summaries, scored with archaic dialogue. The stilted prose of the exercise serves to distance any immediate sense of a living Winnebago culture. In fact, Radin bought a written transcript of the texts from Sam Blowsnake, an acculturated Winnebago whom Radin himself characterizes as "facile of speech, sociable, superficial, self-important, possessed of very little religious feeling and with little interest in the past" (p. 112). Sam Blowsnake said that he heard the cycle narrated by an unnamed storyteller. As reported, the text was then translated by two young bilingual Winnebagos, and lastly "revised" and annotated by Radin himself.

That the editor-folklorist did not witness the telling, less engage the living teller, registers throughout *The Trickster* and leaves the performance flat as essentially a "written" document. A reader misses a sense of performing narrator, any presence of an audience, or a feeling for style, tonality, or artistic context. Barre Toelken, as well as Dell Hymes, Dennis Tedlock, Robert Georges, Alan Dundes, and others, refers to these literary aspects of translated oral culture by way of "texture" and "mode," beneath a surface text and structure. See J. Barre Toelken, "The 'Pretty Language' of Yellowman: Genre, Mode, and Texture in Navajo Coyote Narratives," *Genre*, vol. 2 (September 1969) and his recent *The Dynamics of Folklore* (Boston: Houghton Mifflin, 1979).

This is not to discredit Radin's folklore for what it is, a rich compendium of narrative motifs; but it is to ask for a more complete act of ethnographic translation from oral cultures, in effect, *literature*. The new term for such translation seems to be "ethnopoetics," as used by Rothenberg, Pearce, and others. "A real translation is transparent; it does not cover the original, does not block its light, but allows the pure language, as though reinforced by its own medium, to shine upon the original all the more fully." Walter Benjamin, "The Task of the Translator" in *Illuminations*, ed. Hannah Arendt, trans. Harry Zohn, 2d ed. (1955; London: William Collins Sons, 1973), p. 79.

Leonard Bloomfield's Cree translations, collected in the summer of 1925 on the Sweet Grass Reserve in Saskatchewan, come closer to the origins of Trickster tale telling, though they remain out of print. The collected Bloomfield texts were recorded in Cree from four distinct informants, sketched and stylized in the English translations. The tales concern the basics of courting, jealousy, marriage, child-raising, in-laws, hunting, murder, war, the two-headed cannibal *windigos* with ice hearts, and always the blessed beast, Wisahketchahk, tricking his way through a tangle of epic foolishness.

"Once upon a time, long ago—I am now telling a sacred story," begins Louis Moosomin, blind from childhood, "—once upon a time, of old, a certain man dwelt in a lone lodge with his wife and his two children" (*Sacred Stories of the Sweet Grass Cree*, Anthropological Series of the National Museum of Canada, Department of Mines, Bulletin no. 60. Anthropological Series no. 11 [Ottawa; F. A. Acland, 1930], p. 14). Complex and compactly told, the opening story winds through sexual betrayal, talking "things," regenerated children, a Trickster who changes shape turning into a wolf (successfully) and then a moose (unsuccessfully), chasing and killing enemies, a Flood and the big Canoe, the creation of the four first Indians, and a final injunction against Christianity. There are no gods as such here, but magical animals, objects, and culture heroes with preternatural powers, as though spirits appeared through the bodies of people, animals, stones, blood clots, hunting gear, or any other part of the world magically animate.

9. Preston, *Cree Narrative*, p. 149.

10. A student in my seminar on Native American Tricksters, UCLA, 13 February 1980, asked Norman, the guest lecturer, why the translations of Indian materials seemed "unsophisticated" and "childlike" to Western ears. Norman responded: "Well, I'm always amazed, not at the complexity of the Cree language but in its economy. There's so much that can be assimilated into so little phrasing. My favorite anecdote about this is . . . there are hermits scattered all throughout the north. A lot of them are Indians, and they live in isolated places, but you usually stop to talk to them before you go further. There were three of us traveling, two older people and myself, and we came upon this hermit. Now we all had packs with a lot of things, and we were trying to find out what we needed to carry with us. We also wanted to know how far and what direction the next village was. The hermit came out on the porch, and this was the exchange: '[Cree] Where was this village?' Basically, 'how far?'

"And he said a phrase back, and everybody reacted by taking certain things out of their packs, and leaving them on his porch, and then setting out. No other words were spoken in reaction, except a kind of perfunctory thank you. The term he said, when we asked how far to the village, was '[Cree],' basically, 'Two porcupines to the north.'

"Now as a phrase, just objectively, you could say that it's simple. It would be poetic in a sense. But under the circumstances that phrase, given a context you're walking in, is extraordinarily helpful, and very succinct. The reason is that you have to know a lot about the area you're walking. So first of all, you know which direction you're going, you're going north; secondly, porcupines, you know, are very territorial—there's usually one every three to five miles, roughly speaking—so you know that if it's two porcupines to the north, it's at least a five or six mile walk. You know what porcupines eat—they eat birch and aspen, basically speaking—so you know what kind of terrain you're going to be walking over. And you know what feeds on porcupines—martins, fishers, wolverines occasionally come into that area, coyotes, occasionally wolves, things like that—so you know possibly what other kinds of activity there will be, based on what they eat, which is fish and small animals, and the climate, and area, specifically, you're going into. And then you base what you take with you, and your behavior, and what kinds of shoes you wear and things, on that. So while on the surface level it's kind of a simple statement, it has assimilated and balanced a whole evolution, a complex statement about the ecosystem basically in that one phrase.

"To get back to the poetry, I think that it's interesting that you use the term *childlike*, because I think that's pretty equivocable to what the people generally say about a lot of Indian poetry. The emotions might be very simple, and unpolluted somehow, but I think the way the Cree talk about their language is that it's easy to use a lot of words, but it's hard to use a few words in a lot of different ways."

11. Sapir was quoted in Preston, *Cree Narrative*, p. 19. Edward Sapir, *Language* (New York: Harcourt, Brace, 1921), p. 228.
12. William Butler Yeats, "Why the Blind Man in Ancient Times was Made a Poet" (1906) in *W. B. Yeats: Selected Criticism*, ed. A. Norman Jeffares (London: Macmillan, 1964), p. 153.
13. Mircea Eliade quoted in Ramsey, *Coyote Was Going There*, p. xxiii.
14. Boyce Richardson, *James Bay: The Plot To Drown the North Woods* (San Francisco: Sierra Club, 1972), pp. 171–172.
15. Ibid., p. 172.
16. Jarold Ramsey, "From 'Mythic' to 'Fictive' in a Nez Percé Orpheus Myth," *Western American Literature* 13 (August 1978): 126.
17. Howard A. Norman, proposal to the National Endowment for the Humanities Fellowships, 10 May 1979.
18. "In the boreal forests of subartic Canada, as in the taiga and tundra above the tree line, winter may arrive as early as September and stay into June. When the fur around the hindlegs of the snowshoe hair turns brown, winter for a time is gone. The great flocks of geese and ducks and other migrant birds 'land with summer' as the spring thaw spreads and rushes through the vast maze of lakes, rivers, and streams that eventually route into the Bay. The surface thunder of the Bay ice sectioning into floes makes a paradoxical accompaniment to the sprouting of spring flowers." Howard Norman, *Where the Chill Came From: Cree Windigo Tales and Journeys* (San Francisco: North Point Press, 1982), pp. 11–12.
19. Norman, NEH proposal.

20. See Northrop Frye, "The Mythos of Spring: Comedy" in *Anatomy of Criticism*, 2d ed. (1957; Princeton: Princeton University Press, 1971), pp. 163–186; also see Arthur Koestler's discussion of "bisociation," or split-level comic unities, over disparate levels of thinking in *Insight and Outlook* (n.d.; Lincoln: University of Nebraska Press, 1949).

21. Norman, *Where the Chill Came From*, p. 17.

22. A Carrier Indian once remarked, "We have lived here thousands of years and were taught long ago by the animals themselves. The white man writes everthing down in a book so that it will not be forgotten; but our ancestors married the animals, learned their ways, and passed on the knowledge from one generation to another." Quoted in Claude Lévi-Strauss, *The Savage Mind*, 2d ed. (1962; Chicago: University of Chicago Press, 1966), p. 10.

23. Walter Benjamin writes in "The Storyteller" that wisdom reveals itself as "counsel woven into the fabric of real life." *Illuminations*, pp. 86–87.

24. Margot Astrov, *American Indian Prose and Poetry* (Capricorn: New York, 1962), p. 79. Originally published in 1946 as *The Winged Serpent*. The song comes from Frances Densmore, *Chippewa Music I*, Bureau of American Ethnology Bulletin no. 45 (Washington, D.C.: Government Printing Office, 1910), p. 89.

25. Preston, *Cree Narrative*, p. 264.

26. Ibid., pp. 223, 226.

27. Howard Norman, trans., *Who Met The Ice Lynx* (Ann Arbor: Bear Claw Press, 1978), pp. I–II.

28. Peruvian tribes once used different colors, thicknesses, and lengths of knotted twines, *quipus*, for mnemonic "writing." Daniel G. Brinton, "Aboriginal American Authors and Their Productions" (1883) in *Literature of the American Indians: Views and Interpretations*, ed. Abraham Chapman (New York: New American Library, 1975), p. 192.

29. Job Walks and Howard Norman, "The Killing of the Moss Falls Windigo," *Alcheringa* 4 (1978): 87.

30. Howard Norman, *Born Tying Knots: Swampy Cree Naming Stories* (Ann Arbor: Bear Claw Press, 1976), p. i.

31. Lévi-Strauss, *The Savage Mind*, chapter 1.

32. Gary Snyder, "The Incredible Survival of Coyote" in *The Old Ways: Six Essays* (San Francisco: City Lights Books, 1977).

33. Howard Norman talk on *windigos*, UCLA, 14 February 1980, and class discussions January–April 1981. Norman was relating a "walking" incident as a translator during the James Bay hydroelectric hearings. See "James Bay" in *Cultural Survival Newsletter*, 4 (Winter 1980): 1–2.

34. Benjamin, "The Storyteller."

35. Knud Rasmussen recalls such sacred parody with the Netsilingmiut Eskimo in the arctic. "A curious form of pastime, popular especially among the children, was the Tunangussartut, or 'spirit game,' which consists in 'taking off' the seances of the angakoq, often in a really humorous manner. . . . I asked one of my friends here how it could be that they were not afraid of incurring the anger of the spirits by these disrespectful harlequinades. But he answered that 'of course' the spirits understood it was only in fun; and surely they

knew how to take a joke! He seemed, indeed, astonished that anyone could raise the question at all." Knud Rasmussen, *Across Arctic America: Narrative of the Fifth Thule Expedition* (London and New York: G. P. Putnam's Sons, 1927), pp. 208–209.

36. Victor Turner, *The Forest of Symbols* (Ithaca: Cornell University Press, 1967).

37. "I am just doing what he is doing," explains the Winnebago Wakdjunkaga in Radin's text, pointing his finger at a "black-shirted" figure, really a tree stump, that has stood across a lake for days. In the end he realizes his comic error. "Indeed, it is on this account," he finally sees, "that the people call me the Foolish One." Radin, *The Trickster*, pp. 13–14.

38. See the ninety or more tribal versions of "The Eye-juggler" incident in Barry Lopez's Coyote retellings, *Giving Birth to Thunder, Sleeping with His Daughter: Coyote Builds North America* (Mission, Kan.: Sheed, Andrews and McMeel, 1977), p. 184. Trickster tales must have been told, traded, retold, and passed around vast terrains and tribes, no less than the wanderer myths of Medieval Europe, woodsman stories in frontier America, or traveling salesman escapades today.

39. Consistent with their belief in a cannibal shadowing every fool in the natural food chain, the Cree say that anyone presuming complete control over an environment must be crazy, Norman recounts. Southern Cree dialects refer to the cannibal monster as "Witigo," northern dialects as "Windigo," and eastern dialects as "A-too-oosh," a name imitative perhaps of the wind. See *Where the Chill Came From: Cree Windigo Tales and Journeys.*

Chapter 7: Blackfeet Winter Blues

Page numbers cited in the text refer to James Welch, *Winter in the Blood* (New York: Harper & Row, 1974; Bantam paperback ed., 1975), cited as *WIB* in the text; and *The Death of Jim Loney* (New York: Harper & Row, 1979), cited as *DJL* in the text.

1. "Picnic Weather" and "The Man from Washington," along with all the other poems by Welch quoted in this chapter, are to be found in *Riding the Earthboy 40*, a volume of poetry first issued by Harper and Row in 1971 and reissued in 1976, with some changes in the order of the poems.

2. Interview by Dana Loy, "James Welch: Finding His Own Voice," *Four Winds* (Spring 1980), p. 35.

3. James Welch, "The Only Good Indian," interview and fragment from a work-in-progress that in revised form became *Winter in the Blood*, *South Dakota Review* 9 (Summer, 1971), 54.

4. George Bird Grinnell, *Blackfeet Lodge Tales: The Story of a Prairie People* (1892; reprint ed., Lincoln: University of Nebraska Press, 1962), p. 177.

5. Malcolm McFee, *Modern Blackfeet: Montanans on a Reservation* (New York: Holt, Rinehart, and Winston, 1972), p. 52.

6. Dana Loy interview, p. 39.

7. Clark Wissler and D. C. Duvall, *Mythology of the Blackfoot Indians*, Anthropological Papers of the American Museum of Natural History 2, 1 (Washington, 1908), 19–21.

8. William W. Thackeray, " 'Crying for Pity' in *Winter in the Blood*," *MELUS* 7 (Spring 1980), 62–63.

9. Theodora Kroeber, *Ishi in Two Worlds: A Biography of The Last Wild Indian in North America*, 2d ed. (1961; Berkeley and Los Angeles: University of California Press, 1976), pp. 127–128.

10. William Carlos Williams, "Pere Sabastian Rasles," *In the American Grain*, 2d ed. (1925; New York: New Directions, 1956), p. 128. Peter L. Berger in *Pyramids of Sacrifice* discusses political ethics and social change in the modern world, and he describes the struggle to find a way home facing all peoples today: "Both the oppressions and the discontents of modernity have engendered passionate quests for new ways of being 'at home' socially, religiously, and within the individual psyche. The central mythic motif in these quests is the hope for a *redemptive community* in which each individual will once more be 'at home' with others and with himself." Peter L. Berger, *Pyramids of Sacrifice* (1974; Garden City, N.Y.: Doubleday, 1976), pp. 23–24.

11. Luther Standing Bear recalls the first class of Carlisle Indian schoolboys being assigned Christian names written on a blackboard, chosen with a pointer randomly, and taped on their shirts. "Soon we all had the names of white men sewed on our backs," he remembers in stark contrast to the Lakota tradition of finding a name on vision quest, or by an act of bravery, or other noteworthy event. *My People the Sioux* (1928; Lincoln: University of Nebraska Press, 1975), p. 37.

12. Alan Velie documents the surrealist influences of Cesar Vallejo and James Wright on Welch in "James Welch's Poetry," UCLA *American Indian Culture and Research Journal* 3 (Spring 1979), 19–38. The essay is reprinted in Velie's *Four American Indian Literary Masters* (Norman: University of Oklahoma Press, 1982), pp. 65–90.

13. Edward S. Curtis, *The North American Indian: The Indians of the United States and Alaska*, 3 (1908; New York: Johnson, 1970), p. 66.

14. Welch told Dana Loy, "For poetry, I like to read Yeats, Eliot, and many of the poets from the 1930s to today, including those writing now, such as William Stafford and Richard Hugo" (p. 39). T. S. Eliot's uses of cultural anthropology to background the modern malaise in *The Waste Land* are major influences on Welch, in particular Jessie L. Weston's collation of sources to the Grail Legend, *From Ritual to Romance*, and James Fraser's *The Golden Bough*. Section I of *The Waste land*, "The Burial of the Dead," refers obliquely through World War I to the ancient Nile ritual of burying an earthen effigy of the slain Egyptian god, Osiris, with ears of corn.

> "That corpse you planted last year in your garden,
> "Has it begun to sprout? Will it bloom this year?
> "Or has the sudden frost disturbed its bed?
> "Oh keep the Dog far hence, that's friend to men,
> "Or with nails he'll dig it up again!
> "You! hypocrite lecteur!—mon semblable,—mon frère!" [71–76]

According to Egyptian custom, when the spring rains flooded the river, the effigy was exhumed to reveal sprouting corn and the return of the vegetation god, Osiris, gathered by Isis and her dog Sirius. Eliot sees this ritual as precursor to the Christian resurrection, the wounded Fisher King and his dying lands brought back to life in springtime. Eliot's mythic reading of history draws on Fraser's studies of fertility and vegetation gods transformed in religious cults that spread from the fertile crescent across the Mediterranean. Christianity synthesized the resurrection myths of these earlier religions. An ironic echo of these myths is felt throughout the graveyard humor of *Winter in the Blood*.

15. Grinnell, *Blackfeet Lodge Tales*, p. 220.
16. John C. Ewers, *The Blackfeet: Raiders of the Northwestern Plains* (Norman: University of Oklahoma Press, 1958), p. 258.
17. Wallace Stegner, senior American man of letters, was also raised in Blackfeet country along the forty-ninth parallel. He writes of northwestern life in the autobiographical *Wolf Willow*: "This world is very large, the sky even larger, and you are very small. But also the world is flat, empty, nearly abstract, and in its flatness you are a challenging upright thing, as sudden as an exclamation mark, as enigmatic as a question mark. It is a country to breed mystical people, egocentric people, perhaps poetic people. But not humble ones." *Wolf Willow: A History, a Story and a Memory of the Last Plains Frontier* (1955; New York: Viking, 1973), p. 8.
18. In Section III, "The Fire Sermon," of Eliot's *The Waste Land*, Tiresias the blind, hermaphroditic prophet watches "the young man carbuncular" mechanically copulate with a typist. "I Tiresias, old man with wrinkled dugs / Perceived the scene, and foretold the rest—" (228–229). Eliot annotates, "Tiresias, although a mere spectator and not indeed a 'character,' is yet the most important personage in the poem, uniting all the rest." Eliot goes on to quote Ovid relating the story of Tiresias' blind prophecy. Juno and Jove were arguing over whether a man or a woman received most sexual pleasure, and Tiresias was called to arbitrate. One day walking in the forest, he had witnessed two snakes copulating, struck them with his staff, and been fated to live seven years as a woman. Tiresias, the hermaphrodite, said women were most gratified by sex, and Juno blinded him. Jove gave Tiresias the gift of prophecy in compensation. Welch's hundred-year-old Yellow Calf, the young widow's provider and illicit mate, derives in part from this figure of the blind seer who knows things to be "cockeyed" in a Montana wasteland.
19. Eliot wrote *The Waste Land* in a sanatorium on the banks of Lake Geneva, its older name Lake Leman ("lover"), while his wife was recuperating from a breakdown in Paris. He heard "Datta, dayadhvam, damyata" in the thunder's "Da," that is, according to the Sanskrit texts, "Give, sympathize, control." These redemptive messages were given to gods, mortals, and demons in the Upanishads. Welch's own Blackfeet myths of the original "Speakthunder" in natural events correlate with these ancient records of a first language and culture in India.
20. Grinnell, *Blackfeet Lodge Tales*, p. 256.
21. William W. Thackeray, "Crying for Pity," p. 71.
22. Ewers, *Raiders*, pp. 65–66, and Curtis, *North American Indian*, p. 6.
23. Grinnell, *Blackfeet Lodge Tales*, p. 272.
24. Ibid. p. 284.
25. William Brandon, ed., "Pima chant" in *The Magic World: American Indian Songs and Poems* (New York: William Morrow, 1971), p. 37.
26. Ewers, *Raiders*, p. 172.

27. See Dennis and Barbara Tedlock, eds., *Teachings from the American Earth: Indian Religion and Philosophy* (New York: Liveright, 1975).

28. *The Death of Jim Loney* contains a prose description of Snake Butte ending: "he never got over the feeling that there were lives out there" (p. 47).

29. "Paiute Ghost Dance Song," in Brandon, *The Magic World*, p. 129.

30. The narrator at the end of *Winter in the Blood* recalls: "Somewhere in my mind I could hear the deep rumble of thunder, or maybe it was the rumble of energy, the rumble of guts—it didn't matter. There was only me, a white horse and a cow" (p. 191). Signaled by the voice of spring Thunder, or animal flatulence, Welch's Blackfeet carry on, not questioning the source, surviving the present.

31. See Ewers, *Raiders*, chapter eight, "All In Fun," on traditional Blackfeet winter sports of sliding and sledding, ice tops, blanket tossing games, etc.

32. See, in particular, the anthropologist's "neolithic" identification as an extended kin to Indians in Claude Lévi-Strauss's *Triste Tropique*, trans. John and Doreen Weightman (1955; New York: Atheneum, 1974) and *The Savage Mind*, 2d ed. (1962; Chicago: University of Chicago Press, 1966).

33. *Wassaja* (August–September 1978).

Chapter 8: "The Now Day Indi'ns"

Research and interviewing in the first section of this chapter was supported by funds from the National Institute of Alcohol and Alcohol Abuse, 1981–1983. The author conducted field work on traditional Indian healing approaches to alcohol and substance abuse, working with Professor Joan Weibel, UCLA anthropologist, and Professor Al Logan Slagle, UCB Cherokee lawyer.

Quotations to Simon J. Ortiz's work in the text refer to *Going for the Rain* (New York: Harper & Row, 1976), *A Good Journey* (Berkeley: Turtle Island, 1977) and *Howbah Indians* (Tucson: Blue Moon, 1978). Quotations from Wendy Rose refer to *Hopi Road-runner Dancing* (Greenfield Center, N.Y.: Greenfield Review Press, 1973), *Long Division: A Tribal History* (New York: Strawberry Press, 1977), *Academic Squaw: Reports to the World from the Ivory Tower* (Marvin, S.D.: Blue Cloud Press, 1978), *Builder Kachina: A Home-Going Cycle* (Marvin, S.D.: Blue Cloud Press, 1979), and *Lost Copper* (Banning, Ca.: Malki Museum Press, 1980).

1. Wendy Rose, "American Indian Poets—and Publishing" in a Special Issue of *Book Forum*, "American Indians Today: Their Thought, Their Literature, Their Art," ed. Elaine Jahner, 4, 3 (1981), 402.

2. Gary Witherspoon, *Language and Art in the Navajo Universe* (Ann Arbor: University of Michigan Press, 1977), p. 154.

3. Simon J. Ortiz, "Song/Poetry and Language—Expression and Perception," *Sun Tracks* 3 (Spring 1977), 9, 12.

4. Ward Alan Minge, *Acoma: Pueblo in the Sky* (Albuquerque: University of New Mexico Press, 1976), p. 1.

5. Ortiz, *Sun Tracks*, p. 9.
6. Ibid., p. 10.
7. Conversation with Simon Ortiz, Albuquerque, April 1980.
8. Ortiz, *Sun Tracks*, p. 9.
9. Margot Astrov, *American Indian Prose and Poetry*, originally published in 1946 as *The Winged Serpent* (New York: Capricorn, 1962), p. 40. The quotation comes from Ruth Underhill, *The Autobiography of a Papago Woman* (Menasha, Wisc.: The American Anthropological Association, *Memoirs*, 1936), vol. 46.
10. Witherspoon, *Language and Art*, p. 29.
11. John Bierhorst, *In the Trail of the Wind: American Indian Poems and Ritual Orations* (New York: Farrar, Straus and Giroux, 1971), p. 19.
12. Conversation with Paula Gunn Allen, September 1980, Los Angeles. Simon Ortiz was editor of the Navajo *Rough Rock News* in 1971, when Shirley Hill Witt and Stan Steiner published *The Way: An Anthology of American Indian Literature* (New York: Knopf, 1972), collecting Ortiz's work with other contemporary Indian writers. Ortiz's most recent work bears an overtly political thrust: *Fight Back: For the Sake of the People, For the Sake of the Land* (Albuquerque: University of New Mexico, Institute for Native American Development, 1980) and *From Sand Creek* (New York: Thunder's Mouth Press, 1981).
13. Simon J. Ortiz, *Howbah Indians* (Tucson: Blue Moon Press, 1978), p. 27.
14. Ortiz, *Sun Tracks*, p. 11.
15. Frank Waters writes in *Pumpkin Seed Point*, his personal notes while compiling *The Book of the Hopi*: "Defensively practical as the shapes of these great pueblos were, they also reflected the people's primary concern with the inner values of their lives. They were great mandalas. A mandala, the Sanskrit word for circle, is a geometrical design expressive of the unity and wholeness of all Creation, a design which produces an effect upon its maker. Its basic form is that of a four-petaled lotus with infinite variations in the shape of a cross, a square, or a circle divided by four, but always with four as the basis of the structure. . . . The Hopi concept of a four-world universe, each world designated by a directional color, is itself a symbol of the soul-form of all Creation—a mandala. The superlative sandpaintings of the Navajos are undoubtedly the finest examples today. . . . The ancient pueblos, whose terraced walls enclosed an inner court with circular or rectangular kivas in the center, were in effect great structural mandalas; and the subterranean kivas themselves—so diametrically opposite to the Christian church with its phallic spire—further symbolized the depths of the unconscious which held its meaning. The Plaza, then, was the center of the people's outward communal life and the focus of their religious thought and ceremonies." *Pumpkin Seed Point* (Chicago: The Swallow Press, 1969), pp. 46–47.

    Alfonso Ortiz writes of complementary differentiation among the Tewa Pueblo, a unity across differences through the winter and summer moieties, contesting Lévi-Strauss on cultural dualism: "The answer the Tewa present is, in a word, *time*. The asymmetrical relationship which obtains *at any given time* between the moieties becomes symmetrical over a period of a year or two years. . . . How can the society be united and divided at the same time? The answer here is simply that since there is temporal overlap, no clear and consistent line of division can emerge; the moieties can never really be uniformly divided on a major structural issue." *The Tewa World: Space, Time, Being, and Becoming in a Pueblo Society* (Chicago: University of Chicago Press, 1969), p. 84.

So divisions among moieties oscillate in balance over time; one slice of synchronic asymmetry or stop-action time, with a shifting center across diachronic or sequential time, eventually balances in cultural symmetry through time. It is the same with the moving balance in ceremonial dance steps: a dancer's weight never evenly divides in the frozen moment, but shifts rhythmically and evenly in continuous organic symmetry. This continuous unity of division, an aspect of common walls in Simon Ortiz's poetry, is reflected in a Tewa saying to Alfonso Ortiz: "In the very beginning we were one people. Then we divided into Summer people and Winter people; in the end we came together again as we are today. But you can see we are still Summer people and Winter people" (*The Tewa World*, p. 16).

16. Ortiz, *Sun Tracks*, p. 12.
17. See Ruth Underhill's *Singing For Power: The Song Magic of the Papago Indians of Southern Arizona* (Berkeley: University of California Press, 1938) and Ruth Benedict's *Patterns of Culture* (Boston: Houghton Mifflin, 1934) for early discussions of the ceremonial significance of rain in southwest deserts. Ezra Pound translates one of the Confucian odes in the *Shih-Ching* simply: "Soft rain / high grain." *Shih-Ching: The Classic Anthology Defined by Confucius* (Cambridge: Harvard University Press, 1954).
18. Paula Gunn Allen, "A Stranger in My Own Life: Alienation in American Indian Prose and Poetry" in *MELUS* 7 (Summer 1980), 18–19.
19. N. Scott Momaday, "The Man Made of Words" in *Literature of the American Indians: Views and Interpretations*, ed. Abraham Chapman (New York: New American Library, 1975), p. 97.

To further this end, UCLA has supported a cultural American Indian Studies research center since 1968. The Native American Series publishes first volumes of emerging Indian poets; it is an artists' forum sponsored within the context of academic teaching, research, and publication in Indian studies. The poets gathered in this series represent some of the many hundreds of voices scattered in periodicals: *"A": A Journal of Contemporary Literature, Akwesasne Notes, Alcheringa, American Indian Quarterly, Arizona Highways, Arizona Quarterly, Sail Newsletter, Blue Cloud Quarterly, The Cimarron Review, Dacotah Territory, Greenfield Review, The Indian Historian, La Confluencia, MELUS, New America, Nimrod, The Prairie Schooner, Shantih, The South Dakota Review, Sun Tracks, The Southwest Review, Wambli Ho,* and *Wassaja*. These new tribal voices have received some attention through small presses such as "A" Press, Ahsahta Press, Blackberry Press, Blue Moon Press, Cold Mountain Press, Crossing Press, Dakota Press, Greenfield Review Press, Indian Historian Press, Navajo Community College Press, Puerto del Sol Press, Red Earth Press, San Marcos Press, Strawberry Press, Territorial Press, and Turtle Island Foundation.

With Indian administrators, faculty, staff, and students, the UCLA American Indian Studies Center serves as a clearing house for research and publication, sponsoring undergraduate, graduate, and postdoctoral studies. Its library is among the most complete in the field. The Center publishes a quarterly, the *American Indian Culture and Research*

Journal, monographs, books, and research series in history, law, music, and literature. It recruits and counsels Indian students in higher education, serves as a liaison with Indian communities and reservations, and draws faculty and scholars from across America. For six years running the UCLA Center has sponsored an annual symposium on national issues in American Indian Studies and published the proceedings. In the fall of 1982, the Center began the country's first Master's Program in American Indian Studies, utilizing over forty UCLA faculty.

20. Selection from Frances Densmore's *Papago Music* (Washington: Bureau of American Ethnology Bulletin 90, 1929) in Astrov, *American Indian Prose and Poetry*, p. 196.

21. Selection from Leo W. Simmons's *Sun Chief, The Autobiography of a Hopi Indian* (New Haven: Yale University Press, 1942) in Astrov, p. 250.

22. Ralph Ellison, "Richard Wright's Blues" in *Shadow and Act* (New York: Random House, 1964), p. 78.

23. Vine Deloria, Jr., "Indian Humor," in *Custer Died for Your Sins: An Indian Manifesto* (New York: Macmillan, 1969)

24. John (Fire) Lame Deer and Richard Erdoes, *Lame Deer Seeker of Visions: The Life of a Sioux Medicine Man* (New York: Simon and Schuster, 1972), p. 49.

25. John G. Neihardt, trans., *Black Elk Speaks; Being the Life Story of a Holy Man of the Oglala Sioux* (1932; New York: Pocket, 1972), p. 142.

26. Ruth M. Underhill, *First Penthouse Dwellers of America*, 2d ed. rev. (Santa Fe: Laboratory of Anthropology, 1946), p. 86.

27. Adolph F. Bandelier and Edgar L. Hewett, *Indians of the Rio Grande Valley* (1937; reprint ed., New York: Cooper Square Publications, 1973), p. 23.

28. Paula Gunn Allen, "A Stranger in My Own Life: Alienation in American Indian Prose and Poetry," *MELUS* 7 (Summer 1980), 5.

29. Paula Gunn Allen, "The Trick Is Consciousness" in *Coyote's Daylight Trip* (Albuquerque: La Confluencia, 1978), pp. 38–40.

Chapter 9: Grandmother Storyteller

Page numbers cited in the text refer to Leslie Marmon Silko, *Ceremony* (New York: Viking, 1977), cited as *C.*

1. Simon J. Ortiz, "Notes by the Contributors" in *The Man to Send Rain Clouds: Contemporary Stories by American Indians*, ed. Kenneth Rosen (1974; New York: Vintage, Random House, 1975), p. 174.

2. Leslie Marmon Silko, "Contributors' Biographical Notes" in *Voices of the Rainbow: Contemporary Poetry by American Indians*, ed. Kenneth Rosen (New York: Seaver, 1975), p. 230.

3. "Lullaby" was chosen as one of the twenty best short stories of 1975 and collected in Martha Foley's *Best Short Stories of 1975.* Much of Silko's short fiction appears in Kenneth Rosen's *The Man to Send Rain Clouds*: "The Man to Send Rain Clouds," "Yellow

Woman," "Tony's Story," "Uncle Tony's Goat," "A Geronimo Story," "Bravura," and "*from* Humaweepi, the Warrior Priest," fully half of Rosen's gathering of contemporary Indian short stories. "Storyteller" is anthologized in Geary Hobson's *The Remembered Earth: An Anthology of Contemporary Native American Literature* (Albuquerque: Red Earth Press, 1979), Dexter Fisher's *The Third Woman: Minority Writers of the United States* (Boston: Houghton Mifflin, 1980), and Leslie Silko, *The Storyteller* (New York: Viking, 1981).

4. Knud Rasmussen, *Intellectual Culture of the Iglulik Eskimos* 7, 1 of *Report of the Fifth Thule Expedition, 1921–1924* (Copenhagen: Gylkendalske Boghandel, Nordisk Forlag, 1929). Reprinted as "A Shaman's Journey to the Sea Spirit Takánakapsâluk" in *Teachings from the American Earth: Indian Religion and Philosophy*, ed. Dennis and Barbara Tedlock (New York: Liveright, 1975), pp. 13–19. Rasmussen, a native Greenlander accompanied by an Eskimo man and woman, traveled 20,000 miles in three and a half years, 1921–1924, filling 30 notebooks on native cultures of Siberian North America. Silko most probably read Rasmussen during her prolonged stay in Ketchikan, especially this essay in the popular Tedlock anthology; at the least she would have heard Alaskan stories of Takánakapsâluk.

5. "We use media to destroy cultures, but we first used media to create a false record of what we are about to destroy." Edmund Carpenter, *Oh, What A Blow That Phantom Gave Me!* (New York: Holt, Rinehart & Winston, 1972), p. 99.

6. Leslie Silko, Biographical Note in *The Next World: Poems by Third World Americans*, ed. Joseph Bruchac (Trumansburg, N.Y.: The Crossing Press, 1978), p. 173. Silko updates her own place in the Marmon house and family: "I was born in 1948 in Albuquerque, New Mexico. I grew up in the house at Laguna where my father was born. The house was built ninety years ago with rock and adobe mortar walls two feet thick. Outside there was a great old mountain cottonwood tree, five feet around at its base. Our house was next to my great-grandmother's house. My mother had to work, so I spent most of my time with my great-grandma, following her around her yard while she watered the hollyhocks and blue morning glories.

   "When I got older I carried the coal bucket inside for her. Her name was Maria Anaya and she was born in Paguate Village, north of Old Laguna. She came to Laguna when she married my great-grandfather, who was a white man. She took care of me and my sisters, and she told us about how things were when she was a little girl." "Leslie Silko, Laguna Poet and Novelist," in *This Song Remembers: Self-Portraits of Native Americans in the Arts*, ed. Jane B. Katz (Boston: Houghton Mifflin, 1980), p. 187. A number of personal photographs, including some of Maria Anaya, prototype for Grandmother in *Ceremony*, are in Silko's *The Storyteller*.

7. Elsie Clews Parsons, *Laguna Genealogies*, Anthropological Papers of the American Museum of Natural History 19, pt. 4 (New York: The Trustees, 1920), p. 142.

8. Ibid., p. 242.

9. Franz Boas, *Keresan Texts*, Publications of the American Ethnological Society 8, pt. 1 (1928; reprint ed. New York: AMS Press Reprint, 1974), p. 299.

10. Boas, *Keresan Texts*, p. 292.

11. Ibid., pp. 294–295.

12. Adolph F. Bandelier and Edgar L. Hewett, *Indians of the Rio Grande Valley* (1937; reprint ed. New York: Cooper Square Publications, 1973), p. 45.

13. Hamilton A. Tyler, *Pueblo Gods and Myths* (Norman: University of Oklahoma Press, 1964), p. 17.

14. Boas, *Keresan Texts*, p. 292. Perhaps too, Tayo echoes *Oyoyewi*, the younger of the sun twins who function as Laguna culture heroes, or even the Hopi *Taiowa*, the flute-playing demigod of the sun.

15. Fisher, Silko interview in *The Third Woman*, p. 20.

16. Parsons noted a high incidence of illegitimacy at Laguna, called *yani wahshtyi* or "a stolen child," and Silko recalls her great aunt Alice, who told Yellow Woman stories often, as a village character known by such gossip. Leslie Silko reading, Modern Language Association Conference for Teachers of Native American Literature, July 1977, Flagstaff, Arizona.

17. There is a significant difference here, Alfonso Ortiz says, between Navajo sand paintings, which grow centrifugally outward, and Pueblo sand paintings, which develop centripetally inward from a beginning border. Personal conversation, February 1978, UCLA.

18. Edgar L. Hewett and Bertha P. Dutton, *The Pueblo Indian World: Studies on the Natural History of the Rio Grande Valley in Relation to Pueblo Indian Culture* (Albuquerque: University of New Mexico Press, 1945), p. 160 illustration. The pan-Pueblo mythic Salt Woman, *Tsi'ty'icots'a*, associated with pure water, is adumbrated in Ts'eh. See Tyler, *Pueblo Gods and Myths*, p. 190. According to Parsons's *Notes on Acoma and Laguna* (1918), pilgrimage to Mount Taylor shrines is made only in time of drought. The southeast slopes at 7,000–8,000 feet are favorite summer pasturages. "Montaño Grant" and ruins of houses lie due east of Mount Taylor, beyond the Cebolleta Grant. Florence H. Ellis, "Anthropology of Laguna Pueblo Land Claims" in *Pueblo Indians III* (New York: Garland, 1974), map p. 93, description of house site ruins p. 97.

19. Silko reading, Flagstaff, July 1977. Prologue talk to the poem "Storytelling."

20. Silko, *Sun Tracks* interview, 29–30.

21. Fred Eggan describes a *cheani* ceremony still practiced: "The shaman sets up an altar and uses a crystal to search for the heart of the patient which has been stolen by witches; with a bear's paw he rushes out and finds the patient's 'heart.' " Fred Eggan, *Social Organization of the Western Pueblos* (Chicago: University of Chicago Press, 1950), p. 281.

22. Hamilton A. Tyler, *Pueblo Animals and Myths* (Norman: University of Oklahoma Press, 1975), pp. 213, 227.

23. Boas, *Keresan Texts*, p. 282.

24. Against Tayo's sense of dislocation, place the ceremonial "attention to boundaries, to detail and order, and to the center," ideally speaking, in what Alfonso Ortiz sees as the Pueblo world view: "everything—animate and inanimate—counts and everything has its place in the cosmos. All things are thought to have two aspects, essence and matter. Thus everything in the cosmos is believed to be knowable and, being knowable, controllable. Effective control comes only from letter-perfect attention to detail and correct performance, thus the Pueblo emphasis on formulas, ritual, and repetition revealed in ritual drama. Among human beings the primary causal factors are mental and psychological

states; if these are harmonious, the supernaturals will dispense what is asked and expected of them. If they are not, untoward consequences will follow just as quickly, because within this relentlessly interconnected universal whole the part can affect the whole, just as like can come from like. Men, animals, plants and spirits are intertransposable in a seemingly unbroken chain of being." Alfonso Ortiz, "Ritual Drama and the Pueblo World View" in *New Perspectives on the Pueblos*, ed. Alfonso Ortiz (Albuquerque: University of New Mexico Press, 1972), p. 143.

In an interview with Dexter Fisher, Silko explains what it means for a storyteller to "make accessible certain ways of seeing things. This is the beauty of the old way": "Things about relationships. That's all there really is. There's your relationship with the dust that just blew in your face, or with the person who just kicked you end over end. That's all I'm interested in. You have to come to terms, to some kind of equilibrium with those people around you, those people who care for you, your environment." Leslie Marmon Silko and Dexter Fisher, "Stories and Their Tellers—A Conversation with Leslie Marmon Silko" in *The Third Woman*, p. 22.

In 1957 four informants gave Florence Ellis a Laguna Origin Legend, including the statement: "The Whites came out from the underworld, which we call Shipap, and went to Europe and South America as Your Father told them. Our Mother told her people they were to go south. She made a song naming all the places which they were to go. The people were in a kiva for several days trying to learn the song, which we still have today, but some went to sleep and when they awoke they heard only parts of it. When they left to go south they knew they would find Laguna because the song was like a map in their memory. Everything the people had done or were to do was in the song made for the Lagunas by Our Mother." Ellis, *Anthropology of Laguna Pueblo Land Claims*, p. 13.

25. There are 43 uranium mines, 5 mills, and 31 mining companies digging up Indian lands in the Four Corners area, according to Simon Ortiz's *Fight Back: For the Sake of The People, For the Sake of The Land*, INAD Literary Journal 1, 1 (Albuquerque: Institute for Native American Development, 1980). The Jackpile open-pit uranium mine, on the Laguna Reservation, is the largest in the country. Grants, New Mexico advertises itself "The Uranium Capital of the World, " with a park dedicated to a Navajo, Paddy Martinez, who carried in a chunk of uranium ore lying outside his hogan one afternoon in 1953 (cf. Ortiz's "It Was That Indian" in *Fight Back*). Los Alamos, New Mexico, at the hub of the Pueblo crescent, is a small city of nuclear scientists spearheading the government's atomic energy research.

26. Pueblo witches or Two-Hearts are seen as "simply ordinary humans," Tyler notes, "who possess a special degree of supernatural power and direct it toward antisocial ends." Tyler, *Pueblo Gods and Myths*, p. 259.

27. An older oral tradition of type characterization may be at work here. The ethno-psychology of Pueblo narrative, Tedlock observes in Zuñi tales, implodes motive and character development in ritualized cultural types whose actions spell out their names. Dennis Tedlock, "Pueblo Literature" in Ortiz, ed., *New Perspectives*, pp. 230–237.

28. Ortiz, "Ritual Drama and the Pueblo World View" in Ortiz, ed., *New Perspectives*, p. 142.

SELECTED BIBLIOGRAPHY

PRIMARY NATIVE AMERICAN LITERATURE

POETRY

Allen, Paula Gunn. *The Blind Lion.* Berkeley: Thorp Springs Press, 1975.

————. *A Cannon Between My Knees.* New York: Strawberry Press, 1981.

————. *Coyote's Daylight Trip.* Albuquerque: La Confluencia, 1978.

————. *Shadow Country.* Native American Series no. 6. Los Angeles: UCLA American Indian Studies Center, 1982.

————. *Starchild.* Marvin, S.D.: Blue Cloud Press, 1982.

Arnett (Gogisgi), Carroll. *Come.* New Rochelle, N.Y.: Elizabeth Press, 1973.

————. *Tsalagi.* New Rochelle: Elizabeth Press, 1976.

Big Eagle, Duane. *Bidato: Ten Mile River Poems.* Berkeley: Workingman's Press, 1975.

Blue Cloud (Aroniawenrate), Peter. *Back Then Tomorrow.* Brunswick, Me.: Blackberry Press, 1978.

————. *Coyote & Friends.* Brunswick, Me.: Blackberry Press, 1974.

————. *Turtle, Bear & Wolf.* Rooseveltown, N.Y.: Akwesasne Notes, 1976.

————. *White Corn Sister.* New York: Strawberry Press, 1979.

Boas, Franz. *Keresan Texts.* Publications of the American Ethnological Society, vol. 8, part 1, 1928. New York: AMS Press Reprint, 1974.

Bush, Barney. *My Horse And a Jukebox.* Native American Series no. 4. Los Angeles: UCLA American Indian Studies Center, 1979.

Campbell, Janet. *Custer Lives in Humbolt County.* Greenfield, N.Y.: Greenfield Review Press, 1978.

Cardiff, Gladys. *To Frighten a Storm.* Port Townsend, Wash.: Copper Canyon Press, 1976.

Concha, Joseph L. *Chokecherry Hunters.* Santa Fe, N.M.: The Sunstone Press, n.d.

Cook-Lynn, Elizabeth. *Then Badger Said This.* New York: Vantage, 1977.

Harjo, Joy. *The Last Song.* Las Cruces, N.M.: Puerto del Sol, 1975.

————. *What Moon Drove Me to This.* New York: I. Reed Books, 1979.

Hanson, Lance. *Keeper of Arrows.* Chickasaw, Okla.: Renaissance Press, 1972.

————. *Naming the Dark.* Norman, Okla.: Point Riders Press, 1974.

————. *Mistah.* New York: Strawberry Press, 1977.

Hobson, Geary. *The Road Where People Cried.* Marvin, S.D.: Blue Cloud Press, 1979.

Hogan, Linda. *Calling Myself Home.* Greenfield, N.Y.: Greenfield Review Press, 1979.

Karoniaktatie (Jacobs, Alex). *Native Colours.* Rooseveltown, N.Y.: Akwesasne Notes, 1974.

Kenny, Maurice. *Dancing Back Strong the Nation.* Marvin, S.D.: Blue Cloud Quarterly, 1979.

————. *I Am The Sun.* New York: Strawberry Press, n.d.; reissued, Buffalo, N.Y.: White Pine, 1979.

————. *North: Poems from Home.* Marvin, S.D.: Blue Cloud Quarterly, 1977.

Louis, Adrian C. *The Indian Cheap Wine Seance.* Providence, R.I.: Gray Flannel Press, n.d.

SELECTED BIBLIOGRAPHY

————. *Muted War Drums*. Marvin, S.D.: Blue Cloud Press, 1977.

Momaday, N. Scott. *The Colors of Night*. San Francisco: Arion Press, 1976. A Broadside of 500 copies.

————. *The Gourd Dancer*. New York: Harper & Row, 1976.

Niatum, Duane. *Ascending Red Cedar Moon*. New York: Harper & Row, 1973.

————. *Digging Out The Roots*. New York: Harper & Row, 1978.

————. *Taos Pueblo*. Greenfield, N.Y.: Greenfield Review Press, 1973.

Norman, Howard A., trans. *The Wishing Bone Cycle: Narrative Poems from the Swampy Cree Indians*. New York: Stonehill, 1976. Second edition expanded to include "Who Met the Ice Lynx" and "Why Owls Die With Wings Outspread." Santa Barbara: Ross-Erikson, 1982.

northsun, nila. *Diet Pepsi and Nacho Cheese*. Fallon, Nev.: Duck Down Press, 1977.

Oandasan, William. *A Branch of California Redwood*. Native American Series no. 5. Los Angeles: UCLA American Indian Studies Center, 1980.

————. *Earth and Sky*. Laguna, N.M.: A Press, 1976.

————. *Taking Off*. Laguna, N.M.: A Press, 1977.

Ortiz, Simon. *From Sand Creek*. New York: Thunder's Mouth Press, 1981.

————. *A Good Journey*. Berkeley: Turtle Island, 1977.

————. *Going for the Rain.*. New York: Harper & Row, 1976.

Palmanteer, Ted, and Rogers, Ron. *Man-Spirit*. Greenfield, N.Y.: Greenfield Review Press, 1979.

Red Bird. "Opening Lakota Sun Dance Prayer,"*American Indian Literature: An Anthology*. Norman: University of Oklahoma Press, 1979. First published by Frances Densmore. *Teton Sioux Music*. Smithsonian Institution, Bureau of American Ethnology Bulletin no. 61, Washington, D.C., 1918.

Rose, Wendy. *Academic Squaw: Reports to the World from the Ivory Tower*. Marvin, S.D.: Blue Cloud Press, 1978.

————. *Builder Kachina: A Home-Going Cycle*. Marvin, S.D.: Blue Cloud Press, 1979.

————. *Hopi Roadrunner Dancing*. Greenfield Center, N.Y.: Greenfield Review Press, 1973.

————. *Long Division: A Tribal History*. New York: Strawberry Press, 1977.

————. *Lost Copper*. Banning, Calif.: Malki Museum Press, 1980.

Russell, Norman H. *Collected Poems*. Stafford, Va.: Northwoods Press, 1974.

————. *Indian Thoughts; I Am Old*. Albuquerque, N.M.: San Marcos Press, n.d.

————. *Indian Thoughts: The Childen of God*. Native American Series no. 2. Los Angeles: UCLA American Indian Studies Center, 1975.

————. *Open the Flower*. Mt. Horeb, Wis.: The Perishable Press, 1977.

Sanchez, Carol Lee. *Message Bringer Woman*. San Francisco: Taurean Horn Press, 1977.

Silko, Leslie Marmon. *Laguna Woman*. Greenfield, N.Y.: Greenfield Review Press, 1974.

Tall Mountain, Mary. *Nine Poems*. San Francisco: Friars Press, 1979.

————. *There Is No Word for Goodbye*. Marvin, S.D.: Blue Cloud Quarterly, 1981.

Tedlock, Dennis, trans. *Finding the Center: Narrative Poetry of the Zuñi Indian*. 1972. Lincoln: University of Nebraska Press, Bison, 1978.

Vizenor, Gerald. *Summer in the Spring: Ojibwe Lyric Poems and Tribal Stories*. Minneapolis: Nodin, 1981.

SELECTED BIBLIOGRAPHY

Volborth, J. Ivaloo. *Thunder-Root: Traditional and Contemporary Native American Verse.* Native American Series no. 3. Los Angeles: UCLA American Indian Studies Center, 1978.

Walsh, Marnie. *A Taste of the Knife.* Boise, Idaho: Ahsahte Press, 1976.

Welch, James. *Riding the Earthboy 40.* New York: Harper & Row, 1971, reissued 1976.

Young Bear, Ray A. *Waiting to be Fed.* Seattle: Graywolf Press, 1975.

————. *Winter of the Salamander.* New York: Harper & Row, 1980.

PROSE

Bad Heart Bull, Amos. *A Pictographic History of the Oglala Sioux.* Edited by Helen H. Blish. Lincoln: University of Nebraska Press, 1967.

Bloomfield, Leonard. *Sacred Stories of the Sweet Grass Cree.* Anthropological Series of the National Museum of Canada, Department of Mines, Bulletin no. 60, Anthropological Series no. 11. Ottawa: F. A. Acland, 1930.

Brown, Joseph Epes. *The Sacred Pipe.* 1953. 2d rev. ed. Baltimore: Penguin Books, 1971.

Carter, Forrest. *Watch for Me on the Mountain.* New York: Delacorte, 1978.

Cushman, Dan. *Stay Away Joe.* Great Falls, Mont.: Stay Away Joe Publishers, 1953.

Eastman (Ohiyesa), Charles Alexander. *The Soul of the Indian.* Boston and New York: Houghton Mifflin, 1911.

Fire, John (Lame Deer) and Richard Erdoes. *Lame Deer, Seeker of Visions: The Life of a Sioux Medicine Man.* New York: Simon and Schuster, 1972.

Gunn, John M. *Schat-Chen: History, Tradition and Narratives of the Queres Indians of Laguna and Acoma.* Albuquerque, N.M.: Albright and Anderson, 1917.

Hale, Janet Campbell. *The Owl's Song.* New York: Doubleday, 1974.

Highwater, Jamake. *Anpao: An American Indian Odyssey.* New York: Lippincott, 1977.

————. *Journey to the Sky.* New York: Thomas Y. Crowell, 1978.

Hungry Wolf, Beverly. *The Ways of My Grandmothers.* New York: William Morrow, 1980.

Left Handed. *Son of Old Man Hat.* Recorded by Walter Dyk. 1938. 2d ed. Lincoln: University of Nebraska Press, 1970.

Linderman, Frank B. *Plenty-Coups, Chief of the Crows.* 1930. Reprint. New York: John Day Co., 1972.

"The Longest Walk," *Wassaja* 6 (August–September 1978): 9–10.

McNickle, D'Arcy. *Runner in the Sun: A Story of Indian Maise.* New York: Holt, Rinehart & Winston, 1954.

————. *The Surrounded.* 1936. Reprint. Albuquerque: University of New Mexico Press, 1978.

————. *Wind From an Enemy Sky.* New York: Harper & Row, 1978.

Mails, Thomas E. *Fools Crow.* New York: Doubleday Avon, 1980.

Momaday, N. Scott. "An American Land Ethic," *Sierra Club Bulletin* 55 (February 1970): 8–11.

————. *House Made of Dawn.* New York: Harper & Row, 1968.

————. *The Journey of Tai-me.* Limited Edition of 100. Hand printed at the University of California in collaboration with D. E. Carlsen and Bruce S. McCurdy. 1967.

————. "The Man Made of Words," *Literature of the American Indians: Views and Interpretations.* Edited by Abraham Chapman. New York: New American Library, 1975.

————. "The Morality of Indian Hating," *Ramparts* (Summer 1964): 30–40.

————. *The Names*. New York: Harper & Row, 1976.

————. "To the Singing, to the Drums," *Ants, Indians, and Little Dinosaurs*. Edited by Alan Ternes. New York: Scribner's Sons, 1975.

————. "Tsoai and the Shieldmaker,"*Four Winds* 1 (Summer 1980): 34–43.

————. *The Way to Rainy Mountain*. 1969. Albuquerque: University of New Mexico Press, paperback edition, 1976.

Momaday, N. Scott, and Munsch, David. *Colorado*. Chicago, New York, San Francisco: Rand McNally & Co., 1973.

Mourning Dove (Humishuma). *Co-Ge-We-a, The Half-Blood: A Depiction of the Great Montana Cattle Range*. Boston: Four Seas Press, 1927. Reprint ed. Lincoln: University of Nebraska Press, Bison, 1981.

Neihardt, John G., trans. *Black Elk Speaks: Being the Life Story of a Holy Man of the Oglala Sioux*. 1932. New York: Pocket Books, 1972.

Neihardt, John G. *John G. Neihardt, Flaming Rainbow*. Three long-playing records of Neihardt readings. Los Angeles: United Artists Records, 1973.

Norman, Howard A. "James Bay," *Cultural Survival Newsletter* 4 (Winter 1980): 1–2.

————, trans. *Born Tying Knots: Swampy Cree Naming Stories*. Ann Arbor, Mich.: Bear Claw, 1976.

————, trans. *Where the Chill Came From: Cree Windigo Tales and Journeys*. San Francisco: North Point Press, 1982.

————, trans. *Who Met the Ice Lynx*. Ann Arbor, Mich.: Bear Claw, 1978.

Ortiz, Simon. *Fight Back: For the Sake of the People, For the Sake of the Land*. Albuquerque: University of New Mexico, Institute for Native American Development, 1980.

————. *Howbah Indians*. Tucson, Ariz.: Blue Moon Press, 1978.

————. "Notes by Contributors," *The Man to Send Rain Clouds: Contemporary Stories by American Indians*. Edited by Kenneth Rosen. New York: Vintage Books, Random House, 1974, 1975.

————. "Song/Poetry and Language—Expression and Perception, " *Sun Tracks* 3 (Spring 1977): 9–12.

Radin, Paul. *The Autobiography of a Winnebago Indian*. 1920. New York: Dover, 1963. First published in University of California Publications in American Archaeology & Ethnology, vol. 16, no. 7.

————. *The Trickster. A Study in American Indian Mythology*. 1956. New York: Shocken, 1972.

Radin, Paul, ed. *Crashing Thunder: The Autobiography of an American Indian*. New York and London: D. Appleton & Co., 1926.

Ramsey, Jarold, ed. *Coyote Was Going There: Indian Literature of the Oregon Country*. Seattle: University of Washington Press, 1977.

"Red Cloud's Speech to the Cooper Union, 16 June 1870." *Literature of the American Indian*. Thomas E. Sanders and Walter W. Peek, comps. Beverly Hills, Calif.: Glencoe, 1976.

Rose, Wendy. "For the White Poets Who Would Be Indian," *The Third Woman: Minority Women Writers of the United States*. Edited by Dexter Fisher. Boston, Mass.: Houghton

Mifflin, 1980. First appearing in *Academic Squaw: Reports to the World from the Ivory Tower*. Marvin, S.D.: Blue Cloud Press, 1978.

Sandoz, Mari. *Crazy Horse, the Strange Man of the Oglalas*. 1942. Lincoln: University of Nebraska Press, Bison, 1968.

Silko, Leslie. "An Old-Time Indian Attack Conducted in Two Parts," *Yardbird Reader*. Berkeley: Yardbird Publishing Co., 1977. Reprinted in the Native American Issue of *Shantih* 4 (Summer–Fall 1979). Also reprinted in *The Remembered Earth: An Anthology of Contemporary Native American Literature*. Edited by Geary Hobson, Albuquerque: N.M.: Red Earth Press, 1979.

———. Biographical Note in *The Next World: Poems by 32 Third World Americans*. Edited by Joseph Bruchac. Trumansburg, N.Y.: The Crossing Press, 1978.

———. *Ceremony*. New York: Viking Press, 1977.

Silko, Leslie Marmon. "Contributors' Biographical Notes," *Voices of the Rainbow: Contemporary Poetry by American Indians*. Edited by Kenneth Rosen. New York: Viking, 1975.

———. "A Conversation with Leslie Marmon Silko," from taping in late March of 1976, by Larry Evers and Denny Carr. *Sun Tracks* 3 (Fall 1976): 28–33.

———. "Stories and Their Tellers—A Conversation with Leslie Marmon Silko," *The Third Woman: Minority Women Writers of the United States*. Edited by Dexter Fisher. Boston: Houghton Mifflin, 1980.

———. *Storyteller*. New York: Seaver, 1981.

"Simon Ortiz, Acoma Poet," *This Song Remembers: Self-Portraits of Native Americans in the Arts*. Edited by Jane B. Katz. Boston: Houghton Mifflin, 1980.

Standing Bear, Luther. *Land of the Spotted Eagle*. 1933. Lincoln: University of Nebraska Press, Bison, 1978.

———. *My People the Sioux*. Edited by E. A. Briminstool. 1928. Lincoln: University of Nebraska Press, Bison, 1975.

Storm, Hyemeyohsts. *Heyokah*. New York: Harper & Row, 1981.

———. *Seven Arrows*. New York: Harper & Row, 1972.

Strete, Craig Lee. *Paint Your Face on a Drowning in the River*. New York: William Morrow, 1978.

Talayesva, Don C. *Sun Chief: The Autobiography of a Hopi Indian*. Edited by Leo W. Simmons. New Haven, Conn.: Yale University Press, 1942.

Underhill, Ruth. *The Autobiography of a Papago Woman*. Menasha, Wis.: American Anthropological Association, 1936.

Vizenor, Gerald. *The Darkness in Saint Louis Bearheart*. St. Paul: Truck Press, 1978.

———. *Wordarrows: Indians and Whites in the New Fur Trade*. Minneapolis: University of Minnesota Press, 1978.

Walks, Job, and Norman, Howard. "The Killing of the Moss Falls Windigo," *Alcheringa* 4 (1978):84–88.

Waters, Frank. *The Book of the Hopi*. New York: Viking Press, 1963.

———. *Pumpkin Seed Point*. Chicago: The Swallow Press, 1969.

Welch, James. *The Death of Jim Loney*. New York: Harper & Row, 1979.

SELECTED BIBLIOGRAPHY

———. "The Only Good Indian," interview and fragment from work-in-progress, *South Dakota Review* 9 (Summer 1971): 49–74.

———. *Winter in the Blood.* New York: Harper & Row, 1974. Bantam Edition, 1975.

ANTHOLOGIES

Allen, Terry, ed. *The Whispering Wind: Poetry by Young American Indians.* Garden City, N.Y.: Doubleday, 1972.

Astrov, Margot, ed. *American Indian Prose and Poetry.* Originally published in 1946 as *The Winged Serpent.* New York: Capricorn, 1962.

Bierhorst, John, ed. *Four Masterworks of American Indian Literature.* New York: Farrar, Straus and Giroux, 1974.

———, ed. *In the Trail of the Wind: American Indian Poems and Ritual Orations.* New York: Farrar, Straus and Giroux, 1971.

———, ed. *The Red Swan: Myths and Tales of the American Indians.* New York: Farrar, Straus and Giroux, 1976.

Brandon, William, ed. *The Magic World: American Indian Songs and Poems.* New York: William Morrow, 1971.

Bruchac, Joseph. *The Next World: Poems by Third World Americans.* Trumansburg, N.Y.: Crossing Press, 1978.

Burlin (Curtis), Natalie. *The Indians' Book.* New York and London: Harper, 1907, 1923, 1935. Reissued. New York: Dover, 1950, 1968.

Cronyn, George, ed. *The Path on the Rainbow: An Anthology of Songs and Chants from the Indians of North America.* Intro. by Mary Austin. New York: Boni and Liveright, 1918, 1934. Republished as *American Indian Poetry: The Standard Anthology of Songs and Chants.* New York: Liveright, 1973.

Day, A. Grove. *The Sky Clears: Poetry of the American Indians.* 1951. Reprint ed. Lincoln: University of Nebraska Press, 1964.

Dodge, Robert K., and McCullough, Joseph B., eds. *Voices from Wah'Kon-Tah: Contemporary Poetry of Native Americans.* New York: International Publishers, 1974.

Fisher, Dexter, ed. *The Third Woman: Minority Women Writers of the United States.* Boston: Houghton Mifflin, 1980.

Heth, Charlotte. *Songs of Love, Luck, Animals, and Magic. Music of the Yurok and Tolowa Indians.* New York: New World Records, 1977.

Hobson, Geary, ed. *The Remembered Earth: An Anthology of Contemporary Native American Literature.* Albuquerque: Red Earth Press, 1979.

Levitas, Gloria; Vivelo, Frank; and Vivelo, Jaqueline, eds. *American Indian Prose and Poetry: We Wait in the Darkness.* New York: G. P. Putnam's Sons, 1974.

Lopez, Barry. *Giving Birth to Thunder, Sleeping with His Daughter: Coyote Builds North America.* Mission, Kan.: Sheed Andrews and McMeel, 1977.

Lourie, Dick. *Come to Power: Eleven Contemporary American Indian Poets.* Trumansburg, N.Y.: Crossing Press, 1974.

Lowenfels, Walter, ed. *From the Belly of the Shark: Poems by Chicanos, Eskimos, Hawaiians, Indians, Puerto Ricans in the U.S.A., With Related Poems by Others.* New York: Vintage, 1973.

SELECTED BIBLIOGRAPHY

Milton, John, ed. *The American Indian Speaks*. Vermillion, S.D.: University of South Dakota Press, 1969.

——. *American Indian II*. Vermillion, S.D.: University of South Dakota Press, 1971.

——. *Four Indian Poets*. Vermillion, S.D.: University of South Dakota Press, 1974.

Momaday, Natachee Scott, ed. *American Indian Authors*. Boston: Houghton Mifflin, 1972.

Nabokov, Peter. *Native American Testimony. An Anthology of Indian and White Relations: First Encounter to Dispossession*. New York: Harper & Row, Colophon, 1978.

Niatum, Duane, ed. *Carriers of the Dream Wheel: Contemporary Native American Poetry*. New York: Harper & Row, 1975.

Ortiz, Alfonso and Margaret. *To Carry Forth the Vine*. New York: Columbia University Press, forthcoming.

Rosen, Kenneth, ed. *The Man to Send Rain Clouds. Contemporary Stories by American Indians*. 1974. New York: Random House, Vintage, 1975.

——. *Voices of the Rainbow: Contemporary Poetry by American Indians*. New York: Seaver, 1975.

Rothenberg, Jerome, ed. *Shaking the Pumpkin: Traditional Poetry of the Indian North Americas*. Garden City, N.Y.: Doubleday, 1972.

Sanders, Thomas E., and Peek, Walter W. *Literature of the American Indian*. Beverly Hills: Glencoe, 1976.

Turner, Frederick W., III, ed. and intro. *The Portable North American Indian Reader*. 1973. New York: Penguin, 1977.

Velie, Alan R., ed. *American Indian Literature: An Anthology*. Norman: University of Oklahoma Press, 1979.

White, James L., ed. *The First Skin Around Me: Contemporary American Tribal Poetry*. Moorehead, Minn.: Territorial Press, 1976.

Witt, Shirley Hill, and Steiner, Stan. *The Way: An Anthology of American Indian Literature*. New York: Knopf, 1972.

JOURNALS

"A": A Journal of Contemporary Literature

Akwesasne Notes

Alcheringa

American Indian Art Magazine

American Indian Culture and Research Journal

American Indian Quarterly

Arizona Highways

Arizona Quarterly

Blue Cloud Quarterly

The Cimarron Review

Contact II

Coyote's Journal

Dakota Territory

El Nahuatzen

Four Winds

SELECTED BIBLIOGRAPHY

Greenfield Review
The Indian Historian
La Confluencia
Maize
Many Smokes
MELUS
New America
New Wilderness Letter
Nimrod
Parabola
The Prairie Schooner
SAIL Newsletter
Scree
Shantih
The South Dakota Review
The Southwest Review
Spawning the Medicine River
Sun Tracks
Wambli Ho
Wassaja
Wood Ibis

SCHOLARSHIP

Abrams, David M., and Sutton-Smith, Brian. "The Development of the Trickster in Children's Narrative," *Journal of American Folklore* 90 (1977): 29–47.

Allen, Paula Gunn. " 'The Grace that Remains'—American Indian Women's Literature," *Book Forum* 5 (1981): 376–382.

———. "The Sacred Hoop: A Contemporary Indian Perspective on American Indian Literature," *Literature of the American Indian: Views and Interpretations*. Edited by Abraham Chapman. New York: New American Library, Meridian Books, 1975. Reprinted in *Cross Currents* 26 (1977) and in *The Remembered Earth: An Anthology of Contemporary Native American Literature*. Edited by Geary Hobson. Albuquerque: Red Earth Press, 1979.

———. "A Stranger in My Own Life: Alienation in American Indian Prose and Poetry," *MELUS* 7 (Summer 1980): 3–19.

Auerbach, Eric. *Mimesis. The Representation of Reality in Western Literature*. 1946. Rev. ed. Translated by Willard R. Trask. Princeton: Princeton University Press, 1974.

Austin, Mary. "Aboriginal American Literature" in *American Writers on American Literature*, ed. John A. Macy. New York: Liveright, 1931.

Baker, Houston, ed. *Three American Literatures*. Modern Language Association anthology of critical essays on Asian-American, Chicano, and American Indian literatures. New York: MLA, 1982.

SELECTED BIBLIOGRAPHY

Bandelier, Adolf F., and Hewett, Edgar L. *Indians of the Rio Grande Valley*. 1937. Reprint. New York: Cooper Square Publications, 1973.

Bartón, Paulé. *The Woe Shirt: Caribbean Folk Tales*. Translated by Howard A. Norman. Lincoln, Neb.: Penmaen, 1980.

Bataille, Gretchen. "American Indian Literature: Traditions and Translations," *MELUS* 6 (Winter 1979): 17–26.

Benedict, Ruth. *Patterns of Culture*. Boston: Houghton Mifflin, 1934.

Benjamin, Walter. "The Storyteller" and "The Task of the Translator," *Illuminations*. 1955. 2d ed. Translated by Harry Zohn. Edited by Hannah Arendt. London: William Collins Sons, 1973.

Berger, Thomas. *Little Big Man*. New York: Dial, 1964.

Bevis, William. "American Indian Verse Translations," *Literature of the American Indians: Views and Interpretations*. Edited by Abraham Chapman. New York: New American Library, 1975. First published in *College English*, March 1974.

Bieder, Robert E. "Scientific Attitudes Toward Indian Mixed-Bloods in Early Nineteenth-Century America," *The Journal of Ethnic Studies* 8 (Summer 1980): 17–30.

Billard, Jules B., ed. *The World of the American Indian*. Washington, D.C.: National Geographic Society, 1974.

Borges, Jorge Luis. "The Oral Poetry of the Indians," *Literature of the American Indians: Views and Introductions*. Edited by Abraham Chapman. New York: New American Library, 1975.

Brinton, Daniel G. "Aboriginal American Authors and Their Productions (1883)," *Literature of the American Indians: Views and Interpretations*. Edited by Abraham Chapman. New York: New American Library, 1975.

Brotherston, Gordon. *Images of the New World: The American Continent Portrayed in Native Texts*. Translations prepared in collaboration with Ed Dorn. London: Thames and Hudson, 1979.

Brown, Dee. *Bury My Heart at Wounded Knee*. New York: Holt, Rinehart, and Winston, 1970.

Brown, Joseph Epes. "The Wisdom of the Contrary: A Conversation with Joseph Epes Brown," *Parabola* 4 (February 1979): 54–65.

Cahn, Edgar S. *Our Brother's Keeper: The Indian in White America*. Washington, D.C: World Publishing, 1969.

Canby, Thomas Y. "The Search for the First Americans," *National Geographic* 156 (September 1979): 330–363.

Capps, Walter Holden. *Seeing with a Native Eye. Essays on Native American Religion*. New York: Harper and Row, 1976.

Carmichael, Elizabeth. *Turquoise Mosaics from Mexico*. London: Trustees of the British Museum, 1970.

Cassirer, Ernst. *Language and Myth*. 1946. 2d ed. Translated by Susanne K. Langer. New York: Dover, 1953.

Castaneda, Carlos. *A Separate Reality: Further Conversations with Don Juan*. New York: Simon & Schuster, 1971. This Simon and Schuster series includes: *The Teachings of Don Juan, Journey to Ixtlan, Tales of Power, The Second Ring of Power,* and *The Eagle's Gift*.

SELECTED BIBLIOGRAPHY

Channing, Walter. "Essay on American Language and Literature," *North American Review and Miscellaneous Journal* 1 (1815), reprinted *American Indian Culture and Research Journal* 1 (1976):6.

Chapman, Abraham, ed. *Literature of the American Indians: Views and Interpretations.* New York: New American Library, 1975.

Chiappelli, Fredi, et al. *First Images of America: The Impact of the New World on the Old.* 2 vols. Berkeley, Los Angeles, London: University of California Press, 1976.

Curtis, Edward S. *The North American Indian. The Indians of the United States and Alaska*, vol. 3. (1908). 20 vols. New York: Johnson, 1970.

Deloria, Vine, Jr. *Custer Died for Your Sins: An Indian Manifesto.* New York: The Macmillan Co., 1969.

———. *God Is Red.* New York: Grosset and Dunlap, 1973.

———. *Of Utmost Good Faith.* San Francisco: Straight Arrow Books, 1971.

DeMallie, Raymond J., Jr., and Jahner, Elaine. *Lakota Belief and Ritual: James R. Walker Papers.* 1917. Reprint. Lincoln: University of Nebraska Press, 1980. [See Walker, James R.]

DeMallie, Raymond J., Jr., and Lavenda, Robert H. "*Wakan*: Plains Siouan Concepts of Power," *The Anthropology of Power: Ethnographic Studies from Asia, Oceania, and the New World.* New York: Academic Press, 1977.

Densmore, Frances. *Chippewa Music* I. Bureau of American Ethnology, Bulletin 45. Washington, D.C.: Government Printing Office, 1910.

———. *Teton Sioux Music.* Smithsonian Institution Bureau of American Ethnology, Bulletin 61. Washington, D.C., 1918. New York: Da Capo Press Reprint, 1972.

Devereux, George. *Reality and Dream: Psychotherapy of a Plains Indian.* New York: International University Press, 1951.

Dickinson-Brown, Roger. "The Art and Importance of N. Scott Momaday," *Southern Review* 14 (January 1978): 30–45.

Dobyns, Henry F. "Estimating Aboriginal American Population: An Appraisal of Techniques with a New Hemispheric Estimate," *Current Anthropology* 7 (1966): 395–449.

Dorris, Michael. "Native American Literature in an Ethnohistorical Context," *College English* 41 (October 1979): 147–162.

Driver, Harold E. *Indians of North America.* 1961. 2d rev. ed. Chicago: University of Chicago Press, 1969.

Dundes, Alan. "Texture, Text, and Context," *Southern Folklore Quarterly* 28 (December 1964): 251–265.

Eggan, Frederick Russell. *Social Organization of the Western Pueblos.* Chicago: University of Chicago Press, 1950.

Eliade, Mircea. *Myth and Reality.* Translated by Willard R. Trask. New York: Harper and Row, 1963.

Ellis, Florence H. "Anthropology of Laguna Pueblo Land Claims," *Pueblo Indians* 3. New York: Garland, 1974.

Ewers, John C. *The Blackfeet: Raiders of the Northwestern Plains.* Norman: University of Oklahoma Press, 1958.

Fiedler, Leslie. *The Return of the Vanishing American.* New York: Stein and Day, 1969.

SELECTED BIBLIOGRAPHY

Fletcher, Alice C. *The Emblematic Use of the Tree in the Dakotan Group.* Proclamations of the American Association of Advanced Sciences, 1896. Salem, 1897.

Foster, Michael K. *From the Earth to Beyond the Sky: An Ethnographic Approach to Four Longhouse Iroquois Speech Events.* Canadian Ethnology Service Paper no. 20. National Museum of Man Mercury Series. Ottawa: National Museums of Canada, 1974.

Fox, Robin. *The Keresan Bridge.* New York: Humanities Press, 1967.

Frye, Northrop. "The Mythos of Spring: Comedy," *Anatomy of Criticism.* 1957. 2d ed. Princeton: Princeton University Press, 1971.

Greenway, John. "Will the Indians Get Whitey?" *National Review* 21 (11 March 1969): 223–228, 245.

Grinnell, George Bird. *Blackfeet Lodge Tales: The Story of a Prairie People.* 1892. Reprint. Lincoln: University of Nebraska Press, 1962.

———. *The Fighting Cheyenne.* 1915. 2d ed. Norman: University of Oklahoma Press, 1956.

Haines, Francis. *The Buffalo.* New York: Crowell, 1970.

Hewett, Edgar L., and Dutton, Bertha P. *The Pueblo Indian World: Studies on the Natural History of the Rio Grande Valley in Relation to Pueblo Indian Culture.* Albuquerque: University of New Mexico Press, 1945.

Hirschfelder, Arlene B. *American Indian Authors: A Representative Bibliography.* New York: Association of American Indian Affairs, 1970.

Hobson, Geary. "The Rise of the White Shaman as a New Version of Cultural Imperialism," *Yardbird Reader.* Berkeley: Yardbird Publishing Co., 1976. Reprinted in *The Remembered Earth: An Anthology of Contemporary Native American Literature.* Albuquerque, N.M.: Red Earth Press, 1979.

Honour, Hugh. *The New Golden Land: European Images of America from the Discoveries to the Present Time.* New York: Random House, 1975.

Huizinga, Johan. *Homo Ludens: A Study of the Play Element in Culture.* 1950. 2d ed. Boston: Beacon, 1972.

Huffaker, Clair. *Nobody Loves a Drunken Indian.* 1967. New York: Paperback Library Edition, 1969.

Huntsman, Jeffrey F. "Traditional Native American Literature: The Translation Dilemma," Native American Issue of *Shantih* 4 (Summer–Fall 1979): 5–9.

Hymes, Dell. "Discovering Oral Performance and Measured Verse in American Indian Narrative," *New Literary History* 8 (1976–1977): 431–457.

———. *"In Vain I Tried to Tell You": Essays in Native American Ethnopoetics.* Philadelphia: University of Pennsylvania Press, 1981.

———. "Louis Simpson's 'The deserted boy,' " *Poetics* 5 (1976): 119–155.

Irwin, John T. *American Hieroglyphics: The Symbol of the Egyptian Hieroglyphics in the American Renaissance.* New Haven: Yale University Press, 1980.

Jennings, Francis. *The Invasion of America. Indians, Colonialism, and the Cant of Conquest.* Chapel Hill: University of North Carolina Press, 1975.

Katz, Jane B., ed. "Leslie Silko, Laguna Poet and Novelist," *This Song Remembers: Self-Portraits of Native Americans in the Arts.* Boston: Houghton Mifflin, 1980.

Keeling, Richard. "Songs of the Brush Dance and their Basis in Oral-Expressive Magic: Music and Culture of the Yurok, Hupa, and Karok Indians of Northwestern California,"

Dissertation for the Doctor of Philosophy in Music, University of California at Los Angeles, 1982.

Kopit, Arthur. *Indians*. New York: Hill and Wang, 1969.

Kroeber, Alfred L. *Gros Ventre Myths and Tales*. Anthropological Papers of the Museum of Natural History, vol. 1, pt. 3, New York, 1907.

Kroeber, Karl, comp. and ed. *Traditional American Indian Literatures: Texts and Interpretations*. Lincoln: University of Nebraska Press, 1981.

Kroeber, Theodora. *Ishi in Two Worlds: A Biography of the Last Wild Indian in North America*. 1961. 2d ed. Berkeley, Los Angeles, London: University of California Press, 1976.

Larson, Charles A. *American Indian Fiction*. Albuquerque: University of New Mexico Press, 1978.

Lawrence, D. H. "Fenimore Cooper's White Novels," *Studies in Classic American Literature*. 1923. 2d ed. New York: Viking, 1966.

————. *Mornings in Mexico*. 1927. Reprint. London: William Heinemann, 1956.

Lévi-Strauss, Claude. "The Making of an Anthropologist," *Tristes Tropique*. 1955. Translated by John and Doreen Weightman. New York: Atheneum, 1974.

————. *The Savage Mind*. 1962. 2d ed. Chicago: University of Chicago Press, 1966.

Lincoln, Kenneth, ed. *Word Senders*. Special Issue on American Indian Translation, *American Indian Culture and Research Journal*. Los Angeles: UCLA American Indian Studies Center 4, nos. 1–2, 4 (1980).

Littlefield, Jr., Daniel F., and Parins, James W. *A Biobibliography of Native American Writers, 1772–1924*. Native American Bibliography Series, no. 2. Metuchen, N.J.: The Scarecrow Press, 1981.

Lord, Albert B. *The Singer of Tales*. 1960. Reprint. New York: Atheneum, 1965.

McAllister, H. S. " 'The Language of Shamans': Jerome Rothenberg's Contribution to American Indian Literature," *Western American Literature* 10 (February 1976): 293–309.

McCluskey, Salley. "*Black Elk Speaks*: and So Does John Neihardt," *Western American Literature* 6 (Winter 1972): 231–242.

McHugh, Tom. *The Time of the Buffalo*. New York: Knopf, 1972.

McNickle, D'Arcy. *Native American Tribalism. Indian Survivals and Renewals*. 1973. Reprint. New York: Oxford, 1979.

Matthews, Washington. *The Night Chant: A Navajo Ceremony*. New York: The Knickerbocker Press, 1902.

Matthiessen, F. O. *American Renaissance: Art and Expression in the Age of Emerson and Whitman*. London: Oxford, 1941.

Mayhall, Mildred P. *The Kiowas*. Norman: University of Oklahoma Press, 1962.

Meeker, Joseph W. *The Comedy of Survival: In Search of an Environmental Ethic*. "Foreword" by Konrad Lorenz. 1974. 2d ed. Reprint. Los Angeles: Guild of Tutors, 1980.

Merwin, W. S. *Selected Translations 1968–1978*. New York: Atheneum, 1979.

Minge, Ward Alan. *Acoma: Pueblo in the Sky*. Albuquerque: University of New Mexico Press, 1976.

Momaday, N. Scott, ed. *The Complete Poems of Frederick Goddard Tuckerman*. Oxford: Oxford University Press, 1965.

SELECTED BIBLIOGRAPHY

Mooney, James. *Calendar History of the Kiowa Indians*. U.S. Bureau of American Ethnology, 17th Annual Report, 1895–96. Washington, D.C., 1898, pp. 141–444.

Nabokov, Peter. "American Indian Literature: A Tradition of Renewal," *ASAIL Newsletter* 2 (Autumn 1978): 37.

Newman, Anne, and Suk, Tulie, eds. *Bear Crossings: An Anthology of North American Poets*. New York: Persea Books Inc., 1978.

Olson, Charles. *Selected Writings*. Edited by Robert Creeley. New York: New Directions, 1966.

Ortiz, Alfonso. "Ritual Drama and the Pueblo World View," *New Perspectives on the Pueblos*. Edited by Alfonso Ortiz. Albuquerque: University of New Mexico, 1972.

————. *The Tewa World: Space, Time, Being and Becoming in a Pueblo Society*. Chicago: University of Chicago Press, 1969.

Parsons, Elsie Clews. *Kiowa Tales*. American Folk-lore Society, New York: G. E. Stechert, 1929. Reprint. New York: Kraus Reprint, 1969.

————. *Laguna Genealogies*. Anthropological Papers of the American Museum of Natural History, vol. 19, part 5. New York: The Trustees, 1923.

————. "Notes on Acoma and Laguna," *American Anthropologist* n.s. 20 (April–June 1918): 162–186.

————. *Notes on Ceremonialism at Laguna*. Anthropological Papers of the American Museum of Natural History, vol. 19, part 4. New York: The Trustees, 1920.

————. *Pueblo Indian Religion*. vol. 2. Chicago: University of Chicago Press, 1939.

Paz, Octavio. *In Praise of Hands: Contemporary Crafts of the World*. Greenwich, Conn.: New York Graphic Society, 1974.

Pearce, Roy Harvey. *The Savages of America: A Study of the Indian and the Idea of Civilization*. Baltimore: Johns Hopkins University Press, 1953. Revised edition published as *Savagism and Civilization: A Study of the Indian and the American Mind* (1965).

Peyer, Bernd. *Hyemeyohsts Storm's "Seven Arrows": Fiction and Anthropology in the Native American Novel*. Wiesbaden: Steiner, 1979.

Pound, Ezra. "Warning," *A B C of Reading*. 1934. New York: New Directions, 1960.

————, trans. *Shih-Ching: The Classic Anthology Defined by Confucius*. Cambridge: Harvard University Press, 1954.

Powers, William K. "The Arachic Illusion," Review of *Hanto Yo: An American Saga* by Ruth Beebe Hill. *American Indian Art Magazine* 5 (Winter 1979): 68–71.

————. "Oglala Song Terminology," *Selected Reports in Ethnomusicology*, vol. 3. Edited by Charlotte Heth. Berkeley, Los Angeles, London: University of California Press, 1980, 23–41.

————. *Yuwipi: Vision and Experience in Oglala Ritual*. Lincoln: University of Nebraska Press, 1982.

Preston, Richard J. *Cree Narrative: Expressing the Personal Meanings of Events*. National Museum of Man Mercury Series. Canadian Ethnology Service Paper no. 30. Ottawa: National Museum of Canada, 1975.

Raines, Howell. "American Indians Struggling for Power and Identity," *The New York Times Magazine* (11 February 1979):21.

SELECTED BIBLIOGRAPHY

Ramsey, Jarold. "From 'Mythic' to 'Fictive' in a Nez Percé Orpheus Myth," *Western American Literature* 13 (August 1978): 119–131.

———. "The Teacher of Modern American Indian Writing as Ethnographer and Critic," *College English* 41 (October 1979): 163–169.

Rands, Robert L. "Acoma Land Utilization: An Ethnohistorical Report," *Pueblo Indians* 3. New York: Garland, 1974.

Rasmussen, Knud. *Across Arctic America. Narrative of the Fifth Thule Expedition.* London and New York: G. P. Putnam's Sons, 1927.

———. *Intellectual Culture of the Iglulik Eskimos.* vol. 7, no. 1. *Report of the Fifth Thule Expedition, 1921–1924.* Copenhagen: Gyldendalske Boghandel, Nordisk Forlag, 1929. Reprinted as: "A Shaman's Journey to the Sea Spirit Takánakapsâluk," *Teachings from the American Earth: Indian Religion and Philosophy.* Edited by Dennis and Barbara Tedlock. New York: Liveright, 1975.

———. *The Netsilik Eskimos, Social Life and Spiritual Culture.* Copenhagen: Gyldendal, 1931.

Rilke, Rainer Maria. Letter of 11 August 1924, quoted in Martin Heidegger's "What Are Poets For?" *Poetry, Language, Thought.* Translated by Albert Hofstader. 1971. New York: Harper and Row, 1975.

Rothenberg, Jerome. "Total Translation. An Experiment in the Presentation of American Indian Poetry," *Literature of the American Indians: Views and Interpretations.* Edited by Abraham Chapman. New York: New American Library, A Meridian Book, 1975.

Rourke, Constance. "The Indian Background of American Theatricals," *Literature of the American Indians: Views and Interpretations.* Edited by Abraham Chapman. New York: New American Library, A Meridian Book, 1975.

Ruppert, Jim. "The Uses of Oral Tradition in Six Contemporary Native American Poets," UCLA *American Indian Culture and Research Journal* 4 (Winter 1980): 87–110.

Ruskin, John. "The Pathetic Fallacy," *Modern Painters* 3. 1856. Reprint. New York: E. P. Dutton & Co., 1923.

Sapir, Edward. *Language.* New York: Harcourt, Brace, 1921.

Sayre, Robert F. "Vision and Experience in *Black Elk Speaks,*" *College English* 32 (February 1971): 509–535.

Schiller, Johann. "On Simple (or Naive) and Sentimental Poetry," (1795) *Criticism: The Major Texts.* Edited by Walter Jackson Bate. New York: Harcourt Brace Jovanovich, 1952.

Slotkin, Richard. *Regeneration Through Violence: The Mythology of the American Frontier, 1600–1860.* Middletown, Conn.: Wesleyan University Press, 1973.

Snyder, Gary. "The Incredible Survival of Coyote," *The Old Ways, Six Essays.* San Francisco: City Lights Books, 1977.

Spindler, George D., and Spindler, Louise S. "American Indian Personality Types and Their Sociocultural Roots," *The Annals of the American Academy of Political and Social Science* 311 (May 1957): 147–157.

Sontag, Susan. *Against Interpretation, and Other Essays.* 1966. 2d ed. New York: Farrar, Straus and Giroux, 1967.

Stegner, Wallace. *Wolf Willow: A History, a Story, and a Memory of the Last Plains Frontier.* 1955. New York: The Viking Press, 1973.

Steinmetz, Paul B., S. J. *Pipe, Bible and Peyote Among the Oglala Lakota: a Study in Religious Identity.* Stockholm Studies in Comparative Religion. Motala, Sweden: Borgströms Tryckeri, 1980.

Stirling, Matthew William. *Origin Myth of Acoma and Other Records*. Washington, D.C.: U.S. Government Printing Office, 1942.

Taylor, Alan. "The Literary Offenses of Ruth Beebe Hill," Review Essay in UCLA *American Indian Culture and Research Journal* 4 (1980): 75–85.

Tedlock, Dennis. "Pueblo Literature: Style and Verisimilitude," *New Perspectives on the Pueblos*. Edited by Alfonso Ortiz. Albuquerque: University of New Mexico, 1972.

Tedlock, Dennis, and Tedlock, Barbara, eds. *Teachings from the American Earth: Indian Religion and Philosophy*. New York: Liveright, 1975.

Toelken, J. Barre. *The Dynamics of Folklore*. Boston: Houghton Mifflin, 1979.

——. "The 'Pretty Language' of Yellowman: Genre, Mode, and Texture in Navajo Coyote Narratives," *Genre* 2 (September 1969): 211–235.

——. "Seeing with a Native Eye: How Many Sheep Will It Hold?" *Seeing with a Native Eye. Essays on Native American Religion*. Edited by Walter Holden Capps. New York: Harper and Row, 1976.

Trennert, Robert A. "The Indian Role in the 1876 Centennial Celebration," UCLA *American Indian Culture and Research Journal* 4 (1980): 7–13.

Turner, Frederick. *Beyond Geography: The Western Spirit Against the Wilderness*. New York: Viking Press, 1980.

Turner, Victor. *The Forest of Symbols*. Ithaca, N.Y.: Cornell University Press, 1967.

Tyler, Hamilton A. *Pueblo Animals and Myths*. Norman: University of Oklahoma Press, 1975.

——. *Pueblo Gods and Myths*. Norman: University of Oklahoma Press, 1964.

Underhill, Ruth M. *First Penthouse Dwellers of America*. 2d rev. ed. Santa Fe, N.M.: Laboratory of Anthropology, 1946.

——. *Singing for Power: The Song Magic of the Papago Indians of Southern Arizona*. Berkeley: University of California Press, 1938.

Velie, Alan R. *Four American Indian Literary Masters: N. Scott Momaday, James Welch, Leslie Marmon Silko, and Gerald Vizenor*. Norman: University of Oklahoma Press, 1982.

——. "James Welch's Poetry," UCLA *American Indian Culture and Research Journal* 3 (Spring 1979): 19–38.

Vestal, Stanley. *Sitting Bull: Champion of the Sioux*. Boston and New York: Houghton Mifflin Co., 1932.

Vogel, Virgil J. "American Indian Influence on the American Pharmacopoeia," UCLA *American Indian Culture and Research Journal* 2 (1977): 3–7.

——. *American Indian Medicine*. Norman: University of Oklahoma Press, 1970. New York: Ballantine, paperback reprint edition, 1973.

Walker, J. R. *The Sun Dance and Other Ceremonies of the Oglala Division of the Teton Dakota*. New York: The Trustees, 1917. Revised and reprinted as *Lakota Belief and Ritual*, ed. Raymond J. DeMallie and Elaine A. Jahner. Lincoln: University of Nebraska Press, 1980.

Wallace, Anthony F. C. *The Death and Rebirth of the Seneca*. New York: Random House, 1969.

Washburn, Wilcomb E. *The Indian in America*. New York: Harper and Row, 1975.

Welsh, Andrew. *Roots of Lyric: Primitive Poetry and Modern Poetics*. Princeton: Princeton University Press, 1978.

Wesling, Donald. *The Chances of Rhyme: Device and Modernity*. Berkeley, Los Angeles, London: University of California Press, 1980.

Williams, William Carlos. *In the American Grain*. 1925. 2d ed. New York: New Directions, 1956.

———. *Selected Poems*. 1949. 2d ed. New York: New Directions, 1969.

Wissler, Clark, and Duvall, D. C. *Mythology of the Blackfoot Indians*. Anthropological Papers of the American Museum of Natural History, vol 2, part 1. New York: The Trustees, 1908.

Witherspoon, Gary. *Language and Art in the Navajo Universe*. Ann Arbor: University of Michigan Press, 1977.

The World of the American Indian, Vine Deloria, Jr. and William C. Sturtevant, consultants. Washington, D.C.: National Geographic Society, 1974.

Worth, Lawrence C. "The Indian Treaty as Literature," *Literature of the American Indians: Views and Interpretations*. Edited by Abraham Chapman. New York: New American Library.

Yeats, William Butler. "Why the Blind Man in Ancient Times Was Made a Poet" (1906), *W. B. Yeats: Selected Criticism*. Edited by A. Norman Jeffares. London: Macmillan, 1964.

Zolla, Elémire. *The Writer and the Shaman. A Mythology of the American Indian*. 1969. Translated by Raymond Rosenthal. New York: Harcourt Brace Jovanovich, 1973.

⸙ INDEX ⸙

INDEX

INDEX

Makidemewabe, Samuel (Swampy Cree), means "Turtle Wait," 138; as tribal historian, 135

Malta, Montana, 152, 157

Mammedaty, 111

Man to Send Rain Clouds, The (Rosen), 72

Maricopa, 51

Marmon, Robert G., 234, 241; Marmon household, 282 n. 6

Marshall, John, Supreme Court Justice: and opinion of 1831 defining Indian tribes as "domestic dependent nations," 22

Marx, Karl, 189

Maximilian, Prince (Ferdinand Maximilian Joseph), 6

Mayan, 51

Mayhall, Mildred P., *The Kiowas*, 103

Mornings in Mexico (Lawrence), 7

Means, Russell, 188

Medicine man, 53

Melville, Herman, 30; *Moby Dick*, 159

Menominee, terminated, 13

Merwin, W. S., 126; and Lowie "Crow Versions," 32; *Selected Translations 1968–1978*, 29

Mesa Verde, 192, 233

Milk River, 149, 152, 153, 156

Milton, John, 63

Minimal presence, 48–49

Mining: Four Corners, 284n; in Grants, New Mexico, 284n; Jackpile open-pit uranium, 284n

Mistabeo or "animal overseer" (Swampy Cree), 137

Mitakuye oyasin or "All my relatives," 2

Mitchell, Emerson Blackhorse, 62, 66

Moby Dick (Melville), 159

Modoc, chant, 55

Mohawk, steel workers, 186

Momaday, Al (Kiowa), 102, 113

Momaday, N. Scott (Kiowa), 77, 82–121, 206, 224: on the Indian generalized, 39; on Kiowa arrowmaker, 44

Momaday, Natachee Scott (Cherokee), 102; *American Indian Authors*, 62

Monroe, Harriet, "aboriginal number" in *Poetry*, 3

Monroe, Mark (Lakota), 187; "now day Indi'n," 185

Mooney, James, *A Calendar History of the Kiowa Indians*, 103; on Kiowa naming, 110

Moore, Marianne, *The Dial* (July 1921), 4

Moose Jaw, Montana, 149, 152

Moses, 154

Mourning Dove (Okanogan), 60; *Cogewea*, 61; on coyote tales, 78

My Horse And a Jukebox (Bush), 207, 211–214

Myth and Reality (Eliade): on "eternal return" to mythic reality, 88; on "open" mythic world, 126

Nabokov, Peter, 25

Nahuatl, singer, 51

Name stories, *The Wishing Bone Cycle* (Swampy Cree), 134–142

Names, The (Momaday), 104–105, 112

Naone, Dana, 69

Na'pi or "Old Man" (Blackfeet), 150–163 passim, 176, 181

Native American Church, 111, 112, 186

Native American Studies. *See* American Indian Studies

Native American Tribalism (McNickle), 42

Nature (Emerson), 109

Navajo: against Hopi. 9; Beautyway ceremony, 186; 140,000 *Diné*, 15; healing ceremony, 117; healing chant, 54; "house made of dawn," 92; "in-standing windsoul," 203; Night Chant, 47, 54, 112, 117; origin myth, 34, 195

Nebraska, means "flat river" in Omaha, 93

Neihardt, John, 9, 78; *Black Elk Speaks*, 82–95

Nez Percé, 50; Dreamer Religion, Smohalla, 54; Orphic myths, 128

Niatum, Duane (Klallam), 64, 65, 69; *Carriers of the Dream Wheel*, 69

307

INDEX

INDEX

INDEX

INDEX

Designer:	Kitty Maryatt
Compositor:	Freedmen's Organization
Printer:	Braun-Brumfield
Binder:	Braun-Brumfield
Text:	Bembo (Bem)
Display:	Optima (Oracle II)